Basic

MATHEMATICS

Concepts

Level G

Master the Basics One Step at a Time

edited by
**Bearl Brooks,
Marie-Jose Shaw,
and
Robin Sydorenko**

Student's Edition

**ESP Publishing, Inc.
Largo, Florida 33773**

Authors: Marie-Jose Shaw and Robin Sydorenko

Book Design: Bearl Brooks

Editors: Bearl Brooks, Marie-Jose Shaw, and Robin Sydorenko

Cover Design: Barbara Heer

Graphic Arts Credits: Nancy Baldridge, Susan E. Gist, Barbara Heer, Margie Luster, Donna Morrow, Donna C. Seegraves, Janet E. Thiel, Judy Warren

Student's Edition

Order number: BMC-G

ISBN 0-8209-0651-4

Published by
ESP Publishing, Inc. Largo, FL 33773

Copyright © 1999

Number Sequence

We will learn to place numbers in their proper sequence.

Sequence is the order in which things follow one another.

EXAMPLES:

The four numbers following 151 are 152, 153, 154, and 155.

The four numbers following 267 are 268, 269, 270, and 271.

The four numbers following 636 are 637, 638, 639, and 640.

The four numbers following 997 are 998; 999; 1,000; and 1,001.

A Fill in the blanks with the missing numbers.

① 22 __23__ 24 25 26

② 37 38 _____ 40 41

③ 48 49 50 _____ 52

④ 66 67 68 69 _____

⑤ 82 _____ 84 85 86

⑥ _____ 11 12 13 14

⑦ 93 _____ 95 96 97

⑧ 88 89 _____ 91 92

⑨ 55 56 57 _____ 59

⑩ 70 71 72 73 _____

⑪ 301 _____ 303 304

⑫ 576 577 _____ 579

⑬ 783 784 785 _____

⑭ _____ 444 445 446

⑮ 901 _____ 903 904

⑯ 799 800 _____ 802

⑰ 246 247 248 _____

⑱ 666 _____ 668 669

⑲ 111 112 _____ 114

⑳ _____ 893 894 895

㉑ _____ 1,000 1,001 1,002

㉒ _____ 992 993 994

㉓ 1,089 _____ 1,091 1,092

㉔ 997 998 _____ 1,000

㉕ 999 1,000 1,001 _____

㉖ 993 994 _____ 996

㉗ 996 _____ 998 999

㉘ _____ 2,001 2,002 2,003

㉙ 995 _____ 997 998

㉚ _____ 1,005 1,006 1,007

B Fill in the blanks.

① ninety-two __ninety-three__ ninety-four ninety-five __ninety-six__

② nine hundred   nine hundred one _____ nine hundred three

③ seven hundred six _____ seven hundred eight   seven hundred nine

④ one thousand   one thousand, one   one thousand, two _____

⑤ one thousand, nine hundred one _____ one thousand, nine hundred three

⑥ six hundred thirty-one _____ six hundred thirty-three _____

⑦ fifty-two _____ fifty-four _____ _____

⑧ _____ _____ one thousand, sixty-seven

⑨ _____ eight hundred eighty-five _____

⑩ four thousand, seven _____ _____

REMINDER: Write the definition of sequence.

_____

_____

Unit 1 cont'd ☞

C Rearrange these numbers in proper sequence.

① 114 112 111 110 113   <u>*110*</u> <u>*111*</u> <u>*112*</u> <u>*113*</u> <u>*114*</u>

② 1,003 1,000 999 1,001 1,002   ____ ____ ____ ____ ____

③ 992 994 990 991 993   ____ ____ ____ ____ ____

④ 666 669 670 668 667   ____ ____ ____ ____ ____

⑤ 555 558 556 559 557   ____ ____ ____ ____ ____

⑥ 337 334 335 333 336   ____ ____ ____ ____ ____

⑦ 224 225 223 226 222   ____ ____ ____ ____ ____

⑧ 1,111 1,115 1,112 1,114 1,113 ____ ____ ____ ____ ____

⑨ 1,113 1,110 1,112 1,109 1,111 ____ ____ ____ ____ ____

⑩ 1,913 1,909 1,912 1,910 1,911 ____ ____ ____ ____ ____

⑪ 1,810 1,811 1,808 1,807 1,809 ____ ____ ____ ____ ____

⑫ 1,605 1,606 1,607 1,609 1,608 ____ ____ ____ ____ ____

⑬ 1,883 1,881 1,879 1,880 1,882 ____ ____ ____ ____ ____

D Write the numbers in sequence.

① Jeremy mowed lawns for six months to save enough money for a motor scooter. He already had 612 dollars. He needed 88 dollars more. He earned 20 dollars from the Robison's, 15 dollars from the Headly's, 16 dollars from the King's, 20 dollars from the Dison's, and 17 dollars from the Comb's. Everyone paid Jeremy with one dollar bills. Did he have enough money to buy the motor scooter?

612 _____

_____

_____

_____

_____

② Carl's Cucumber Farm employs five cucumber pickers. Monday they picked 500 cucumbers. Tuesday they had to pick 1,000 to reach their quota. At noon Tuesday they had picked 887 cucumbers. How many more had they to pick?

887 _____

_____

_____

_____

_____

_____

Cardinal and Ordinal Numbers   Unit 2

Learning Objective: *We will learn to recognize cardinal and ordinal numbers.*

Cardinal numbers are used in simple counting to explain how many there are in a group. Ordinal numbers tell what place the number has in a group.

EXAMPLE: "Four" tells how many.   Four is a cardinal number.
"Fourth" tells which one.   Fourth is an ordinal number.
Mary picked four flowers.
The fourth one was red.

A Underline the cardinal numbers.

① 1 2nd 3 4 5 6 7th 8th 9th

② 6th 7th 8 9 10 11 12 13th 14th

③ 11th 12th 13 14 15 16th 17 18th 19

④ 16 17 18 19th 20th 21 22 23

⑤ 21 22nd 23rd 24 25 26th 27

⑥ 39 40th 41st 42nd 43 44 45

⑦ 7th 8th 9th 10 11 12 13 14

⑧ 12th 13 14 15th 16th 17 18

⑨ 17 18th 19th 20 21 22nd

⑩ 22 23rd 24 25 26th 27

⑪ 39th 40th 41 42 43 44 45th

⑫ 52nd 53 54th 55th 56th

B Underline the ordinal numbers.

① 1 2 3 4 5th 6th 7th 8th 9

② 30th 31st 32 33 34 35th 36th

③ 86th 87 88 89 90 91st 92 93rd

④ 112th 113th 114 115 116 117th 118

⑤ 125 126 127th 128 129 130 131st

⑥ 100 101st 102nd 103rd 104 105th

⑦ 50 51st 52nd 53rd 54th 55

⑧ 119th 120th 121st 122nd 123 124th

⑨ 132nd 133 134th 135th 136th 137

⑩ 10 11 12th 13th 14th 15th 16

⑪ 63rd 64th 65 66 67th 68th 69

⑫ 70 71st 72nd 73rd 74 75 76

C Write the number or word equivalent.

① first ___1st___   ⑦ 8th _____   ⑬ one hundred thirty-first _____

② second _____   ⑧ 9th _____   ⑭ six hundred ninety-nine _____

③ 3rd _____   ⑨ tenth _____   ⑮ 576th _____

④ 4th _____   ⑩ 76 _____   ⑯ 734th _____

⑤ fifth _____   ⑪ 63 _____   ⑰ 833rd _____

⑥ sixth _____   ⑫ fifty-seven _____   ⑱ three hundred twenty-second _____

REMINDER: Write the definitions of cardinal and ordinal numbers.

_____

_____

Unit 2 cont'd 👉

D Match each word name with the number.

① thirty	40		⑱ ninety	220
② twenty-second	34th		⑲ two hundred twenty	90
③ thirty-fourth	30		⑳ ninetieth	220th
④ forty	22nd		㉑ one hundred	90th
⑤ eightieth	22		㉒ two hundred twentieth	100
⑥ twenty-two	50		㉓ forty-second	42nd
⑦ fifty	40th		㉔ two hundred	10th
⑧ fortieth	80th		㉕ one hundredth	200
⑨ thirtieth	60		㉖ tenth	100th
⑩ sixty	30th		㉗ four hundred	400
⑪ fiftieth	50th		㉘ three thousand, eleventh	2,000
⑫ fifteenth	15th		㉙ four hundredth	196
⑬ seventy	1,088		㉚ two thousand	400th
⑭ one thousand, eighty-eight	34		㉛ six hundred twelfth	3,011th
⑮ thirty-four	80		㉜ two thousandth	2,000th
⑯ eighty	70		㉝ one hundred ninety-six	612th
⑰ seventieth	70th		㉞ nine hundred ninety-ninth	999th

E Fill the blanks with the cardinal or ordinal numbers.

The football team held its 7th (___seventh___) annual try-outs on September 1st (_____). 46 (_____) boys tried out for the team. They were divided into 5 (_____) groups. The 1st (_____) group, made up of 6 (_____) boys, tried for the position of 1st (_____) string, 2nd (_____) string, and 3rd (_____) string quarterbacks. 3 (_____) boys were cut. The 2nd (_____) group, made up of 15 (_____) boys, tried for 13 (_____) defensive positions. The 1st (_____) through 10th (_____) boys made the team, as did the 12th (_____), 13th (_____), and 14th (_____). The 3rd (_____) group, made up of 14 (_____) boys, tried out for various back positions. Only 2 (_____) boys were cut. 5 (_____) became running backs, 4 (_____) became tailbacks, and 3 (_____) became cornerbacks. The 4th (_____) group, made up of 10 (_____) boys, tried out for special teams' positions. 6 (_____) boys were cut, but 1 (_____) was very happy because he was chosen as the school's 1st (_____) barefoot kicker. The 5th (_____) group consisted of 1 (_____) boy. He was the waterboy. Of 46 (_____) boys, 33 (_____) made the team. This was the 3rd (_____) largest group of boys to make the team. The 1st (_____) group, chosen in 1979 (_____) consisted of 40 (_____) boys. The 2nd (_____) largest, chosen in 1982 (_____) consisted of 36 (_____).

Roman Numerals

Unit 3

Learning Objective: *We will learn to recognize the Roman numerals* I *through* $\overline{M}$.

A Roman numeral is part of the system of numbering that was developed by the ancient Romans.

Our system of numbering is called the Arabic system. The Arabic numeral 1 was written as I by the ancient Romans.

1	I	9	IX	4,000			$\overline{MV}$
2	II	10	X	5,000			$\overline{V}$
3	III	40	XL	10,000			$\overline{X}$
4	IV	50	L	15,000			$\overline{XV}$
5	V	100	C	50,000			$\overline{L}$
6	VI	500	D	75,000			$\overline{LXXV}$
7	VII	1,000	M	100,000			$\overline{C}$
8	VIII	3,000	MMM	1,000,000			$\overline{M}$

A Match the Arabic and Roman numerals.

① 28	XIV	⑥ 100	CV	⑪ 596	DXCVI
② 67	LXVII	⑦ 55	C	⑫ 738	MCXI
③ 14	XXVIII	⑧ 105	LV	⑬ 999	CMXCIX
④ 44	XXXIV	⑨ 115	CLV	⑭ 1,111	DCCXXXVIII
⑤ 34	XLIV	⑩ 155	CXV	⑮ 1,578	MDLXXVIII

B Write the Roman numerals that equal these Arabic numerals.

① 102 _CII_　　⑧ 6,069 _____　　⑮ 3,079 _____

② 120 _____　　⑨ 7,566 _____　　⑯ 8,078 _____

③ 1,020 _____　　⑩ 8,656 _____　　⑰ 7,983 _____

④ 1,112 _____　　⑪ 8,066 _____　　⑱ 6,938 _____

⑤ 1,222 _____　　⑫ 4,068 _____　　⑲ 4,683 _____

⑥ 2,020 _____　　⑬ 4,757 _____　　⑳ 4,646 _____

⑦ 2,220 _____　　⑭ 6,356 _____　　㉑ 6,464 _____

REMINDER: Write the definition of a Roman numeral.

_____

_____

C Write the Arabic numeral that is the same as each Roman numeral.

① MMMX ___3,010___

② MMI _____

③ $\overline{V}$CLVII _____

④ $\overline{LMV}$CCCVII _____

⑤ $\overline{XV}$DLV _____

⑥ $\overline{V}$IV _____

⑦ $\overline{XV}$ _____

⑧ $\overline{XXVC}$CXXV _____

⑨ $\overline{C}$ _____

⑩ $\overline{M}$ _____

⑪ CMXXIX _____

⑫ CCXXIV _____

⑬ $\overline{MC}$X _____

⑭ $\overline{CCC}$C _____

⑮ $\overline{MMMC}$CCV _____

⑯ $\overline{CXX}$V _____

⑰ $\overline{M}$C _____

⑱ $\overline{MV}$CCII _____

⑲ CCCLV _____

⑳ $\overline{XI}$ _____

㉑ $\overline{XVD}$V _____

㉒ $\overline{VMMD}$CC _____

㉓ $\overline{MXD}$CXLVIII _____

㉔ MMMCCXCVII _____

㉕ $\overline{MVD}$CLXXXVIII _____

㉖ $\overline{VMD}$CXLV _____

㉗ $\overline{MX}$LXXVIII _____

D Write the Roman numerals that mean the same as the Arabic numerals.

① Laurie worked hard in her flower garden during early spring. Her labor was evident during the late spring and summer. Laurie had 24 (___XXIV___) white roses, 28 (_____)red roses, 32 (_____) pink roses, and 47 (_____) yellow roses. Laurie counted many flowers in her bulb garden. She had 53 (_____) purple iris, 67 (_____) orange iris, and 74 (_____) yellow iris. Laurie also counted 89 (_____) blue ragged robins. She was very proud of her 106 (_____) pink surprise lilies and her 111 (_____) tiger lilies.

② There are over 1,000,000 (_____) residents of Carterston and its suburbs. Approximately 2,350 (_____) of the residents live in the inner part of the city. There are 5 (_____) other parts of Carterston and several suburbs. One (_____) part is called Garden Hill, and approximately 3,620 (_____) live in this area. A much larger district of the city, called Near North Side, houses about 24,500 (_____) people. Two very large districts, one called Marina and one called the Inland, each house approximately 50,900 (_____) residents. The rest of the approximate 867,730 (_____) residents of Carterston live in the suburbs. There are seven (_____) major suburbs, each housing approximately 123,961 (_____) residents.

Greater Than or Less Than; Equal or Not Equal

Learning Objective: *We will learn to recognize numbers of equal or various values.*

Numbers that are greater than, less than, or not equal have different values. Numbers that are equal have the same value.

EXAMPLES:

100 > 99	One hundred is greater than ninety-nine.
99 < 100	Ninety-nine is less than one hundred.
99 ≠ 100	Ninety-nine is not equal to one hundred.
99 = XCIX	Ninety-nine is equal to ninety-nine.

A Supply the >, <, ≠, or = sign. (Several have two answers.)

① 17 __< ≠__ 71

② 28 _____ 27

③ 19 _____ 19

④ 43 _____ 34

⑤ 22 _____ 29

⑥ 13 _____ 3

⑦ 11 _____ 11

⑧ 194 _____ 194

⑨ 176 _____ 776

⑩ 200 _____ 200

⑪ 798 _____ 898

⑫ 999 _____ 991

⑬ 347 _____ 346

⑭ 567 _____ 557

⑮ 1,000 _____ 900

⑯ 1,123 _____ 1,121

⑰ 3,946 _____ 2,999

⑱ 1,976 _____ 1,076

⑲ 9,776 _____ 8,776

⑳ 1,986 _____ 1,986

㉑ 7,352 _____ 7,288

㉒ 10,567 _____ 10,566

㉓ 12,765 _____ 12,765

㉔ 73,894 _____ 63,894

㉕ 15,476 _____ 15,476

㉖ 97,621 _____ 17,621

㉗ 79,300 _____ 79,200

㉘ 60,222 _____ 20,222

B Supply the > or < sign.

① 1,010 __>__ 1,001

② 6,934 _____ 6,933

③ 7,343 _____ 7,342

④ 2,927 _____ 6,927

⑤ 4,638 _____ 9,638

⑥ 5,947 _____ 7,495

⑦ 7,890 _____ 6,890

⑧ 8,901 _____ 9,901

⑨ 9,108 _____ 9,106

⑩ 1,112 _____ 1,114

⑪ 3,233 _____ 3,231

⑫ 4,674 _____ 4,764

C Supply the = or ≠ sign.

① CCC __=__ 300

② CCC _____ 210

③ XIV _____ XVI

④ LXV _____ 65

⑤ MI _____ MIX

⑥ XIII _____ 8

⑦ CLXI _____ CLIX

⑧ XX _____ CC

⑨ XC _____ CX

⑩ CLV _____ CLX

⑪ DLV _____ 555

⑫ DC _____ 600

⑬ CD _____ 40

⑭ DCCV _____ 750

⑮ MDV _____ CLV

⑯ MV _____ 1005

REMINDER: Write the definition of greater than, less than, not equal, or equal.

_____

_____

Unit 4 cont'd 👉

D In each problem, check (✓) the number that has a different value from the others.

① ✓ 200
___ MM
___ two thousand
___ 2,000

② ___ 100
___ M
___ one hundred
___ C

③ ___ 555
___ D
___ five hundred
___ 500

④ ___ 606
___ DCCX
___ six hundred six
___ DCVI

⑤ ___ 7,001
___ XVI
___ seven thousand, one
___ VMMI

⑥ ___ MCCLV
___ 1,255
___ twelve hundred fifty-five
___ CCLV

⑦ ___ 912
___ 902
___ nine hundred two
___ CMII

⑧ ___ 209
___ CCXI
___ two hundred nine
___ CCIX

⑨ ___ 3,467
___ 346
___ three hundred forty-six
___ CCCXLVI

⑩ ___ 9,099
___ CXXCIX
___ nine thousand, ninety-nine
___ CMIX

⑪ ___ $\overline{\text{MMM}}$
___ CCC
___ three hundred
___ 300

⑫ ___ DLV
___ six thousand, seven
___ 6,007
___ $\overline{\text{VMVII}}$

⑬ ___ CCCXXXIII
___ 3,033
___ three thousand, thirty-three
___ MMMXXXIII

⑭ ___ 10,011
___ ten thousand, eleven
___ XXI
___ XXI

⑮ ___ $\overline{\text{M}}$
___ M
___ one million
___ 1,000,000

E In each paragraph, underline the number which is greater. Answer the questions.

① Marolyn has nine sisters. Robin is 23, Liz is 20, Sue is 18, Lori is 16, Carmen is 14, Angie is 12, Marci is 10, Linda is 8, and Debra is 6. Marolyn also has one brother, Tony, who is 18. If Tony has a twin, who is it? _____

② The Kansas Can Company ships out canned peanuts. They ship 20,000 cans a week to St. Louis; 30,000 cans a week to Des Moines; 40,000 cans a week to Jefferson City; and 60,000 cans a week to Chicago. If Memphis orders half the cans that Chicago does, which city's order does Memphis match? _____

③ The Clark National Forest is home to 8,567,322 squirrels. 7,567,232 blue jays also live there. Rangers have counted 567,322 raccoons and 7,002 black bears. The government estimates that 567,322 ducks come to live in Clark National Forest every winter. 8,567,322 geese fly in to live there too. 9,873,000 foxes like to hunt the geese. What animal of equal number as the geese could the foxes hunt? _____

④ Armeda works in a department store selling make-up and perfume. During her first week at work she sold $4,632 of merchandise and made $460 on commission. The second week she sold $5,784 of merchandise and made $570 on commission. The third week she sold $4,689 of merchandise and made $460 on commission. The fourth week she sold $5,984 of merchandise and made $590 on commission. During which weeks did Armeda sell different values of merchandise but make the same amount on commission? _____

12

Place Value

Learning Objective: *We will learn to identify place value in multi-digit numbers.*

Place value is determined by the position of a digit in relation to the other digits of a number.

EXAMPLE:

In the number 987,654 the 9 is in the hundred thousands' place, the 8 is in the ten thousands' place, the 7 is in the thousands' place, the 6 is in the hundreds' place, the 5 is in the tens' place, and the 4 is in the ones' place.

A Underline the digits that occupy the hundred thousands' place.

① 6̲78,943	⑦ 646,667	⑬ 829,845	⑲ 417,819	㉕ 622,621
② 397,777	⑧ 877,812	⑭ 901,332	⑳ 998,664	㉖ 303,331
③ 896,896	⑨ 741,161	⑮ 100,853	㉑ 937,237	㉗ 820,000
④ 498,393	⑩ 562,409	⑯ 161,000	㉒ 711,246	㉘ 112,321
⑤ 678,349	⑪ 387,188	⑰ 261,837	㉓ 483,566	㉙ 531,321
⑥ 499,999	⑫ 129,133	⑱ 483,401	㉔ 459,865	㉚ 619,312

B Underline the digits that occupy the thousands' place.

① 687̲,777	⑦ 667,646	⑬ 845,829	⑲ 819,417	㉕ 621,622
② 943,397	⑧ 812,877	⑭ 332,901	⑳ 664,998	㉖ 311,303
③ 896,393	⑨ 161,741	⑮ 853,100	㉑ 237,937	㉗ 802,888
④ 896,498	⑩ 409,562	⑯ 611,000	㉒ 246,711	㉘ 112,321
⑤ 349,678	⑪ 188,387	⑰ 837,261	㉓ 566,483	㉙ 532,131
⑥ 999,499	⑫ 133,129	⑱ 401,483	㉔ 865,459	㉚ 312,619

C Underline the digits that occupy the hundreds' and the tens' places.

① 777̲,3̲9̲7	⑥ 349,999	⑪ 797,446	⑯ 829,901	㉑ 237,246
② 393,498	⑦ 110,100	⑫ 102,299	⑰ 100,000	㉒ 556,483
③ 678,499	⑧ 467,111	⑬ 845,332	⑱ 261,483	㉓ 865,544
④ 100,393	⑨ 121,667	⑭ 853,611	⑲ 405,746	㉔ 734,444
⑤ 212,111	⑩ 812,161	⑮ 831,401	⑳ 161,242	㉕ 410,109

REMINDER: Write the definition of place value.

_____

_____

Unit 5 cont'd ☞

D How many ten thousands are in these numbers?

① 678,397 ___seven___   ⑨ 829,901 _____   ⑰ 621,311 _____

② 896,656 _____   ⑩ 100,583 _____   ⑱ 802,112 _____

③ 489,321 _____   ⑪ 161,223 _____   ⑲ 532,312 _____

④ 678,901 _____   ⑫ 322,161 _____   ⑳ 837,102 _____

⑤ 488,884 _____   ⑬ 261,483 _____   ㉑ 756,432 _____

⑥ 100,111 _____   ⑭ 834,612 _____   ㉒ 123,456 _____

⑦ 393,322 _____   ⑮ 746,139 _____   ㉓ 789,101 _____

⑧ 111,222 _____   ⑯ 161,616 _____   ㉔ 100,999 _____

E Identify the highest place value in each number.

① 45,290 ___ten thousand___   ⑩ 789,616 _____   ⑲ 600,616 _____

② 100 _____   ⑪ 67,198 _____   ⑳ 624 _____

③ 6 _____   ⑫ 1,986 _____   ㉑ 50,550 _____

④ 398 _____   ⑬ 999 _____   ㉒ 34,455 _____

⑤ 1 _____   ⑭ 10 _____   ㉓ 89 _____

⑥ 1,000 _____   ⑮ 63 _____   ㉔ 860,600 _____

⑦ 10,900 _____   ⑯ 6,335 _____   ㉕ 90 _____

⑧ 6,543 _____   ⑰ 74,999 _____   ㉖ 999 _____

⑨ 7 _____   ⑱ 90,955 _____   ㉗ 3 _____

F Fill in the blanks.

① The number 834,468 has ___eight___ hundred thousands, three ten thousands, ___four___ thousands, four hundreds, ___six___ tens, and eight ones.

② The number 923,124 has nine hundred thousands, _____ ten thousands, _____ thousands, one hundred, _____ tens, and four ones.

③ The number 634,564 has _____ hundred thousands, three ten thousands, _____ thousands, five hundreds, _____ tens, and _____ ones.

④ The number 230,163 has _____ hundred thousands, _____ ten thousands, _____ thousands, one hundred, _____ tens, and _____ ones.

⑤ The number 123,456 has _____ hundred thousand, _____ ten thousands, _____ thousands, _____ hundreds, _____ tens, and _____ ones.

⑥ The number 756,998 has seven _____ , five ten thousands, six thousands, nine _____ , nine tens, and eight ones.

⑦ The number 621,303 has six _____ , two _____ , one _____ , three hundreds, zero tens, and three ones.

Comprehension Check

A Fill in the blanks.

① 1 2 3 4 _5_ _6_   ⑥ 50 ___ ___ ___   ⑪ 100 ___ ___ 103 ___ ___ 106

② 10 11 12 ___ 14   ⑦ 63 ___ ___ ___   ⑫ 989 ___ ___ 992 ___ ___ 995

③ 23 ___ ___ 26   ⑧ 47 ___ ___ 50   ⑬ 997 ___ ___ 1,000 ___ ___ 1,003

④ 27 ___ 29 ___   ⑨ 89 ___ 91 ___   ⑭ 643 ___ ___ 646 ___ ___ 649

⑤ 35 ___ 37 ___   ⑩ 76 ___ ___ 79   ⑮ 435 ___ ___ 438 ___ ___ 441

B Write "c" beside the cardinal numbers and "o" beside the ordinal numbers.

① 735 _c_   ⑥ 2079th ___   ⑪ 3043 ___   ⑯ 2021st ___

② 356th ___   ⑦ 100,434 ___   ⑫ 991st ___   ⑰ 648,100 ___

③ 999th ___   ⑧ 101,123 ___   ⑬ 333rd ___   ⑱ 438,439 ___

④ 3rd ___   ⑨ 3,000th ___   ⑭ 564th ___   ⑲ 4041st ___

⑤ 1013 ___   ⑩ 6,453rd ___   ⑮ 520,198 ___   ⑳ 3934th ___

C Fill in the blanks with >, <, =, or ≠ sign. (Several have two answers.)

① CCX _>_ _≠_ 205   ⑬ CCC ___ 30th   ㉕ one ___ first

② LX ___ 67   ⑭ 30 ___ MMXX   ㉖ second ___ thirtieth

③ D ___ 50th   ⑮ 520 ___ 198th   ㉗ fifty-five ___ DLV

④ 500th ___ M   ⑯ MXX ___ 522   ㉘ sixty-nine ___ 69th

⑤ 1st ___ C   ⑰ DV ___ 515th   ㉙ seventy ___ 69th

⑥ 42 ___ 3rd   ⑱ 2,384 ___ XXXVIII   ㉚ 4,041 ___ 4,000th

⑦ 393 ___ 399   ⑲ CCCXXIII ___ 332nd   ㉛ fortieth ___ XLIII

⑧ 960 ___ 690   ⑳ 20th ___ XX   ㉜ 2,627 ___ MMDCXXVI

⑨ 565 ___ 65th   ㉑ 321st ___ XXXII   ㉝ 300 ___ CCC

⑩ 41st ___ 14th   ㉒ 1,442nd ___ XVII   ㉞ 2,400th ___ 2,200th

⑪ 423 ___ 423   ㉓ 1,700th ___ MD   ㉟ 3,526 ___ 3,635

⑫ 990 ___ 991   ㉔ 4,385th ___ 3,499th   ㊱ 2,016 ___ CCXVI

D Underline the digits that occupy the hundred thousands' place.

① <u>1</u>01,394	⑤ 229,196	⑨ 666,555	⑬ 743,968	⑰ 111,232
② 493,110	⑥ 392,229	⑩ 313,194	⑭ 347,394	⑱ 181,191
③ 336,638	⑦ 243,196	⑪ 331,369	⑮ 493,743	⑲ 192,001
④ 894,992	⑧ 819,624	⑫ 639,399	⑯ 491,331	⑳ 100,555

E Underline the digits that occupy the ten thousands' place.

① 6<u>2</u>4,342	⑤ 101,493	⑨ 313,941	⑬ 673,894	⑰ 987,763
② 229,229	⑥ 363,694	⑩ 111,811	⑭ 494,532	⑱ 815,597
③ 196,392	⑦ 894,624	⑪ 191,192	⑮ 153,698	⑲ 972,815
④ 243,624	⑧ 819,666	⑫ 100,515	⑯ 698,355	⑳ 686,215

Tell how many hundred thousands, ten thousands, thousands, hundreds, tens, and ones are in each number.

① 121,314 = *one hundred thousand + two ten thousands + one thousand + three hundreds + one ten + four ones*

② 436,998 = _____

③ 698,344 = _____

④ 567,777 = _____

⑤ 910,100 = _____

⑥ 688,888 = _____

⑦ 543,123 = _____

⑧ 999,545 = _____

⑨ 910,111 = _____

⑩ 213,145 = _____

⑪ 167,890 = _____

⑫ 124,486 = _____

16

Zero as a Place Holder
Unit 6

Learning Objective: *We will learn to recognize zero as a part of a multi-digit number.*

The numeral zero has no value. When combined with other digits to form a number, zero means there is nothing in that particular place.

EXAMPLE: In the number 105 there are 1 hundred and 5 ones. There are no tens because the numeral 0 is in the tens' place.

A What place does each zero hold?

#			#			#	
①	20,698 *thousands'*		㉑	105,666 _____		㊶	698,105 _____
②	34,058 _____		㉒	230,328 _____		㊷	201,544 _____
③	92,104 _____		㉓	909,545 _____		㊸	709,776 _____
④	33,033 _____		㉔	806,832 _____		㊹	908,325 _____
⑤	24,240 _____		㉕	809,382 _____		㊺	240,468 _____
⑥	10,593 _____		㉖	804,232 _____		㊻	908,334 _____
⑦	15,093 _____		㉗	905,657 _____		㊼	543,031 _____
⑧	15,903 _____		㉘	567,809 _____		㊽	238,051 _____
⑨	15,930 _____		㉙	999,012 _____		㊾	236,078 _____
⑩	39,690 _____		㉚	987,014 _____		㊿	210,112 _____
⑪	96,390 _____		㉛	345,067 _____		51	222,806 _____
⑫	39,069 _____		㉜	190,765 _____		52	210,211 _____
⑬	43,204 _____		㉝	760,532 _____		53	240,555 _____
⑭	90,324 _____		㉞	489,031 _____		54	570,666 _____
⑮	84,609 _____		㉟	570,632 _____		55	489,520 _____
⑯	82,024 _____		㊱	680,815 _____		56	190,345 _____
⑰	53,201 _____		㊲	550,868 _____		57	815,970 _____
⑱	48,021 _____		㊳	978,320 _____		58	972,810 _____
⑲	90,281 _____		㊴	980,996 _____		59	686,780 _____
⑳	30,222 _____		㊵	238,051 _____		60	785,027 _____

REMINDER: Write the definition of zero as a place holder.

_____

_____

Unit 6 cont'd ☞

B Check (✓) the answer that tells in which place zero is a place holder.

① 120,487 ____ hundred thousand ____ ten thousand ✓ thousand ____ hundred ____ ten ____ one

② 780,699 ____ hundred thousand ____ ten thousand ____ thousand ____ hundred ____ ten ____ one

③ 209,324 ____ hundred thousand ____ ten thousand ____ thousand ____ hundred ____ ten ____ one

④ 504,619 ____ hundred thousand ____ ten thousand ____ thousand ____ hundred ____ ten ____ one

⑤ 341,032 ____ hundred thousand ____ ten thousand ____ thousand ____ hundred ____ ten ____ one

⑥ 320,954 ____ hundred thousand ____ ten thousand ____ thousand ____ hundred ____ ten ____ one

⑦ 403,632 ____ hundred thousand ____ ten thousand ____ thousand ____ hundred ____ ten ____ one

⑧ 140,872 ____ hundred thousand ____ ten thousand ____ thousand ____ hundred ____ ten ____ one

⑨ 505,555 ____ hundred thousand ____ ten thousand ____ thousand ____ hundred ____ ten ____ one

⑩ 960,672 ____ hundred thousand ____ ten thousand ____ thousand ____ hundred ____ ten ____ one

⑪ 687,098 ____ hundred thousand ____ ten thousand ____ thousand ____ hundred ____ ten ____ one

⑫ 780,123 ____ hundred thousand ____ ten thousand ____ thousand ____ hundred ____ ten ____ one

⑬ 709,824 ____ hundred thousand ____ ten thousand ____ thousand ____ hundred ____ ten ____ one

⑭ 507,666 ____ hundred thousand ____ ten thousand ____ thousand ____ hundred ____ ten ____ one

⑮ 841,023 ____ hundred thousand ____ ten thousand ____ thousand ____ hundred ____ ten ____ one

⑯ 320,148 ____ hundred thousand ____ ten thousand ____ thousand ____ hundred ____ ten ____ one

⑰ 920,262 ____ hundred thousand ____ ten thousand ____ thousand ____ hundred ____ ten ____ one

C Fill in the blanks.

① Mrs. MacFarlin sent her daughter to the grocery store to buy food for their family reunion. The grocery list included forty cans of pork and beans, three hundred hot dogs, three hundred hot dog buns, one hundred twenty cans of soda, forty bags of potato chips, and thirty quarts of potato salad. Rewrite the grocery list using Arabic numbers.

_____

_____

② Jimmy tried to guess the number of jelly beans in jars at the fair to win a prize. He guessed one hundred twenty thousand, seven hundred ninety-nine jelly beans were in the blue jar. He guessed six hundred seventy-eight thousand, four hundred twenty were in the red jar. Jimmy said there were nine hundred nine thousand, nine hundred ninety-nine jelly beans in the green jar. For the yellow jar Jimmy guessed seven hundred sixty-four thousand, thirty-two. To remember Jimmy's guesses, the man behind the counter wrote them down. Jimmy won, but what did the man write?

_____

_____

Place Value Through Millions

Learning Objective: *We will learn to identify place value through 999,999,999.*

Place value is determined by the position of a digit in relation to the other digits of a number.

EXAMPLE: In the number 129,867,543 the 1 is in the hundred millions' place, the 2 is in the ten millions' place, the 9 is in the millions' place, and the 8 is in the hundred thousands' place.

A Underline the digits that occupy the hundred millions' place.

① <u>6</u>43,989,654   ⑥ 659,876,511   ⑪ 654,777,666   ⑯ 210,671,651

② 936,412,876   ⑦ 468,972,654   ⑫ 812,346,781   ⑰ 619,864,468

③ 432,101,999   ⑧ 488,321,123   ⑬ 916,724,813   ⑱ 723,197,199

④ 223,465,791   ⑨ 909,179,679   ⑭ 101,121,134   ⑲ 111,111,112

⑤ 912,312,676   ⑩ 458,210,923   ⑮ 987,654,268   ⑳ 618,714,443

B Underline the digits that occupy the ten millions' place.

① 649,865,989   ⑥ 785,432,469   ⑪ 218,977,561   ⑯ 261,671,651

② 101,112,432   ⑦ 686,217,900   ⑫ 121,312,460   ⑰ 769,100,000

③ 936,102,989   ⑧ 461,334,433   ⑬ 909,606,707   ⑱ 801,764,433

④ 694,431,561   ⑨ 369,211,924   ⑭ 101,679,814   ⑲ 431,630,531

⑤ 236,636,736   ⑩ 479,442,555   ⑮ 325,814,321   ⑳ 671,817,654

C Underline the digits that occupy the millions' place.

① 231,676,771   ⑥ 817,654,865   ⑪ 494,949,633   ⑯ 657,768,921

② 921,444,561   ⑦ 101,121,131   ⑫ 365,414,216   ⑰ 700,800,900

③ 248,971,652   ⑧ 900,000,000   ⑬ 517,648,921   ⑱ 241,658,976

④ 249,973,379   ⑨ 666,174,923   ⑭ 121,212,314   ⑲ 679,111,221

⑤ 697,451,214   ⑩ 651,924,314   ⑮ 134,431,699   ⑳ 314,431,614

D Underline the digits that occupy the hundred thousands' and ten thousands' places.

① 654,<u>22</u>2,461   ③ 345,678,911   ⑤ 978,654,321   ⑦ 764,365,721

② 511,231,645   ④ 123,456,789   ⑥ 167,765,346   ⑧ 786,465,321

REMINDER: Write the definition of place value.

_____

_____

E How many hundred millions are in each number?

① 493,865,215
four

⑤ 100,679,349

⑨ 659,101,653

⑬ 691,321,461

② 694,568,515

⑥ 567,719,101

⑩ 743,245,197

⑭ 431,468,459

③ 210,617,701

⑦ 696,717,121

⑪ 798,164,241

⑮ 951,428,961

④ 100,210,460

⑧ 659,421,989

⑫ 328,717,929

⑯ 812,368,972

F How many ten millions are in each number?

① 468,936,813
six

⑤ 107,819,171

⑨ 619,381,148

⑬ 175,654,146

② 491,126,517

⑥ 643,619,213

⑩ 458,174,832

⑭ 189,610,346

③ 111,216,436

⑦ 444,676,197

⑪ 821,924,167

⑮ 521,651,231

④ 506,709,908

⑧ 637,121,611

⑫ 706,968,676

⑯ 667,787,921

G Fill in the blanks.

① The number 325,814,103 has _____ hundred millions, _____ ten millions, five millions, eight hundred thousands, one ten thousand, _____ thousands, _____ hundred, zero tens, and three ones.

② The number 439,961,932 has _____ hundred millions, _____ ten millions, _____ millions, nine hundred thousands, _____ ten thousands, one thousand, _____ hundreds, three tens, and two ones.

③ The number 764,355,721 has seven hundred millions, _____ ten millions, _____ millions, three hundred thousands, _____ ten thousands, five thousands, _____ hundreds, _____ tens, and _____ one.

④ The number 909,606,707 has nine hundred millions, zero ten millions, _____ millions, _____ hundred thousands, _____ ten thousands, _____ thousands, _____ hundreds, _____ tens, and _____ ones.

⑤ The number _____ has five hundred millions, seven ten millions, six millions, nine hundred thousands, four ten thousands, nine thousands, two hundreds, two tens, and one one.

A Number Line

Unit 8

Learning Objective: *We will learn to compare numbers on a number line.*

A number line is a scale along which numbers are positioned according to their values.

EXAMPLE: As we move toward the right on a number line, we can see that each number has a larger value than those to the left.

A Fill in the missing numbers.

①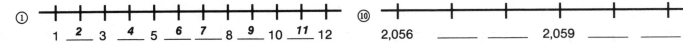
1 **2** 3 **4** 5 **6** **7** 8 **9** 10 **11** 12

②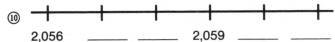
30 ___ ___ ___ 34 ___ ___ ___ 38 ___ ___ ___

③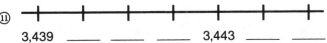
50 51 52 ___ ___ ___ ___ ___ ___ 59 60 ___

④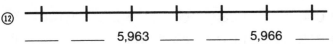
___ ___ 72 ___ ___ ___ ___ ___ ___ 80 ___

⑤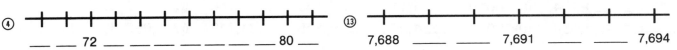
___ ___ ___ ___ 90 ___ ___ ___ 94 ___ ___ ___

⑥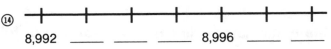
97 ___ ___ ___ ___ 102 ___ ___ ___ ___

⑦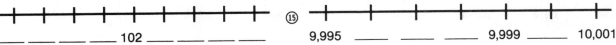
201 ___ ___ ___ ___ 206 ___ ___ ___ 210

⑧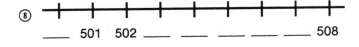
___ 501 502 ___ ___ ___ ___ ___ 508

⑨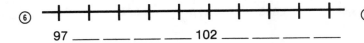
753 ___ ___ ___ ___ 758 759 ___ ___

⑩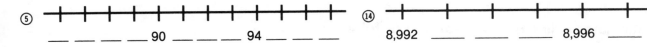
2,056 ___ ___ 2,059 ___ ___

⑪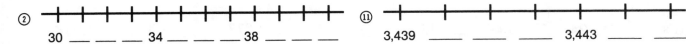
3,439 ___ ___ ___ 3,443 ___ ___

⑫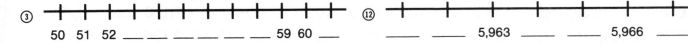
___ ___ 5,963 ___ ___ 5,966 ___

⑬
7,688 ___ ___ 7,691 ___ ___ 7,694

⑭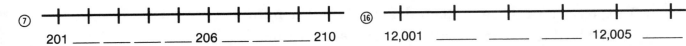
8,992 ___ ___ 8,996 ___ ___

⑮
9,995 ___ ___ ___ 9,999 ___ 10,001

⑯
12,001 ___ ___ ___ 12,005 ___

⑰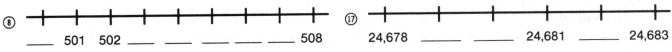
24,678 ___ ___ 24,681 ___ 24,683

⑱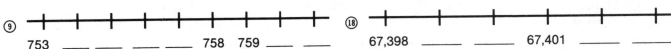
67,398 ___ ___ 67,401 ___ ___

REMINDER: Write the definition of a number line.

_____

_____

21 **Unit 8 cont'd** ☞

B Study the number lines and tell whether the numbers are greater than (>), less than (<), or equal (=).

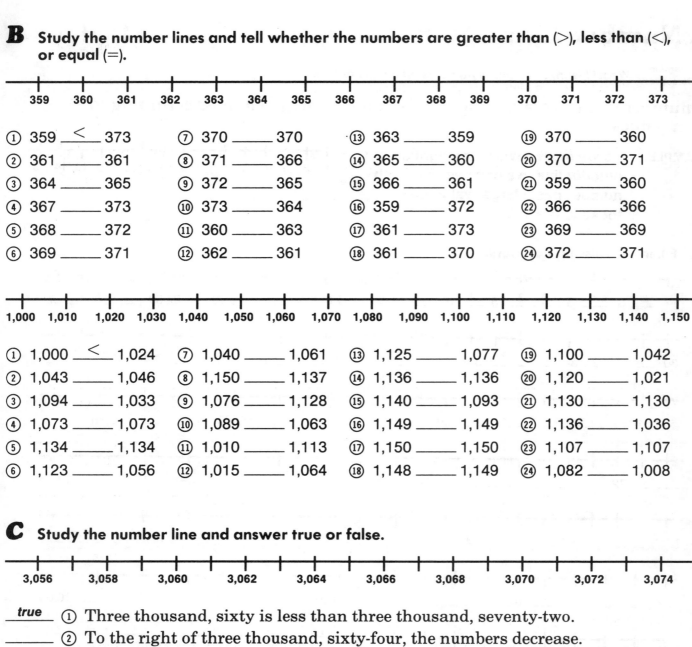

| 359 | 360 | 361 | 362 | 363 | 364 | 365 | 366 | 367 | 368 | 369 | 370 | 371 | 372 | 373 |

① 359 _<_ 373
② 361 _____ 361
③ 364 _____ 365
④ 367 _____ 373
⑤ 368 _____ 372
⑥ 369 _____ 371

⑦ 370 _____ 370
⑧ 371 _____ 366
⑨ 372 _____ 365
⑩ 373 _____ 364
⑪ 360 _____ 363
⑫ 362 _____ 361

⑬ 363 _____ 359
⑭ 365 _____ 360
⑮ 366 _____ 361
⑯ 359 _____ 372
⑰ 361 _____ 373
⑱ 361 _____ 370

⑲ 370 _____ 360
⑳ 370 _____ 371
㉑ 359 _____ 360
㉒ 366 _____ 366
㉓ 369 _____ 369
㉔ 372 _____ 371

| 1,000 | 1,010 | 1,020 | 1,030 | 1,040 | 1,050 | 1,060 | 1,070 | 1,080 | 1,090 | 1,100 | 1,110 | 1,120 | 1,130 | 1,140 | 1,150 |

① 1,000 _<_ 1,024
② 1,043 _____ 1,046
③ 1,094 _____ 1,033
④ 1,073 _____ 1,073
⑤ 1,134 _____ 1,134
⑥ 1,123 _____ 1,056

⑦ 1,040 _____ 1,061
⑧ 1,150 _____ 1,137
⑨ 1,076 _____ 1,128
⑩ 1,089 _____ 1,063
⑪ 1,010 _____ 1,113
⑫ 1,015 _____ 1,064

⑬ 1,125 _____ 1,077
⑭ 1,136 _____ 1,136
⑮ 1,140 _____ 1,093
⑯ 1,149 _____ 1,149
⑰ 1,150 _____ 1,150
⑱ 1,148 _____ 1,149

⑲ 1,100 _____ 1,042
⑳ 1,120 _____ 1,021
㉑ 1,130 _____ 1,130
㉒ 1,136 _____ 1,036
㉓ 1,107 _____ 1,107
㉔ 1,082 _____ 1,008

C Study the number line and answer true or false.

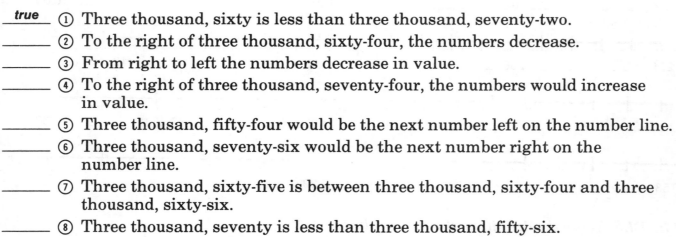

| 3,056 | 3,058 | 3,060 | 3,062 | 3,064 | 3,066 | 3,068 | 3,070 | 3,072 | 3,074 |

true ① Three thousand, sixty is less than three thousand, seventy-two.

_____ ② To the right of three thousand, sixty-four, the numbers decrease.

_____ ③ From right to left the numbers decrease in value.

_____ ④ To the right of three thousand, seventy-four, the numbers would increase in value.

_____ ⑤ Three thousand, fifty-four would be the next number left on the number line.

_____ ⑥ Three thousand, seventy-six would be the next number right on the number line.

_____ ⑦ Three thousand, sixty-five is between three thousand, sixty-four and three thousand, sixty-six.

_____ ⑧ Three thousand, seventy is less than three thousand, fifty-six.

_____ ⑨ Three thousand, sixty-four is the least number on the number line.

_____ ⑩ Three thousand, seventy-four is the greatest number on this number line.

Positive Numbers

Learning Objective: *We will learn to identify positive numbers.*

A positive number is one which is to the right of zero on the number line.

EXAMPLE: The numbers on a number line continue right and left of zero. Numbers to the right of zero are positive, and numbers to the left of zero are negative.

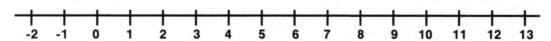

A Underline the positive numbers.

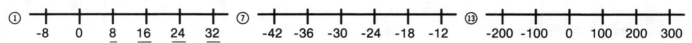

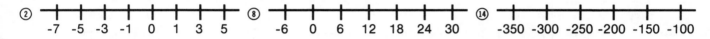

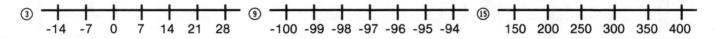

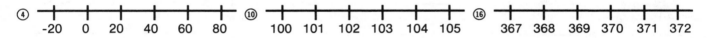

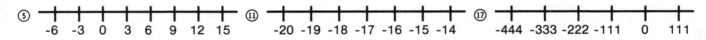

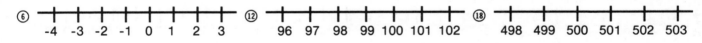

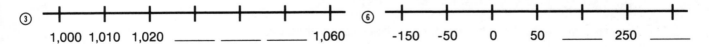

B Fill in the blanks.

① 0 __1__ __2__ __3__ 4 5 __6__ __7__ __8__ 9

② -500 -250 0 250 ___ ___ ___

③ 1,000 1,010 1,020 ___ ___ ___ 1,060

④ -1,000 -500 0 500 ___ ___ ___

⑤ 250 300 ___ ___ ___ ___ ___

⑥ -150 -50 0 50 ___ 250 ___

REMINDER: Write the definition of a positive number.

_____

_____

Unit 9 cont'd ☞

C Do these thermometers show positive or negative readings?

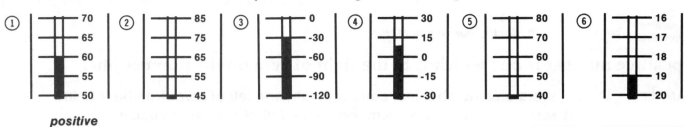

① _positive_ ② _____ ③ _____ ④ _____ ⑤ _____ ⑥ _____

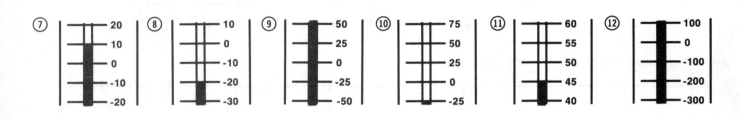

⑦ _____ ⑧ _____ ⑨ _____ ⑩ _____ ⑪ _____ ⑫ _____

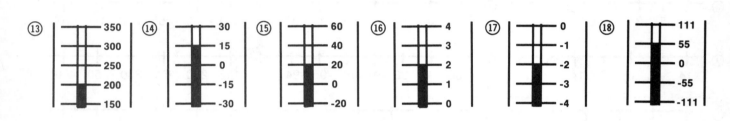

⑬ _____ ⑭ _____ ⑮ _____ ⑯ _____ ⑰ _____ ⑱ _____

D Study the number line and answer true or false.

false ① Moving left to right from zero, the numbers become negative.

_____ ② Moving from zero to the right, the numbers become positive.

_____ ③ The numbers on the right side of zero are negative.

_____ ④ The fourteen on the right side of zero is positive.

_____ ⑤ The six on the right side of zero is positive.

_____ ⑥ The six on the left side of zero is negative.

_____ ⑦ From left to right, the numbers become positive.

_____ ⑧ Four is to the right of twenty-two on the number line.

_____ ⑨ Minus one is left of ten on the number line.

_____ ⑩ Nine is to the right of eight on the number line.

Negative Numbers

Learning Objective: **We will learn to identify negative numbers.**

A negative number is one which is to the left of zero on the number line.

EXAMPLE: The numbers on a number line continue right and left of zero. Numbers to the left of zero are negative, and numbers to the right of zero are positive.

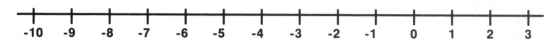

A Underline the negative numbers.

① -3 -2 -1 0 1 2 3 4 5 6

② -60 -50 -40 -30 -20

③ -10 0 10 20 30 40 50

④ -77 -76 -75 -74 -73 -72

⑤ -54 -53 -52 -51 -50 -49

⑥ -10 -9 -8 -7 -6 -5 -4

⑦ -120 -110 -100 -90 -80

⑧ -365 -360 -355 -350 -345

⑨ 660 670 680 690 700

⑩ 800 900 1,000 1,100 1,200

⑪ -1,000 -500 0 500 1,000

⑫ -900 -800 -700 -600 -500 -400

⑬ -200 -100 0 100 200 300

⑭ -350 -300 -250 -200 -150 -100

⑮ -777 -666 -555 -444 -333 -222

⑯ -398 -298 -198 -98 0 98

⑰ 96 97 98 99 100 101 102

⑱ -36 -35 -34 -33 -32 -31 -30

B Fill in the blanks.

① -10 **-9** **-8** **-7** **-6** -5 **-4** **-3** **-2** -1

② -30 ___ ___ 0 ___ ___ ___ 40 50 ___

③ -100 -90 ___ ___ ___ ___ ___ ___ -20

④ -999 ___ ___ -666 ___ ___

⑤ ___ -200 ___ ___ 100 ___

⑥ -367 ___ ___ -364 ___ ___

REMINDER: Write the definition of a negative number.

_____

_____

Unit 10 cont'd ☞

C Do these thermometers show positive or negative readings?

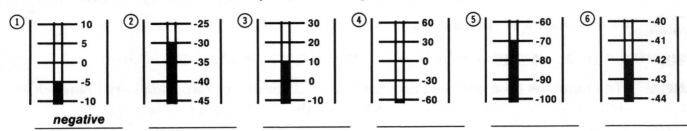

① negative

②

③

④

⑤

⑥

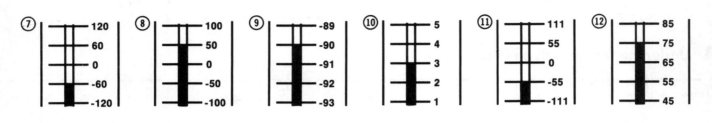

⑦

⑧

⑨

⑩

⑪

⑫

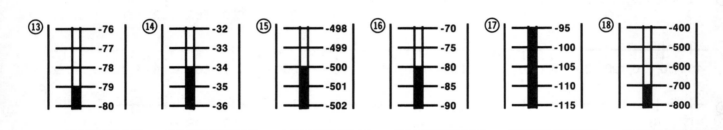

⑬

⑭

⑮

⑯

⑰

⑱

D Study the number line and answer true or false.

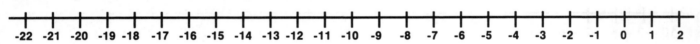

false ① Moving left to right from zero, the numbers become negative.

_____ ② Moving from zero to the right, the numbers become positive.

_____ ③ The numbers on the right side of zero are negative.

_____ ④ The fourteen on the left side of zero is positive.

_____ ⑤ The two on the right side of zero is positive.

_____ ⑥ The two on the left side of zero is negative.

_____ ⑦ From left to right, the numbers become positive.

_____ ⑧ Minus sixteen is on the right of zero.

_____ ⑨ Minus twenty-two is on the left of zero.

_____ ⑩ Minus two is equal to two.

Comprehension Check

A Identify what place the zero holds.

① 965,704,989 _____ *ten thousands'* _____
② 698,776,240 _____
③ 211,806,555 _____
④ 109,345,815 _____
⑤ 972,065,871 _____
⑥ 643,990,835 _____
⑦ 235,921,013 _____
⑧ 507,148,149 _____

⑨ 240,666,439 _____
⑩ 659,852,940 _____
⑪ 101,121,161 _____
⑫ 480,969,721 _____
⑬ 844,015,653 _____
⑭ 364,514,609 _____
⑮ 832,045,666 _____
⑯ 999,909,999 _____

B Underline the digits that occupy the hundred millions' place.

① 6̲45,977,345
② 504,345,921
③ 678,910,111
④ 686,215,678
⑤ 910,112,134

⑥ 212,223,242
⑦ 876,543,241
⑧ 611,760,437
⑨ 776,554,929
⑩ 634,983,389

⑪ 201,019,684
⑫ 921,212,121
⑬ 690,000,000
⑭ 800,000,101
⑮ 654,789,654

C Underline the digits that occupy the ten millions' place.

① 6̲98,754,651
② 341,864,961
③ 996,811,766
④ 220,123,456
⑤ 619,916,696

⑥ 768,972,851
⑦ 651,434,221
⑧ 421,665,473
⑨ 541,221,673
⑩ 947,613,100

⑪ 976,451,651
⑫ 607,921,817
⑬ 102,676,121
⑭ 721,678,910
⑮ 821,345,678

D Fill in the blanks.

①
-1 0 *1 2 3 4 5 6 7*

②
-300 _____ -100 _____ _____ _____ _____ _____

③
36 ___ ___ ___ 40 ___ ___ ___ ___

④
49 ___ ___ ___ ___ ___ ___ ___

⑤
-720 _____ _____ -690 _____ _____ _____

⑥
156 _____ _____ 159 _____ _____ _____

⑦
210 _____ _____ _____ _____ 260 270

⑧
-70 ___ ___ ___ -20 ___ 0 ___

Test 2 cont'd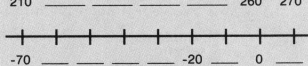

E How many hundred millions are in each number?

① 105,666,698
   one
   _____

② 876,543,211
   _____

③ 111,232,466
   _____

④ 230,328,545
   _____

⑤ 922,636,465
   _____

⑥ 123,456,777
   _____

⑦ 909,806,997
   _____

⑧ 789,101,234
   _____

⑨ 678,001,000
   _____

⑩ 804,232,899
   _____

⑪ 993,448,632
   _____

⑫ 121,134,567
   _____

F How many ten thousands are in each number?

① 686,215,678
   one
   _____

② 815,972,932
   _____

③ 935,271,216
   _____

④ 612,170,833
   _____

⑤ 593,222,438
   _____

⑥ 667,778,990
   _____

⑦ 789,101,000
   _____

⑧ 596,384,901
   _____

⑨ 832,433,222
   _____

⑩ 101,000,222
   _____

⑪ 101,121,314
   _____

⑫ 989,726,853
   _____

G Underline the digits that occupy the millions' place.

① 554,678,321
② 496,770,123
③ 987,654,321
④ 123,455,666
⑤ 700,600,500
⑥ 701,201,333
⑦ 980,999,321
⑧ 787,666,000

Study the number line and answer true or false.

___*false*___ ① Minus twenty-five is to the right of zero.

_____ ② Moving left to right from zero, the numbers become negative.

_____ ③ The numbers left of zero are positive.

_____ ④ The numbers left of minus eleven are negative.

_____ ⑤ The number right of minus six is negative.

_____ ⑥ The numbers left of minus twenty-five are twenty-four, twenty-three, twenty-two, etc.

_____ ⑦ The numbers right of one would continue two, three, four, etc.

_____ ⑧ Minus twelve is a negative number.

_____ ⑨ Zero divides negative and positive numbers.

_____ ⑩ Minus sixteen is to the right of minus seventeen.

28

Prime Numbers

Learning Objective: *We will learn to recognize prime numbers.*

A prime number is divisible only by itself and one.

EXAMPLE: All prime numbers are whole numbers.
1 is not a prime number.
2 is a prime number.

$$2\overline{)2}^{\,1} \qquad 1\overline{)2}^{\,2}$$

A Place a check (✓) beside all prime numbers.

① __ 1 ✓ 2 ✓ 3 __ 4 ✓ 5

② __ 6 __ 7 __ 8 __ 9 __ 10

③ __ 11 __ 12 __ 13 __ 14 __ 15

④ __ 16 __ 17 __ 18 __ 19 __ 20

⑤ __ 21 __ 22 __ 23 __ 24 __ 25

⑥ __ 26 __ 27 __ 28 __ 29 __ 30

⑦ __ 31 __ 32 __ 33 __ 34 __ 35

⑧ __ 36 __ 37 __ 38 __ 39 __ 40

⑨ __ 41 __ 42 __ 43 __ 44 __ 45

⑩ __ 46 __ 47 __ 48 __ 49 __ 50

⑪ __ 51 __ 52 __ 53 __ 54 __ 55

⑫ __ 56 __ 57 __ 58 __ 59 __ 60

⑬ __ 61 __ 62 __ 63 __ 64 __ 65

⑭ __ 66 __ 67 __ 68 __ 69 __ 70

⑮ __ 71 __ 72 __ 73 __ 74 __ 75

⑯ __ 76 __ 77 __ 78 __ 79 __ 80

⑰ __ 81 __ 82 __ 83 __ 84 __ 85

⑱ __ 86 __ 87 __ 88 __ 89 __ 90

⑲ __ 91 __ 92 __ 93 __ 94 __ 95

⑳ __ 96 __ 97 __ 98 __ 99 __ 100

㉑ __ 101 __ 102 __ 103 __ 104 __ 105

㉒ __ 106 __ 107 __ 108 __ 109 __ 110

㉓ __ 111 __ 112 __ 113 __ 114 __ 115

㉔ __ 116 __ 117 __ 118 __ 119 __ 120

㉕ __ 121 __ 122 __ 123 __ 124 __ 125

㉖ __ 126 __ 127 __ 128 __ 129 __ 130

㉗ __ 131 __ 132 __ 133 __ 134 __ 135

㉘ __ 136 __ 137 __ 138 __ 139 __ 140

㉙ __ 141 __ 142 __ 143 __ 144 __ 145

㉚ __ 146 __ 147 __ 148 __ 149 __ 150

㉛ __ 151 __ 152 __ 153 __ 154 __ 155

㉜ __ 156 __ 157 __ 158 __ 159 __ 160

㉝ __ 161 __ 162 __ 163 __ 164 __ 165

㉞ __ 166 __ 167 __ 168 __ 169 __ 170

REMINDER: Write the definition of a prime number.

_____

_____

Unit 11 cont'd ☞

B Check (✓) if the number is prime. If it is not prime, explain why.

① 52 __ _divisible by 2, 26, 1, 52, 4, and 13_

② 7 __ _____

③ 61 __ _____

④ 94 __ _____

⑤ 13 __ _____

⑥ 41 __ _____

⑦ 83 __ _____

⑧ 82 __ _____

⑨ 167 __ _____

⑩ 131 __ _____

⑪ 173 __ _____

⑫ 29 __ _____

⑬ 34 __ _____

⑭ 2 __ _____

⑮ 55 __ _____

⑯ 113 __ _____

⑰ 59 __ _____

⑱ 143 __ _____

C Find the answer. Check (✓) if the number is prime.

① Rick took inventory of his school books from college. He had 3 math books, 4 English books, 2 history books, 1 science book, 1 sociology book, 1 health book, 3 accounting books, 2 data processing books, 4 business theory books, and 2 Spanish books. How many text books did Rick own?

___23___   ___✓___

② Marci decided to write a novel. She wrote 42 pages on Monday and 36 pages on Tuesday. The next three days she wrote 278 pages. Over the weekend she wrote another 30 pages. How many pages did she write?

_____   _____

③ Jody voted in the primary election. He voted for a sheriff, a county clerk, a school board member, a state representative, a congressman, a bond issue, a judge, and a sales tax. How many votes did he cast?

_____   _____

④ Robert and John went fishing. They caught 7 bass, 2 catfish, and 4 brim. How many fish did they catch?

_____   _____

⑤ Linda brushes her hair 100 strokes every night. How many nights a week does she brush her hair?

_____   _____

⑥ Jeremy and Tony played 43 computer games Saturday and 46 on Sunday. How many did they play?

_____   _____

Composite Numbers

Learning Objective: **We will learn to recognize composite numbers.**

A composite number is divisible by itself, one, and at least one other number. Except for one and zero, all whole numbers that are not prime are composite.

EXAMPLE:

12 is a composite number. $12\overline{)12}^{\,1}$ $1\overline{)12}^{\,12}$ $3\overline{)12}^{\,4}$ $4\overline{)12}^{\,3}$ $6\overline{)12}^{\,2}$ $2\overline{)12}^{\,6}$

106 is a composite number. $106\overline{)106}^{\,1}$ $1\overline{)106}^{\,106}$ $2\overline{)106}^{\,53}$ $53\overline{)106}^{\,2}$

7 is not a composite number. It is prime. $7\overline{)7}^{\,1}$ $1\overline{)7}^{\,7}$

A Place a check (✓) beside all composite numbers.

① __ 1 __ 2 __ 3 ✓ 4 __ 5   ② __ 6 __ 7 __ 8 __ 9 __ 10

③ __ 11 __ 12 __ 13 __ 14 __ 15   ④ __ 16 __ 17 __ 18 __ 19 __ 20

⑤ __ 21 __ 22 __ 23 __ 24 __ 25   ⑥ __ 26 __ 27 __ 28 __ 29 __ 30

⑦ __ 31 __ 32 __ 33 __ 34 __ 35   ⑧ __ 36 __ 37 __ 38 __ 39 __ 40

⑨ __ 41 __ 42 __ 43 __ 44 __ 45   ⑩ __ 46 __ 47 __ 48 __ 49 __ 50

⑪ __ 51 __ 52 __ 53 __ 54 __ 55   ⑫ __ 56 __ 57 __ 58 __ 59 __ 60

⑬ __ 61 __ 62 __ 63 __ 64 __ 65   ⑭ __ 66 __ 67 __ 68 __ 69 __ 70

⑮ __ 71 __ 72 __ 73 __ 74 __ 75   ⑯ __ 76 __ 77 __ 78 __ 79 __ 80

⑰ __ 81 __ 82 __ 83 __ 84 __ 85   ⑱ __ 86 __ 87 __ 88 __ 89 __ 90

⑲ __ 91 __ 92 __ 93 __ 94 __ 95   ⑳ __ 96 __ 97 __ 98 __ 99 __ 100

㉑ __ 101 __ 102 __ 103 __ 104 __ 105   ㉒ __ 106 __ 107 __ 108 __ 109 __ 110

㉓ __ 111 __ 112 __ 113 __ 114 __ 115   ㉔ __ 116 __ 117 __ 118 __ 119 __ 120

㉕ __ 121 __ 122 __ 123 __ 124 __ 125   ㉖ __ 126 __ 127 __ 128 __ 129 __ 130

㉗ __ 131 __ 132 __ 133 __ 134 __ 135   ㉘ __ 136 __ 137 __ 138 __ 139 __ 140

㉙ __ 141 __ 142 __ 143 __ 144 __ 145   ㉚ __ 146 __ 147 __ 148 __ 149 __ 150

㉛ __ 151 __ 152 __ 153 __ 154 __ 155   ㉜ __ 156 __ 157 __ 158 __ 159 __ 160

㉝ __ 161 __ 162 __ 163 __ 164 __ 165   ㉞ __ 166 __ 167 __ 168 __ 169 __ 170

REMINDER: Write the definition of a composite number.

_____

_____

B Check (✓) if the number is composite. If it is not composite, explain why.

① 3   ___   *divisible only by 1 and itself*   ⑩ 59   ___ _____

② 14   ___ _____   ⑪ 23   ___ _____

③ 12   ___ _____   ⑫ 178   ___ _____

④ 11   ___ _____   ⑬ 103   ___ _____

⑤ 84   ___ _____   ⑭ 143   ___ _____

⑥ 40   ___ _____   ⑮ 126   ___ _____

⑦ 55   ___ _____   ⑯ 200   ___ _____

⑧ 60   ___ _____   ⑰ 186   ___ _____

⑨ 61   ___ _____   ⑱ 310   ___ _____

C Find the answer. Check (✓) if the number is composite.

① While Mr. and Mrs. Casey were out of town, Jeremy watered their plants. He watered their 3 ferns, 5 palms, and 6 violets. How many plants did Jeremy water?

     _____ 14 _____   ___ ✓ ___

② Robin has 6 pictures of her sister, 3 pictures of her father, 2 pictures of her mom, 4 pictures of her sons, and 5 pictures of her entire family hanging in the living room. How many pictures does she have hanging on the wall in the living room?

     _____   _____

③ Alex has a band saw, a jigsaw, a bow saw, a hack saw, a chain saw, and a wood saw. How many saws does he own?

     _____   _____

④ Tony jogs every day. During the week he jogs 76 miles and on weekends he jogs 7 miles. How many miles does he jog in a week?

     _____   _____

⑤ Marolyn works in a restaurant. Monday night she cooked 5 fish dinners, 6 hamburger dinners, 7 steak dinners, and 9 shrimp dinners. How many dinners did she cook Monday night?

     _____   _____

⑥ Lori typed 9 memos, 16 letters, 24 reports, and 13 product reports in one day. How many items did she type?

     _____   _____

Sets

Learning Objective: *We will learn to identify and combine sets.*

A set is a group of things that belong together.

EXAMPLE:

Here is a set of helicopters and a set of airplanes.

Combined, they look like this.

A Match the name of the set with its members.

① 10 hearts

② 3 squares

③ 6 hangers

④ 12 clubs

⑤ 9 buses

⑥ 7 envelopes

⑦ 5 dots

⑧ 8 question marks

⑨ 6 arrows

⑩ 10 cups and saucers

a. ■ ■ ■

b. ♣ ♣ ♣ ♣ ♣ ♣ ♣ ♣ ♣ ♣ ♣ ♣

c. ♥ ♥ ♥ ♥ ♥ ♥ ♥ ♥ ♥ ♥

d. ⌂ ⌂ ⌂ ⌂ ⌂ ⌂

e. ● ● ● ● ●

f. ⑦ ⑦ ⑦ ⑦ ⑦ ⑦ ⑦ ⑦

g. ✉ ✉ ✉ ✉ ✉ ✉ ✉

h. 🚌 🚌 🚌 🚌 🚌 🚌 🚌 🚌 🚌

i. ☕ ☕ ☕ ☕ ☕ ☕ ☕ ☕ ☕ ☕

j. ← ← ← ← ← ←

B Combine the sets.

① ◇◇◇◇◇◇ + ◇◇◇◇◇◇ = ◇◇◇◇◇◇◇◇◇◇◇◇

② 🚗🚗🚗🚗🚗🚗🚗🚗🚗 + 🚗🚗🚗 =

③ ✚ ✚ ✚ ✚ + ✚ ✚ ✚ ✚ =

④ ⇨⇨ + ⇨⇨⇨⇨⇨ =

⑤ ♠♠ + ♠♠♠♠♠♠♠ =

⑥ ○○○○○○ + ○○○○ =

⑦ ▼▼▼▼▼ + ▼▼▼▼▼ =

REMINDER: Write the definition of a set.

_____

_____

Unit 13 cont'd ☞

C Make two sets from each group.

	Set A	Set B
① ✿ 🏃 🍁 ✿ 🏃 🍁 🏃 ✿ 🍁	✿ 🍁 ✿ ✿ 🍁 ✿	🏃 🏃 🏃
② 🎭 🎭 🎭 🎭 🎭 🎭 🎭 🎭 🎭		
③ ▶▶ ▶▶ ▷▷ ▶▶ ▶▶ ▷▷ ▶▶ ▷▷ ▶▶ ▷▷ ▶▶ ▷▷		
④ ◣ ◥ ◣ ◣ ◣ ◥ ◣ ◣ ◣ ◥		
⑤ ■ □ ■ □ □ ■ ■ ■ □ ■ □		
⑥ ♤ ♠ ♣ ♠ ♣ ♠ ♣ ♠ ♣ ♠ ♣		
⑦ ▶ ◀ ▶ ▶ ◀ ▶ ▶ ◀ ▶		
⑧ ◆ ◇ ◆ ◇ ◇ ◆ ◇ ◇ ◆ ◇		

D Match the sets.

_b_ ① Paula has 2 puppies and 4 kittens.

___ ② Paula has 1 brother and 3 sisters.

___ ③ Paula's family has a blue truck and a red station wagon.

___ ④ Paula's best friends are Suzy, Marolyn, and Lynn.

___ ⑤ Paula sent letters to Suzy, Mike, Robert, and Lynn.

___ ⑥ Paula likes to swim, run, ride her bike, and snow ski.

___ ⑦ Paula ate salad, pizza, and cake at dinner.

___ ⑧ Paula made B's in math, English, and history.

___ ⑨ Paula made A's in physical education, science, and home economics.

___ ⑩ Paula has shoes that are red, blue, brown, black, and white.

a. Paula has four siblings.

b. Paula has six pets.

c. Paula has three best friends.

d. Paula wrote four letters.

e. Paula's family has two vehicles.

f. Paula ate three foods at dinner.

g. Paula likes four sports.

h. Paula made three A's.

i. Paula made three B's.

j. Paula has five pairs of shoes.

34

Subsets

Learning Objective: *We will learn to identify subsets of larger sets.*

A subset is a group that is made up of certain members of a larger set.

EXAMPLE: B and C are subsets of A.

A = {▶, ▷, ▶, ▷, ▶, ▷, ▶, ▷, ▶, ▷, ▶, ▷, ▶, ▷}

B = {▶, ▶, ▶, ▶, ▶, ▶, ▶}

C = {▷, ▷, ▷, ▷, ▷, ▷, ▷}

A Match the sets and subsets.

① A = {⊠, ⊠, ⌂, ⌂, ⌂, ⊠, ⊠}————————— B = {⊠, ⊠, ⊠, ⊠}   C = {⌂, ⌂, ⌂}

② A = {♣, ♧, ♣, ♧, ♣, ♧, ♣, ♧, ♣}   B = {♣, ♣, ♣, ♣, ♣}   C = {♧, ♧, ♧, ♧}

③ A = {▲, ▲, △, ▲, △, △, △, ▲, △, △}   B = {▲, ▲, ▲, ▲}   C = {△, △, △, △, △, △}

④ A = {◇, ◇, ◆, ◆, ◆, ◆, ◆, ◆, ◇, ◇}   B = {★, ★, ★, ★, ★}   C = {☆, ☆, ☆, ☆, ☆}

⑤ A = {♠, ♠, ♠, ♠, ♤, ♤, ♤}   B = {🚌, 🚌, 🚌, 🚌}   C = {🚗, 🚗, 🚗, 🚗}

⑥ A = {★, ★, ★, ☆, ☆, ☆, ★, ★, ☆, ☆}   B = {◇, ◇, ◇, ◇}   C = {◆, ◆, ◆, ◆, ◆, ◆}

⑦ A = {🚌, 🚌, 🚗, 🚗, 🚗, 🚌, 🚗, 🚌}   B = {♠, ♠, ♠, ♠}   C = {♤, ♤, ♤}

⑧ A = {1, 2, 3, 4, 5, 6, 7, 8, 9, 10}   B = {2, 4, 6, 8, 10, 12}   C = {14, 16, 18}

⑨ A = {2, 4, 6, 8, 10, 12, 14, 16, 18}   B = {10, 20, 30}   C = {40, 50, 60, 70}

⑩ A = {10, 20, 30, 40, 50, 60, 70}   B = {1, 2, 3, 4, 5}   C = {6, 7, 8, 9, 10}

⑪ A = {2, 22, 32, 52, 62, 82, 92}   B = {3, 13, 23}   C = {33, 43, 53, 63}

⑫ A = {5, 10, 15, 20, 25, 30, 35}   B = {2, 22, 32}   C = {52, 62, 82, 92}

⑬ A = {3, 13, 23, 33, 43, 53, 63}   B = {4, 16, 20, 24, 28}   C = {32, 36}

⑭ A = {6, 16, 7, 17, 8, 18, 9, 19}   B = {5, 10, 15, 20}   C = {25, 30, 35}

⑮ A = {4, 16, 20, 24, 28, 32, 26}   B = {6, 16, 7, 17}   C = {8, 18, 9, 19}

REMINDER: Write the definition of a subset.

_____

_____

Unit 14 cont'd ☞

A = {△, △, △, ▲, ▲}

B = {▲, ▲}

B ⊆ A	B is a subset of Set A.
△ ∈ A	△ is a member of Set A.
△ ∉ B	△ is not a member of Set B.

B Study the sets below and mark the following statements true or false.

① A = {1, 2, 3, 4, 5}
B = {1, 2}
C = {3, 4, 5}

② A = {20, 30, 40, 50, 60}
B = {20, 30}
C = {40, 50, 60}

③ A = {2, 12, 22, 32, 42, 52}
B = {2, 12, 22}
C = {32, 42, 52}

_t_ B ⊆ A   ___ A ∈ B   ___ 20 ∈ A   ___ B ⊆ C   ___ 22 ∈ C

_t_ C ⊆ A   ___ C ∈ B   ___ 60 ∈ B   ___ B ⊆ A   ___ 32 ∈ B

_f_ 2 ∈ C   ___ C ⊆ A   ___ 50 ∈ A   ___ B ∈ C   ___ 22 ⊆ A

④ A = {6, 7, 8, 9, 10}
B = {6, 7, 8}
C = {8, 9, 10}

⑤ A = {5, 10, 15, 20, 25, 30, 35}
B = {5, 15, 25, 35}
C = {10, 20, 30}

⑥ A = {9, 19, 29, 39, 49, 59}
B = {9}
C = {19, 29, 39, 49, 59}

___ C ∈ B   ___ C ⊆ A   ___ 5 ∈ A   ___ C ⊆ A   ___ 29 ∈ B

___ 8 ∈ B   ___ B ⊆ A   ___ 5 ∈ B   ___ B ⊆ A   ___ 59 ∈ A

___ 8 ∉ C   ___ A ⊆ C   ___ 15 ∉ C   ___ 9 ∈ B   ___ 9 ∈ C

C Fill in the blanks.

① Set A includes all even numbers. Set B includes all even numbers up to fifty. Set C includes all even numbers beyond fifty. Set B _____ Set A. Set C _____ Set A. The number 426 _____ Set A and C.

② Set A includes all children. Set B includes all male children. Set C includes all female children. Set B _____ Set A. Set C _____ Set A. Set A _____ Set C. John, Roy, and Nick _____ Set C. Mary and Linda _____ Set C.

③ Set A includes all whole numbers. Set B includes all numbers that have 9 as a digit. Set C includes all numbers that have 3 as a digit. Set B _____ Set A. The number 999,999 _____ Set C. The number 3,939 _____ Set A.

④ Set A includes the alphabet. Set B includes letters "a" through "m." Set C includes letters "n" through "z." Set C _____ Set A. Set B _____ Set A. Set C _____ Set B. The letter "g" _____ Set B. The letter "y" _____ Set A.

⑤ Set A includes all numbers. Set B includes Roman numerals. Set C includes Arabic numerals. Set A _____ Set B. Set B _____ Set A. Set C _____ Set A. 9 _____ Set C. XV _____ Set C. All even numbers _____ Set A.

Intersection and Union   Unit 15

Learning Objective: *We will learn to identify the intersection and union of sets.*

The intersection of a set occurs when there are two sets made up of like members. A third set of those like members is the intersection of the sets. When all members of two sets are combined to form a third set, the third set is called the union of the two sets.

EXAMPLE:

A = {☆ ☆ ★ ★}   The intersection of   A = {☆ ☆ ★ ★}   The union of
B = {★ ★}   A and B is   B = {● ●}   A and B is
A ∩ B = {★ ★}   {★ ★}.   A ∪ B = {☆ ☆ ★ ★ ● ●}   {☆ ☆ ★ ★ ● ●}.

A Underline the members that are included in both sets.

① A = {1, 2, 3, 4, <u>5</u>, <u>6</u>, <u>7</u>}   ④ A = {37, 38, 39, 40}   ⑦ A = {6, 16, 26, 36, 46, 56}
   B = {<u>5</u>, <u>6</u>, <u>7</u>, 8, <u>9</u>, 10, 11}   B = {37, 39, 41, 42}   B = {6, 12, 18, 24, 30, 36}
② A = {<u>2</u>, <u>4</u>, <u>6</u>, 8, 10, 12}   ⑤ A = {5, 10, 15, 20, 25}   ⑧ A = {2, 12, 22, 32, 42, 52}
   B = {2, 6, 8, 10}   B = {5, 15, 25}   B = {12, 22, 32, 42, 52, 62}
③ A = {1, 3, 5, 7, 9}   ⑥ A = {5, 15, 25, 35, 45}   ⑨ A = {3, 33, 333, 3,333}
   B = {1, 3, 7, 9, 13}   B = {10, 15, 20, 25, 30}   B = {3, 13, 53, 93, 133}

B Match the sets and their unions.

① A = {a, b, c} B = {d, e, f}   C = {Ed, Tom, Kay, Liz}
② A = {Ed, Tom} B = {Kay, Liz}   C = {a, b, c, d, e, f}
③ A = {▲, ▲, ▲, ▲, ▲} B = {△, △, △, △, △}   C = {▲, ▲, ▲, ▲, ▲, △, △, △, △, △}
④ A = {L, LL, LLL} B = {M, MM, MMM}   C = {A, a, B, b, C, c, D, d, E}
⑤ A = {A, a, B, b} B = {C, c, D, d, E}   C = {a, e, i, o, u, y, w}
⑥ A = {a, e, i, o, u} B = {y, w}   C = {L, LL, LLL, M, MM, MMM}

C Study the sets and fill in the blanks.

A = {1, 2, 3, 4, 5, 6, 7, 8, 9, 10} B = {8, 9, 10, 11, 12, 13, 14, 15, 16, 17, 18}
C = {1, 2, 3, 4, 5, 6, 7, 8, 9, 10, 11, 12, 13, 14, 15, 16, 17, 18}

① Set A __⊄__ Set B   ⑦ {1, 2} _____ Set A   ⑬ A ∪ B = {_____
② Set B _____ Set A   ⑧ {8, 9} _____ Set B   _____}
③ Set B _____ Set C   ⑨ {8, 9} _____ Set A   ⑭ A ∩ C = {_____}
④ Set A _____ Set C   ⑩ {10, 11} _____ Set B   ⑮ B ∩ C = {_____}
⑤ Set C _____ Set A   ⑪ {1, 2} _____ Set C   ⑯ B ∪ C = {_____
⑥ Set C _____ Set B   ⑫ {8, 9} _____ Set C   _____}

REMINDER: Write the definition of intersection and union of sets.

_____
_____

D Identify the intersection or union of the sets.

① A = {1, 2, 3, 4, 5}
B = {1, 4, 8}
A ∪ B = { __1, 2, 3,__ __4, 5, 8__ }

② A = {a, b, c, d, e, f}
B = {c, d, e, f, g, h}
A ∩ B = { _____ }

③ A = {▲, ▲, ▲, ▲}
B = {△, △, △, △}
A ∪ B = { _____ }

④ A = {55, 66, 77, 88}
B = {66, 77, 66, 77}
A ∩ B = { _____ }

⑤ A = {♡, ♡, ♡, ♡}
B = {♥, ♡, ♡, ♥}
A ∪ B = { _____ }

⑥ A = {103, 104, 105, 106}
B = {102, 103, 104, 105}
A ∩ B = { _____ }

⑦ A = {8, 88, 8, 88, 8, 88}
B = {86, 87, 88, 89}
A ∩ B = { _____ }

⑧ A = {100, 99, 98, 97, 96}
B = {94, 95, 96, 97, 98}
A ∪ B = { _____ }

⑨ A = {⇨, ⇨, ⇨, ⇨}
B = {⇦, ⇦, ⇦, ⇦}
A ∪ B = { _____ }

⑩ A = {X, XI, XII, XIII}
B = {VI, VII, VIII, IX, X}
A ∩ B = { _____ }

⑪ A = {3, 6, 9, 12, 15}
B = {2, 4, 6, 8, 10, 12}
A ∩ B = { _____ }

⑫ A = {X, X, X, X, X}
B = {O, O, O, O, O}
A ∪ B = { _____ }

E Fill in the blanks.

① Red, yellow, orange, blue, green, indigo, and violet are the seven main colors of the rainbow. Maroon, blue-green, pink, white, brown, grey, green, and blue are the colors in Susan's carpet. Set A = {seven main colors}. Set B = {the colors in the carpet}.

Set A ∩ Set B = { _____ }

② Robin, Alex, Liz, and Tommy are members of the Beta Club. Lynn, Ann, Mike, Liz, Tony, and Alex are members of the tennis team. Set A = {the Beta club members}. Set B = {the tennis team members}.

Set A ∪ Set B = { _____ }

③ Lassie, Rover, Tiny, Boots, and Chief are popular dog names. Boots, Friskey, Spot, and Tiny are popular cat names. Set A = {dog names}. Set B = {cat names}.

Set A ∩ Set B = { _____ }

Set A ∪ Set B = { _____ }

④ Some red flowers are roses, gladioluses, peonies, lilies, irises, and rose of Sharons. Some yellow flowers are daisies, daffodils, dandelions, roses, irises, lilies, gladioluses, and tulips. Some pink flowers are roses, peonies, irises, and tulips. Set A = {red flowers}. Set B = {yellow flowers}. Set C = {pink flowers}.

Set A ∩ Set B = { _____ }

Set A ∩ Set C = { _____ }

Set B ∩ Set C = { _____ }

Comprehension Check   Test 3

A Place a ✓ beside the prime numbers and a X beside the composite numbers.

① _X_ 1 _✓_ 2 _✓_ 3 _X_ 4 _✓_ 5   ⑪ ___ 51 ___ 52 ___ 53 ___ 54 ___ 55

② ___ 6 ___ 7 ___ 8 ___ 9 ___ 10   ⑫ ___ 56 ___ 57 ___ 58 ___ 59 ___ 60

③ ___ 11 ___ 12 ___ 13 ___ 14 ___ 15   ⑬ ___ 61 ___ 62 ___ 63 ___ 64 ___ 65

④ ___ 16 ___ 17 ___ 18 ___ 19 ___ 20   ⑭ ___ 66 ___ 67 ___ 68 ___ 69 ___ 70

⑤ ___ 21 ___ 22 ___ 23 ___ 24 ___ 25   ⑮ ___ 71 ___ 72 ___ 73 ___ 74 ___ 75

⑥ ___ 26 ___ 27 ___ 28 ___ 29 ___ 30   ⑯ ___ 76 ___ 77 ___ 78 ___ 79 ___ 80

⑦ ___ 31 ___ 32 ___ 33 ___ 34 ___ 35   ⑰ ___ 81 ___ 82 ___ 83 ___ 84 ___ 85

⑧ ___ 36 ___ 37 ___ 38 ___ 39 ___ 40   ⑱ ___ 86 ___ 87 ___ 88 ___ 89 ___ 90

⑨ ___ 41 ___ 42 ___ 43 ___ 44 ___ 45   ⑲ ___ 91 ___ 92 ___ 93 ___ 94 ___ 95

⑩ ___ 46 ___ 47 ___ 48 ___ 49 ___ 50   ⑳ ___ 96 ___ 97 ___ 98 ___ 99 ___ 100

B Identify if each number is prime or composite and why.

① 53 ____*prime*____ _____*divisible only by 1 and itself*_____

② 14 _____ _____

③ 59 _____ _____

④ 10 _____ _____

⑤ 17 _____ _____

⑥ 12 _____ _____

⑦ 173 _____ _____

⑧ 61 _____ _____

⑨ 13 _____ _____

⑩ 25 _____ _____

C Make two sets from each group.

                                          Set A   Set B

①

②

③

④

⑤

⑥

⑦

⑧

Test 3 cont'd ☞

D Study the sets and fill in the blanks with ⊆, ∈, ∉, ∩, and ∪.
There may be more than one answer.

① A = {1, 2, 3, 4, 5}
B = {6, 7, 8, 9, 10}
C = {1, 2, 3, 4, 5, 6, 7, 8, 9, 10}

1 ___∈___ Set A and Set C
6 ___∈___ Set B and Set C
6 ___∉___ Set A

④ A = {3, 6, 9, 12}
B = {4, 5, 7, 8, 10}
C = {3, 4, 5, 6, 7, 8, 9, 10, 12}

{3, 4, 5, 6, 7, 8, 9, 10, 12} = A _____ B
{4, 5, 7, 8, 10} _____ Set A
{4, 5, 7, 8} _____ Set B and Set C

② A = {11, 12, 13, 14}
B = {15, 16, 17, 18}
C = {11, 12, 13, 14, 15, 16, 17, 18}

15 _____ Set A
15 _____ Set B
15 _____ Set C

⑤ A = {5, 10, 15, 20}
B = {15, 20}
C = {5, 10, 15, 20}

Set B _____ Set A
Set B _____ Set C
Set C _____ Set A and B

③ A = {10, 20, 30, 40, 50}
B = {40, 50, 60}
C = {10, 20, 30, 40, 50, 60}

{40, 50} _____ Set A and Set B
{10, 20} _____ Set B
{10, 20} _____ Set C

⑥ A = {8, 10}
B = {2, 4, 6}
C = {2, 4, 6, 8, 10}

Set A _____ Set C
Set B _____ Set C
Set C _____ Set A and Set B

Define these terms and symbols.

① prime number _____

② composite number _____

③ ⊆ _____

④ ∩ _____

⑤ ∪ _____

⑥ ∉ _____

⑦ ∈ _____

⑧ set _____

⑨ subset _____

⑩ intersection _____

⑪ union _____

Finite Sets

Learning Objective: *We will learn to identify finite sets.*

A finite set is one whose members can be counted.

EXAMPLE:
finite sets include
a) all numbers between 23 and 232,232
b) all varieties of oak trees
c) all boys in the New York public school system

A Answer "t" if the members of the set can be counted. Answer "f" if they cannot be counted.

__t__ ① the number of birdcages that house canaries

_____ ② the number of Swedish cooks that believe in Santa Claus

_____ ③ the number of streets in Chicago that are not paved

_____ ④ the number of sand grains in the deserts of the world

_____ ⑤ the numbers between 1 and 234,567,890

_____ ⑥ the number of popsicles in a box bought on July 4, 1980

_____ ⑦ the number of people at any picnic who ate outside

_____ ⑧ the number of Americans with the name "Smith"

_____ ⑨ the number of men under 56 and over 30 years old

_____ ⑩ the number of stars, planets, and universes that we cannot see

_____ ⑪ the number of Thursdays that it snowed since 1907

_____ ⑫ the number of students in the fourth grade who eat lunch at school

_____ ⑬ the number of gallons of gas it takes the fill the family car

_____ ⑭ the number of pages in the New York Times of June 7, 1943

REMINDER: Write the definition of a finite set.

_____

_____

Unit 16 cont'd ☞

n(A) = 10	The number of members of Set A is 10.

B How many members are in each set?

① A = { the number of pages in this book}
n (A) = _____400_____

② B = {how many eyes you have}
n (B) = _____

③ C = {how many toes and fingers you have}
n (C) = _____

④ D = { 999, 998, 997, 996}
n (D) = _____

⑤ E = {green, blue, yellow}
n (E) = _____

⑥ F = {1, 2, 3, 4, 5, 6, 7}
n (F) = _____

⑦ G = { 2, 4, 6, 8, . . . 16}
n (G) = _____

⑧ H = {a, e, i, o, u, y}
n (H) = _____

⑨ I = {1 dog, 2 cats, 1 fish}
n (I) = _____

⑩ J = { a, b, c, d, e, f, . . . z}
n (J) = _____

⑪ K = {Angie, Stella}
n (K) = _____

⑫ L = {1, 2, 3, 4, 5, . . . 50}
n (L) = _____

⑬ M = { 50, 51, . . . 100}
n (M) = _____

⑭ N = {1,001; 1,002; . . . 1,100}
n (N) = _____

⑮ O = {1, 2, 3, 4, 5, . . . 667}
n (O) = _____

C How many members are in each set?

n (A) = ___60___ ① Set A includes all the minutes in an hour.

n (B) = _____ ② Set B includes all the seconds in a minute.

n (C) = _____ ③ Set C includes all the days in a week.

n (D) = _____ ④ Set D includes all the weeks in a year.

n (E) = _____ ⑤ Set E includes all the months in a year.

n (F) = _____ ⑥ Set F includes all the years in a decade.

n (G) = _____ ⑦ Set G includes all the years in a century.

n (H) = _____ ⑧ Set H includes all the males in your class.

n (I) = _____ ⑨ Set I includes all the men over 40 in your family.

n (J) = _____ ⑩ Set J includes all the women under 35 in your family.

n (K) = _____ ⑪ Set K includes all the money in your pockets.

Infinite Sets   Unit 17

An infinite set is one whose members cannot be counted. An infinite set has no end.

EXAMPLE:
We show an infinite set by adding three dots on to the end of a set. The set of whole numbers is infinite, so we show it by writing $\{0, 1, 2, 3, 4, \ldots\}$. This means the set goes on forever.

A Answer "t" if the members of the set cannot be counted. Answer "f" if they can be counted.

_t___ ① the number of galaxies

_____ ② time

_____ ③ the history of the world

_____ ④ the history of living creatures

_____ ⑤ the number of air molecules

_____ ⑥ the number of males in your class with blonde hair

_____ ⑦ the number of females in Pittsburgh that like pizza

_____ ⑧ the number of stars in the sky

_____ ⑨ the set of even numbers

_____ ⑩ the set of odd numbers

_____ ⑪ the set of odd prime numbers after 3,009,101,782,346

_____ ⑫ the set of all sunrises after the year 2673

_____ ⑬ the number of all boys that will ever play baseball

_____ ⑭ the number of all grandfathers who will spoil their granddaughters

REMINDER: Write the definition of an infinite set.

_____

_____

Unit 17 cont'd ☞

B How many members are in each set?

① A = { 1, 2, 3,...}
n (A) = ___infinite___

⑦ A = {...-1, 0, 1,...}
n (A) = _____

⑬ A = {...0, 1, 2}
n (A) = _____

② B = { 4, 6, 8, 10,...}
n (B) = _____

⑧ B = {...1, 2, 3}
n (B) = _____

⑭ B = {-4, -3, -2, -1}
n (B) = _____

③ C = { 5, 10, 15}
n (C) = _____

⑨ C = {...4, 5, 6,...}
n (C) = _____

⑮ C = {-5, -4, -3,...}
n (C) = _____

④ D = { 3, 6, 9,...}
n (D) = _____

⑩ D = {10, 11, 12}
n (D) = _____

⑯ D = {-6, -3, -1, 0}
n (D) = _____

⑤ E = { 2, 4, 6, 8}
n (E) = _____

⑪ E = {6, 7, 8, 9,...}
n (E) = _____

⑰ E = {100, 200, 300,...}
n (E) = _____

⑥ F = { 9, 10, 11,...}
n (F) = _____

⑫ F = {1, 2, 3, 4}
n (F) = _____

⑱ F = {5, 10, 5, 10, 5, 10}
n (F) = _____

C Write "i" if the set is infinite or "f" if the set is finite.

___f___ ① the number of men who died in World War II

_____ ② the amount of money collected by toll booths on any given day

_____ ③ the stars that are within 3,000 light years of earth

_____ ④ the sand grains of the deserts of the world

_____ ⑤ the population of Mars

_____ ⑥ the number of popcorns in a bowl

_____ ⑦ all the men born after the year 1999

_____ ⑧ the number of times it will snow after December 6, 1989

_____ ⑨ the number of high school seniors who will enroll in college

_____ ⑩ the number of years after 2006

_____ ⑪ the number of fish caught in the future

Set Notation

Learning Objective: **We will learn to use set notation.**

The symbol ∈ stands for "is a member of."   The symbol ∩ stands for "intersection."
The symbol ∉ stands for "is not a member of."   The symbol ⊆ stands for "is a subset of."
The symbol ∪ stands for "union."

EXAMPLE: **Set A = {1, 2, 3, 4}   Set B = {3, 4, 5, 6}   Set C = {1, 2, 3, 4, 5, 6}**
These sentences are notations of Sets A, B, and C.
3 ∈ Set A   2 ∉ Set B   Set C ∪ Set A and Set B
{3, 4} ∩ Set A and Set B   Set B ⊆ Set C   Set A ⊆ Set C

A Fill in the blanks to make set notation sentences. There may be more than one possible answer.

Set A = {0, 1, 2, 3, 4, 5}   Set B = {5, 6, 7, 8, 9, 10, 11, 12}   Set C = {0, 1, 2, 3, 4, 5, 6, 7, 8, 9, 10, 11, 12}

① __0__ ∈ Set A   ④ _____ ∉ Set A   ⑦ Set A _____ Set C
② _____ ∈ Set B   ⑤ 4 _____ Set B   ⑧ Set B _____ Set C
③ _____ ∈ Set C   ⑥ 5 _____ Set C   ⑨ Set C _____ Set A and Set B

Set A = {3, 6, 9, 12}   Set B = {3, 5, 7, 9, 12, 15}   Set C = {3, 5, 6, 7, 9, 12, 15}

① __3__ ∈ Set A   ④ 3 _____ Set A   ⑦ 3, 9, 12 _____ Set A and Set B
② _____ ∈ Set B   ⑤ 3 _____ Set B   ⑧ Set B _____ Set C
③ _____ ∈ Set C   ⑥ 3 _____ Set C   ⑨ Set C _____ Set A and Set B

Set A = {5, 10, 15, 20, 25}   Set B = {10, 20, 30, 40, 50, 60}   Set C = {5, 10, 15, 20, 25, 30, 40, 50, 60}

① __5__ ∈ Set A   ⑥ 5 _____ Set C   ⑪ {10, 20} _____ Set A
② _____ ∈ Set B   ⑦ 10 _____ Set C   ⑫ {10, 20} _____ Set B
③ _____ ∈ Set C   ⑧ 10 _____ Set A   ⑬ {10, 20} _____ Set C
④ 30 _____ Set A   ⑨ 60 _____ Set C   ⑭ {10, 20} _____ Set A and Set B
⑤ 5 _____ Set B   ⑩ Set A _____ Set C   ⑮ Set C _____ Set A and Set B

Set A = {1, 10, 11, 20, 21, 30, 31, 40}   Set B = {30, 33, 40, 43, 50, 53, 60}
Set C = {1, 10, 11, 20, 21, 30, 31, 33, 40, 43, 53, 60}

① __1__ ∈ Set A   ⑥ 20 _____ Set A   ⑪ {10, 20, 30} _____ Set A
② _____ ∈ Set B   ⑦ 30 _____ Set B   ⑫ {10, 20, 30} _____ Set B
③ _____ Set C   ⑧ 30 _____ Set C   ⑬ {30, 40} _____ Set B and Set A
④ 21 _____ Set B   ⑨ Set B _____ Set C   ⑭ Set A _____ Set C
⑤ 33 _____ Set A   ⑩ Set A _____ Set C   ⑮ Set B _____ Set C

REMINDER: Write the definition of set notation.

_____

_____

Unit 18 cont'd 👉

B Fill in the blanks.

Set A = {...5, 6, 7, 8}   Set B = {...9, 10, 11...}

① 4 $\in$ Set A
② -206 ___ Set A
③ 399 ___ Set B
④ -9 ___ Set A
⑤ -30 ___ Set A

⑥ 11 ___ Set B
⑦ 103 ___ Set B
⑧ 406 ___ Set B
⑨ {5, 6} ___ Set A
⑩ {...7, 8} ___ Set A and Set B

⑪ {...8, 9, 10...} ___ Set A and Set B
⑫ {9, 10, 11} ___ Set B
⑬ {...5, 6, 7, 8} ___ Set A and Set B
⑭ {11, 12, 13...} ___ Set B
⑮ {...8} ___ Set A and B

Set A = {...3, 6, 9, 12, 15}   Set B = {15, 18, 21...}

① -3 $\in$ Set A
② -6 ___ Set A
③ 23 ___ Set B
④ 33 ___ Set B
⑤ 63 ___ Set B

⑥ 3 ___ Set A
⑦ 9 ___ Set A
⑧ {18, 21} ___ Set B
⑨ {...3} ___ Set A
⑩ {3, 6, 9} ___ Set A

⑪ {15, 18, 21} ___ Set B
⑫ {15} ___ Set A and Set B
⑬ {...3, 6, 9} ___ Set A
⑭ {18, 21...} ___ Set B
⑮ {...12, 15...} ___ Set A and Set B

Set A = {...5, 10, 15, 20}   Set B = {...20, 25, 30...}

① 5 $\in$ Set A
② 5 ___ Set B
③ 20 ___ Set B
④ ___ $\in$ Set A
⑤ ___ $\in$ Set B

⑥ {...20} ___ Set A
⑦ {...20} ___ Set B
⑧ {-10, -5, 0} ___ Set A
⑨ {-10, -5, 0} ___ Set B
⑩ {-50, -45} ___ Set B

⑪ {50, 55} ___ Set B
⑫ 15, 20 ___ Set A
⑬ {...15, 20} ___ Set A and Set B
⑭ {...15, 20} ___ Set A and Set B
⑮ {...20, 25...} ___ Set A and Set B

C Fill in the blanks.

① Marolyn, Lisa, and Kim went swimming at the lake on Tuesday. Marolyn, Lisa, Amos, and John went swimming at the lake on Wednesday. On Thursday, Lisa, Marolyn, John, Amos, and Kim went swimming at the lake. Set A = {Tuesday's swimmers}   Set B = {Wednesday's swimmers}   Set C = {Thursday's swimmers}   Set A ∩ Set B = { _____ }
Set B ∩ Set C = { _____ }   Set A ∪ Set B = { _____
_____ }   Set A ∪ Set B = Set _____

② On Friday, Liz, Carmen, and Connie went to the mall. Liz bought a pair of pink sandals. After much deliberation, Carmen decided she wanted a pair also. On Saturday, Carmen, Sue, and Frannie went to the mall and each bought a pair of pink sandals. On Sunday, since the mall was closed, Liz, Carmen, Sue, and Frannie, all in pink sandals, went to the beach to meet Connie, who wore old tennis shoes, to watch boys surf. Set A = {Friday's shoppers}
Set B = {Saturday's shoppers}   Set C = {Beach goers}   Set A ___ Set C   Set B ___ Set C
Set A ∩ Set B = { _____ }   Set A ___ Set B = Set C   Set A ∪ Set B = { _____
_____ }

46

Simple Addition

Unit 19

Learning Objective: ***We will learn to add.***

Addition is the combining of numbers to obtain the total value, or sum.

EXAMPLE:
Addition is combining numbers.
2 apples + 3 apples is 5 apples. We combined to obtain the total number of apples.

A Combine the numbers.

① 36 + 1 = *37*	② 50 + 29	③ 9 + 4	④ 61 + 8	⑤ 60 + 3	⑥ 16 + 13	⑦ 12 + 0
⑧ 12 + 11	⑨ 73 + 20	⑩ 36 + 32	⑪ 73 + 11	⑫ 47 + 22	⑬ 27 + 22	⑭ 89 + 1
⑮ 9 + 7	⑯ 50 + 33	⑰ 5 + 1	⑱ 61 + 17	⑲ 69 + 10	⑳ 14 + 3	㉑ 81 + 13
㉒ 13 + 13	㉓ 71 + 5	㉔ 54 + 22	㉕ 43 + 43	㉖ 9 + 8	㉗ 9 + 9	㉘ 54 + 32
㉙ 46 + 23	㉚ 82 + 13	㉛ 86 + 10	㉜ 33 + 11	㉝ 10 + 11	㉞ 94 + 2	㉟ 14 + 5
㊱ 85 + 14	㊲ 9 + 6	㊳ 77 + 22	㊴ 50 + 47	㊵ 32 + 16	㊶ 6 + 2	㊷ 37 + 10
㊸ 8 + 2	㊹ 10 + 11	㊺ 18 + 3	㊻ 45 + 1	㊼ 17 + 10	㊽ 45 + 17	㊾ 50 + 3
㊿ 65 + 13	(51) 23 + 5	(52) 31 + 26	(53) 10 + 10	(54) 40 + 40	(55) 56 + 23	(56) 22 + 11

REMINDER: Write the definition of addition.

____

____

Unit 19 cont'd

B Find the sums.

① 41 + 22 = **63**   ⑩ 9 + 11 =   ⑲ 47 + 11 =   ㉘ 23 + 1 =

② 17 + 32 =   ⑪ 2 + 2 =   ⑳ 9 + 5 =   ㉙ 17 + 2 =

③ 79 + 0 =   ⑫ 4 + 4 =   ㉑ 75 + 24 =   ㉚ 14 + 42 =

④ 33 + 32 =   ⑬ 14 + 4 =   ㉒ 30 + 15 =   ㉛ 95 + 2 =

⑤ 33 + 11 =   ⑭ 44 + 24 =   ㉓ 12 + 12 =   ㉜ 89 + 1 =

⑥ 9 + 3 =   ⑮ 5 + 4 =   ㉔ 13 + 13 =   ㉝ 56 + 10 =

⑦ 5 + 2 =   ⑯ 13 + 0 =   ㉕ 21 + 7 =   ㉞ 14 + 13 =

⑧ 30 + 12 =   ⑰ 86 + 3 =   ㉖ 10 + 9 =   ㉟ 12 + 15 =

⑨ 56 + 22 =   ⑱ 55 + 20 =   ㉗ 15 + 13 =   ㊱ 90 + 7 =

C Find the sums. Use the space to work the problems.

① Marci and Rick picked 88 peaches in one hour. Then Marci picked one more. How many did they have?

89
+ 1
89

_____**89**_____

② Liz drove 33 miles to visit a friend. Then she drove 6 miles down her friend's driveway. How far did she drive to see her friend?

_____

③ Jeremy caught 20 fish before noon. He only caught one after noon. How many did he catch?

_____

④ Jerry and Cathy made seventeen baskets for the Homeless Children's Fair. Cathy also made eleven lunch buckets. How many items did they make altogether?

_____

⑤ Lori and Eddie dated for 12 years. Then they got married. They have been married for eighteen years. How many years have they been together?

_____

⑥ Robin bought nine loaves of bread for her family's picnic. During the picnic, they ran out of bread and Lizabeth went to town to buy 2 more loaves. How many loaves were bought for the picnic?

_____

Carrying

Learning Objective: *We will learn to carry to the tens' and hundreds' column.*

Carrying is moving any amount over 9 into the next column.

EXAMPLE:

When we add 7 to 73, we must carry to the tens' column.

$$\begin{array}{r} 1 \\ 73 \\ + 7 \\ \hline 80 \end{array}$$

When we add 37 to 73, we must carry to the hundreds' column.

$$\begin{array}{r} 1\,1 \\ 73 \\ + 37 \\ \hline 110 \end{array}$$

A Combine the numbers.

① $\begin{array}{r} 1 \\ 50 \\ + 69 \\ \hline 119 \end{array}$ ② $\begin{array}{r} 43 \\ + 17 \\ \hline \end{array}$ ③ $\begin{array}{r} 29 \\ + 62 \\ \hline \end{array}$ ④ $\begin{array}{r} 48 \\ + 4 \\ \hline \end{array}$ ⑤ $\begin{array}{r} 49 \\ + 11 \\ \hline \end{array}$ ⑥ $\begin{array}{r} 18 \\ + 8 \\ \hline \end{array}$ ⑦ $\begin{array}{r} 11 \\ + 19 \\ \hline \end{array}$

⑧ $\begin{array}{r} 33 \\ + 77 \\ \hline \end{array}$ ⑨ $\begin{array}{r} 85 \\ + 99 \\ \hline \end{array}$ ⑩ $\begin{array}{r} 63 \\ + 34 \\ \hline \end{array}$ ⑪ $\begin{array}{r} 25 \\ + 48 \\ \hline \end{array}$ ⑫ $\begin{array}{r} 18 \\ + 3 \\ \hline \end{array}$ ⑬ $\begin{array}{r} 9 \\ + 9 \\ \hline \end{array}$ ⑭ $\begin{array}{r} 25 \\ + 25 \\ \hline \end{array}$

⑮ $\begin{array}{r} 87 \\ + 4 \\ \hline \end{array}$ ⑯ $\begin{array}{r} 14 \\ + 66 \\ \hline \end{array}$ ⑰ $\begin{array}{r} 37 \\ + 80 \\ \hline \end{array}$ ⑱ $\begin{array}{r} 50 \\ + 45 \\ \hline \end{array}$ ⑲ $\begin{array}{r} 73 \\ + 17 \\ \hline \end{array}$ ⑳ $\begin{array}{r} 48 \\ + 26 \\ \hline \end{array}$ ㉑ $\begin{array}{r} 41 \\ + 90 \\ \hline \end{array}$

㉒ $\begin{array}{r} 90 \\ + 40 \\ \hline \end{array}$ ㉓ $\begin{array}{r} 39 \\ + 42 \\ \hline \end{array}$ ㉔ $\begin{array}{r} 38 \\ + 42 \\ \hline \end{array}$ ㉕ $\begin{array}{r} 80 \\ + 60 \\ \hline \end{array}$ ㉖ $\begin{array}{r} 48 \\ + 17 \\ \hline \end{array}$ ㉗ $\begin{array}{r} 46 \\ + 7 \\ \hline \end{array}$ ㉘ $\begin{array}{r} 57 \\ + 73 \\ \hline \end{array}$

㉙ $\begin{array}{r} 10 \\ + 94 \\ \hline \end{array}$ ㉚ $\begin{array}{r} 29 \\ + 13 \\ \hline \end{array}$ ㉛ $\begin{array}{r} 35 \\ + 5 \\ \hline \end{array}$ ㉜ $\begin{array}{r} 64 \\ + 18 \\ \hline \end{array}$ ㉝ $\begin{array}{r} 44 \\ + 72 \\ \hline \end{array}$ ㉞ $\begin{array}{r} 39 \\ + 84 \\ \hline \end{array}$ ㉟ $\begin{array}{r} 85 \\ + 7 \\ \hline \end{array}$

㊱ $\begin{array}{r} 50 \\ + 91 \\ \hline \end{array}$ ㊲ $\begin{array}{r} 17 \\ + 48 \\ \hline \end{array}$ ㊳ $\begin{array}{r} 47 \\ + 13 \\ \hline \end{array}$ ㊴ $\begin{array}{r} 27 \\ + 18 \\ \hline \end{array}$ ㊵ $\begin{array}{r} 84 \\ + 61 \\ \hline \end{array}$ ㊶ $\begin{array}{r} 68 \\ + 3 \\ \hline \end{array}$ ㊷ $\begin{array}{r} 24 \\ + 27 \\ \hline \end{array}$

㊸ $\begin{array}{r} 17 \\ + 17 \\ \hline \end{array}$ ㊹ $\begin{array}{r} 73 \\ + 8 \\ \hline \end{array}$ ㊺ $\begin{array}{r} 19 \\ + 16 \\ \hline \end{array}$ ㊻ $\begin{array}{r} 67 \\ + 13 \\ \hline \end{array}$ ㊼ $\begin{array}{r} 28 \\ + 7 \\ \hline \end{array}$ ㊽ $\begin{array}{r} 94 \\ + 17 \\ \hline \end{array}$ ㊾ $\begin{array}{r} 47 \\ + 19 \\ \hline \end{array}$

REMINDER: Write the definition of carrying.

_____

_____

Unit 20 cont'd ☞

B Find the sums.

① 81 + 19 = **100**   ② 96 + 45 =   ③ 43 + 27 =   ④ 90 + 81 =

⑤ 61 + 94 =   ⑥ 46 + 55 =   ⑦ 73 + 99 =   ⑧ 76 + 35 =

⑨ 75 + 17 =   ⑩ 27 + 74 =   ⑪ 39 + 14 =   ⑫ 84 + 48 =

⑬ 27 + 13 =   ⑭ 88 + 14 =   ⑮ 94 + 66 =   ⑯ 16 + 14 =

⑰ 80 + 40 =   ⑱ 90 + 19 =   ⑲ 15 + 16 =   ⑳ 94 + 26 =

㉑ 49 + 12 =   ㉒ 32 + 9 =   ㉓ 77 + 77 =   ㉔ 66 + 49 =

㉕ 56 + 65 =   ㉖ 15 + 7 =   ㉗ 46 + 39 =   ㉘ 27 + 26 =

㉙ 99 + 94 =   ㉚ 27 + 18 =   ㉛ 12 + 8 =   ㉜ 44 + 19 =

㉝ 62 + 50 =   ㉞ 84 + 84 =   ㉟ 41 + 19 =   ㊱ 70 + 36 =

C Add these figures and write the sums.

① At the 4th of July picnic, Dean grilled 84 t-bone steaks and 20 sirloin strips. How many steaks did he cook?

104

② Robin has 56 fiction books at home. She has another 38 fiction books in her office. How many books of fiction does Robin own?

③ Christy had 39 pairs of shoes. In the last year her mother has bought her 12 more pair. How many pairs of shoes does Christy now own?

④ Mary canned 38 quarts of cherries this year. Last year she only canned 12 quarts. How many quarts of cherries has Mary canned in the past two years?

⑤ Janet paddled seventeen miles in one day. The next day she was tired and only paddled nine miles. How many miles did Janet paddle altogether?

⑥ Marie ate 34 cookies one night watching television. The next evening she ate 28 cookies while reading a book. How many cookies did Marie eat in those two nights?

Comprehension Check

Ⓐ Write "f" if the set is finite and "i" if the set is infinite.

_f_ ① {1, 2, 3, 4, 5}

____ ② {101, 102, 103, 104, 105, 106, 107}

____ ③ {-20, -15, -10, -5, 0, 5, 10,...}

____ ④ {...24, 48, 72, 96, 102,...}

____ ⑤ {6, 7, 8, 9, 10}

____ ⑥ {1, 2, 3, 4,...}

____ ⑦ {26, 27, 28, 29, 36, 37, 38, 39}

____ ⑧ {2, 4, 8, 16, 32,...}

____ ⑨ {-256, -128, -64, -32, -16,...}

____ ⑩ {-20, -10, 0, 10, 20}

____ ⑪ {-46, -47, -48, -49, -50}

____ ⑫ {3, 6, 9, 12, 15, 18,...}

____ ⑬ the number of Idaho potatoes consumed after 1926

____ ⑭ the number of thumbnails clipped after 1976

____ ⑮ the number of men between the age of 17 and 21 in Little Rock

____ ⑯ the number of Big Boy tomatoes grown in July in Jonesboro

____ ⑰ the number of blue Fords bought during September in New York

____ ⑱ the number of big-mouth bass caught after 1956

____ ⑲ the number of dictionaries printed after 1894

____ ⑳ {2, 4, 6, 8, 10, 12, 14, 16, 18, 16, 14, 12, 10, 8, 6, 4, 2}

____ ㉑ the number of roses in Maggie O'Reilly's garden

____ ㉒ the number of green-eyed girls at Milton High School in 1963

____ ㉓ the number of oak trees in old Winchester's front yard

____ ㉔ the number of white socks, sized 9-11, made after 1984

Ⓑ Complete the mathematical sentences.

Set A = {...-10, -9, -8, -7, -6, -5, -4, -3, -2, -1, 0, 1}

Set B = {0, 1, 2, 3, 4, 5, 6, 7, 8, 9, 10, 11, 12,...}

Set C = {...-10, -9, -8, -7, -6, -5, -4, -3, -2, -1, 0, 1, 2, 3, 4, 5, 6, 7, 8, 9, 10, 11, 12,...}

① _-9_ ∈ Set A

② ____ ∈ Set B

③ ____ ∈ Set C

④ ____ ∈ Set A

⑤ ____ ∈ Set B

⑥ ____ ∈ Set C

⑦ ____ ∉ Set A

⑧ ____ ∉ Set B

⑨ ____ ∉ Set B

⑩ ____ ∈ Set A

⑪ 5 ____ Set A

⑫ {7} ____ Set B

⑬ 9 ____ Set C

⑭ {-9} ____ Set A

⑮ -7 ____ Set B

⑯ -5 ____ Set C

⑰ {-3} ____ Set A

⑱ {0} ____ Set B

⑲ {20} ____ Set C

⑳ {-20} ____ Set A

㉑ {-30, -29, -28} ____ Set A

㉒ {-29, -28, -27} ____ Set C

㉓ {0, 1} ____ Set A and Set B

㉔ {...-10, -9, -8} ____ Set C

㉕ Set A ____ Set B = {0, 1}

㉖ {1, 2, 3, 4, 5, 6, 7} ____ Set C

㉗ Set B ____ Set C = {0, 1, 2, 3, 4,...}

㉘ {...-16, -15, -12, -11} ____ Set A

㉙ {...15, 16, 17, 18, 19} ____ Set B

㉚ Set A ∪ Set B ____ Set C

Test 4 cont'd ☞

C Find the sums.

① 7
  + 5
  12

② 10
  + 10

③ 16
  + 1

④ 72
  + 12

⑤ 40
  + 15

⑥ 3
  + 13

⑦ 96
  + 3

⑧ 54
  + 6

⑨ 22
  + 17

⑩ 22
  + 57

⑪ 42
  + 10

⑫ 2
  + 2

⑬ 11
  + 12

⑭ 16
  + 4

⑮ 13
  + 13

⑯ 84
  + 3

⑰ 33
  + 33

⑱ 92
  + 8

⑲ 2
  + 4

⑳ 6
  + 26

㉑ 54
  + 23

㉒ 24
  + 6

㉓ 29
  + 1

㉔ 64
  + 6

㉕ 1
  + 1

㉖ 17
  + 4

㉗ 16
  + 2

㉘ 19
  + 1

㉙ 64
  + 1

㉚ 42
  + 8

㉛ 22
  + 33

㉜ 48
  + 31

D Find the sums. Show where numbers were carried to the next column.

① 11
  58
  + 46
  104

② 42
  + 19

③ 38
  + 13

④ 59
  + 11

⑤ 78
  + 12

⑥ 92
  + 78

⑦ 78
  + 42

⑧ 33
  + 77

⑨ 92
  + 18

⑩ 65
  + 65

⑪ 66
  + 14

⑫ 27
  + 36

⑬ 24
  + 36

⑭ 43
  + 68

⑮ 78
  + 13

⑯ 77
  + 88

⑰ 16
  + 27

⑱ 14
  + 67

⑲ 32
  + 29

⑳ 69
  + 69

㉑ 42
  + 99

㉒ 66
  + 65

㉓ 91
  + 19

㉔ 56
  + 66

Define these symbols and terms.

① ∩ _____

_____

② ∪ _____

_____

③ set notation _____

_____

④ finite set _____

_____

⑤ infinite set _____

_____

⑥ addition _____

_____

Mental Addition

Learning Objective: *We will learn to add mentally.*

Mental addition is the combining of numbers to obtain the total value, or sum, in one's mind.

EXAMPLE: Mental addition is adding figures in one's mind. We know that $5 + 5 = 10$, $3 + 2 = 5$, and that $2 + 1 = 3$, so we can add 235 to 125 in our heads, carry the 1, and conclude 360.

$$\begin{array}{r} 235 \\ +125 \\ \hline 360 \end{array}$$

A Add.

①	②	③	④	⑤	⑥	⑦
$\begin{array}{r}1\\+1\\\hline 2\end{array}$	$\begin{array}{r}11\\+13\end{array}$	$\begin{array}{r}56\\+78\end{array}$	$\begin{array}{r}73\\+50\end{array}$	$\begin{array}{r}396\\+404\end{array}$	$\begin{array}{r}197\\+204\end{array}$	$\begin{array}{r}434\\+547\end{array}$

⑧	⑨	⑩	⑪	⑫	⑬	⑭
$\begin{array}{r}2\\+1\end{array}$	$\begin{array}{r}20\\+32\end{array}$	$\begin{array}{r}93\\+39\end{array}$	$\begin{array}{r}82\\+96\end{array}$	$\begin{array}{r}569\\+322\end{array}$	$\begin{array}{r}567\\+664\end{array}$	$\begin{array}{r}789\\+344\end{array}$

⑮	⑯	⑰	⑱	⑲	⑳	㉑
$\begin{array}{r}3\\+2\end{array}$	$\begin{array}{r}48\\+53\end{array}$	$\begin{array}{r}11\\+99\end{array}$	$\begin{array}{r}99\\+24\end{array}$	$\begin{array}{r}596\\+232\end{array}$	$\begin{array}{r}928\\+113\end{array}$	$\begin{array}{r}815\\+597\end{array}$

㉒	㉓	㉔	㉕	㉖	㉗	㉘
$\begin{array}{r}4\\+3\end{array}$	$\begin{array}{r}32\\+64\end{array}$	$\begin{array}{r}74\\+64\end{array}$	$\begin{array}{r}66\\+32\end{array}$	$\begin{array}{r}667\\+348\end{array}$	$\begin{array}{r}925\\+606\end{array}$	$\begin{array}{r}856\\+678\end{array}$

㉙	㉚	㉛	㉜	㉝	㉞	㉟
$\begin{array}{r}5\\+4\end{array}$	$\begin{array}{r}77\\+60\end{array}$	$\begin{array}{r}53\\+34\end{array}$	$\begin{array}{r}75\\+25\end{array}$	$\begin{array}{r}597\\+668\end{array}$	$\begin{array}{r}733\\+248\end{array}$	$\begin{array}{r}471\\+777\end{array}$

㊱	㊲	㊳	㊴	㊵	㊶	㊷
$\begin{array}{r}7\\+2\end{array}$	$\begin{array}{r}55\\+49\end{array}$	$\begin{array}{r}90\\+17\end{array}$	$\begin{array}{r}33\\+67\end{array}$	$\begin{array}{r}345\\+549\end{array}$	$\begin{array}{r}533\\+678\end{array}$	$\begin{array}{r}567\\+664\end{array}$

㊸	㊹	㊺	㊻	㊼	㊽	㊾
$\begin{array}{r}8\\+3\end{array}$	$\begin{array}{r}73\\+82\end{array}$	$\begin{array}{r}83\\+65\end{array}$	$\begin{array}{r}47\\+64\end{array}$	$\begin{array}{r}600\\+799\end{array}$	$\begin{array}{r}436\\+507\end{array}$	$\begin{array}{r}333\\+667\end{array}$

REMINDER: *Write the definition of mental addition.*

_____

_____

Unit 21 cont'd ☞

B Find the sums.

① 20 + 30 = **50**

② 47 + 38 =

③ 42 + 58 =

④ 91 + 79 =

⑤ 32 + 76 =

⑥ 77 + 81 =

⑦ 93 + 47 =

⑧ 99 + 11 =

⑨ 48 + 36 =

⑩ 734 + 598 =

⑪ 322 + 309 =

⑫ 784 + 667 =

⑬ 555 + 555 =

⑭ 666 + 434 =

⑮ 201 + 709 =

⑯ 397 + 323 =

⑰ 982 + 898 =

⑱ 181 + 909 =

⑲ 666 + 334 =

⑳ 493 + 377 =

㉑ 473 + 398 =

㉒ 567 + 898 =

㉓ 955 + 400 =

㉔ 454 + 980 =

㉕ 890 + 457 =

㉖ 663 + 763 =

㉗ 927 + 360 =

㉘ 732 + 555 =

㉙ 708 + 561 =

㉚ 908 + 809 =

㉛ 111 + 999 =

㉜ 211 + 877 =

㉝ 409 + 302 =

㉞ 900 + 111 =

㉟ 333 + 888 =

㊱ 489 + 777 =

C Find the sums.

① Roger and Jana walk 3 miles a day. Jana also walks 2 miles every day to work. How many miles a day does Jana walk?
5

② Roger grades 106 mid-term exams and 106 final exams every semester. How many tests does he grade per semester?

③ Roger planted 28 iris bulbs in his yard. Jana planted another 13. How many did they plant altogether?

④ Roger and Jana have invited 366 people to a party. Each person will bring one other. If the 366 guests bring 366 more people, how many guests will there be?

⑤ Jana made 396 cookies for her daughter's girl scout meeting. She also baked 146 brownies. How many sweets did she make?

⑥ Roger and his son caught 400 minnows in Lake Charles one day. The next day they caught 697. How many little fish did they catch?

⑦ Jana bought 10 pieces of china to go with her existing 50 pieces. How many pieces does she have now?

⑧ On the way to camp, Roger drove 257 miles. On the way home he drove 260 miles. How many miles did he drive altogether?

⑨ Jana picked 679 cherries on Monday, and 531 on Tuesday. How many did she pick?

Three-Digit Addition

Learning Objective: *We will learn to add three-digit numbers.*

A three-digit number has digits in the ones' place, the tens' place, and the hundreds' place.

EXAMPLE:
When we add three-digit numbers, we sometimes carry to the thousands' column.

$$
\begin{array}{r}
{}^{1\ 1\ 1} \\
333 \\
222 \\
+555 \\
\hline
1,110
\end{array}
$$

A Add these three-digit numbers.

① 185 +369 = 554   ② 550 +330   ③ 352 +352   ④ 120 +506   ⑤ 403 +403   ⑥ 774 +111   ⑦ 456 +156

⑧ 729 +203   ⑨ 336 +639   ⑩ 104 +401   ⑪ 442 +304   ⑫ 180 +180   ⑬ 111 +222   ⑭ 250 +250

⑮ 123 +819   ⑯ 569 +333   ⑰ 118 +115   ⑱ 654 +120   ⑲ 555 +444   ⑳ 222 +555   ㉑ 336 +265

㉒ 321 +213   ㉓ 633 +111   ㉔ 336 +226   ㉕ 520 +366   ㉖ 222 +559   ㉗ 357 +159   ㉘ 239 +456

㉙ 205 +520   ㉚ 103 +103   ㉛ 554 +332   ㉜ 633 +200   ㉝ 781 +156   ㉞ 258 +369   ㉟ 148 +598

㊱ 544 +445   ㊲ 336 +336   ㊳ 889 +100   ㊴ 654 +108   ㊵ 601 +319   ㊶ 147 +147   ㊷ 456 +125

㊸ 200 +300   ㊹ 522 +225   ㊺ 500 +389   ㊻ 458 +458   ㊼ 699 +249   ㊽ 204 +304   ㊾ 125 +458

REMINDER: Write the definition of a three-digit number.

_____

_____

Unit 22 cont'd ☞

B Find the sums.

① $123 + 147 = $ **270**

② $587 + 203 = $

③ $800 + 150 = $

④ $459 + 354 = $

⑤ $654 + 321 = $

⑥ $603 + 333 = $

⑦ $789 + 125 = $

⑧ $230 + 650 = $

⑨ $128 + 560 = $

⑩ $147 + 369 = $

⑪ $258 + 105 = $

⑫ $182 + 181 = $

⑬ $158 + 654 = $

⑭ $458 + 500 = $

⑮ $159 + 192 = $

⑯ $114 + 225 = $

⑰ $308 + 304 = $

⑱ $375 + 275 = $

⑲ $587 + 145 = $

⑳ $445 + 502 = $

㉑ $560 + 440 = $

㉒		㉓		㉔		㉕		㉖		㉗	
	363		932		560		783		128		148
	653		105		730		536		560		456
	+724		+106		+333		+814		+192		+458

C Find the sums.

① Oregon county steel workers worked 329 days in 1981, 307 days in 1982, 300 days in 1983, and only 100 days the following year. How many days did the workers work during the four years?

1,036

② Six hundred seventy-five Oregon county residents subscribe to The Oregon News. Three hundred eighty-nine people outside the county also receive the paper. How many subscribers are there?

③ The mayor of Oregon City gave 46 speeches in 1983. In 1984 he gave 57, and in 1985 the mayor gave 63 speeches. How many speeches did the mayor give during the three years?

④ The Oregon City Police Department raised $967 at their annual ball for charity. The fire department raised $898 at a similar ball for the same charity. How much did the charity receive?

⑤ The Oregon county garden club planted 397 rose bushes around the courthouse. They also planted 260 iris bulbs around the sheriff's office. How many flowers did the garden club plant?

⑥ There are 297 students at Oregon County High School. There are 276 students at the junior high school. There are 481 students at the elementary school. How many students are there?

56

Four-Digit Addition

Learning Objective: *We will learn to add four-digit numbers.*

A four-digit number has digits in the ones' place, the tens' place, the hundreds' place, and the thousands' place.

EXAMPLE: When we add four-digit numbers, we sometimes carry to the ten thousands' column.

```
  1 1 1 1
   3,333
   4,444
 + 4,444
  12,221
```

A Add these four-digit numbers.

① 1,234 +4,563 **5,797**	② 5,236 +6,521	③ 1,023 +5,554	④ 9,226 +3,246	⑤ 1,254 +1,254	⑥ 3,209 +9,632
⑦ 3,000 +2,000	⑧ 5,612 +3,215	⑨ 1,111 +1,111	⑩ 2,503 +3,650	⑪ 2,222 +3,658	⑫ 3,502 +3,502
⑬ 5,023 +6,325	⑭ 2,020 +5,050	⑮ 2,222 +2,222	⑯ 8,920 +6,302	⑰ 5,556 +2,228	⑱ 5,688 +2,222
⑲ 9,632 +1,000	⑳ 6,654 +3,365	㉑ 5,555 +5,555	㉒ 4,563 +4,563	㉓ 9,635 +9,635	㉔ 1,052 +1,052
㉕ 5,600 +5,600	㉖ 2,231 +5,555	㉗ 3,330 +2,225	㉘ 8,952 +8,952	㉙ 3,332 +3,255	㉚ 5,555 +9,632
㉛ 6,000 +2,101	㉜ 6,663 +5,555	㉝ 3,369 +6,602	㉞ 1,147 +2,352	㉟ 1,235 +6,666	㊱ 5,688 +2,222
㊲ 6,600 +2,101	㊳ 8,882 +3,110	㊴ 4,568 +5,690	㊵ 2,220 +3,335	㊶ 7,852 +7,852	㊷ 5,692 +5,602

REMINDER: Write the definition of a four-digit number.

_____

_____

Unit 23 cont'd ☞

B Add these four-digit numbers.

① $7,777 + 7,774 =$ **15,551** ② $3,214 + 2,103 =$ ③ $5,503 + 1,111 =$

④ $4,456 + 2,256 =$ ⑤ $5,123 + 8,521 =$ ⑥ $2,222 + 1,102 =$

⑦ $2,356 + 8,956 =$ ⑧ $3,025 + 4,120 =$ ⑨ $4,402 + 3,023 =$

⑩ $2,589 + 8,521 =$ ⑪ $7,120 + 2,300 =$ ⑫ $9,000 + 1,235 =$

⑬ $3,232 + 1,212 =$ ⑭ $3,300 + 5,500 =$ ⑮ $4,560 + 2,359 =$

⑯ $5,689 + 6,598 =$ ⑰ $3,302 + 5,551 =$ ⑱ $3,210 + 5,642 =$

⑲ $7,789 + 3,369 =$ ⑳ $6,600 + 4,400 =$ ㉑ $5,550 + 6,650 =$

| ㉒ | 3,350 | ㉓ | 5,523 | ㉔ | 1,148 | ㉕ | 2,245 | ㉖ | 5,560 | ㉗ | 4,423 |
| | +2,225 | | +5,525 | | +4,582 | | +3,356 | | +3,302 | | +8,812 |

C Find the sums.

① At the Butler County Fair last year, 3,301 people ate hamburgers for lunch and 8,801 people bought hot dogs for lunch. How many lunches were bought?
____**12,102**____

② Liz saved $1,258 working in a restaurant. She saved another $4,569 when she became a reporter. She saved all this in two years. How much did she save?
_____

③ The Charity League collected 4,176 cans of food for needy families. It also collected 1,052 packages of foods such as rice, noodles, and beans. How many items of food were collected?
_____

④ The senior class of 1983 raised $1,401 for the prom. They also raised $2,501 for a senior trip. How much did they raise?
_____

⑤ It takes 2,500 sheets of paper to fill a small box. It takes 3,750 sheets to fill a large box. How many sheets of paper are in the two boxes?
_____

⑥ Robin drove 1,600 miles to visit her cousin. On the way back home she drove 1,650 miles. How many miles did she drive?
_____

Five-Digit Addition

Learning Objective: **We will learn to add five-digit numbers.**

A five-digit number has digits in the ones' place, the tens' place, the hundreds' place, the thousands' place, and the ten thousands' place.

EXAMPLE: When we add five-digit numbers, we sometimes carry to the hundred thousands' column.

```
 1 1 1 1 1
    22,222
    44,444
  + 44,444
   111,110
```

A Add these five-digit numbers.

① 42,580
  +42,580
  85,160

② 78,945
  +61,230

③ 86,868
  +86,868

④ 65,498
  +12,369

⑤ 70,583
  +36,987

⑥ 11,111
  +22,222

⑦ 96,302
  +58,741

⑧ 66,665
  +55,556

⑨ 45,687
  +23,235

⑩ 45,871
  +45,821

⑪ 33,333
  +44,444

⑫ 23,009
  +23,569

⑬ 12,345
  +56,894

⑭ 56,984
  +45,683

⑮ 78,945
  +54,987

⑯ 66,666
  +33,333

⑰ 11,112
  +33,336

⑱ 55,512
  +78,945

⑲ 55,512
  +23,269

⑳ 58,744
  +55,864

㉑ 23,569
  +23,569

㉒ 33,333
  +66,669

㉓ 56,894
  +22,256

㉔ 45,689
  +33,324

㉕ 89,745
  +63,258

㉖ 55,552
  +66,663

㉗ 33,333
  +66,666

㉘ 10,102
  +20,203

㉙ 77,412
  +88,456

㉚ 20,153
  +23,562

㉛ 55,653
  +65,239

㉜ 95,953
  +56,563

㉝ 56,894
  +50,003

㉞ 32,658
  +74,102

㉟ 11,025
  +85,214

REMINDER: Write the definition of a five-digit number.

Unit 24 cont'd 👉

B Find the sums.

①
```
  45,780
  25,023
  70,000
 +70,025
 ───────
 210,828
```

②
```
  65,656
  96,699
  33,335
 +66,668
```

③
```
  23,579
  98,743
  65,559
 +66,559
```

④
```
  56,123
  10,101
  30,253
 +20,360
```

⑤
```
  56,023
  89,560
  55,876
 +55,555
```

⑥
```
  95,680
  54,785
  55,565
 +23,650
```

⑦
```
  54,123
  88,805
  89,456
 +98,745
```

⑧
```
  66,669
  44,449
  99,874
 +33,325
```

⑨
```
  95,203
  62,100
  56,200
 +98,708
```

⑩
```
  44,520
  22,250
  66,520
 +33,210
```

⑪
```
  44,445
  56,559
  77,771
 +22,210
```

⑫
```
  12,457
  23,568
  24,658
 +98,756
```

⑬
```
  55,698
  22,222
  22,503
 +66,520
```

⑭
```
  60,325
  63,025
  12,300
 +32,000
```

⑮
```
  33,350
  66,650
  99,980
 +99,950
```

C Find the sums.

① An inventory at Sunny Bread shows 25,698 loaves of wheat bread and 22,223 loaves of white bread. How many loaves are there?

47,921

② Rocky High Ski Resort hosted 10,768 skiers in the first week of January. The second week brought 10,312 skiers. How many skiers were there?

③ A total of 12,839 students toured foreign countries through World Tours, Inc. A total of 15,971 tourists visited foreign countries through the same agency. How many clients did World Tours, Inc., handle?

④ Across the country 26,800 boxes of candy were sold during a fund-raising drive to feed starving people in Africa. In addition, 15,650 posters were sold. How many total items were sold?

⑤ On Monday, telephone operators connected 23,579 long distance calls. On Tuesday, they connected 12,300 calls. On Wednesday, the operators connected 10,101 long distance calls. How many calls were connected?

⑥ Burgers, Inc., sold 36,520 hamburgers in 1983. They sold another 36,570 in 1984. In 1985 they hit an all-time sales high by selling 43,469 burgers. How many hamburgers did they sell during the three years?

60

Six-Digit Addition

Learning
Objective: *We will learn to add six-digit numbers.*

A six-digit number has digits in the ones' place, the tens' place, the hundreds' place, the thousands' place, the ten thousands' place, and the hundred thousands' place.

EXAMPLE: When we add six-digit numbers, we sometimes carry to the millions' column.

```
  1 1 1 1  1 1
    777,333
  + 333,777
  1,111,110
```

A Add these six-digit numbers.

① 666,598
  +666,542
  1,333,140

② 745,874
  +852,145

③ 777,556
  +222,659

④ 123,456
  +123,456

⑤ 445,500
  +223,301

⑥ 112,546
  +456,789

⑦ 123,456
  +456,987

⑧ 333,336
  +998,456

⑨ 775,213
  +777,563

⑩ 669,982
  +665,540

⑪ 124,569
  +126,951

⑫ 123,456
  +784,561

⑬ 120,236
  +236,902

⑭ 995,203
  +995,230

⑮ 556,689
  +110,022

⑯ 457,855
  +556,523

⑰ 123,789
  +456,123

⑱ 124,569
  +456,895

⑲ 123,789
  +456,258

⑳ 112,369
  +114,752

㉑ 999,999
  +666,665

㉒ 111,123
  +111,256

㉓ 112,233
  +112,569

㉔ 123,000
  +336,600

㉕ 220,230
  +303,035

㉖ 121,236
  +121,583

㉗ 635,236
  +666,659

㉘ 200,569
  +445,693

㉙ 550,023
  +556,230

㉚ 333,360
  +444,456

㉛ 202,036
  +365,239

㉜ 101,012
  +235,696

㉝ 888,952
  +111,156

㉞ 885,522
  +994,563

㉟ 888,852
  +111,102

REMINDER: *Write the definition of a six-digit number.*

_____

_____

Unit 25 cont'd ☛

B Find the sums.

①
```
   333,698
   111,236
 + 456,321
   901,255
```

②
```
   789,456
   789,456
 + 789,456
```

③
```
   456,123
   303,210
 + 369,520
```

④
```
   789,456
   741,258
 + 963,025
```

⑤
```
   451,200
   366,698
 + 866,968
```

⑥
```
   963,695
   555,555
 + 665,983
```

⑦
```
   102,030
   605,040
 + 908,070
```

⑧
```
   456,123
   333,201
 + 698,740
```

⑨
```
   708,090
   605,040
 + 302,010
```

⑩
```
   784,560
   331,025
 + 575,255
```

⑪
```
   555,569
   202,020
 + 321,032
```

⑫
```
   603,030
   505,203
 + 120,321
```

⑬
```
   456,123
   963,258
 + 741,258
```

⑭
```
   360,250
   654,980
 + 707,070
```

⑮
```
   852,036
   741,025
 + 147,205
```

C Find the sums.

① There are 444,425 books on Johnston Library's main floor. There are another 222,254 books on the second floor. How many books are there in Johnston's Library?
666,679

② There are 147,852 people living in Corning. There are 222,258 people living in Cartersville. If all the residents of both cities meet to discuss land-fill sharing, how many people will be at the meeting?

③ The Morrow Company grossed $107,000 last year. The previous year it grossed $121,500. How much did it gross the last two years?

④ The national headquarters of The Foreign Stamp Collectors' Guild took a survey of how many stamps its current members possessed. The members were divided into two groups. One group held 451,176 stamps. The other group held 387,902 stamps. What was the total number of stamps?

⑤ The state fair held a contest whereby contestants had to guess how many marbles were in a giant jar. Blake guessed 247,000. Richard guessed 266,000. If they had combined their guesses, they would have been exactly right. How many marbles were in the jar?

⑥ Over the past ten years Mr. Johnson has hoarded pennies. One day he decided to count how many pennies he had collected. On Monday he counted 100,000 pennies. On Tuesday he counted 125,000 pennies. How many pennies did he have?

Comprehension Check

A Add these problems mentally and write the sums.

① 6
  +6
  ——
  12

② 8
  +9

③ 5
  +5

④ 11
  +17

⑤ 32
  +34

⑥ 102
  +309

⑦ 556
  +433

⑧ 400
  +600

⑨ 1
  +7

⑩ 9
  +5

⑪ 5
  +4

⑫ 23
  +13

⑬ 56
  +57

⑭ 406
  +798

⑮ 783
  +991

⑯ 550
  +450

⑰ 9
  +3

⑱ 6
  +8

⑲ 9
  +2

⑳ 15
  +16

㉑ 38
  +49

㉒ 883
  +911

㉓ 564
  +382

㉔ 350
  +650

㉕ 7
  +6

㉖ 4
  +6

㉗ 9
  +4

㉘ 17
  +18

㉙ 56
  +63

㉚ 164
  +308

㉛ 197
  +235

㉜ 333
  +776

㉝ 3
  +1

㉞ 3
  +7

㉟ 8
  +5

㊱ 19
  +13

㊲ 79
  +81

㊳ 371
  +173

㊴ 225
  +575

㊵ 932
  +483

㊶ 5
  +2

㊷ 7
  +7

㊸ 6
  +7

㊹ 20
  +23

㊺ 86
  +12

㊻ 411
  +141

㊼ 770
  +330

㊽ 999
  +111

B Add these three-digit numbers.

① 102
  +201
  ——
  303

② 666
  +334

③ 544
  +644

④ 523
  +327

⑤ 390
  +399

⑥ 246
  +802

⑦ 306
  +194

⑧ 789
  +334

⑨ 101
  +999

⑩ 802
  +888

⑪ 402
  +688

⑫ 135
  +791

⑬ 335
  +777

⑭ 808
  +102

⑮ 111
  +219

⑯ 159
  +161

⑰ 911
  +119

⑱ 232
  +425

⑲ 567
  +303

⑳ 889
  +702

㉑ 996
  +444

㉒ 160
  +660

㉓ 337
  +773

㉔ 267
  +999

Test 5 cont'd ☞

C Add these four-digit numbers.

①	3,019 +2,621	②	5,555 +6,666	③	8,910 +1,089	④	3,562 +9,191	⑤	1,333 +7,777	⑥	1,099 +9,901

① 3,019
　+2,621
　5,640

② 5,555
　+6,666

③ 8,910
　+1,089

④ 3,562
　+9,191

⑤ 1,333
　+7,777

⑥ 1,099
　+9,901

⑦ 3,894
　+5,264

⑧ 3,333
　+2,975

⑨ 8,496
　+5,321

⑩ 2,456
　+7,890

⑪ 4,646
　+6,464

⑫ 2,468
　+3,579

D Add these five-digit numbers.

① 77,332
　21,111
　+10,992
　109,435

② 58,112
　38,279
　+12,345

③ 52,567
　66,776
　+93,321

④ 56,655
　71,832
　+94,666

⑤ 84,811
　23,322
　+49,499

⑥ 11,121
　94,638
　+34,368

⑦ 11,234
　44,576
　+33,001

⑧ 68,621
　89,765
　+54,321

⑨ 99,333
　67,891
　+21,345

⑩ 61,621
　27,911
　+93,482

⑪ 66,666
　55,555
　+44,444

⑫ 49,356
　63,598
　+24,848

E Add these six-digit numbers.

① 100,000
　+999,666
　1,099,666

② 222,567
　+372,009

③ 525,616
　+789,101

④ 999,234
　+111,876

⑤ 246,810
　+121,416

⑥ 562,437
　+289,001

⑦ 123,465
　+789,011

⑧ 113,020
　+927,091

⑨ 777,566
　+333,544

⑩ 932,815
　+568,621

Define these terms.

① mental addition _____

_____

② three-digit number _____

_____

③ four-digit number _____

_____

④ five-digit number _____

_____

⑤ six-digit number _____

_____

The Associative Property

Learning Objective: *We will learn to use the associative property of addition.*

The associative property of addition holds that the sum will be the same regardless of the way in which a series of numbers is combined.

EXAMPLE:
$$[a + b] + c = d \qquad a + [b + c] = d$$
$$[1 + 2] + 3 = 6 \qquad 1 + [2 + 3] = 6$$

A Below each set of brackets, write the sum of the two addends within the brackets. Add to this sum the third addend and write the final sum.

① $[7 + 3] + 2 = $ ___12___
      10

   $7 + [3 + 2] = $ ___12___
        5

② $[27 + 14] + 35 = $ _____
      _____

   $27 + [14 + 35] = $ _____
      _____

③ $[111 + 76] + 44 = $ _____
      _____

   $111 + [76 + 44] = $ _____
      _____

④ $[338 + 150] + 512 = $ _____
      _____

   $338 + [150 + 512] = $ _____
      _____

⑤ $[1,299 + 1,275] + 1,300 = $ _____
      _____

   $1,299 + [1,275 + 1,300] = $ _____
      _____

⑥ $[3,462 + 143] + 786 = $ _____
      _____

   $3,462 + [143 + 786] = $ _____
      _____

⑦ $[10,211 + 2,075] + 388 = $ _____
      _____

   $10,211 + [2,075 + 388] = $ _____
      _____

⑧ $[30,219 + 14,876] + 9,210 = $ _____
      _____

   $30,219 + [14,876 + 9,210] = $ _____
      _____

⑨ $[832 + 1,509] + 67 = $ _____
      _____

   $832 + [1,509 + 67] = $ _____
      _____

⑩ $[13,323 + 7,877] + 3,333 = $ _____
      _____

   $13,323 + [7,877 + 3,333] = $ _____
      _____

REMINDER: Write the definition of the associative property of addition.

_____

_____

Unit 26 cont'd 🖝

B Study each problem and write a second problem that demonstrates the associative property of addition.

① $[911 + 486] + 52 = 1,449$ $911 + [486 + 52] = 1,449$

② $[692 + 847] + 10 = 1,549$

③ $[1,459 + 1,011] + 1,765 = 4,235$

④ $[762 + 8,913] + 2,428 = 12,103$

⑤ $[99 + 5,436] + 10,419 = 15,954$

⑥ $[1,274 + 7,861] + 3,862 = 12,997$

⑦ $[22,416 + 46,811] + 11,876 = 81,103$

⑧ $[77 + 10,814] + 87,202 = 98,093$

⑨ $[137 + 6,414] + 2,198 = 8,749$

⑩ $914 + [1,477 + 10,001] = 12,392$

⑪ $[784 + 361] + 980 = 2,125$

⑫ $51,430 + [15,007 + 721] = 67,158$

⑬ $1,213 + [8,460 + 7,100] = 16,773$

⑭ $[488 + 2,098] + 1,416 = 4,002$

⑮ $922 + [6,401 + 10,972] = 18,295$

C Study the paragraphs. Then write two addition sentences that demonstrate the associative property.

① Jamison sold 716 boxes of candy for the fund-raising drive. Albert sold 248. But Ralph sold the most, 912 boxes. How many boxes did the three sell?

a. _____
b. _____

② Stephen collected 4,600 pennies; 2,110 nickels; and 1,862 dimes. How many coins

a. _____
b. _____

③ Reba traveled 550 miles on Monday, 491 miles on Tuesday, and 142 miles on Wednesday. How many miles were traveled in three days?

a. _____
b. _____

④ Jacyln made 112 cookies. Robert made 121. Dana made 96. How many cookies did they make?

a. _____
b. _____

⑤ Gina read 267 pages on Tuesday, 241 on Thursday, and 172 on Friday. How many pages did she read?

a. _____
b. _____

Using the Associative Property   Unit 27

Learning Objective: *We will learn to apply the associative property of addition.*

The associative property of addition holds that the sum will be the same regardless of the way in which a series of numbers is combined.

EXAMPLES:

$$[10 + 61] + 42 = 113$$
$$10 + [61 + 42] = 113$$

$$[900 + 400] + 200 = 1,500$$
$$900 + [400 + 200] = 1,500$$

A   Write two addition sentences that illustrate the associative property.

① 17
   30
+81
_____
128

$[17 + 30] + 81 = 128$
$17 + [30 + 81] = 128$

② 100
   72
+56
_____
228

③ 43
   80
+94
_____
217

④ 161
   129
+107
_____
397

⑤ 491
   203
+652
_____
1,346

⑥ 999
   434
+147
_____
1,580

⑦ 1,291
   3,461
+6,772
_____
11,524

⑧ 4,806
   7,622
+1,335
_____
13,763

⑨ 14,711
   36,875
+12,748
_____
64,334

⑩ 75,001
   11,413
+32,334
_____
118,748

REMINDER: Write the definition of the associative property of addition.

_____

_____

'Unit 27 cont'd 👉

B Match the addition sentences that illustrate the associative property.

① [1 + 2] + 3 = 6   10 + [5 + 7] = 22   ⑨ [a + b] + c = d   90 + [10 + 1] = 101

② [1 + 3] + 2 = 6   1 + [2 + 3] = 6   ⑩ [90 + 10] + 1 = 101   a + [b + c] = d

③ [10 + 5] + 7 = 22   1 + [3 + 2] = 6   ⑪ 12 + [11 + 6] = 29   3 + [6 + 2] = 11

④ [7 + 5] + 10 = 22   20 + [4 + 2] = 26   ⑫ 7 + [3 + 8] = 18   [7 + 3] + 8 = 18

⑤ [9 + 0] + 8 = 17   8 + [0 + 9] = 17   ⑬ [3 + 6] + 2 = 11   [12 + 11] + 6 = 29

⑥ [8 + 0] + 9 = 17   7 + [5 + 10] = 22   ⑭ [20 + 10] + 7 = 37   20 + [10 + 7] = 37

⑦ [20 + 4] + 2 = 26   9 + [0 + 8] = 17   ⑮ 13 + [6 + 11] = 30   [5 + 4] + 3 = 12

⑧ [4 + 20] + 2 = 26   4 + [20 + 2] = 26   ⑯ 5 + [4 + 3] = 12   [13 + 6] + 11 = 30

C Match the addition sentences that illustrate the associative property.

① Nine plus the sum of two and four equals fifteen.

② Ten plus the sum of one and eight equals nineteen.

③ Three plus the sum of six and seven equals sixteen.

④ Twenty plus the sum of ten and five equals thirty-five.

⑤ Eleven plus the sum of two and four equals seventeen.

⑥ Fifty plus the sum of ten and twenty equals eighty.

⑦ One plus the sum of ninety-six and three equals one hundred.

a. The sum of ten and one plus eight equals nineteen.

b. The sum of eleven and two plus four equals seventeen.

c. The sum of one and ninety-six plus three equals one hundred.

d. The sum of nine and two plus four equals fifteen.

e. The sum of three and six plus seven equals sixteen.

f. The sum of fifty and ten plus twenty equals eighty.

g. The sum of twenty and ten plus five equals thirty-five.

The Commutative Property

Learning
Objective: *We will learn to apply the commutative property of addition.*

The commutative property of addition holds that the sum will be the same if the order of the addends is reversed.

EXAMPLES: (1) a + b = c
                    or b + a = c

(2) a + b + c = d
     or a + c + b = d   or   b + c + a = d
     or b + a + c = d   or   c + b + a = d
     or c + a + b = d

A Apply the commutative property of addition and write one other way the addends could be combined.

① x + y = z
   y + x = z

② 1 + 2 = 3

③ 7 + 8 = 15

④ 10 + 1 = 11

⑤ 31 + 18 = 49

⑥ a + c = b

⑦ 27 + 6 = 33

⑧ 19 + 40 = 59

⑨ 100 + 50 = 150

⑩ 90 + 22 = 112

⑪ x + 2 = 10

⑫ 31 + 32 = 63

⑬ 57 + a = 100

⑭ 44 + 36 = 80

⑮ 12 + 84 = 96

⑯ q + n = o

B Apply the commutative property of addition and write two other ways the addends could be combined.

① 1 + 2 + 3 = 6
   2 + 1 + 3 = 6
   3 + 2 + 1 = 6

② a + z + x = 88

③ 19 + 2 + 9 = 30

④ 21 + 48 + 11 = 80

⑤ 15 + 72 + 8 = 95

⑥ 62 + a + 9 = 76

⑦ x + y + z = a

⑧ 111 + 11 + 1 = 123

⑨ 44 + 24 + 54 = 122

⑩ 51 + 92 + 22 = 165

⑪ 4 + z + x = y

⑫ 27 + 20 + 140 = 187

REMINDER: Write the definition of the commutative property of addition.

Unit 28 cont'd ☛

C Write two ways to combine each set of numbers. Then solve the problems.

① 6, 10, 21

  6 + 10 + 21 = 37

  10 + 6 + 21 = 37

② 98, 13

_____

_____

③ 100, 20, 60

_____

_____

④ 1, 57, 35

_____

_____

⑤ 41, 40, 43

_____

_____

⑥ 11, 8, 33, 14

_____

_____

⑦ 71, 22, 49, 90

_____

_____

⑧ 121, 150, 86

_____

_____

⑨ 307, 82, 109, 4

_____

_____

⑩ 15, 150, 12, 120

_____

_____

⑪ 6, 19, 62, 41

_____

_____

⑫ 36, 40, 2, 50

_____

_____

⑬ 13, 28, 113, 60

_____

_____

⑭ 17, 18, 19, 20

_____

_____

⑮ 133, 21, 17, 99

_____

_____

D Read each problem. Then write two addition sentences which illustrate the commutative property.

① Sonyer's Flower Shop sold 813 corsages for the Celebrity Ball. 518 corsages were orchids, 212 were rosebuds, and 83 were daisies.

  518 + 212 + 83 = 813

  83 + 212 + 518 = 813

② Joanna made cookies for the family reunion. She baked 200 chocolate chip cookies, 150 peanut-butter cookies, and 175 coconut-almond cookies. All 525 cookies were eaten.

_____

_____

③ Donnie ate 22 potato chips for lunch. Edna ate 31, Paul ate 15, and Sid ate 1. None of the 69 chips were left.

_____

_____

④ On his vacation, Stan drove 112 miles to his aunt's house. Then he drove 83 miles to his grandparents' house. A week later he drove 195 miles home. His mileage showed 390 miles.

_____

_____

⑤ Lisa worked 4 hours on her essay. Then she went shopping for 3 hours. That afternoon she attended a tea that lasted 2 hours. In the evening she went to dinner and a movie and returned 4 hours later. It had been a busy 13-hour day.

_____

_____

⑥ Joe's brothers are ages 12, 14, 17, and 20. Joe is 15. Together their ages total 78 years.

_____

_____

Using the Commutative Property

Learning
Objective: *We will learn to apply the commutative property of addition.*

The commutative property of addition holds that the sum will be the same if the order of the addends is reversed.

EXAMPLES: **(a)**
```
  2,142      1,001        (b)    8,347        714
 +1,001     +2,142             + 714       +8,347
 ------     ------             ------       ------
  3,143      3,143             9,061        9,061
```

A Find the sums.

①
```
   24       78
  +78      +24
  ----     ----
  102      102
```

②
```
  111       59
  +59      +111
```

③
```
  418      130
 +130     +418
```

④
```
  780      291
 +291     +780
```

⑤
```
  555      620
 +620     +555
```

⑥
```
  604       22
  +22     +604
```

⑦
```
 1,280     1,112
+1,112    +1,280
```

⑧
```
 4,367     3,900
+3,900    +4,367
```

⑨
```
 9,002      450
 +450    +9,002
```

⑩
```
 4,811     2,650
+2,650    +4,811
```

⑪
```
 1,987     1,804
+1,804    +1,987
```

⑫
```
 2,118     4,999
+4,999    +2,118
```

⑬
```
10,416     4,423
+4,423   +10,416
```

⑭
```
 8,300    11,366
+11,366   +8,300
```

⑮
```
 5,082     6,082
+6,082    +5,082
```

⑯
```
  415      123
  876      876
 +123     +415
```

⑰
```
 1,400     2,301
   811     1,400
+2,301     +811
```

⑱
```
 7,162     1,238
 1,238     7,162
+5,086    +5,086
```

⑲
```
10,240     6,875
 6,875     3,901
+3,901   +10,240
```

⑳
```
11,896    17,352
14,860    11,896
+17,352  +14,860
```

㉑
```
22,222    42,424
13,131    13,131
+42,424  +22,222
```

REMINDER: Write the definition of the commutative property of addition.

_____

_____

Unit 29 cont'd ☞

B Match the problems which illustrate the commutative property of addition.

① $72 + 18 = 90$ $84 + 101 = 185$ ⑨ $715 + 173 = 888$ $42 + 76 = 118$

② $421 + 97 = 518$ $18 + 72 = 90$ ⑩ $76 + 42 = 118$ $173 + 715 = 888$

③ $101 + 84 = 185$ $109 + 490 = 599$ ⑪ $374 + 651 = 1,025$ $651 + 374 = 1,025$

④ $63 + 802 = 865$ $97 + 421 = 518$ ⑫ $1,180 + 3,472 = 4,652$ $662 + 20 = 682$

⑤ $490 + 109 = 599$ $802 + 63 = 865$ ⑬ $20 + 662 = 682$ $99 + 612 = 711$

⑥ $651 + 610 = 1,261$ $572 + 620 = 1,192$ ⑭ $1,417 + 5,803 = 7,220$ $3,472 + 1,180 = 4,652$

⑦ $490 + 331 = 821$ $331 + 490 = 821$ ⑮ $612 + 99 = 711$ $990 + 711 = 1,701$

⑧ $620 + 572 = 1,192$ $610 + 651 = 1,261$ ⑯ $711 + 990 = 1,701$ $5,803 + 1,417 = 7,220$

C Read each problem. Then write two addition sentences which illustrate the commutative property. Solve the problems.

① Edward needs 250 more roses to finish his display. So far he has used 150 white roses, 300 red roses, 125 yellow roses, and 50 pink roses.

$250 + 150 + 300 + 125 + 50 = 875$

$50 + 125 + 150 + 250 + 300 = 875$

④ Jetta read 115 pages of her new book on Saturday. She read 76 on Sunday. On Monday she read 95. She finished the last 27 pages on Tuesday.

_____

_____

② Sarah counted 75 words in her introductory paragraph. Her second paragraph totaled 136 words. Her third paragraph was the longest at 183 words. Her conclusion was 79 words.

_____

_____

⑤ Dennis sold 16 tickets to his father, 12 tickets to his mother, 6 tickets to his friend Ralphie, and 8 tickets to his neighbor Roberta.

_____

_____

③ Candace collects postcards. So far she has 67 from the United States, 41 from Asia, and 52 from Europe.

_____

_____

⑥ Betsy decorated 36 clown cookies, 45 teddy bear cookies, 24 tree-shaped cookies, and 24 house-shaped cookies.

_____

_____

Identifying Properties

Learning Objective: *We will learn to distinguish between the associative and commutative properties of addition.*

The associative property of addition holds that the sum will be the same regardless of the way in which a series of numbers is combined.

$[a + b] + c = d$ $\qquad\qquad$ $a + [b + c] = d$

The commutative property of addition holds that the sum will be the same if the order of the addends is reversed.

$a + b = c$ $\qquad\qquad$ $b + a = c$

A Apply the associative property and solve the problems.

① $[18 + 20] + 10 =$ _____

$\qquad$ _____

$\quad$ $18 + [20 + 10] =$ _____

$\qquad$ _____

② $[31 + 46] + 24 =$ _____

$\qquad$ _____

$\quad$ $31 + [46 + 24] =$ _____

$\qquad$ _____

③ $912 + [400 + 167] =$ _____

$\qquad$ _____

$\quad$ $[912 + 400] + 167 =$ _____

$\qquad$ _____

④ $333 + [182 + 729] =$ _____

$\qquad$ _____

$\quad$ $[333 + 182] + 729 =$ _____

$\qquad$ _____

B Apply the commutative property and solve the problems.

①		②		③		④	
17	13	77	41	101	38	710	450
+ 13	+ 17	+ 41	+ 77	+ 38	+ 101	+ 450	+ 710
30	**30**						

⑤		⑥		⑦		⑧	
1,201	672	2,009	1,478	8,326	2,100	10,765	21,431
+ 672	+ 1,201	+ 1,478	+ 2,009	+ 2,100	+ 8,326	+ 21,431	+ 10,765

REMINDER: Write the definitions of the associative and commutative properties of addition.

_____

_____

_____

_____

Unit 30 cont'd ☞

C Does each set of addition problems illustrate the associative (a) or commutative (c) property?

__c__ ① 236 + 118 = 354
    118 + 236 = 354

____ ② 100 + [50 + 25] = 175
    [100 + 50] + 25 = 175

____ ③ 1,401 + 814 = 2,215
    814 + 1,401 = 2,215

____ ④ [12 + 8] + 11 = 31
    12 + [8 + 11] = 31

____ ⑤ 621 + [220 + 82] = 923
    [621 + 220] + 82 = 923

____ ⑥ 3,549 + 7,076 = 10,625
    7,076 + 3,549 = 10,625

____ ⑦ 60 + 40 = 100
    40 + 60 = 100

____ ⑧ [199 + 452] + 311 = 962
    199 + [452 + 311] = 962

____ ⑨ 6,431 + 6,430 = 12,861
    6,430 + 6,431 = 12,861

____ ⑩ 9 + 31 + 56 = 96
    56 + 31 + 9 = 96

____ ⑪ 2,682 + 4,198 = 6,880
    4,198 + 2,682 = 6,880

____ ⑫ 80 + 40 = 120
    40 + 80 = 120

____ ⑬ [400 + 11] + 200 = 611
    400 + [11 + 200] = 611

____ ⑭ 75 + [16 + 90] = 181
    [75 + 16] + 90 = 181

____ ⑮ [274 + 610] + 70 = 954
    274 + [610 + 70] = 954

____ ⑯ 10,467 + 46,801 = 57,268
    46,801 + 10,467 = 57,268

____ ⑰ [12,100 + 1,200] + 6 = 13,306
    12,100 + [1,200 + 6] = 13,306

____ ⑱ 1 + 2 + 3 = 6
    3 + 2 + 1 = 6

D Work the problems.

① Kevin sold 18 roses, 22 daisies, and 9 orchids. How many flowers did he sell?

    __18 + 22 + 9 = 49__

② Steve counted 81 men and 86 women at the meeting. How many people did he count?

    _____

③ Nicole collected 67 stamps from Europe, 10 from Australia, and 111 from the United States. How many stamps did she collect?

    _____

④ Barry listed 100 nouns, 125 verbs, 75 adjectives, and 25 prepositions. How many words did Barry list?

    _____

⑤ Wallace worked on math for 53 minutes, on science for 41 minutes, and on English for 61 minutes. How many minutes did he work?

    _____

⑥ Tammy read 120 pages on Friday and 260 pages on Saturday. How many pages did she read?

    _____

Comprehension Check

A Show how the associative property can apply to each problem.

① $[20 + 30] + 40 = 90$

    $20 + [30 + 40] = 90$

② $16 + [41 + 87] = 144$

③ $[61 + 50] + 44 = 155$

④ $100 + [150 + 155] = 405$

⑤ $[209 + 172] + 333 = 714$

⑥ $[525 + 600] + 269 = 1,394$

⑦ $[281 + 516] + 411 = 1,208$

⑧ $[421 + 686] + 900 = 2,007$

⑨ $4,183 + [266 + 662] = 5,111$

⑩ $[388 + 672] + 198 = 1,258$

⑪ $2,011 + [67 + 148] = 2,226$

⑫ $760 + [810 + 1,988] = 3,558$

⑬ $1,301 + [975 + 295] = 2,571$

⑭ $1,199 + [384 + 10] = 1,593$

⑮ $[75 + 75] + 250 = 400$

B Show how the commutative property can apply to each problem.

①		②	③	④
37	*17*	50	48	100
+ 17	*+ 37*	+ 25	+ 60	+ 286
54	*54*	75	108	386

⑤	⑥	⑦	⑧
444	610	777	500
+ 380	+ 745	+ 333	+ 300
824	1,355	1,110	800

⑨	⑩	⑪	⑫
1,410	10,172	13,811	50,000
+ 3,486	+ 25,381	+ 17,410	+ 16,861
4,896	35,553	31,221	66,861

⑬	⑭	⑮	⑯
9	25	185	1,418
11	75	315	2,222
6	50	492	4,917
+ 15	+ 80	+ 258	+ 6,458
41	230	1,250	15,015

Test 6 cont'd ☞

C Match the problems which illustrate the associative property.

① $[12 + 30] + 6 = 48$ $[a + b] + c = d$ ⑥ $10 + [5 + 4] = 19$ $[m + n] + o = p$

② $a + [b + c] = d$ $12 + [30 + 6] = 48$ ⑦ $m + [n + o] = p$ $[10 + 5] + 4 = 19$

③ $d + [b + a] = c$ $[d + b] + a = c$ ⑧ $3 + [4 + 6] = 13$ $[3 + 4] + 6 = 13$

④ $9 + [1 + 8] = 18$ $4 + [5 + 1] = 10$ ⑨ $[3 + 8] + 2 = 13$ $7 + [7 + 2] = 16$

⑤ $[4 + 5] + 1 = 10$ $[9 + 1] + 8 = 18$ ⑩ $[7 + 7] + 2 = 16$ $3 + [8 + 2] = 13$

D Match the problems which illustrate the commutative property.

① $39 + 80 = 119$ $1 + 20 + 16 = 37$ ⑥ $481 + 300 = 781$ $b + a = 500$

② $22 + 55 = 77$ $55 + 22 = 77$ ⑦ $781 + 300 = 1,081$ $300 + 481 = 781$

③ $16 + 20 + 1 = 37$ $80 + 39 = 119$ ⑧ $250 + 150 = 400$ $300 + 781 = 1,081$

④ $9 + 8 + 7 = 24$ $7 + 8 + 9 = 24$ ⑨ $175 + 225 = 400$ $150 + 250 = 400$

⑤ $14 + 2 + 1 = 17$ $1 + 2 + 14 = 17$ ⑩ $a + b = 500$ $225 + 175 = 400$

E Which property has been applied?

                     associative (a)   commutative (c)

__c__ ① $a + b + c + d = 200$ ____ ④ $[170 + 200] + 185 = 555$

        $d + c + b + a = 200$ $170 + [200 + 185] = 555$

____ ② $[721 + 256] + 900 = 1,877$ ____ ⑤ $4,870 + 9,281 = 14,151$

        $721 + [256 + 900] = 1,877$ $9,281 + 4,870 = 14,151$

____ ③ $10,625 + 42,347 = 52,972$ ____ ⑥ $a + [b + c] = 1,000$

        $42,347 + 10,625 = 52,972$ $[a + b] + c = 1,000$

Write a paragraph explaining how the associative and commutative properties of addition work.

_____

_____

_____

_____

_____

_____

Addition Practice

Learning Objective: *We will learn to identify parts of an addition problem.*

Two or more numbers to be added are called addends. The combined values of two or more addends make up the sums.

EXAMPLE:

	1	addend	23	addend	12	addend
	+1	addend	+16	addend	30	addend
					+22	addend
	2	sum	39	sum	64	sum

A Determine the addends and sums. Write each problem correctly.

① 47   **11**   ② 76   ③ 55   ④ 98
    11   **+36**   115   45   160
    36   **47**   39   100   62

⑤ 13   ⑥ 8   ⑦ 266   ⑧ 33
    41   86   88   28
   114   70   67   135
    60   164   111   74

⑨ 43   ⑩ 113   ⑪ 82   ⑫ 18
    26   4   53   57
   244   97   230   34
    85   12   66   189
    90   226   29   80

⑬ 394   ⑭ 410   ⑮ 263   ⑯ 701
   811   652   177   964
 1,205   1,062   86   263

⑰ 1,427   ⑱ 20,623   ⑲ 101,711
  7,748   10,254   256,999
  6,321   10,369   358,710

⑳ 1,798   ㉑ 145,132   ㉒ 100,000
  3,811   86,000   200,000
  2,364   13,131   600,000
  7,973   46,001   300,000

REMINDER: What are the parts of an addition problem?

_____

_____

     Unit 31 cont'd 👉

B Find the missing parts.

① 18 + _____32_____ = 50   ② 71 + 96 = _____   ③ _____ + 44 = 79

④ _____ + 111 = 188   ⑤ 245 + _____ = 500   ⑥ 1,000 + 361 = _____

⑦ _____ + 970 = 2,308   ⑧ _____ + 72 = 674   ⑨ 2,381 + _____ = 3,933

⑩ 4,107 + _____ = 4,825   ⑪ 10,746 + 11,801 = _____   ⑫ 87,213 + 13,466 = _____

⑬ 12 + _____ + 62 = 99   ⑭ 90 + _____ + 60 + 20 = 200

⑮ _____ + 295 + 411 = 1,000   ⑯ 736 + 891 + _____ = 2,300

⑰ 672 + 198 + 1,258 = _____   ⑱ 750 + 1,291 + 876 = _____

⑲ 4,850 + 9,760 + 1,000 = _____   ⑳ _____ + 2,980 + 4,300 = 9,865

㉑ 6,871 + _____ + 3,719 = 14,977   ㉒ _____ + 876 + 345 + 669 = 3,811

㉓ 12,653 + 11,951 + _____ = 60,102   ㉔ 2,439 + 10,982 + 40,464 = _____

C Read each paragraph and write the addition problem.

① Nancy needed 1,000 names on the anti-closed campus petition. On Monday she collected 476 names. On Tuesday she collected 451 names. On Wednesday she collected 73 names.

_____

② Tad had to write a 500-word essay for English class. His first page contained 165 words. His second page contained 212 words. His last page contained 123 words.

_____

③ Cooley spends 264 minutes a week practicing tennis. She spends 176 minutes practicing dancing. And she spends 300 minutes practicing the piano. Altogether, Cooley spends 740 minutes a week on her hobbies.

_____

④ Lezli drove 67 miles. David drove 112 miles. Willard drove 89 miles. The three drove 268 miles.

_____

Sums

Learning
Objective: *We will learn to find the sum.*

The sum is the combined value of two or more addends.

EXAMPLE:

	a.	8	b.	750	c.	10,877	d.	104,600
		+ 3		+ 304		+ 4,932		131,496
								+ 231,946
		11		1,054		15,809		468,042

A Find the sums.

① 8
  + 6
  14

② 14
  + 17

③ 49
  + 86

④ 100
  + 179

⑤ 4,777
  + 2,111

⑥ 10,712
  + 11,216

⑦ 1
  + 5

⑧ 87
  + 42

⑨ 99
  + 88

⑩ 382
  + 228

⑪ 9,064
  + 2,721

⑫ 42,860
  + 21,121

⑬ 6
  5
  + 4

⑭ 30
  41
  + 65

⑮ 82
  27
  + 11

⑯ 193
  337
  + 268

⑰ 2,462
  7,610
  + 8,908

⑱ 28,006
  14,973
  + 60,087

⑲ 3
  9
  + 1

⑳ 75
  25
  + 15

㉑ 106
  81
  + 39

㉒ 472
  683
  + 717

㉓ 8,196
  2,348
  + 6,541

㉔ 42,800
  31,501
  + 10,000

㉕ 1
  8
  4
  + 7

㉖ 33
  67
  22
  + 80

㉗ 170
  70
  107
  + 25

㉘ 341
  500
  789
  + 120

㉙ 5,842
  1,600
  3,762
  + 4,800

㉚ 25,410
  62,001
  87,248
  + 10,990

㉛ 142,679
  + 500,812

㉜ 1,412,000
  + 236,762

㉝ 434,875
  + 240,198

㉞ 976,045
  + 380,762

REMINDER: Write the definition of a sum.

_____

_____

Unit 32 cont'd ☞

B Find the sums.

① $12 + 12 = $ **24**

② $91 + 50 = $

③ $87 + 21 = $

④ $173 + 250 = $

⑤ $487 + 272 = $

⑥ $960 + 673 = $

⑦ $4,652 + 7,258 = $

⑧ $2,176 + 3,857 = $

⑨ $6,500 + 5,600 = $

⑩ $11,111 + 12,850 = $

⑪ $32,132 + 60,541 = $

⑫ $19,850 + 26,504 = $

⑬ $27,853 + 11,250 + 10,000 = $

⑭ $996 + 991 + 990 + 993 = $

⑮ $4,118 + 3,267 + 7,800 = $

⑯ $269 + 177 + 852 + 414 = $

⑰ $12,856 + 31,986 + 26,431 = $

⑱ $1,400 + 806 + 777 + 385 = $

⑲ $37,377 + 22,961 + 41,876 = $

⑳ $895 + 900 + 750 + 606 = $

㉑ $50,126 + 48,974 + 18,575 = $

㉒ $2,410 + 7,852 + 16,719 = $

㉓ $2,780 + 3,418 + 70,913 = $

㉔ $36,711 + 42,615 + 72,888 = $

C Work the problems.

① Dirk's community service club washes cars every Saturday to raise money. On the first Saturday in August, the members washed 67 cars. On the second and third Saturdays, they washed 172 cars. On the fourth Saturday, they washed 58 cars. How many cars did they wash in August?

_____

② A total of 261 hamburgers were sold at the Wescott-Tyler football game last week. Also sold were 380 cheeseburgers and 400 hot dogs. Only 51 tuna sandwiches were sold. What was the total hot and cold sandwiches sold at the game?

_____

③ Deborah mails letters for the Mail Order Company. Monday she mailed 251 letters; Tuesday she mailed 480 letters; Friday she mailed 1,641 letters. How many letters did Deborah mail?

_____

④ Casey has four boxes of pencils. In one box are 250 pencils. In another box are 460 pencils. In a third box are 375 pencils. And in the fourth box are 62 pencils. How many pencils does Casey have?

_____

Simple Subtraction

Unit 33

Learning Objective: *We will learn to subtract.*

Subtraction is the deducting of one number from another to find the difference of the two numbers.

EXAMPLE:

When we subtract, we find the difference between two numbers.

The difference between 5 and 3 is 2.

▲▲▲▲▲   5
−▲▲▲   − 3
  ▲▲   2

A Subtract.

① 7 − 5 = 2   ② 7 − 3   ③ 5 − 1   ④ 13 − 2   ⑤ 36 − 35   ⑥ 13 − 12   ⑦ 94 − 93

⑧ 3 − 2   ⑨ 8 − 1   ⑩ 9 − 8   ⑪ 45 − 5   ⑫ 22 − 11   ⑬ 26 − 13   ⑭ 18 − 1

⑮ 10 − 8   ⑯ 8 − 3   ⑰ 10 − 7   ⑱ 26 − 12   ⑲ 86 − 34   ⑳ 81 − 11   ㉑ 17 − 15

㉒ 9 − 6   ㉓ 9 − 3   ㉔ 29 − 8   ㉕ 24 − 12   ㉖ 54 − 22   ㉗ 29 − 0   ㉘ 37 − 11

㉙ 7 − 7   ㉚ 2 − 1   ㉛ 25 − 3   ㉜ 18 − 3   ㉝ 99 − 8   ㉞ 79 − 19   ㉟ 88 − 47

㊱ 3 − 1   ㊲ 1 − 1   ㊳ 76 − 14   ㊴ 17 − 3   ㊵ 80 − 60   ㊶ 42 − 22   ㊷ 33 − 11

㊸ 8 − 4   ㊹ 4 − 2   ㊺ 33 − 1   ㊻ 21 − 10   ㊼ 95 − 75   ㊽ 32 − 31   ㊾ 70 − 60

REMINDER: Write the definition of subtraction.

_____

_____

Unit 33 cont'd 🖝

B Subtract.

① $58 - 58 = 0$ ② $51 - 40 =$ ③ $43 - 21 =$ ④ $86 - 81 =$ ⑤ $10 - 1 =$

⑥ $62 - 31 =$ ⑦ $62 - 32 =$ ⑧ $18 - 16 =$ ⑨ $13 - 11 =$ ⑩ $23 - 12 =$

⑪ $87 - 76 =$ ⑫ $90 - 10 =$ ⑬ $31 - 30 =$ ⑭ $23 - 3 =$ ⑮ $16 - 5 =$

⑯ $45 - 10 =$ ⑰ $66 - 30 =$ ⑱ $99 - 19 =$ ⑲ $79 - 13 =$ ⑳ $66 - 44 =$

㉑ $91 - 60 =$ ㉒ $19 - 3 =$ ㉓ $94 - 12 =$ ㉔ $32 - 20 =$ ㉕ $81 - 30 =$

㉖ $39 - 32 =$ ㉗ $40 - 10 =$ ㉘ $76 - 71 =$ ㉙ $99 - 56 =$ ㉚ $30 - 20 =$

㉛ $25 - 13 =$ ㉜ $33 - 22 =$ ㉝ $58 - 3 =$ ㉞ $57 - 32 =$ ㉟ $25 - 6 =$

㊱ $37 - 6 =$ ㊲ $56 - 24 =$ ㊳ $66 - 22 =$ ㊴ $41 - 40 =$ ㊵ $12 - 1 =$

㊶ $62 - 42 =$ ㊷ $60 - 50 =$ ㊸ $73 - 30 =$ ㊹ $27 - 6 =$ ㊺ $39 - 7 =$

C Subtract to find the answers.

① Sixteen students tried out for the cheerleading squad. Only 8 were chosen. How many were not picked as a cheerleader?

_____8_____

② There are 26 students on the school newspaper staff. Sixteen of them are reporters and the rest are writers. How many are writers?

_____

③ Fifty students drive their cars to school every day, but there are only 20 parking places. How many students do not get parking places?

_____

④ Of the 31 members of the high school marching band, 7 play brass instruments. The rest of the members play woodwind or percussion instruments. How many members do not play brass instruments?

_____

⑤ There are 76 students in the NHS senior class. Thirteen plan to go to college. The rest will try to get a job after graduation. How many will will not go to college?

_____

⑥ There are 72 students in NHS's ninth grade. Only 4 made straight A's at the end of the nine week's grading period. How many had less than straight A's?

_____

Renaming

Unit 34

Learning Objective: *We will learn to borrow in subtraction.*

Renaming is necessary when the value of a digit to be subtracted is greater than the value of the digit to be subtracted from.

EXAMPLE: Three tens and 3 ones are equal to 2 tens and 13 ones. When we make the 3 into a 13, we have renamed.

$$\begin{array}{r} 2\ 13 \\ \cancel{3}\ \cancel{3} \\ -\ 2\ 5 \\ \hline 8 \end{array}$$

	2 tens,	13 ones
−	2 tens,	5 ones
	0 tens,	8 ones = 8

A Show how to rename numbers to perform the subtractions.

① 94 − 26 } __8__ ten(s), __14__ one(s) / −2 ten(s), 6 one(s) / __6__ ten(s), __8__ one(s) = __68__

② 43 − 27 } ____ ten(s), ____ one(s) / −2 ten(s), 7 one(s) / ____ ten(s), ____ one(s) = ____

③ 47 − 28 } ____ ten(s), ____ one(s) / −2 ten(s), 8 one(s) / ____ ten(s), ____ one(s) = ____

④ 32 − 28 } ____ ten(s), ____ one(s) / −2 ten(s), 8 one(s) / ____ ten(s), ____ one(s) = ____

⑤ 76 − 37 } ____ ten(s), ____ one(s) / −3 ten(s), 7 one(s) / ____ ten(s), ____ one(s) = ____

⑥ 21 − 16 } ____ ten(s), ____ one(s) / −1 ten(s), 6 one(s) / ____ ten(s), ____ one(s) = ____

⑦ 85 − 47 } ____ ten(s), ____ one(s) / −4 ten(s), 7 one(s) / ____ ten(s), ____ one(s) = ____

⑧ 53 − 45 } ____ ten(s), ____ one(s) / −4 ten(s), 5 one(s) / ____ ten(s), ____ one(s) = ____

⑨ 94 − 58 } ____ ten(s), ____ one(s) / −5 ten(s), 8 one(s) / ____ ten(s), ____ one(s) = ____

⑩ 62 − 54 } ____ ten(s), ____ one(s) / −5 ten(s), 4 one(s) / ____ ten(s), ____ one(s) = ____

⑪ 73 − 69 } ____ ten(s), ____ one(s) / −6 ten(s), 9 one(s) / ____ ten(s), ____ one(s) = ____

⑫ 74 − 65 } ____ ten(s), ____ one(s) / −2 ten(s), 5 one(s) / ____ ten(s), ____ one(s) = ____

⑬ 82 − 79 } ____ ten(s), ____ one(s) / −7 ten(s), 9 one(s) / ____ ten(s), ____ one(s) = ____

⑭ 85 − 37 } ____ ten(s), ____ one(s) / −3 ten(s), 7 one(s) / ____ ten(s), ____ one(s) = ____

REMINDER: Write the definition of renaming.

_____

_____

83

Unit 34 cont'd 🖝

B Subtract these two-digit figures.

① $37 - 8 = 29$ ⑩ $31 - 9 =$ ⑲ $21 - 9 =$ ㉘ $83 - 66 =$

② $11 - 6 =$ ⑪ $47 - 9 =$ ⑳ $73 - 25 =$ ㉙ $74 - 56 =$

③ $52 - 6 =$ ⑫ $58 - 9 =$ ㉑ $51 - 37 =$ ㉚ $44 - 23 =$

④ $53 - 9 =$ ⑬ $57 - 8 =$ ㉒ $51 - 39 =$ ㉛ $96 - 78 =$

⑤ $45 - 9 =$ ⑭ $54 - 9 =$ ㉓ $43 - 34 =$ ㉜ $72 - 36 =$

⑥ $12 - 3 =$ ⑮ $36 - 8 =$ ㉔ $42 - 36 =$ ㉝ $75 - 66 =$

⑦ $45 - 8 =$ ⑯ $25 - 7 =$ ㉕ $56 - 38 =$ ㉞ $62 - 26 =$

⑧ $25 - 6 =$ ⑰ $12 - 5 =$ ㉖ $93 - 56 =$ ㉟ $35 - 27 =$

⑨ $41 - 3 =$ ⑱ $14 - 6 =$ ㉗ $96 - 77 =$ ㊱ $61 - 55 =$

C Solve these problems. Use the blank space to work the problems.

① Thirty-two dogs were in the dog pound. In one week 17 were adopted. How many were left?

$$\begin{array}{r} \scriptstyle 2\ \ 12 \\ \mathbf{32} \\ -\ \mathbf{17} \\ \hline \mathbf{15} \end{array}$$

___15___

② Twenty-four flowers grew in a pot in Marissa's front yard. She picked 15. How many did she have left?

_____

③ Lezli owns 92 books. Lori took 13. How many books does Lezli have left?

_____

④ Forty-two people took the state's driving test. Nineteen failed. How many passed?

_____

⑤ Fifty-two presents were under the McFee's Christmas tree. Eighteen were for Suzy McFee. How many were for other members of the family?

_____

⑥ Alex bought a fan at Reid's for $32. When he got home, he saw in the paper that he could have bought one at Miller's for $28. How much money could he have saved?

_____

84

Mental Borrowing

Learning Objective: *We will learn to borrow mentally.*

Mental borrowing is subtracting in one's head and borrowing from a higher column than the ones' column.

EXAMPLE:

When we borrow mentally, we are subtracting without crossing out numbers or writing new ones. We borrow in our heads.

$$\begin{array}{r} 14 \\ -\ 7 \\ \hline 7 \end{array} \qquad \begin{array}{r} 18 \\ -\ 9 \\ \hline 9 \end{array} \qquad \begin{array}{r} 23 \\ -\ 5 \\ \hline 18 \end{array}$$

A Subtract.

① $\begin{array}{r} 41 \\ -\ 9 \\ \hline 32 \end{array}$
② $\begin{array}{r} 76 \\ -\ 8 \\ \hline \end{array}$
③ $\begin{array}{r} 90 \\ -79 \\ \hline \end{array}$
④ $\begin{array}{r} 23 \\ -\ 8 \\ \hline \end{array}$
⑤ $\begin{array}{r} 80 \\ -14 \\ \hline \end{array}$
⑥ $\begin{array}{r} 41 \\ -25 \\ \hline \end{array}$
⑦ $\begin{array}{r} 35 \\ -19 \\ \hline \end{array}$

⑧ $\begin{array}{r} 12 \\ -\ 7 \\ \hline \end{array}$
⑨ $\begin{array}{r} 80 \\ -57 \\ \hline \end{array}$
⑩ $\begin{array}{r} 74 \\ -39 \\ \hline \end{array}$
⑪ $\begin{array}{r} 73 \\ -\ 8 \\ \hline \end{array}$
⑫ $\begin{array}{r} 23 \\ -\ 8 \\ \hline \end{array}$
⑬ $\begin{array}{r} 18 \\ -\ 9 \\ \hline \end{array}$
⑭ $\begin{array}{r} 50 \\ -33 \\ \hline \end{array}$

⑮ $\begin{array}{r} 52 \\ -26 \\ \hline \end{array}$
⑯ $\begin{array}{r} 10 \\ -\ 9 \\ \hline \end{array}$
⑰ $\begin{array}{r} 63 \\ -\ 9 \\ \hline \end{array}$
⑱ $\begin{array}{r} 61 \\ -45 \\ \hline \end{array}$
⑲ $\begin{array}{r} 34 \\ -19 \\ \hline \end{array}$
⑳ $\begin{array}{r} 22 \\ -\ 3 \\ \hline \end{array}$
㉑ $\begin{array}{r} 27 \\ -\ 9 \\ \hline \end{array}$

㉒ $\begin{array}{r} 83 \\ -79 \\ \hline \end{array}$
㉓ $\begin{array}{r} 94 \\ -\ 7 \\ \hline \end{array}$
㉔ $\begin{array}{r} 11 \\ -\ 9 \\ \hline \end{array}$
㉕ $\begin{array}{r} 98 \\ -\ 9 \\ \hline \end{array}$
㉖ $\begin{array}{r} 12 \\ -\ 5 \\ \hline \end{array}$
㉗ $\begin{array}{r} 52 \\ -13 \\ \hline \end{array}$
㉘ $\begin{array}{r} 55 \\ -17 \\ \hline \end{array}$

㉙ $\begin{array}{r} 17 \\ -\ 8 \\ \hline \end{array}$
㉚ $\begin{array}{r} 67 \\ -59 \\ \hline \end{array}$
㉛ $\begin{array}{r} 92 \\ -56 \\ \hline \end{array}$
㉜ $\begin{array}{r} 100 \\ -20 \\ \hline \end{array}$
㉝ $\begin{array}{r} 60 \\ -17 \\ \hline \end{array}$
㉞ $\begin{array}{r} 93 \\ -28 \\ \hline \end{array}$
㉟ $\begin{array}{r} 60 \\ -49 \\ \hline \end{array}$

㊱ $\begin{array}{r} 33 \\ -\ 9 \\ \hline \end{array}$
㊲ $\begin{array}{r} 50 \\ -16 \\ \hline \end{array}$
㊳ $\begin{array}{r} 82 \\ -\ 9 \\ \hline \end{array}$
㊴ $\begin{array}{r} 13 \\ -\ 8 \\ \hline \end{array}$
㊵ $\begin{array}{r} 42 \\ -\ 9 \\ \hline \end{array}$
㊶ $\begin{array}{r} 30 \\ -11 \\ \hline \end{array}$
㊷ $\begin{array}{r} 54 \\ -\ 8 \\ \hline \end{array}$

㊸ $\begin{array}{r} 54 \\ -27 \\ \hline \end{array}$
㊹ $\begin{array}{r} 22 \\ -\ 9 \\ \hline \end{array}$
㊺ $\begin{array}{r} 58 \\ -39 \\ \hline \end{array}$
㊻ $\begin{array}{r} 92 \\ -58 \\ \hline \end{array}$
㊼ $\begin{array}{r} 11 \\ -\ 7 \\ \hline \end{array}$
㊽ $\begin{array}{r} 94 \\ -87 \\ \hline \end{array}$
㊾ $\begin{array}{r} 21 \\ -17 \\ \hline \end{array}$

REMINDER: Write the definition of mental borrowing.

_____

_____   _____

Unit 35 cont'd ☞

B Subtract.

① 91 − 9 = **82**   ② 61 − 18 =   ③ 90 − 89 =   ④ 43 − 7 =

⑤ 44 − 19 =   ⑥ 33 − 7 =   ⑦ 45 − 17 =   ⑧ 25 − 8 =

⑨ 62 − 16 =   ⑩ 77 − 28 =   ⑪ 77 − 68 =   ⑫ 96 − 58 =

⑬ 31 − 18 =   ⑭ 56 − 48 =   ⑮ 11 − 8 =   ⑯ 52 − 48 =

⑰ 86 − 8 =   ⑱ 22 − 7 =   ⑲ 85 − 7 =   ⑳ 78 − 59 =

㉑ 78 − 69 =   ㉒ 73 − 7 =   ㉓ 13 − 7 =   ㉔ 86 − 18 =

㉕ 33 − 18 =   ㉖ 42 − 18 =   ㉗ 98 − 49 =   ㉘ 33 − 18 =

㉙ 91 − 86 =   ㉚ 81 − 68 =   ㉛ 24 − 7 =   ㉜ 10 − 9 =

㉝ 50 − 2 =   ㉞ 94 − 36 =   ㉟ 30 − 5 =   ㊱ 70 − 3 =

C Subtract.

① During three games that Little League players played on Saturday, 24 balls were hit out of the park. Only 7 were returned. How many were lost?

_____**17**_____

② Of the 20 problems on her semester math test, Sara only got 9 correct. How many did she get wrong?

_____

③ LeeAnn had 92 plants in her apartment. While she was on vacation, 8 of them died. How many plants were alive when she got home?

_____

④ Laurie had 71 pencils when school started. She used 66 during the school year. How many did she have left at the end of the year?

_____

⑤ Kevin and Mike caught 56 large mouth bass on a fishing trip. They had to throw 8 fish back because they were too small. How many fish did they take home?

_____

⑥ Sixty students tried out for the school play. As there were only 17 roles, some students were cut from the play. How many students were not chosen?

_____

Comprehension Check

A Determine the addends and the sums. Write each problem correctly.

① 26　　　**11**　　② 47
　 11　　 **+15**　　　 86
　 15　　 　**26**　　　 39

③ 13　　　　　　④ 22
　 28　　　　　　　 63
　 15　　　　　　　 41

⑤ 241　　　　　⑥ 480
　 369　　　　　　 561
　 610　　　　　　 81

⑦ 2,346　　　　⑧ 413
　 4,042　　　　　 911
　 1,696　　　　　 1,324

B Find the missing parts.

① $63 + 59 = \underline{\ 122\ }$　② $17 + \underline{\hspace{1cm}} = 64$

③ $48 + \underline{\hspace{1cm}} = 132$　④ $\underline{\hspace{1cm}} + 48 = 97$

⑤ $\underline{\hspace{1cm}} + 62 = 94$　⑥ $\underline{\hspace{1cm}} + 53 = 100$

⑦ $93 + 15 = \underline{\hspace{1cm}}$　⑧ $37 + 57 = \underline{\hspace{1cm}}$

⑨ $113 + 6,390 + \underline{\hspace{1.5cm}} = 8,492$

⑩ $131 + 531 + 699 = \underline{\hspace{1cm}}$

⑪ $\underline{\hspace{1cm}} + 2,399 + 4,573 = 11,627$

⑫ $6,573 + \underline{\hspace{1cm}} + 3,349 = 13,271$

C From each group of numbers, determine which are sums and which are addends. Label sums "s" and label addends "a." Write each problem correctly.

① 67　**a**　　**67**　② 112 ___　③ 35 ___　④ 74 ___
　 21　**a**　**+21**　　 80 ___　　 51 ___　　 89 ___
　 88　**s**　　**88**　　 32 ___　　 86 ___　　 15 ___

⑤ 91 ___　　⑥ 92 ___　　⑦ 397 ___　⑧ 706 ___
　 133 ___　　 14 ___　　 156 ___　　 1,143 ___
　 42 ___　　 106 ___　　 241 ___　　 437 ___

⑨ 4,273 ___　⑩ 8,721 ___　⑪ 10,243 ___　⑫ 2,156 ___
　 3,269 ___　　 11,160 ___　　 6,027 ___　　 7,969 ___
　 1,004 ___　　 2,439 ___　　 4,216 ___　　 5,813 ___

⑬ 22,391 ___　　⑭ 74,000 ___　　⑮ 29,856 ___
　 62,348 ___　　 106,364 ___　　 101,857 ___
　 84,739 ___　　 32,364 ___　　 72,001 ___

D Subtract.

① 14　② 21　③ 10　④ 7　⑤ 12　⑥ 32　⑦ 61　⑧ 27
　−7　　−7　　−5　　−3　　−2　　−30　　−60　　−0
　 7

⑨ 64　⑩ 73　⑪ 82　⑫ 91　⑬ 30　⑭ 46　⑮ 72　⑯ 55
　−43　　−41　　−71　　−50　　−27　　−35　　−61　　−34

Test 7 cont'd

E **Rename and subtract.**

① $\begin{array}{r} 32 \\ -29 \end{array}$ } _2_ ten(s), _12_ one(s)
　　　　　　-2 ten(s), 9 one(s)
　　　　　　_0_ ten(s), _3_ one(s) = _3_

② $\begin{array}{r} 92 \\ -48 \end{array}$ } ____ ten(s), ____ one(s)
　　　　　　-4 ten(s), 8 one(s)
　　　　　　____ ten(s), ____ one(s) = ____

③ $\begin{array}{r} 22 \\ -19 \end{array}$ } ____ ten(s), ____ one(s)
　　　　　　-1 ten(s), 9 one(s)
　　　　　　____ ten(s), ____ one(s) = ____

④ $\begin{array}{r} 81 \\ -69 \end{array}$ } ____ ten(s), ____ one(s)
　　　　　　-6 ten(s), 9 one(s)
　　　　　　____ ten(s), ____ one(s) = ____

⑤ $\begin{array}{r} 76 \\ -68 \end{array}$ } ____ ten(s), ____ one(s)
　　　　　　-6 ten(s), 8 one(s)
　　　　　　____ ten(s), ____ one(s) = ____

⑥ $\begin{array}{r} 65 \\ -58 \end{array}$ } ____ ten(s), ____ one(s)
　　　　　　-5 ten(s), 8 one(s)
　　　　　　____ ten(s), ____ one(s) = ____

⑦ $\begin{array}{r} 53 \\ -19 \end{array}$ } ____ ten(s), ____ one(s)
　　　　　　-1 ten(s), 9 one(s)
　　　　　　____ ten(s), ____ one(s) = ____

⑧ $\begin{array}{r} 72 \\ -39 \end{array}$ } ____ ten(s), ____ one(s)
　　　　　　-3 ten(s), 9 one(s)
　　　　　　____ ten(s), ____ one(s) = ____

F **Borrow mentally and subtract.**

① $\begin{array}{r} 71 \\ -25 \\ \hline 46 \end{array}$　② $\begin{array}{r} 34 \\ -27 \end{array}$　③ $\begin{array}{r} 42 \\ -29 \end{array}$　④ $\begin{array}{r} 93 \\ -47 \end{array}$　⑤ $\begin{array}{r} 84 \\ -67 \end{array}$　⑥ $\begin{array}{r} 30 \\ -14 \end{array}$　⑦ $\begin{array}{r} 82 \\ -67 \end{array}$　⑧ $\begin{array}{r} 51 \\ -24 \end{array}$

⑨ $\begin{array}{r} 65 \\ -19 \end{array}$　⑩ $\begin{array}{r} 61 \\ -49 \end{array}$　⑪ $\begin{array}{r} 26 \\ -17 \end{array}$　⑫ $\begin{array}{r} 92 \\ -63 \end{array}$　⑬ $\begin{array}{r} 52 \\ -29 \end{array}$　⑭ $\begin{array}{r} 47 \\ -39 \end{array}$　⑮ $\begin{array}{r} 72 \\ -57 \end{array}$　⑯ $\begin{array}{r} 71 \\ -69 \end{array}$

⑰ $\begin{array}{r} 26 \\ -18 \end{array}$　⑱ $\begin{array}{r} 43 \\ -29 \end{array}$　⑲ $\begin{array}{r} 51 \\ -33 \end{array}$　⑳ $\begin{array}{r} 61 \\ -18 \end{array}$　㉑ $\begin{array}{r} 82 \\ -57 \end{array}$　㉒ $\begin{array}{r} 62 \\ -47 \end{array}$　㉓ $\begin{array}{r} 93 \\ -16 \end{array}$　㉔ $\begin{array}{r} 24 \\ -17 \end{array}$

Define these terms.

① addend _____

② sum _____

③ subtraction _____

④ renaming _____

⑤ mental borrowing _____

Three- and Four-Digit Subtraction

Learning Objective: *We will learn to subtract with three- and four-digit numbers.*

A three-digit number has digits in the ones' place, the tens' place, and the hundreds' place. A four-digit number has digits in the ones' place, the tens' place, the hundreds' place, and the thousands' place.

EXAMPLE:

When we subtract three- and four-digit numbers, we may need to borrow.

$$\begin{array}{r} {\scriptstyle 2\ ^{12}_{}{}^{12}13} \\ 3,333 \\ -\ 2,555 \\ \hline 778 \end{array}$$

$$\begin{array}{r} {\scriptstyle 3\ ^{13}_{}{}^{13}14} \\ 44,444 \\ -43,666 \\ \hline 778 \end{array}$$

A Subtract.

① 973
− 258

715

② 975
− 624

③ 267
− 154

④ 444
− 333

⑤ 632
− 543

⑥ 999
− 421

⑦ 500
− 364

⑧ 483
− 345

⑨ 333
− 222

⑩ 547
− 483

⑪ 3,000
− 2,461

⑫ 9,000
− 8,219

⑬ 721
− 567

⑭ 129
− 100

⑮ 348
− 167

⑯ 549
− 142

⑰ 4,000
− 3,333

⑱ 9,469
− 8,433

⑲ 642
− 397

⑳ 246
− 106

㉑ 356
− 242

㉒ 561
− 278

㉓ 5,000
− 4,954

㉔ 7,211
− 6,666

㉕ 321
− 278

㉖ 275
− 115

㉗ 394
− 215

㉘ 432
− 234

㉙ 6,000
− 4,132

㉚ 8,496
− 2,146

㉛ 211
− 177

㉜ 289
− 280

㉝ 377
− 300

㉞ 1,000
− 946

㉟ 7,000
− 5,000

㊱ 6,214
− 5,544

㊲ 666
− 587

㊳ 299
− 199

㊴ 569
− 169

㊵ 2,000
− 1,211

㊶ 8,000
− 4,217

㊷ 9,999
− 6,213

REMINDER: Write the definition of three- and four-digit numbers.

_____

_____

Unit 36 cont'd ☞

B Subtract.

① 432 − 234 = **198**

② 467 − 276 =

③ 889 − 649 =

④ 627 − 287 =

⑤ 724 − 427 =

⑥ 994 − 499 =

⑦ 178 − 108 =

⑧ 849 − 498 =

⑨ 946 − 649 =

⑩ 888 − 628 =

⑪ 777 − 399 =

⑫ 666 − 17 =

⑬ 555 − 499 =

⑭ 444 − 315 =

⑮ 333 − 217 =

⑯ 222 − 22 =

⑰ 111 − 99 =

⑱ 542 − 541 =

⑲ 8,888 − 2,148 =

⑳ 6,666 − 5,143 =

㉑ 7,777 − 1,317 =

㉒ 5,555 − 4,321 =

㉓ 3,333 − 624 =

㉔ 2,222 − 1,222 =

㉕ 6,600 − 461 =

㉖ 4,200 − 2,310 =

㉗ 3,600 − 2,976 =

C Subtract. Use the space to work the problems.

① Frank put 8,221 miles on his car the first year. During the second year he owned the car, he only put 3,715 miles on it. How many more miles did he drive the first year?

$$\begin{array}{r} 8,221 \\ - 3,715 \\ \hline 4,506 \end{array}$$

_____**4,506**_____

② Lori had 200 golf balls in March. By August she only had 92. How many did she lose in six months?

_____

③ John put $9,191 in his savings account in January. In August, he withdrew $6,421 to buy a car. How much money does he have left?

_____

④ Gretta canned 240 jars of dill pickles. Only 225 of the jars sealed properly. How many jars were spoiled?

_____

⑤ Suzy saved $1,986 during the summer. She spent only $219 of her savings during the next three months. How much did she have left?

_____

⑥ Marie had 1,283 recipes in her cookbook. Of these, 842 were for desserts. How many were not for desserts?

_____

Five-Digit Subtraction

Learning
Objective: *We will learn to subtract five-digit numbers.*

A five-digit number has digits in the ones' place, the tens' place, the hundreds' place, the thousands' place, and the ten thousands' place.

EXAMPLE:

$$^2_{12}\ ^{12}_{12}{}^{13}$$
$$\begin{array}{r} 33,333 \\ -25,555 \\ \hline 7,778 \end{array}$$

2 ten thousands, 12 thousands, 12 hundreds, 12 tens, 13 ones
− 2 ten thousands, 5 thousands, 5 hundreds, 5 tens, 5 ones
0 ten thousands, 7 thousands, 7 hundreds, 7 tens, 8 ones = 7,778

A Subtract these five-digit numbers.

① 37,329
− 21,671

15,658

② 93,756
− 84,867

③ 37,231
− 32,466

④ 86,899
− 36,999

⑤ 85,633
− 45,623

⑥ 32,564
− 21,548

⑦ 87,965
− 65,423

⑧ 78,945
− 65,498

⑨ 99,999
− 65,423

⑩ 99,875
− 65,423

⑪ 45,698
− 32,156

⑫ 65,498
− 32,556

⑬ 32,916
− 25,555

⑭ 55,555
− 32,165

⑮ 88,795
− 66,542

⑯ 78,956
− 32,165

⑰ 96,581
− 45,632

⑱ 96,354
− 56,482

⑲ 46,587
− 23,156

⑳ 55,668
− 22,335

㉑ 79,612
− 21,678

㉒ 33,256
− 21,156

㉓ 45,689
− 34,578

㉔ 67,852
− 32,194

㉕ 42,100
− 25,789

㉖ 78,568
− 45,896

㉗ 44,458
− 25,252

㉘ 78,965
− 12,345

㉙ 45,668
− 26,548

㉚ 77,899
− 45,623

REMINDER: Write the definition of a five-digit number.

_____

_____

Unit 37 cont'd

B Subtract.

① 99,766 − 85,877 = **13,889**

② 34,521 − 23,251 =

③ 66,555 − 44,333 =

④ 79,801 − 79,779 =

⑤ 86,999 − 66,725 =

⑥ 45,886 − 32,659 =

⑦ 78,564 − 21,365 =

⑧ 44,444 − 21,563 =

⑨ 12,365 − 11,569 =

⑩ 99,577 − 88,899 =

⑪ 77,569 − 45,688 =

⑫ 96,632 − 54,545 =

⑬ 76,258 − 58,623 =

⑭ 59,568 − 25,688 =

⑮ 78,569 − 45,689 =

⑯ 99,887 − 66,558 =

⑰ 33,226 − 21,456 =

⑱ 74,589 − 56,423 =

⑲ 47,655 − 34,789 =

⑳ 49,900 − 34,999 =

㉑ 42,399 − 16,231 =

㉒ 36,591 − 35,555 =

㉓ 44,223 − 43,329 =

㉔ 56,783 − 24,896 =

㉕ 61,322 − 60,322 =

㉖ 79,839 − 18,337 =

㉗ 83,321 − 56,931 =

C Subtract.

① Sharon needed 36,591 jelly beans to fill a giant jar. She only had 34,562. How many more did she need?

2,029

② Mr. Winchester planted 54,321 roses in his garden. Of these, 22,961 died in the spring frost. How many of the roses survived?

③ The Appliance Warehouse's goal for 1985 was to sell 23,649 televisions. They sold 23,213 during that year. By how many sales did they miss their goal?

④ The Reid Lumber Company cut 94,666 cherry trees to sell to a furniture manufacturing company. The furniture company only bought 82,572 of the trees. How many extra trees were cut?

⑤ Club members called 12,564 people to help raise money for charity. Only 11,296 of the people called donated money. How many people did not give to the charity?

⑥ The Reading Society collected 72,394 paperback books. They gave 41,629 of them to a local goodwill store. How many did they have left?

Six-Digit Subtraction

Learning Objective: *We will learn to subtract six-digit numbers.*

A six-digit number has digits in the ones' place, the tens' place, the hundreds' place, the thousands' place, the ten thousands' place, and the hundred thousands' place.

EXAMPLE:

$$\begin{array}{r} {}^{2\ \ 13}{}_{14}{}^{16} \\ 123,456 \\ -\ 122,777 \\ \hline 679 \end{array}$$

1 hundred thousand, 2 ten thousands, 2 thousands, 13 hundreds, 14 tens, 16 ones
−1 hundred thousand, 2 ten thousands, 2 thousands, 7 hundreds, 7 tens, 7 ones
0 hundred thousands, 0 ten thousands, 0 thousands, 6 hundreds, 7 tens, 9 ones

A Subtract these six-digit numbers.

① 333,000
  − 222,111
  110,889

② 455,321
  − 396,333

③ 373,113
  − 159,205

④ 588,757
  − 288,469

⑤ 463,136
  − 153,216

⑥ 666,000
  − 245,000

⑦ 881,019
  − 447,609

⑧ 556,665
  − 499,970

⑨ 477,588
  − 477,578

⑩ 596,832
  − 321,764

⑪ 727,000
  − 123,456

⑫ 170,314
  − 123,917

⑬ 501,934
  − 464,087

⑭ 972,551
  − 393,597

⑮ 427,790
  − 396,111

⑯ 932,812
  − 190,410

⑰ 314,239
  − 173,860

⑱ 610,784
  − 266,499

⑲ 601,171
  − 596,489

⑳ 779,042
  − 654,321

㉑ 997,210
  − 835,239

㉒ 527,734
  − 440,081

㉓ 266,494
  − 144,930

㉔ 448,935
  − 181,801

㉕ 139,670
  − 123,456

㉖ 732,559
  − 672,878

㉗ 927,525
  − 896,863

㉘ 814,946
  − 416,686

㉙ 148,391
  − 102,461

㉚ 196,494
  − 106,200

REMINDER: Write the definition of a six-digit number.

B Find the answers.

① 199,000 − 23,614 = *175,386*

② 232,232 − 111,111 =

③ 649,000 − 549,000 =

④ 238,832 − 213,492 =

⑤ 675,009 − 675,000 =

⑥ 466,836 − 342,109 =

⑦ 340,471 − 219,678 =

⑧ 652,536 − 541,425 =

⑨ 340,471 − 296,432 =

⑩ 652,500 − 555,555 =

⑪ 364,821 − 216,972 =

⑫ 102,245 − 5,518 =

⑬ 309,326 − 68,621 =

⑭ 896,935 − 567,858 =

⑮ 972,815 − 785,581 =

⑯ 568,585 − 320,087 =

⑰ 707,663 − 536,791 =

⑱ 221,322 − 123,456 =

⑲ 121,212 − 7,000 =

⑳ 511,515 − 21,764 =

㉑ 243,324 − 242,166 =

㉒ 913,291 − 313,421 =

㉓ 670,000 − 296,842 =

㉔ 240,000 − 111,222 =

㉕ 775,527 − 623,410 =

㉖ 350,664 − 211,644 =

㉗ 324,094 − 324,000 =

C Solve the problems.

① Ann had to type 133,946 letters in two weeks to help with the governor's reelection campaign. She was only able to type 62,932. How many letters were not sent?
71,014

② Lucy had taught chemistry to 222,646 students in the course of 5 years. Only 4,816 of those students failed. How many students had passed Lucy's chemistry class?

③ The Forms Company printed 876,234 forms in 1986. Of these, 626,810 were invoices. How many were not invoices?

④ Super-S Drug Store had 964,811 capsules of Diet-Trim in March. By May they had only 21,646 pills left. How many pills had been bought by people wanting to lose weight?

⑤ The Desmond Company mailed out 245,000 catalogs to its customers. Of these only 2,615 were returned by the post office. How many reached the customers?

⑥ Combined Charities, Inc., needed $401,032 to build homes for orphans. They only raised $321,987. How much more money did they need?

94

Parts of a Subtraction Problem

Learning Objective: *We will learn to identify the parts of a subtraction problem.*

In a subtraction problem, the minuend is the number to be subtracted from. The subtrahend is the number to be subtracted. The remainder is the difference.

EXAMPLE: In the problem at the right,
87,655 is the minuend,
24,777 is the subtrahend,
and 62,878 is the remainder.

$$\begin{array}{r} 87,655 \\ -\ 24,777 \\ \hline 62,878 \end{array}$$

A Choose the minuend from the box that fits each problem below.

794	630	864	6,629	6,543	75,486
249	321	561	6,500	6,296	87,878
895	672	556	3,215	7,241	85,201
391	999	324	6,194	7,291	96,589

① **391**
$-\ 214$
177

②
$-\ 491$
139

③
$-\ 567$
432

④
$-\ 1,234$
1,981

⑤
$-\ 2,899$
3,601

⑥
$-\ 60,000$
25,201

⑦
$-\ 514$
158

⑧
$-\ 211$
350

⑨
$-\ 106$
143

⑩
$-\ 5,321$
975

⑪
$-\ 2,156$
4,387

⑫
$-\ 22,222$
53,264

⑬
$-\ 167$
154

⑭
$-\ 149$
175

⑮
$-\ 236$
320

⑯
$-\ 4,218$
1,976

⑰
$-\ 6,321$
920

⑱
$-\ 54,545$
33,333

⑲
$-\ 211$
583

⑳
$-\ 348$
516

㉑
$-\ 558$
337

㉒
$-\ 3,211$
3,418

㉓
$-\ 1,269$
6,022

㉔
$-\ 52,145$
44,444

Work Area

REMINDER: Write the definition of a minuend.

Unit 39 cont'd ☞

B Determine the parts of these subtraction problems. Write each problem in the correct order.

① 7,092   **7,543**   ② 6,219   ③ 53,821   ④ 888,253
   451 − **7,092**   3,222   32,101   111,579
 7,543   **451**   2,997   85,922   999,832

⑤ 8,867   ⑥   867   ⑦ 27,832   ⑧ 496,800
  5,657   7,410   36,777   327,243
  3,210   6,543   8,945   169,557

⑨ 3,835   ⑩ 4,361   ⑪ 17,569   ⑫ 569,778
  4,761   3,210   31,999   562,361
  8,596   1,151   49,568   7,417

⑬ 4,606   ⑭ 1,698   ⑮ 55,555   ⑯ 393,853
  8,321   3,410   43,210   956,222
  3,715   5,108   98,765   562,369

C Read the paragraph and determine which numbers are the minuend, subtrahend, and remainder. Write the problem correctly.

① The U-Save-More Store had 3,216 irregular tee shirts to sell at low prices. At the end of the sale, they had only 1,060 remaining. They had sold 2,156 in less time than they had expected.

② Over the 4th of July weekend, state police gave out 43,926 traffic tickets. Only 16,626 were for speeding and 27,300 were for illegal parking.

③ During one shift, the employees of Handy-Tool Company made 112 screwdrivers. That total was 280 less than their goal of 392.

④ During June, the Peachy-Keen Orchard harvested 599,786 peaches. That total was 257,138 less than last year's total of 856,924. Bad weather was blamed for the bad harvest.

Checking Subtraction Problems

Unit 40

Learning Objective: *We will learn to use addition to check subtraction.*

Checking is the process of proving correctness.

EXAMPLE: To check a subtraction
problem, add the subtrahend
to the remainder. The sum
should be the same as
the minuend.

```
  5,432  minuend
- 3,291  subtrahend
  2,141  remainder
+ 3,291  subtrahend
  5,432  minuend
```

A Use addition to check these subtraction problems. Place check (✓) beside each remainder that is correct. Draw an X beside each incorrect answer.

① 200
 − 119
  81   ✓
 + *119*
  200

② 624
 − 547
  77 ____

③ 3,256
 − 2,154
  1,111 ____

④ 8,795
 − 6,588
  2,207 ____

⑤ 25,000
 − 14,569
  17,111 ____

⑥ 563
 − 421
  142 ____

⑦ 989
 − 269
  730 ____

⑧ 8,879
 − 6,589
  2,290 ____

⑨ 4,554
 − 1,558
  2,996 ____

⑩ 78,549
 − 56,982
  21,567 ____

⑪ 322
 − 111
  222 ____

⑫ 764
 − 151
  631 ____

⑬ 4,456
 − 3,265
  1,119 ____

⑭ 9,660
 − 2,001
  7,659 ____

⑮ 144,444
 − 133,333
  122,222 ____

⑯ 999
 − 788
  220 ____

⑰ 863
 − 542
  321 ____

⑱ 7,777
 − 6,598
  1,179 ____

⑲ 5,000
 − 3,232
  1,766 ____

⑳ 165,987
 − 12,555
  44,443 ____

㉑ 762
 − 541
  221 ____

㉒ 942
 − 831
  111 ____

㉓ 4,589
 − 2,222
  2,337 ____

㉔ 1,005
 − 1,000
  10 ____

㉕ 278,923
 − 42,569
  36,333 ____

REMINDER: Write the definition of checking.

_____

_____

Unit 40 cont'd ☛

B Use addition to check these subtraction problems. Place a ✓ before each problem that is correct and an X before each incorrect problem.

____✓ ① 734 − 654 = 80 + **654** = **734**   ____ ⑩ 6,548 − 5,478 = 1,070 +

____ ② 888 − 492 = 395 +   ____ ⑪ 4,588 − 3,256 = 1,333 +

____ ③ 549 − 422 = 116 +   ____ ⑫ 1,414 − 1,222 = 192 +

____ ④ 645 − 561 = 82 +   ____ ⑬ 5,458 − 3,922 = 1,546 +

____ ⑤ 308 − 107 = 201 +   ____ ⑭ 88,569 − 45,698 = 42,871 +

____ ⑥ 662 − 398 = 264 +   ____ ⑮ 78,952 − 69,500 = 9,452 +

____ ⑦ 589 − 432 = 157 +   ____ ⑯ 76,593 − 65,893 = 10,700 +

____ ⑧ 321 − 269 = 51 +   ____ ⑰ 78,455 − 63,333 = 15,111 +

____ ⑨ 210 − 190 = 20 +   ____ ⑱ 47,888 − 21,100 = 26,777 +

C Use addition to check each problem. If the problem is incorrect, find the correct answer.

① At St. Christopher's Hospital they needed 128,935 new bed sheets. If a local department store gave them 100,569 sheets, how many would St. Christopher's still need?

$$\begin{array}{r} 128,935 \\ -100,569 \\ \hline 28,366 \end{array}$$

② On Mother's Day, 85,923 long-distance phone calls were made. Of those, 65,531 were connected. How many calls could not get through?

$$\begin{array}{r} 85,923 \\ -65,531 \\ \hline 20,400 \end{array}$$

③ There are 749 cars in Baldwin's car lot. During an inventory sale, 694 were sold. How many cars did not sell?

$$\begin{array}{r} 749 \\ -694 \\ \hline 65 \end{array}$$

④ Clarksville High School's library has 6,007 books on the shelves. In the course of one school year, 537 books were lost. How many books does the high school have now?

$$\begin{array}{r} 6,007 \\ -537 \\ \hline 5,460 \end{array}$$

Comprehension Check

A Subtract these three- and four-digit numbers.

① 456 − 325 **131**	② 235 − 123	③ 365 − 258	④ 845 − 569	⑤ 1,036 − 1,000	⑥ 666 − 214
⑦ 6,568 − 4,179	⑧ 4,985 − 3,332	⑨ 8,888 − 5,236	⑩ 485 − 256	⑪ 489 − 256	⑫ 6,542 − 389
⑬ 875 − 235	⑭ 879 − 654	⑮ 956 − 345	⑯ 8,432 − 6,549	⑰ 6,489 − 3,297	⑱ 6,210 − 987

B Subtract these five-digit numbers.

① 65,893 − 25,896 **39,997**	② 44,456 − 21,598	③ 25,698 − 12,500	④ 47,856 − 25,896	⑤ 77,777 − 32,658	⑥ 54,986 − 35,625
⑦ 47,586 − 25,641	⑧ 23,659 − 12,589	⑨ 66,598 − 24,589	⑩ 45,698 − 32,547	⑪ 95,642 − 32,556	⑫ 45,896 − 23,569
⑬ 57,896 − 25,698	⑭ 72,003 − 65,239	⑮ 65,231 − 32,555	⑯ 52,874 − 33,300	⑰ 88,820 − 65,231	⑱ 99,631 − 57,789

C Subtract these six-digit numbers.

① 885,632 − 659,321 **226,311**	② 444,563 − 325,698	③ 444,444 − 326,589	④ 775,698 − 365,249	⑤ 553,009 − 202,015
⑥ 662,200 − 365,489	⑦ 745,310 − 623,589	⑧ 425,639 − 258,006	⑨ 896,136 − 363,636	⑩ 555,890 − 424,242
⑪ 159,632 − 102,586	⑫ 445,892 − 222,222	⑬ 569,823 − 262,648	⑭ 888,888 − 333,951	⑮ 663,663 − 215,987

Test 8 cont'd ☞

D Determine the parts of these subtraction problems. Write each problem in correct order.

① 2,365   **4,789**   ② 41,980   ③ 325,674
   4,789   **− 2,365**   78,569   673,980
   2,424   **2,424**   36,589   999,654

④ 5,498   ⑤ 36,547   ⑥ 386,230
   1,846   49,144   200,694
   3,652   85,691   586,924

⑦ 2,525   ⑧ 52,689   ⑨ 215,871
   4,049   32,533   745,238
   6,574   20,156   529,367

E Use addition to check the subtraction problems. If problem is incorrect, find the correct answer.

①   893   ② 4,569   ③ 56,789   ④ 912,312
  − 259   − 3,256   − 29,399   − 799,666
    634   1,343   27,390   112,646
+ 259
 893

⑤   533   ⑥ 7,111   ⑦ 78,232   ⑧ 562,311
  − 499   − 3,569   − 59,798   − 361,987
     32   3,452   18,454   201,224

Define these terms.

① three-digit number _____
_____

② four-digit number _____
_____

③ five-digit number _____
_____

④ six-digit number _____
_____

⑤ minuend _____
_____

⑥ subtraction _____
_____

⑦ checking _____
_____

Subtraction Practice

Unit 41

Learning Objective: *We will practice subtraction.*

Subtraction is the deducting of one number from another to find the difference of the two numbers.

EXAMPLE: Remember, we sometimes must borrow when we subtract.

$$\begin{array}{r} 5\ \ 9\,910 \\ \cancel{6,000} \\ -\,4,999 \\ \hline 1,001 \end{array}$$

A Subtract.

① 10 −1 = **9**	② 7 −5	③ 3 −2	④ 120 −14	⑤ 842 −742	⑥ 362 −351	⑦ 7,856 −3,265	⑧ 4,895 −2,222
⑨ 20 −3	⑩ 32 −17	⑪ 59 −43	⑫ 115 −100	⑬ 906 −837	⑭ 279 −189	⑮ 5,698 −2,541	⑯ 4,865 −2,355
⑰ 6 −4	⑱ 9 −3	⑲ 8 −5	⑳ 209 −164	㉑ 929 −561	㉒ 199 −99	㉓ 9,856 −5,687	㉔ 8,546 −3,215
㉕ 64 −12	㉖ 29 −24	㉗ 66 −34	㉘ 317 −300	㉙ 848 −632	㉚ 235 −227	㉛ 2,569 −1,258	㉜ 7,892 −4,621
㉝ 9 −8	㉞ 6 −2	㉟ 9 −5	㊱ 487 −391	㊲ 727 −550	㊳ 334 −218	㊴ 4,444 −2,569	㊵ 5,421 −4,213
㊶ 51 −1	㊷ 36 −18	㊸ 75 −25	㊹ 592 −211	㊺ 665 −321	㊻ 400 −357	㊼ 7,878 −6,952	㊽ 8,556 −5,698

REMINDER: Write the definition of subtraction.

101 Unit 41 cont'd ☛

B Subtract.

① 85,258 − 52,852 = **32,406**

② 56,239 − 56,230

③ 444,444 − 323,232

④ 542,138 − 235,689

⑤ 775,511 − 259,840

⑥ 32,553 − 24,400

⑦ 99,999 − 56,565

⑧ 789,456 − 456,123

⑨ 412,138 − 256,871

⑩ 236,591 − 100,000

⑪ 60,025 − 41,098

⑫ 25,984 − 12,365

⑬ 894,561 − 237,894

⑭ 776,654 − 456,920

⑮ 485,690 − 321,890

⑯ 60,598 − 35,269

⑰ 63,842 − 23,488

⑱ 945,612 − 378,945

⑲ 456,000 − 252,500

⑳ 942,600 − 512,048

㉑ 74,569 − 63,251

㉒ 45,304 − 32,873

㉓ 654,123 − 123,654

㉔ 369,820 − 157,924

㉕ 555,555 − 231,689

C Solve these problems.

① Acme Tennis Ball Company packaged 724 tennis balls in one morning. The next morning, the company packaged 612 balls. How many fewer tennis balls were packaged the second day?

_____**112**_____

② The Conner's bills for the month of June were $800. In July, their bills only amounted to $299. How much less were their bills in July than June?

_____

③ Karen has to read 257 pages for her history assignment. She has read 183 pages. How many more pages must she read?

_____

④ It takes 416 jelly beans to fill the jar on Mr. Cameron's desk. If he pours a bag of 300 jelly beans into the empty jar, how many more does he need to fill it?

_____

⑤ Over the years Tim has collected 380 base-ball cards. If he sells 57 of them, how many will he have left?

_____

⑥ Jacob bought 5,000 sheets of notebook paper at the beginning of the school year. In February he had 2,600 left. How many sheets had he used?

_____

Add or Subtract?

Learning Objective: *We will learn to determine if a problem calls for addition or subtraction.*

Addition is the combining of numbers to obtain the total value, or sum. Subtraction is the deducting of one number from another to find the difference, or remainder.

EXAMPLE:

		A	B
In problem A, the sum of		222	352
222 and 352 is 574.		+ 352	− 222
In problem B, the difference		574	130
between 352 and 222 is 130.			

A Find the sums or remainders.

① 106
\+ 304
410

② 324
− 106

③ 849
\+ 100

④ 3,396
− 2,196

⑤ 17,971
\+ 61,472

⑥ 32,143
\+ 66,908

⑦ 625
− 100

⑧ 525
\+ 125

⑨ 123
− 100

⑩ 4,117
\+ 2,106

⑪ 72,890
− 60,051

⑫ 23,251
\+ 61,003

⑬ 212
\+ 464

⑭ 869
− 125

⑮ 665
\+ 334

⑯ 6,904
− 2,431

⑰ 12,164
\+ 13,421

⑱ 62,371
\+ 25,257

⑲ 322
− 111

⑳ 237
\+ 692

㉑ 500
− 400

㉒ 9,000
\+ 1,369

㉓ 93,670
− 32,960

㉔ 69,699
− 32,111

㉕ 342
\+ 600

㉖ 626
− 232

㉗ 201
\+ 642

㉘ 3,204
− 2,156

㉙ 96,263
\+ 11,298

㉚ 64,115
− 11,115

㉛ 649
− 102

㉜ 141
\+ 666

㉝ 625
− 525

㉞ 2,111
\+ 6,842

㉟ 80,701
− 80,071

㊱ 23,921
− 14,632

REMINDER: Write the definition of addition and subtraction.

_____

_____

Unit 42 cont'd ☞

B Fill in the blanks with + or − .

① 304 __−__ 292 = 12

② 4,201 _____ 4,310 = 8,511

③ 33,413 _____ 42,915 = 76,328

④ 133 _____ 642 = 775

⑤ 3,264 _____ 1,928 = 5,192

⑥ 21,642 _____ 19,864 = 1,778

⑦ 200 _____ 160 = 40

⑧ 5,261 _____ 3,344 = 1,917

⑨ 67,850 _____ 52,640 = 15,210

⑩ 341 _____ 240 = 581

⑪ 2,114 _____ 6,983 = 9,097

⑫ 78,558 _____ 69,333 = 9,225

⑬ 814 _____ 700 = 114

⑭ 9,116 _____ 1,000 = 10,116

⑮ 23,481 _____ 71,481 = 94,962

⑯ 553 _____ 242 = 795

⑰ 6,780 _____ 4,240 = 2,540

⑱ 13,861 _____ 11,460 = 25,321

⑲ 762 _____ 511 = 251

⑳ 3,210 _____ 2,222 = 988

㉑ 43,332 _____ 83,333 = 126,665

㉒ 394 _____ 284 = 678

㉓ 9,304 _____ 2,116 = 11,420

㉔ 79,350 _____ 32,461 = 46,889

㉕ 933 _____ 647 = 286

㉖ 2,694 _____ 8,321 = 11,015

㉗ 54,367 _____ 34,000 = 20,367

C Study each paragraph and identify each as an addition (a) or subtraction (s) problem.

__s__ ① The Malcom Theater can seat 560 people. At a recent showing of "Gone With the Wind," the theater was only occupied by 483 people. How many seats were not filled?

_____ ② Charlotte had 21 math problems for homework on Tuesday. She also had 27 English problems to write out that night. How much homework did Charlotte have?

_____ ③ Alex read 429 pages in his history book during the first semester. He read 376 pages during the second semester. How many pages did he read those semesters?

_____ ④ There are 394 seniors at Oakdale High School. Of those 389 made passing grades and will graduate. How many students will not graduate from Oakdale High School?

_____ ⑤ Lori put together a landscape jigsaw puzzle. A total of 5,462 pieces were earth tones. A total of 3,246 were blue and white. How many pieces were in Lori's puzzle?

_____ ⑥ Bridgedale's Nursery had 3,469 rosebushes in stock in April. By August they only had 256 left. How many did they sell in those five months?

104

Simple Multiplication   **Unit 43**

Multiplication is a shortcut for adding a number to itself.

EXAMPLE:

$$\begin{array}{r} 15 \\ \times 2 \end{array}\Bigg\}$$
$$\begin{array}{r} \overset{1}{1 \text{ ten, } 5 \text{ ones}} \\ \times 2 \\ \hline 3 \text{ tens, } 0 \text{ ones} \end{array} = \begin{array}{r} 15 \\ +15 \\ \hline 30 \end{array}$$

To multiply 15 by 2, first multiply 2 times 5 ones. From the multiplication tables we know that $2 \times 5 = 10$. Write down 0 and carry the 1 to the tens' column. Multiply 2×10. The answer is 2. Add the 1 that was carried and write down 3 in the tens' column.

A Multiply the ones, then the tens. Check your answers with addition.

① $\begin{array}{r} 16 \\ \times 3 \end{array}\Big\}$ $\begin{array}{r} \overset{1}{1 \text{ ten, } 6 \text{ ones}} \\ \times 3 \\ \hline 4 \text{ tens, } 8 \text{ ones} \end{array} = 48$

② $\begin{array}{r} 27 \\ \times 2 \end{array}\Big\}$

③ $\begin{array}{r} 24 \\ \times 2 \end{array}\Big\}$

④ $\begin{array}{r} 10 \\ \times 5 \end{array}\Big\}$

⑤ $\begin{array}{r} 23 \\ \times 1 \end{array}\Big\}$

⑥ $\begin{array}{r} 15 \\ \times 5 \end{array}\Big\}$

⑦ $\begin{array}{r} 14 \\ \times 7 \end{array}\Big\}$

⑧ $\begin{array}{r} 28 \\ \times 3 \end{array}\Big\}$

⑨ $\begin{array}{r} 41 \\ \times 2 \end{array}\Big\}$

⑩ $\begin{array}{r} 3 \\ \times 6 \end{array}\Big\}$

⑪ $\begin{array}{r} 5 \\ \times 5 \end{array}\Big\}$

⑫ $\begin{array}{r} 34 \\ \times 2 \end{array}\Big\}$

REMINDER: Write the definition of multiplication.

_____

_____

B Multiply.

① 12 × 2 = **24** ② 36 × 2 = ③ 11 × 5 = ④ 55 × 2 =

⑤ 33 × 4 = ⑥ 85 × 2 = ⑦ 99 × 3 = ⑧ 62 × 4 =

⑨ 22 × 5 = ⑩ 2 × 2 = ⑪ 20 × 6 = ⑫ 27 × 3 =

⑬ 6 × 6 = ⑭ 4 × 8 = ⑮ 5 × 2 = ⑯ 14 × 2 =

⑰ 32 × 1 = ⑱ 17 × 2 = ⑲ 21 × 5 = ⑳ 11 × 7 =

㉑ 6 × 3 = ㉒ 2 × 3 = ㉓ 5 × 4 = ㉔ 9 × 6 =

㉕ 7 × 4 = ㉖ 11 × 2 = ㉗ 63 × 1 = ㉘ 45 × 3 =

㉙ 18 × 2 = ㉚ 10 × 3 = ㉛ 12 × 5 = ㉜ 12 × 1 =

㉝ 13 × 4 = ㉞ 25 × 4 = ㉟ 28 × 6 = ㊱ 43 × 3 =

㊲ 50 × 2 = ㊳ 60 × 9 = ㊴ 15 × 3 = ㊵ 26 × 7 =

㊶ 3 × 8 = ㊷ 54 × 9 = ㊸ 4 × 9 = ㊹ 8 × 7 =

C Multiply. Use the space to work the problems.

① Mr. Mankee bought 81 shares of Pel-Tex oil stock. The stock did so well that he bought the same amount each week for the next three weeks. How many shares did Mr. Mankee own?

③ Mr. Arnold bought his wife a basket of 24 peaches to can. She liked them so much that she sent Mr. Arnold to buy 4 more baskets. How many peaches did Mrs. Arnold have to can?

② Mrs. Harmon, the high school French teacher, gave 67 poptests during the school year. If each poptest was worth 2 points, how many possible points could each student have?

④ During a fire damage sale, Mrs. Poiler found an excellent bargain on packages of 8 ball-point pens. If she bought seven packages, how many pens did she buy?

Multiplying by 10, 100, or 1,000

Learning Objective: *We will learn to multiply by 10; 100; or 1,000.*

Multiplying with a power of 10 means adding zeroes to an answer.

EXAMPLE: When we multiply by 10; 100; or 1,000; we can write down the multiplicand and add to it the number of zeroes in the multiplier.

$$10 \times 575 = 5,750 \qquad 100 \times 273 = 27,300 \qquad 1,000 \times 678 = 678,000$$

A Multiply by 10 or 100.

① 81 ×10 **810**	② 631 ×10	③ 52 ×10	④ 100 ×10	⑤ 875 ×10	⑥ 13 ×10
⑦ 9,000 ×10	⑧ 36 ×10	⑨ 7,599 ×10	⑩ 43 ×10	⑪ 6,954 ×10	⑫ 549 ×10
⑬ 5,003 ×100	⑭ 601 ×100	⑮ 5,180 ×100	⑯ 4,409 ×100	⑰ 24 ×100	⑱ 3,227 ×100
⑲ 5,180 ×100	⑳ 2,090 ×100	㉑ 90 ×100	㉒ 963 ×100	㉓ 45 ×100	㉔ 700 ×100
㉕ 5,600 ×10	㉖ 5,514 ×10	㉗ 77 ×10	㉘ 19 ×10	㉙ 8,029 ×10	㉚ 650 ×10
㉛ 900 ×100	㉜ 13 ×100	㉝ 7,000 ×100	㉞ 833 ×100	㉟ 9,080 ×100	㊱ 35 ×100
㊲ 100 ×100	㊳ 990 ×100	㊴ 7,699 ×100	㊵ 1,100 ×100	㊶ 333 ×100	㊷ 7,654 ×100

REMINDER: Write the definition of multiplying by a power of 10.

_____

_____

Unit 44 cont'd ☛

B Multiply by 100 or 1,000.

① $2,400 \times 100 = $ **240,000**   ② $621 \times 100 = $ ③ $100 \times 60 = $

④ $300 \times 100 = $ ⑤ $175 \times 100 = $ ⑥ $1,500 \times 100 = $

⑦ $553 \times 100 = $ ⑧ $100 \times 40 = $ ⑨ $899 \times 100 = $

⑩ $440 \times 100 = $ ⑪ $3,444 \times 100 = $ ⑫ $699 \times 100 = $

⑬ $100 \times 17 = $ ⑭ $320 \times 100 = $ ⑮ $100 \times 66 = $

⑯ $9,899 \times 100 = $ ⑰ $7,001 \times 100 = $ ⑱ $8,000 \times 100 = $

⑲ $1,000 \times 100 = $ ⑳ $1,000 \times 13 = $ ㉑ $1,000 \times 909 = $

㉒ $1,000 \times 330 = $ ㉓ $2,010 \times 1,000 = $ ㉔ $6,504 \times 1,000 = $

C Read each problem and find the answer.

① Mr. Mayberry, a coin collector, gathered 10 rare gold pieces for a buyer to examine. The buyer paid $563 for each of the gold pieces. How many dollars did Mr. Mayberry receive?

$$\begin{array}{r} \$563 \\ \times\ \mathbf{10} \\ \hline \mathbf{\$5,630} \end{array}$$

② A local radio station sold 61 spots on the air for April. If, over the next 10 months, the station sells April's amount of spots each month, how many spots will be sold?

③ Each of 28 people at a charity fair put $1,000 in a drop box. How much money was raised at the fair?

④ A motorcycle race had 34 competitors. The race was 100 miles long. If all competitors finished the race, what was the total of miles driven?

⑤ Larry's mother made the costumes for his school's play. Twenty-six yards of material were used on each of the 100 members' costumes. How many yards of material were used?

⑥ During the summer, Ladd's Photography ran a special for 100 senior photos per package. Seventy-eight students took advantage of the special. How many photos were produced?

Multiplication Tables Through 12 Unit 45

Learning Objective: *We will learn to multiply 1 × 1 through 12 × 12.*

Multiplication is a shortcut for adding a number to itself.

EXAMPLE:

$3 \times 3 = 9$ $3 + 3 + 3 = 9$ $6 \times 6 = 36$ $6 + 6 + 6 + 6 + 6 + 6 = 36$

$4 \times 4 = 16$ $4 + 4 + 4 + 4 = 16$ $7 \times 7 = 49$ $7 + 7 + 7 + 7 + 7 + 7 + 7 = 49$

$5 \times 5 = 25$ $5 + 5 + 5 + 5 + 5 = 25$ $8 \times 8 = 64$ $8 + 8 + 8 + 8 + 8 + 8 + 8 + 8 = 64$

A Multiply.

(1) $\begin{array}{r} 1 \\ \times 1 \\ \hline 1 \end{array}$	(2) $\begin{array}{r} 1 \\ \times 2 \\ \hline \end{array}$	(3) $\begin{array}{r} 1 \\ \times 3 \\ \hline \end{array}$	(4) $\begin{array}{r} 1 \\ \times 4 \\ \hline \end{array}$	(5) $\begin{array}{r} 1 \\ \times 5 \\ \hline \end{array}$	(6) $\begin{array}{r} 1 \\ \times 6 \\ \hline \end{array}$	(7) $\begin{array}{r} 1 \\ \times 7 \\ \hline \end{array}$	(8) $\begin{array}{r} 1 \\ \times 8 \\ \hline \end{array}$	(9) $\begin{array}{r} 1 \\ \times 9 \\ \hline \end{array}$	(10) $\begin{array}{r} 10 \\ \times 1 \\ \hline \end{array}$
(11) $\begin{array}{r} 11 \\ \times 1 \\ \hline \end{array}$	(12) $\begin{array}{r} 12 \\ \times 1 \\ \hline \end{array}$	(13) $\begin{array}{r} 2 \\ \times 1 \\ \hline \end{array}$	(14) $\begin{array}{r} 2 \\ \times 2 \\ \hline \end{array}$	(15) $\begin{array}{r} 2 \\ \times 3 \\ \hline \end{array}$	(16) $\begin{array}{r} 2 \\ \times 4 \\ \hline \end{array}$	(17) $\begin{array}{r} 2 \\ \times 5 \\ \hline \end{array}$	(18) $\begin{array}{r} 2 \\ \times 6 \\ \hline \end{array}$	(19) $\begin{array}{r} 2 \\ \times 7 \\ \hline \end{array}$	(20) $\begin{array}{r} 2 \\ \times 8 \\ \hline \end{array}$
(21) $\begin{array}{r} 2 \\ \times 9 \\ \hline \end{array}$	(22) $\begin{array}{r} 10 \\ \times 2 \\ \hline \end{array}$	(23) $\begin{array}{r} 11 \\ \times 2 \\ \hline \end{array}$	(24) $\begin{array}{r} 12 \\ \times 2 \\ \hline \end{array}$	(25) $\begin{array}{r} 3 \\ \times 1 \\ \hline \end{array}$	(26) $\begin{array}{r} 3 \\ \times 2 \\ \hline \end{array}$	(27) $\begin{array}{r} 3 \\ \times 3 \\ \hline \end{array}$	(28) $\begin{array}{r} 3 \\ \times 4 \\ \hline \end{array}$	(29) $\begin{array}{r} 3 \\ \times 5 \\ \hline \end{array}$	(30) $\begin{array}{r} 3 \\ \times 6 \\ \hline \end{array}$
(31) $\begin{array}{r} 3 \\ \times 7 \\ \hline \end{array}$	(32) $\begin{array}{r} 3 \\ \times 8 \\ \hline \end{array}$	(33) $\begin{array}{r} 3 \\ \times 9 \\ \hline \end{array}$	(34) $\begin{array}{r} 10 \\ \times 3 \\ \hline \end{array}$	(35) $\begin{array}{r} 11 \\ \times 3 \\ \hline \end{array}$	(36) $\begin{array}{r} 12 \\ \times 3 \\ \hline \end{array}$	(37) $\begin{array}{r} 4 \\ \times 1 \\ \hline \end{array}$	(38) $\begin{array}{r} 4 \\ \times 2 \\ \hline \end{array}$	(39) $\begin{array}{r} 4 \\ \times 3 \\ \hline \end{array}$	(40) $\begin{array}{r} 4 \\ \times 4 \\ \hline \end{array}$
(41) $\begin{array}{r} 4 \\ \times 5 \\ \hline \end{array}$	(42) $\begin{array}{r} 4 \\ \times 6 \\ \hline \end{array}$	(43) $\begin{array}{r} 4 \\ \times 7 \\ \hline \end{array}$	(44) $\begin{array}{r} 4 \\ \times 8 \\ \hline \end{array}$	(45) $\begin{array}{r} 4 \\ \times 9 \\ \hline \end{array}$	(46) $\begin{array}{r} 10 \\ \times 4 \\ \hline \end{array}$	(47) $\begin{array}{r} 11 \\ \times 4 \\ \hline \end{array}$	(48) $\begin{array}{r} 12 \\ \times 4 \\ \hline \end{array}$	(49) $\begin{array}{r} 5 \\ \times 1 \\ \hline \end{array}$	(50) $\begin{array}{r} 5 \\ \times 2 \\ \hline \end{array}$
(51) $\begin{array}{r} 5 \\ \times 3 \\ \hline \end{array}$	(52) $\begin{array}{r} 5 \\ \times 4 \\ \hline \end{array}$	(53) $\begin{array}{r} 5 \\ \times 5 \\ \hline \end{array}$	(54) $\begin{array}{r} 5 \\ \times 6 \\ \hline \end{array}$	(55) $\begin{array}{r} 5 \\ \times 7 \\ \hline \end{array}$	(56) $\begin{array}{r} 5 \\ \times 8 \\ \hline \end{array}$	(57) $\begin{array}{r} 5 \\ \times 9 \\ \hline \end{array}$	(58) $\begin{array}{r} 10 \\ \times 5 \\ \hline \end{array}$	(59) $\begin{array}{r} 11 \\ \times 5 \\ \hline \end{array}$	(60) $\begin{array}{r} 12 \\ \times 5 \\ \hline \end{array}$
(61) $\begin{array}{r} 6 \\ \times 1 \\ \hline \end{array}$	(62) $\begin{array}{r} 6 \\ \times 2 \\ \hline \end{array}$	(63) $\begin{array}{r} 6 \\ \times 3 \\ \hline \end{array}$	(64) $\begin{array}{r} 6 \\ \times 4 \\ \hline \end{array}$	(65) $\begin{array}{r} 6 \\ \times 5 \\ \hline \end{array}$	(66) $\begin{array}{r} 6 \\ \times 6 \\ \hline \end{array}$	(67) $\begin{array}{r} 6 \\ \times 7 \\ \hline \end{array}$	(68) $\begin{array}{r} 6 \\ \times 8 \\ \hline \end{array}$	(69) $\begin{array}{r} 6 \\ \times 9 \\ \hline \end{array}$	(70) $\begin{array}{r} 10 \\ \times 6 \\ \hline \end{array}$

REMINDER: Write the definition of multiplication.

_____

_____

Unit 45 cont'd ☞

B Multiply.

① $11 \times 6 =$ **66** ② $12 \times 6 =$ ③ $7 \times 1 =$ ④ $7 \times 2 =$

⑤ $7 \times 3 =$ ⑥ $7 \times 4 =$ ⑦ $7 \times 5 =$ ⑧ $7 \times 6 =$

⑨ $7 \times 7 =$ ⑩ $7 \times 8 =$ ⑪ $7 \times 9 =$ ⑫ $7 \times 10 =$

⑬ $7 \times 11 =$ ⑭ $7 \times 12 =$ ⑮ $8 \times 1 =$ ⑯ $8 \times 2 =$

⑰ $8 \times 3 =$ ⑱ $8 \times 4 =$ ⑲ $8 \times 5 =$ ⑳ $8 \times 6 =$

㉑ $8 \times 7 =$ ㉒ $8 \times 8 =$ ㉓ $8 \times 9 =$ ㉔ $8 \times 10 =$

㉕ $8 \times 11 =$ ㉖ $8 \times 12 =$ ㉗ $9 \times 1 =$ ㉘ $9 \times 2 =$

㉙ $9 \times 3 =$ ㉚ $9 \times 4 =$ ㉛ $9 \times 5 =$ ㉜ $9 \times 6 =$

㉝ $9 \times 7 =$ ㉞ $9 \times 8 =$ ㉟ $9 \times 9 =$ ㊱ $9 \times 10 =$

㊲ $9 \times 11 =$ ㊳ $9 \times 12 =$ ㊴ $10 \times 1 =$ ㊵ $10 \times 2 =$

㊶ $10 \times 3 =$ ㊷ $10 \times 4 =$ ㊸ $10 \times 5 =$ ㊹ $10 \times 6 =$

C Read each problem and write the answer.

① ten times eight equals *eighty* ② ten times nine equals

③ ten times ten equals ④ ten times eleven equals

⑤ ten times twelve equals ⑥ eleven times one equals

⑦ eleven times two equals ⑧ eleven times three equals

⑨ eleven times four equals ⑩ eleven times five equals

⑪ eleven times six equals ⑫ eleven times seven equals

⑬ eleven times eight equals ⑭ eleven times nine equals

⑮ eleven times ten equals ⑯ eleven times eleven equals

⑰ eleven times twelve equals ⑱ twelve times one equals

⑲ twelve times two equals ⑳ twelve times three equals

㉑ twelve times four equals ㉒ twelve times five equals

㉓ twelve times six equals ㉔ twelve times seven equals

㉕ twelve times eight equals ㉖ twelve times nine equals

㉗ twelve times ten equals ㉘ twelve times eleven equals

Comprehension Check

A Subtract these numbers.

① 26
− 14
12

② 38
− 27

③ 57
− 46

④ 73
− 29

⑤ 89
− 79

⑥ 98
− 29

⑦ 56
− 49

⑧ 43
− 29

⑨ 31
− 28

⑩ 399
− 276

⑪ 489
− 325

⑫ 572
− 399

⑬ 447
− 331

⑭ 997
− 899

⑮ 921
− 599

⑯ 308
− 272

⑰ 4,953
− 3,210

⑱ 5,976
− 4,996

⑲ 2,397
− 1,999

⑳ 1,009
− 972

㉑ 9,789
− 5,638

㉒ 8,989
− 7,658

㉓ 99,767
− 56,998

㉔ 97,666
− 56,454

㉕ 57,499
− 43,454

㉖ 44,537
− 32,494

㉗ 95,446
− 87,938

㉘ 999,776
− 655,449

㉙ 102,317
− 97,322

㉚ 667,889
− 543,441

㉛ 329,971
− 222,558

㉜ 857,892
− 569,431

B Listed below are two elements of a problem and its answer. Put a + sign if you would use addition to find the answer, or put a − sign if you would use subtraction to find the answer.

① 23
+ 46
69

② 53
21
32

③ 67
19
48

④ 99
23
122

⑤ 48
28
20

⑥ 92
34
126

⑦ 70
25
45

⑧ 89
72
17

⑨ 70
39
31

⑩ 399
478
877

⑪ 569
321
248

⑫ 569
874
1,443

⑬ 895
369
526

⑭ 569
321
890

⑮ 456
399
57

⑯ 555
223
778

⑰ 4,569
2,369
6,938

⑱ 7,896
2,365
10,261

⑲ 9,845
2,356
7,489

⑳ 1,258
1,113
2,371

㉑ 4,563
2,121
6,684

㉒ 7,894
3,636
4,258

㉓ 45,632
12,586
58,218

㉔ 78,965
45,632
124,597

㉕ 78,523
56,565
21,958

㉖ 98,745
63,258
35,487

㉗ 997,663
544,223
453,440

Test 9 cont'd ☞

Ⓒ Multiply.

① 5 × 5 = *25*	② 6 × 7	③ 3 × 2	④ 5 × 1	⑤ 4 × 3	⑥ 4 × 8	⑦ 9 × 2	⑧ 8 × 8	⑨ 9 × 9	⑩ 7 × 7
⑪ 7 × 3	⑫ 8 × 1	⑬ 7 × 2	⑭ 2 × 9	⑮ 8 × 2	⑯ 7 × 4	⑰ 6 × 1	⑱ 8 × 3	⑲ 6 × 2	⑳ 9 × 1
㉑ 7 × 5	㉒ 9 × 3	㉓ 8 × 4	㉔ 9 × 4	㉕ 9 × 5	㉖ 8 × 5	㉗ 9 × 6	㉘ 7 × 6	㉙ 6 × 3	㉚ 8 × 6
㉛ 7 × 1	㉜ 6 × 4	㉝ 7 × 8	㉞ 8 × 9	㉟ 7 × 9	㊱ 9 × 8	㊲ 6 × 5	㊳ 8 × 7	㊴ 6 × 6	㊵ 9 × 7
㊶ 3 × 10	㊷ 5 × 3	㊸ 6 × 8	㊹ 5 × 6	㊺ 3 × 9	㊻ 4 × 7	㊼ 5 × 8	㊽ 10 × 4	㊾ 4 × 9	㊿ 5 × 9
(51) 5 × 7	(52) 3 × 8	(53) 3 × 4	(54) 6 × 9	(55) 4 × 4	(56) 10 × 2	(57) 4 × 5	(58) 10 × 1	(59) 3 × 3	(60) 5 × 2

Write out the answers.

① ten times twenty-seven equals
② ten times thirty equals
③ ten times ninety-eight equals
④ ten times forty-six equals
⑤ one hundred times three equals
⑥ one hundred times twenty equals
⑦ one hundred times four hundred equals
⑧ one hundred times four hundred twenty equals
⑨ one thousand times sixty-three equals
⑩ one thousand times fifty-eight equals
⑪ one thousand times seventy-nine equals
⑫ one thousand times one hundred eleven equals

Multiplying Two-Digit Numbers

Learning Objective: *We will learn to multiply with two-digit numbers.*

A two-digit number has numbers in the ones' place and the tens' place.

EXAMPLE: When we multiply
two-digit numbers,
we often carry to
the next column.

```
   24
 ×35
  120
   72
  840
```

A Multiply these two-digit numbers.

①
```
  50
 ×17
 350
  50
 850
```

②
```
  35
 ×35
```

③
```
  76
 ×50
```

④
```
  25
 ×12
```

⑤
```
  89
 ×70
```

⑥
```
  90
 ×31
```

⑦
```
  70
 ×55
```

⑧
```
  22
 ×17
```

⑨
```
  51
 ×49
```

⑩
```
  73
 ×25
```

⑪
```
  11
 ×11
```

⑫
```
  30
 ×25
```

⑬
```
  55
 ×22
```

⑭
```
  93
 ×76
```

⑮
```
  38
 ×10
```

⑯
```
  56
 ×33
```

⑰
```
  29
 ×29
```

⑱
```
  44
 ×18
```

⑲
```
  47
 ×20
```

⑳
```
  55
 ×50
```

㉑
```
  70
 ×35
```

㉒
```
  99
 ×81
```

㉓
```
  31
 ×25
```

㉔
```
  25
 ×17
```

㉕
```
  75
 ×43
```

㉖
```
  60
 ×34
```

㉗
```
  18
 ×10
```

㉘
```
  31
 ×18
```

REMINDER: Write the definition of a two-digit number.

_____

_____

Unit 46 cont'd ☞

B Multiply.

① $44 \times 10 = $ **440** ② $40 \times 40 = $ ③ $13 \times 49 = $ ④ $21 \times 23 = $

⑤ $80 \times 32 = $ ⑥ $95 \times 33 = $ ⑦ $29 \times 37 = $ ⑧ $18 \times 16 = $

⑨ $73 \times 73 = $ ⑩ $54 \times 21 = $ ⑪ $80 \times 71 = $ ⑫ $56 \times 85 = $

⑬ $33 \times 23 = $ ⑭ $17 \times 15 = $ ⑮ $97 \times 15 = $ ⑯ $87 \times 10 = $

⑰ $60 \times 13 = $ ⑱ $39 \times 38 = $ ⑲ $47 \times 98 = $ ⑳ $77 \times 11 = $

㉑ $20 \times 72 = $ ㉒ $80 \times 25 = $ ㉓ $18 \times 55 = $ ㉔ $12 \times 30 = $

㉕ $31 \times 18 = $ ㉖ $12 \times 66 = $ ㉗ $53 \times 24 = $ ㉘ $35 \times 15 = $

㉙ $98 \times 99 = $ ㉚ $64 \times 96 = $ ㉛ $66 \times 81 = $ ㉜ $25 \times 25 = $

㉝ $13 \times 56 = $ ㉞ $73 \times 93 = $ ㉟ $70 \times 39 = $ ㊱ $50 \times 10 = $

C Read each paragraph and find the answer.

① In the church choir there are 16 members sitting in each row. If there are 11 rows, how many members are in the choir?

$$
\begin{array}{r}
16 \\
\times 11 \\
\hline
16 \\
16 \\
\hline
176
\end{array}
$$

② During Carmen's first semester at college, she made 28 phone calls home. Each conversation lasted 49 minutes. How many minutes did she talk on the phone to someone at home?

③ Ann studied 14 hours a day for 23 days for her college finals. How many hours did Ann study?

④ Twenty-six high school friends gathered for a reunion. Each person gave out 26 cards with their name and address on it. How many cards were given out?

⑤ Mrs. Laurie's pet shop groomed 18 dogs a day for 38 days. How many dogs were groomed?

⑥ For the office Christmas party, Mr. Williams bought 12 packages of cold drinks. Each package had 12 drinks. How many drinks did Mr. Williams buy?

Multiplying Three-Digit Numbers

Unit 47

Learning Objective: *We will learn to multiply three-digit numbers.*

A three-digit number has digits in the ones' place, the tens' place, and the hundreds' place.

EXAMPLE: When we multiply three-digit numbers, we often carry.

```
     106
   ×333
     318
     318
     318
  35,298
```

A Multiply these three-digit numbers.

① 177
  ×523
  531
  354
  885
  92,571

② 443
  ×918

③ 989
  ×644

④ 505
  ×112

⑤ 648
  ×361

⑥ 150
  ×668

⑦ 936
  ×117

⑧ 320
  ×612

⑨ 800
  ×106

⑩ 945
  ×111

⑪ 200
  ×126

⑫ 554
  ×260

⑬ 700
  ×715

⑭ 565
  ×417

⑮ 799
  ×729

⑯ 780
  ×350

⑰ 399
  ×390

⑱ 675
  ×702

⑲ 532
  ×217

⑳ 800
  ×310

㉑ 660
  ×436

㉒ 221
  ×109

㉓ 922
  ×754

㉔ 753
  ×596

REMINDER: Write the definition of a three-digit number.

_____

_____

Unit 47 cont'd ☞

B Multiply.

① 162 ×103 __486__ __1620__ __16,686__	② 618 ×555	③ 179 ×147	④ 340 ×366	⑤ 701 ×123	⑥ 807 ×247
⑦ 300 ×750	⑧ 930 ×300	⑨ 931 ×286	⑩ 262 ×831	⑪ 314 ×683	⑫ 581 ×642
⑬ 969 ×876	⑭ 194 ×719	⑮ 618 ×191	⑯ 847 ×221	⑰ 610 ×964	⑱ 252 ×738

C Match each problem with the answer.

___c___ ① three hundred thirty-three times ninety-three

_____ ② three hundred times seventy-five

_____ ③ eight hundred eleven times sixty-nine

_____ ④ nine hundred thirty times thirty

_____ ⑤ seven hundred twenty-seven times six hundred

_____ ⑥ six hundred fifty times two hundred ten

_____ ⑦ two hundred fifty-three times six hundred sixty-six

_____ ⑧ one hundred six times one hundred

_____ ⑨ nine hundred thirty-one times twenty-eight

_____ ⑩ five hundred eighty-one times twelve

_____ ⑪ six hundred twenty-four times five hundred ninety-nine

_____ ⑫ three hundred ten times ten

_____ ⑬ two hundred sixty-two times thirty-one

_____ ⑭ eight hundred eighty-eight times one hundred ten

a. one hundred sixty-eight thousand, four hundred ninety-eight

b. twenty-two thousand, five hundred

c. thirty thousand, nine hundred sixty-nine

d. three hundred seventy-three thousand, seven hundred seventy-six

e. ninety-seven thousand, six hundred eighty

f. one hundred thirty-six thousand, five hundred

g. four hundred thirty-six thousand, two hundred

h. ten thousand, six hundred

i. twenty-seven thousand, nine hundred

j. eight thousand, one hundred twenty-two

k. twenty-six thousand, sixty-eight

l. six thousand, nine hundred seventy-two

m. three thousand, one hundred

n. fifty-five thousand, nine hundred fifty-nine

116

Multiplying Four-Digit Numbers

Learning Objective: *We will learn to multiply four-digit numbers.*

A four-digit number has digits in the ones' place, the tens' place, the hundreds' place, and the thousands' place.

EXAMPLE: When we multiply
four-digit numbers,
we sometimes carry.

```
      3,333
    ×2,226
     19998
      6666
      6666
      6666
   7,419,258
```

A Multiply these four-digit numbers.

①
```
    1,290
  ×1,185
    6450
   10320
    1290
    1290
 1,528,650
```

②
```
    6,008
  ×5,632
```

③
```
    5,151
  ×2,243
```

④
```
    7,181
  ×8,744
```

⑤
```
    8,880
  ×7,041
```

⑥
```
    3,123
  ×7,553
```

⑦
```
    2,111
  ×1,490
```

⑧
```
    7,174
  ×9,385
```

⑨
```
    1,222
  ×6,091
```

⑩
```
    3,199
  ×3,239
```

⑪
```
    9,856
  ×4,075
```

⑫
```
    9,916
  ×3,061
```

⑬
```
    5,167
  ×2,232
```

⑭
```
    5,911
  ×7,556
```

⑮
```
    4,532
  ×9,822
```

⑯
```
    2,001
  ×1,616
```

⑰
```
    6,599
  ×7,190
```

⑱
```
    3,092
  ×3,180
```

⑲
```
    2,721
  ×1,360
```

⑳
```
    8,922
  ×5,000
```

REMINDER: Write the definition of a four-digit number.

Unit 48 cont'd ☞

B Match each problem with the answer.

_h_ ① 8,653 × 4,358

_____ ② 8,716 × 1,890

_____ ③ 4,300 × 7,000

_____ ④ 4,428 × 1,130

_____ ⑤ 1,117 × 4,803

_____ ⑥ 3,342 × 5,555

_____ ⑦ 6,969 × 1,212

_____ ⑧ 3,456 × 8,910

_____ ⑨ 7,738 × 9,110

_____ ⑩ 7,596 × 6,248

_____ ⑪ 9,879 × 2,076

_____ ⑫ 8,008 × 7,251

_____ ⑬ 7,357 × 3,206

_____ ⑭ 9,394 × 1,000

_____ ⑮ 2,036 × 3,256

_____ ⑯ 7,890 × 1,226

_____ ⑰ 6,221 × 2,213

_____ ⑱ 4,872 × 6,579

a. 20,508,804
b. 23,586,542
c. 5,364,951
d. 47,459,808
e. 9,394,000
f. 30,100,000
g. 8,446,428
h. 37,709,774
i. 5,003,640
j. 6,629,216
k. 16,473,240
l. 58,066,008
m. 9,673,140
n. 13,767,073
o. 30,792,960
p. 32,052,888
q. 70,493,180
r. 18,564,810

C Read each paragraph and find the answer.

① There are 5,657 cases of cookies in Amece's warehouse. There are 5,524 cookies in each case. How many cookies are in the warehouse?

② If 4,584 different chapters of the YMCA each have 3,025 members, how many members are there in those chapters?

③ There are 1,420 copies of French-English dictionaries in Kansas public schools. Each dictionary has 1,968 pages in it. How many French-English dictionary pages are there altogether?

④ Each member of the International Cooks received 1,350 recipes as a gift from the club. If there are 1,215 members, how many recipes were sent as gifts?

The Associative Property

Learning Objective: *We will learn to use the associative property of multiplication.*

The associative property of multiplication holds that the product will be the same regardless of the way in which a series of numbers is grouped.

EXAMPLE: $[a \times b] \times c = d$ If we multiply the product of a × b by c, the result will be
$a \times [b \times c] = d$ equal to that of multiplying a times the product of b × c.

A Show how the associative property can apply to these problems.

① $[2 \times 3] \times 4 = 24$ ② $6 \times [1 \times 3] = 18$ ③ $[4 \times 2] \times 30 = 240$

   $2 \times [3 \times 4] = 24$

④ $[6 \times 5] \times 2 = 60$ ⑤ $[9 \times 2] \times 4 = 72$ ⑥ $[11 \times 3] \times 6 = 198$

⑦ $10 \times [3 \times 5] = 150$ ⑧ $[3 \times 9] \times 5 = 135$ ⑨ $15 \times [3 \times 3] = 135$

⑩ $[7 \times 8] \times 1 = 56$ ⑪ $[6 \times 8] \times 10 = 480$ ⑫ $4 \times [12 \times 10] = 480$

⑬ $12 \times [5 \times 8] = 480$ ⑭ $[7 \times 4] \times 7 = 196$ ⑮ $[8 \times 7] \times 4 = 224$

⑯ $[3 \times 6] \times 7 = 126$ ⑰ $20 \times [3 \times 15] = 900$ ⑱ $21 \times [2 \times 11] = 462$

⑲ $[13 \times 10] \times 8 = 1,040$ ⑳ $[6 \times 6] \times 3 = 108$ ㉑ $4 \times [8 \times 9 = 288$

REMINDER: Write the definition of the associative property of multiplication.

_____

_____

Unit 49 cont'd ☞

B Match the problems that illustrate the associative property.

① $[a \times b] \times c = 100$ $[11 \times 6] \times 5 = 330$ ⑪ $[7 \times 5] \times 1 = 35$ $10 \times [10 \times 3] = 300$

② $[7 \times 2] \times 1 = 14$ $a \times [b \times c] = 100$ ⑫ $5 \times [6 \times 8] = 240$ $[5 \times 6] \times 8 = 240$

③ $11 \times [6 \times 5] = 330$ $7 \times [2 \times 1] = 14$ ⑬ $[10 \times 10] \times 3 = 300$ $7 \times [5 \times 1] = 35$

④ $[8 \times 3] \times 6 = 144$ $8 \times [3 \times 6] = 144$ ⑭ $9 \times [3 \times 3] = 81$ $[9 \times 3] \times 3 = 81$

⑤ $5 \times [9 \times 4] = 180$ $[2 \times 2] \times 4 = 16$ ⑮ $4 \times [4 \times 4] = 64$ $3 \times [10 \times 2] = 60$

⑥ $2 \times [2 \times 4] = 16$ $[4 \times 4] \times 1 = 16$ ⑯ $[3 \times 10] \times 2 = 60$ $100 \times [2 \times 1] = 200$

⑦ $4 \times [4 \times 1] = 16$ $[5 \times 9] \times 4 = 180$ ⑰ $[11 \times 1] \times 5 = 55$ $[4 \times 4] \times 4 = 64$

⑧ $x \times [y \times z] = 50$ $[3 \times 3] \times 2 = 18$ ⑱ $6 \times [8 \times 50] = 2,400$ $a \times [a \times b] = c$

⑨ $10 \times [8 \times 2] = 160$ $[x \times y] \times z = 50$ ⑲ $[100 \times 2] \times 1 = 200$ $11 \times [1 \times 5] = 55$

⑩ $3 \times [3 \times 2] = 18$ $[10 \times 8] \times 2 = 160$ ⑳ $[a \times a] \times b = c$ $[6 \times 8] \times 50 = 2,400$

C Work the problems.

① Jan, Sue, and Pat each work three hours per day at Hyler's Dress Shop. Each works four days a week. How many hours per week do the three girls work?

_____

② Mr. Warner divided his class into five groups. Each group was made up of five students. Each student was responsible for two class lectures. How many lectures were the students responsible for?

_____

③ Barbara takes two vacations a year. On each vacation she takes 20 pictures a day. Each vacation lasts seven days. How many pictures does Barbara take on vacations in one year?

_____

④ Louis has six boxes. In each box are ten record albums. Louis' friends Rick and Bob also have six boxes, each containing ten records. How many records do the three boys have?

_____

120

Using the Associative Property

Learning Objective: **We will learn to apply the associative property of multiplication.**

The associative property of multiplication holds that the product will be the same regardless of the way in which a series of numbers is grouped.

EXAMPLE: $[2 \times 3] \times 4 = 24$ If we multiply the product of 2×3 by 4, the result will be
   $2 \times [3 \times 4] = 24$ equal to that of multiplying 2 times the product of 3×4.

A Solve the problems.

① $[6 \times 4] \times 2 = $ **48**
   $\underline{24}$

② $8 \times [1 \times 7] = $ ____

③ $[1 \times 6] \times 5 = $ ____

④ $[3 \times 4] \times 9 = $ ____

⑤ $4 \times [7 \times 7] = $ ____

⑥ $[2 \times 9] \times 1 = $ ____

⑦ $3 \times [5 \times 5] = $ ____

⑧ $[9 \times 9] \times 2 = $ ____

⑨ $4 \times [5 \times 7] = $ ____

⑩ $1 \times [5 \times 0] = $ ____

⑪ $5 \times [7 \times 10] = $ ____

⑫ $[11 \times 2] \times 2 = $ ____

⑬ $[8 \times 6] \times 4 = $ ____

⑭ $10 \times [2 \times 2] = $ ____

⑮ $[7 \times 3] \times 8 = $ ____

⑯ $[9 \times 1] \times 6 = $ ____

⑰ $[4 \times 4] \times 2 = $ ____

⑱ $2 \times [1 \times 13] = $ ____

⑲ $5 \times [10 \times 4] = $ ____

⑳ $50 \times [3 \times 2] = $ ____

㉑ $[9 \times 2] \times 10 = $ ____

㉒ $[14 \times 2] \times 1 = $ ____

㉓ $2 \times [50 \times 1] = $ ____

㉔ $4 \times [8 \times 2] = $ ____

㉕ $3 \times [12 \times 1] = $ ____

㉖ $[3 \times 8] \times 3 = $ ____

㉗ $7 \times [1 \times 0] = $ ____

㉘ $[16 \times 1] \times 3 = $ ____

㉙ $6 \times [7 \times 2] = $ ____

㉚ $[15 \times 1] \times 3 = $ ____

㉛ $8 \times [1 \times 1] = $ ____

㉜ $[100 \times 2] \times 5 = $ ____

㉝ $[3 \times 3] \times 20 = $ ____

㉞ $[10 \times 10] \times 1 = $ ____

㉟ $[30 \times 3] \times 2 = $ ____

㊱ $12 \times [1 \times 5] = $ ____

REMINDER: Write the definition of the associative property of multiplication.

_____

_____

Unit 50 cont'd ☛

B Solve the problems.

① $6 \times [4 \times 5] = $ ***120***
   $[6 \times 4] \times 5 = $ ***120***

② $2 \times [3 \times 7] = $
   $[2 \times 3] \times 7 = $

③ $[1 \times 9] \times 5 = $
   $1 \times [9 \times 5] = $

④ $10 \times [2 \times 6] = $
   $[10 \times 2] \times 6 = $

⑤ $[4 \times 4] \times 3 = $
   $4 \times [4 \times 3] = $

⑥ $[5 \times 6] \times 2 = $
   $5 \times [6 \times 2] = $

⑦ $26 \times [2 \times 1] = $
   $[26 \times 2] \times 1 = $

⑧ $[2 \times 3] \times 10 = $
   $2 \times [3 \times 10] = $

⑨ $[1 \times 1] \times 46 = $
   $1 \times [1 \times 46] = $

⑩ $12 \times [3 \times 3] = $
   $[12 \times 3] \times 3 = $

⑪ $25 \times [4 \times 1] = $
   $[25 \times 4] \times 1 = $

⑫ $7 \times [20 \times 3] = $
   $[7 \times 20] \times 3 = $

⑬ $[7 \times 5] \times 1 = $
   $7 \times [5 \times 1] = $

⑭ $[9 \times 7] \times 6 = $
   $9 \times [7 \times 6] = $

⑮ $50 \times [10 \times 5] = $
   $[50 \times 10] \times 5 = $

⑯ $[11 \times 10] \times 2 = $
   $11 \times [10 \times 2] = $

⑰ $31 \times [3 \times 10] = $
   $[31 \times 3] \times 10 = $

⑱ $100 \times [8 \times 8] = $
   $[100 \times 8] \times 8 = $

C Fill in the blanks.

① $7 \times 2 \times 3 = 42$
   If we multiply the product of 7×2 by ____***3***____ , the result will be equal to that of multiplying 7 times the product of ____***2 × 3***____ .

② $1 \times 8 \times 9 = 72$
   If we multiply the product of $1 \times$ _____ by 9, the result will be equal to that of multiplying _____ times the product of 8×9.

③ $5 \times 6 \times 2 = 60$
   If we multiply the product of _____ by 2, the result will be equal to that of multiplying 5 times the product of _____ .

④ $3 \times 8 \times 4 = 96$
   If we multiply the product of _____ $\times 8$ by 4, the result will be _____ to that of multiplying 3 times the _____ of 8×4.

⑤ $10 \times 5 \times 2 = 100$
   If we multiply the product of _____ by _____ , the result will be equal to that of multiplying _____ times the product of _____ .

Comprehension Check

A Multiply these two-digit numbers.

① 22
  ×18
   176
    22
   396

② 56
  ×23

③ 11
  ×38

④ 62
  ×41

⑤ 76
  ×14

⑥ 89
  ×75

⑦ 38
  ×34

⑧ 72
  ×16

⑨ 97
  ×29

⑩ 81
  ×48

⑪ 49
  ×51

⑫ 12
  ×11

B Multiply these three-digit numbers.

① 418
  ×222
   836
   836
   836
 92,796

② 467
  ×338

③ 298
  ×172

④ 823
  ×248

⑤ 781
  ×502

⑥ 671
  ×327

⑦ 519
  ×234

⑧ 781
  ×625

⑨ 375
  ×291

⑩ 677
  ×212

⑪ 857
  ×491

⑫ 928
  ×199

C Multiply these four-digit numbers.

① 1,281
  ×1,174

② 7,241
  ×2,688

③ 3,968
  ×4,255

④ 5,209
  ×4,641

⑤ 6,859
  ×1,426

 Test 10 cont'd ☞

D Apply the associative property of multiplication.

① $[2 \times 8] \times 1 = 16$

    $2 \times [8 \times 1] = 16$

② $[10 \times 3] \times 2 = 60$

③ $[9 \times 5] \times 2 = 90$

④ $7 \times [6 \times 5] = 210$

⑤ $[11 \times 1] \times 8 = 88$

⑥ $20 \times [2 \times 2] = 80$

⑦ $[9 \times 9] \times 2 = 162$

⑧ $5 \times [4 \times 4] = 80$

⑨ $[3 \times 7] \times 6 = 126$

⑩ $[2 \times 12] \times 3 = 72$

⑪ $30 \times [10 \times 10] = 3,000$

⑫ $[19 \times 1] \times 2 = 38$

⑬ $[18 \times 3] \times 5 = 270$

⑭ $6 \times [6 \times 6] = 216$

⑮ $22 \times [4 \times 2] = 176$

⑯ $5 \times [8 \times 1] = 40$

⑰ $[25 \times 2] \times 2 = 100$

⑱ $[10 \times 3] \times 9 = 270$

⑲ $[19 \times 5] \times 2 = 190$

⑳ $15 \times [12 \times 9] = 1,620$

㉑ $[41 \times 3] \times 4 = 492$

㉒ $[75 \times 1] \times 2 = 150$

㉓ $[13 \times 3] \times 5 = 195$

㉔ $80 \times [10 \times 5] = 4,000$

Write a short paragraph explaining the associative property of multiplication.

_____

_____

_____

_____

_____

_____

The Commutative Property

Learning Objective: *We will learn to use the commutative property of multiplication.*

The commutative property of multiplication holds that the product will be the same regardless of the order in which the numbers are multiplied.

EXAMPLE: $10 \times 6 = 60$

$6 \times 10 = 60$

If we multiply ten times six, we will get the same product as when we multiply six times ten.

A Match the problems which illustrate the commutative property.

① $2 \times 3 = 6$ $2 \times 4 = 8$ ⑧ $4 \times 6 = 24$ $12 \times 2 = 24$

② $6 \times 2 = 12$ $3 \times 2 = 6$ ⑨ $3 \times 8 = 24$ $3 \times 7 = 21$

③ $4 \times 2 = 8$ $2 \times 6 = 12$ ⑩ $2 \times 12 = 24$ $8 \times 3 = 24$

④ $3 \times 4 = 12$ $2 \times 8 = 16$ ⑪ $7 \times 3 = 21$ $6 \times 5 = 30$

⑤ $8 \times 2 = 16$ $7 \times 2 = 14$ ⑫ $5 \times 6 = 30$ $6 \times 4 = 24$

⑥ $3 \times 5 = 15$ $4 \times 3 = 12$ ⑬ $3 \times 10 = 30$ $10 \times 3 = 30$

⑦ $2 \times 7 = 14$ $5 \times 3 = 15$ ⑭ $2 \times 15 = 30$ $15 \times 2 = 30$

B Find the products.

① $5 \times 7 = \mathbf{35}$ ② $6 \times 8 =$ ③ $4 \times 9 =$ ④ $10 \times 2 =$
    $7 \times 5 = \mathbf{35}$ $8 \times 6 =$ $9 \times 4 =$ $2 \times 10 =$

⑤ $3 \times 6 =$ ⑥ $18 \times 2 =$ ⑦ $20 \times 2 =$ ⑧ $45 \times 5 =$
    $6 \times 3 =$ $2 \times 18 =$ $2 \times 20 =$ $5 \times 45 =$

⑨ $9 \times 8 =$ ⑩ $4 \times 8 =$ ⑪ $25 \times 3 =$ ⑫ $75 \times 1 =$
    $8 \times 9 =$ $8 \times 4 =$ $3 \times 25 =$ $1 \times 75 =$

⑬ $12 \times 3 =$ ⑭ $11 \times 8 =$ ⑮ $31 \times 3 =$ ⑯ $5 \times 12 =$
    $3 \times 12 =$ $8 \times 11 =$ $3 \times 31 =$ $12 \times 5 =$

REMINDER: Write the definition of the commutative property.

_____

_____

Unit 51 cont'd ☛

C Find the products.

①
```
  12        11
 ×11       ×12
  12        22
  12        11
 132       132
```

②
```
  23        15
 ×15       ×23
```

③
```
  41        27
 ×27       ×41
```

④
```
  76        38
 ×38       ×76
```

⑤
```
 418       211
×211      ×418
```

⑥
```
 855       419
×419      ×855
```

⑦
```
 333       654
×654      ×333
```

⑧
```
 1,410     1,542
×1,542    ×1,410
```

⑨
```
 2,724     3,582
×3,582    ×2,724
```

⑩
```
 6,421     2,973
×2,973    ×6,421
```

D Fill in the blanks.

① The product of five times four equals the product of four times _____*five*_____ .

② The product of six times eight equals the product of eight times _____ .

③ The product of eleven times nine equals the product of _____ times _____ .

④ The product of twenty times one equals the product of _____ times _____ .

⑤ The product of seven times nine equals the product of _____ times _____ .

⑥ The product of twenty times three equals the product of _____ times _____ .

⑦ The product of two times twelve equals the product of _____ times _____ .

⑧ The product of ten times six equals the product of _____ times _____ .

⑨ The product of zero times one equals the product of _____ times _____ .

⑩ The product of fifty times three equals the product of _____ times _____ .

Using the Commutative Property

Learning Objective: *We will learn to apply the commutative property of multiplication.*

The commutative property of multiplication holds that the product will be the same regardless of the order in which the numbers are multiplied.

EXAMPLE: $7 \times 8 = 56$

$8 \times 7 = 56$

If we multiply seven times eight, we will get the same product as when we multiply eight times seven.

A Apply the commutative property of multiplication.

① $2 \times 3 = 6$
$3 \times 2 = 6$

② $4 \times 5 = 20$

③ $7 \times 6 = 42$

④ $10 \times 1 = 10$

⑤ $4 \times 7 = 28$

⑥ $9 \times 8 = 72$

⑦ $20 \times 4 = 80$

⑧ $11 \times 6 = 66$

⑨ $25 \times 4 = 100$

⑩ $3 \times 9 = 27$

⑪ $2 \times 14 = 28$

⑫ $7 \times 12 = 84$

⑬ $19 \times 3 = 57$

⑭ $1 \times 2 = 2$

⑮ $33 \times 3 = 99$

⑯ $80 \times 6 = 480$

⑰ $41 \times 5 = 205$

⑱ $45 \times 7 = 315$

⑲ $13 \times 12 = 156$

⑳ $30 \times 50 = 1,500$

㉑ $50 \times 2 = 100$

㉒ $20 \times 21 = 420$

㉓ $16 \times 24 = 384$

㉔ $11 \times 25 = 275$

㉕ $6 \times 9 = 54$

㉖ $18 \times 10 = 180$

㉗ $101 \times 5 = 505$

㉘ $14 \times 13 = 182$

㉙ $100 \times 4 = 400$

㉚ $55 \times 3 = 165$

㉛ $9 \times 63 = 567$

㉜ $28 \times 10 = 280$

㉝ $56 \times 5 = 280$

㉞ $86 \times 7 = 602$

㉟ $48 \times 8 = 384$

㊱ $1 \times 900 = 900$

REMINDER: Write the definition of the commutative property.

_____

_____

Unit 52 cont'd ☞

B Fill in the missing numbers.

① $10 \times \underline{40} = 400$
   $40 \times \underline{10} = 400$

② $6 \times 2 = \underline{\hspace{1cm}}$
   $2 \times 6 = \underline{\hspace{1cm}}$

③ $4 \times \underline{\hspace{1cm}} = 248$
   $62 \times \underline{\hspace{1cm}} = 248$

④ $36 \times \underline{\hspace{1cm}} = 324$
   $9 \times \underline{\hspace{1cm}} = 324$

⑤ $9 \times 5 = \underline{\hspace{1cm}}$
   $5 \times 9 = \underline{\hspace{1cm}}$

⑥ $25 \times \underline{\hspace{1cm}} = 75$
   $3 \times \underline{\hspace{1cm}} = 75$

⑦ $\underline{\hspace{1cm}} \times 30 = 300$
   $\underline{\hspace{1cm}} \times 10 = 300$

⑧ $\underline{\hspace{1cm}} \times 3 = 153$
   $\underline{\hspace{1cm}} \times 51 = 153$

⑨ $\underline{\hspace{1cm}} \times 8 = 32$
   $\underline{\hspace{1cm}} \times 4 = 32$

⑩ $\underline{\hspace{1cm}} \times 9 = 90$
   $\underline{\hspace{1cm}} \times 10 = 90$

⑪ $22 \times \underline{\hspace{1cm}} = 110$
   $5 \times \underline{\hspace{1cm}} = 110$

⑫ $100 \times 4 = \underline{\hspace{1cm}}$
   $4 \times 100 = \underline{\hspace{1cm}}$

⑬ $22 \times \underline{\hspace{1cm}} = 66$
   $3 \times \underline{\hspace{1cm}} = 66$

⑭ $\underline{\hspace{1cm}} \times 12 = 240$
   $\underline{\hspace{1cm}} \times 20 = 240$

⑮ $77 \times 2 = \underline{\hspace{1cm}}$
   $2 \times 77 = \underline{\hspace{1cm}}$

⑯ $\underline{\hspace{1cm}} \times 22 = 198$
   $\underline{\hspace{1cm}} \times 9 = 198$

⑰ $\underline{\hspace{1cm}} \times 7 = 63$
   $\underline{\hspace{1cm}} \times 9 = 63$

⑱ $13 \times 6 = \underline{\hspace{1cm}}$
   $6 \times 13 = \underline{\hspace{1cm}}$

⑲ $\underline{\hspace{1cm}} \times 11 = 55$
   $\underline{\hspace{1cm}} \times 5 = 55$

⑳ $71 \times 16 = \underline{\hspace{1cm}}$
   $16 \times 71 = \underline{\hspace{1cm}}$

㉑ $30 \times 4 = \underline{\hspace{1cm}}$
   $4 \times 30 = \underline{\hspace{1cm}}$

㉒ $1 \times 17 = \underline{\hspace{1cm}}$
   $17 \times 1 = \underline{\hspace{1cm}}$

㉓ $97 \times 2 = \underline{\hspace{1cm}}$
   $2 \times 97 = \underline{\hspace{1cm}}$

㉔ $\underline{\hspace{1cm}} \times 18 = 360$
   $\underline{\hspace{1cm}} \times 20 = 360$

C Work the problems.

① Nell planted 9 rows of corn. She planted 12 seeds in each row. How much corn did she plant?

   Sam planted 12 rows of tomatoes. He planted 9 seedlings in each row. How many tomatoes did he plant?

② Hester has 31 blue balloons. She needs 4 times that amount. How many blue balloons does she need?

   Hester has 4 red balloons. She needs 31 times that amount. How many red balloons does she need?

③ Tim read 60 pages. Eve read twice that amount. How many pages did Eve read?

   Della read only 2 pages. Chris read 60 times more than Della. How many pages did Chris read?

④ Margie's speech lasted 8 minutes. Hank's speech was 5 times as long as Margie's. How long was Hank's speech?

   Teresa's speech was only 5 minutes long. Her partner's speech was 8 times longer. How long was her partner's speech?

The Distributive Property

Learning Objective: **We will learn to use the distributive property of multiplication.**

The distributive property of multiplication holds that the product of a number and a sum is equal to the sum of the two products.

EXAMPLES:

$a(b + c) = d$
or
$(a \times b) + (a \times c) = d$

If we multiply a times the sum of b plus c, we will get the same answer as when we multiply a times b and add that product to the second product of a times c.

$2(3 + 4) = 14$
or
$(2 \times 3) + (2 \times 4) = 14$

If we multiply 2 times the sum of 3 plus 4 (7), we get 14. This is the same as when we multiply 2×3 (6) and add it to the product of 2 times 4 (8). The answer again is 14.

A Fill in the missing numbers.

① $4(2 + 5) = 28$
(___**4**___ × 2) + (___**4**___ × 5) = 28

② $5(6 + 7) = 65$
(_____ × 6) + (_____ × 7) = 65

③ $3(10 + 6) = 48$
(_____ × 10) + (_____ × 6) = 48

④ $7(4 + 5) = 63$
(7 × ___) + (7 × ___) = 63

⑤ $8(2 + 3) = 40$
(8 × ___) + (8 × ___) = 40

⑥ $6(5 + 6) = 66$
(6 × ___) + (6 × ___) = 66

⑦ $9(2 + 3) = 45$
(9 × ___) + (___ × 3) = 45

⑧ $10(4 + 1) = 50$
(___ × 4) + (10 × ___) = 50

⑨ $4(5 + 9) = 56$
(___ × 5) + (4 × ___) = 56

⑩ $8(8 + 8) = 128$
(___ × ___) + (___ × ___) = 128

⑪ $2(1 + 1) = 4$
(___ × ___) + (___ × ___) = 4

⑫ $1(8 + 2) = 10$
(___ × ___) + (___ × ___) = 10

⑬ $7(7 + 2) = 63$
(___ × ___) + (___ × ___) = 63

⑭ $6(4 + 4) = 48$
(___ × ___) + (___ × ___) = 48

⑮ $12(2 + 3) = 60$
(___ × ___) + (___ × ___) = 60

⑯ $4(9 + 8) = 68$
(___ × ___) + (___ × ___) = 68

⑰ $7(1 + 2) = 21$
(___ × ___) + (___ × ___) = 21

⑱ $11(4 + 2) = 66$
(___ × ___) + (___ × ___) = 66

REMINDER: Write the definition of the distributive property.

_____

_____

Unit 53 cont'd ☞

B Match the problems that illustrate the distributive property.

① 10 (10 + 12) = 220

② 36 (41 + 18) = 2,124

③ 52 (11 + 47) = 3,016

④ 84 (7 + 50) = 4,788

⑤ 25 (25 + 25) = 1,250

⑥ 67 (23 + 71) = 6,298

⑦ 112 (30 + 20) = 5,600

⑧ 150 (70 + 30) = 15,000

(36 × 41) + (36 × 18) = 2,124

(84 × 7) + (84 × 50) = 4,788

(10 × 10) + (10 × 12) = 220

(67 × 23) + (67 × 71) = 6,298

(25 × 25) + (25 × 25) = 1,250

(52 × 11) + (52 × 47) = 3,016

(150 × 70) + (150 × 30) = 15,000

(112 × 30) + (112 × 20) = 5,600

C Work the problems. Apply the distributive property.

① Each student in Ms. Barton's class donated 4 can goods and 2 packages of dried beans to the Thanksgiving goody box. There were 27 students in the class. How many food items did the class donate?

② Kevin, Ben, Liz, Toby, and Mark each took 50 pictures at Disneyland. They also each took 25 pictures at the ocean. How many pictures were taken?

③ Jan and her four brothers each own 20 acres of land at Brownsville. They also each own 15 acres at Owenboro. How many acres do they own?

④ George and nine of his friends each work 18 hours a week at the newspaper office. They also each work 14 hours a week at the police department. How many hours a week do they all work?

Using the Distributive Property

Unit 54

Learning Objective: *We will learn to apply the distributive property of multiplication.*

The distributive property of multiplication holds that the product of a number and a sum is equal to the sum of the two products.

EXAMPLE: If we multiply 4 times the sum of 6 plus 2 (8), we get 32. If we multiply 4 times 6 and 4 times 2 and add the products, we also get 32.

$4(6 + 2) = 32$

$(4 \times 6) + (4 \times 2) = 32$

A Apply the distributive property.

① $3(8 + 1) = 27$

$(3 \times 8) + (3 \times 1) = 27$

② $7(3 + 4) = 49$

③ $11(2 + 1) = 33$

④ $9(5 + 3) = 72$

⑤ $20(2 + 2) = 80$

⑥ $7(6 + 8) = 98$

⑦ $8(6 + 2) = 64$

⑧ $3(10 + 1) = 33$

⑨ $40(1 + 1) = 80$

⑩ $12(3 + 3) = 72$

⑪ $8(6 + 10) = 128$

⑫ $35(3 + 3) = 210$

⑬ $4(4 + 5) = 36$

⑭ $5(3 + 11) = 70$

⑮ $17(3 + 8) = 187$

⑯ $25(1 + 1) = 50$

⑰ $9(9 + 9) = 162$

⑱ $22(10 + 5) = 330$

⑲ $100(2 + 3) = 500$

⑳ $6(100 + 1) = 606$

㉑ $1,000(1 + 7) = 8,000$

REMINDER: Write the definition of the distributive property of multiplication.

_____

_____

Unit 54 cont'd ☛

B Find the answers.

① $7(8 + 6) = \mathbf{98}$

$(7 \times 8) + (7 \times 6) =$

② $4(10 + 10) =$

$(4 \times 10) + (4 \times 10) =$

③ $8(4 + 3) =$

$(8 \times 4) + (8 \times 3) =$

④ $5(5 + 5) =$

$(5 \times 5) + (5 \times 5) =$

⑤ $13(2 + 1) =$

$(13 \times 2) + (13 \times 1) =$

⑥ $9(7 + 7) =$

$(9 \times 7) + (9 \times 7) =$

⑦ $12(4 + 4) =$

$(12 \times 4) + (12 \times 4) =$

⑧ $10(5 + 9) =$

$(10 \times 5) + (10 \times 9) =$

⑨ $21(4 + 8) =$

$(21 \times 4) + (21 \times 8) =$

⑩ $6(7 + 1) =$

$(6 \times 7) + (6 \times 1) =$

⑪ $15(2 + 3) =$

$(15 \times 2) + (15 \times 3) =$

⑫ $3(9 + 8) =$

$(3 \times 9) + (3 \times 8) =$

⑬ $100(4 + 5) =$

$(100 \times 4) + (100 \times 5) =$

⑭ $50(7 + 3) =$

$(50 \times 7) + (50 \times 3) =$

⑮ $1,000(4 + 4) =$

$(1,000 \times 4) + (1,000 \times 4) =$

C Work the problems. Apply the distributive property.

① Ben and Rita each wrote 73 pages for a math project and 52 pages for a history research project. How many pages did they write?

② Four students each sold 26 boxes of candy and 17 magazine subscriptions. How many items did the 4 students sell?

③ Cassie, Lisa, Ann, Terry, Sally, and Marcia each volunteered 25 hours work at the local hospital. The girls also each worked 10 hours on the play publicity committee. How many hours did they work?

④ Wilma bet Celia that she could pick more ears of corn. Each girl picked 48 ears of corn. Then Wilma bet that she could pick more green beans. Again the girls tied at 120. How many vegetables did Wilma and Celia pick?

Products

Learning
Objective: *We will learn to find products.*

A product is the answer to a multiplication problem.

EXAMPLES: 6 is the product of 3 $\times$ 2.
100 is the product of 25 $\times$ 4.
5,058 is the product of 562 $\times$ 9.

A Find the products.

①
$$
\begin{array}{r}
22 \\
\times 76 \\
\hline
\mathbf{132} \\
\mathbf{154} \\
\hline
\mathbf{1,672}
\end{array}
$$

②
$$
\begin{array}{r}
89 \\
\times 43 \\
\hline
\end{array}
$$

③
$$
\begin{array}{r}
32 \\
\times 56 \\
\hline
\end{array}
$$

④
$$
\begin{array}{r}
73 \\
\times 28 \\
\hline
\end{array}
$$

⑤
$$
\begin{array}{r}
87 \\
\times 53 \\
\hline
\end{array}
$$

⑥
$$
\begin{array}{r}
22 \\
\times 85 \\
\hline
\end{array}
$$

⑦
$$
\begin{array}{r}
87 \\
\times 35 \\
\hline
\end{array}
$$

⑧
$$
\begin{array}{r}
72 \\
\times 36 \\
\hline
\end{array}
$$

⑨
$$
\begin{array}{r}
29 \\
\times 47 \\
\hline
\end{array}
$$

⑩
$$
\begin{array}{r}
68 \\
\times 72 \\
\hline
\end{array}
$$

⑪
$$
\begin{array}{r}
18 \\
\times 35 \\
\hline
\end{array}
$$

⑫
$$
\begin{array}{r}
72 \\
\times 89 \\
\hline
\end{array}
$$

⑬
$$
\begin{array}{r}
776 \\
\times 434 \\
\hline
\end{array}
$$

⑭
$$
\begin{array}{r}
569 \\
\times 119 \\
\hline
\end{array}
$$

⑮
$$
\begin{array}{r}
734 \\
\times 689 \\
\hline
\end{array}
$$

⑯
$$
\begin{array}{r}
476 \\
\times 136 \\
\hline
\end{array}
$$

⑰
$$
\begin{array}{r}
190 \\
\times 578 \\
\hline
\end{array}
$$

⑱
$$
\begin{array}{r}
691 \\
\times 242 \\
\hline
\end{array}
$$

⑲
$$
\begin{array}{r}
2,678 \\
\times 9,817 \\
\hline
\end{array}
$$

⑳
$$
\begin{array}{r}
6,978 \\
\times 4,121 \\
\hline
\end{array}
$$

㉑
$$
\begin{array}{r}
8,235 \\
\times 4,792 \\
\hline
\end{array}
$$

㉒
$$
\begin{array}{r}
6,942 \\
\times 9,118 \\
\hline
\end{array}
$$

㉓
$$
\begin{array}{r}
1,332 \\
\times 4,551 \\
\hline
\end{array}
$$

REMINDER: Write the definition of a product.

_____

_____

Unit 55 cont'd ☛

B Work the problems to find the products.

① 342
   ×909
   3078
  30780
 310,878

② 678
  ×149

③ 846
  ×621

④ 147
  ×699

⑤ 267
  ×527

⑥ 842
  ×236

⑦ 6,942
  ×8,653

⑧ 6,298
  ×1,268

⑨ 7,146
  ×3,481

⑩ 4,664
  ×7,668

C Match each product to its problem.

a. 18,624   b. 3,540   c. 701,454   d. 255,801,280   e. 18,648   f. 1,883

_a_ ① Mr. Fleece had 2,328 sheep. Each produced 8 pounds of wool. How many pounds of wool did he have?

___ ② Liz drives 777 miles round trip to and from work each month. How many miles to and from work would she drive in 24 months?

___ ③ Lezli had 7 textbooks her first semester at college. If each book had 269 pages, what was the total number of pages in her textbooks?

___ ④ Jeremy's Shoe Company employs 2,346 people at each of its 299 plants. How many people work for Jeremy's Shoe Company?

___ ⑤ There are 236 classes at U of Q. If there are 15 students in each class, how many students are enrolled at U of Q?

___ ⑥ E.P.S. Manufacturing has 456,788 books in one warehouse. They have 560 other warehouses with the same number of books. How many books are there?

Comprehension Check

Ⓐ Apply the commutative property.

① $10 \times 6 = 60$

　　$\mathbf{6 \times 10 = 60}$

② $9 \times 7 = 63$

③ $22 \times 5 = 110$

④ $7 \times 70 = 490$

⑤ $12 \times 4 = 48$

⑥ $5 \times 6 = 30$

⑦ $11 \times 9 = 99$

⑧ $3 \times 5 = 15$

⑨ $8 \times 20 = 160$

⑩ $25 \times 4 = 100$

⑪ $6 \times 2 = 12$

⑫ $1 \times 75 = 75$

⑬ $31 \times 6 = 186$

⑭ $2 \times 45 = 90$

⑮ $8 \times 13 = 104$

⑯ $51 \times 3 = 153$

⑰ $40 \times 4 = 160$

⑱ $71 \times 2 = 142$

⑲ $27 \times 10 = 270$

⑳ $19 \times 11 = 209$

Ⓑ Apply the distributive property.

① $3(1 + 4) = 15$

　　$\mathbf{(3 \times 1) + (3 \times 4) = 15}$

② $10(3 + 7) = 100$

③ $6(5 + 3) = 48$

④ $7(5 + 5) = 70$

⑤ $2(50 + 4) = 108$

⑥ $8(9 + 2) = 88$

⑦ $25(2 + 2) = 100$

⑧ $4(9 + 9) = 72$

⑨ $6(11 + 11) = 132$

⑩ $1(30 + 25) = 55$

⑪ $5(20 + 4) = 120$

⑫ $50(10 + 5) = 750$

⑬ $16(3 + 3) = 96$

⑭ $33(8 + 4) = 396$

⑮ $100(8 + 8) = 1,600$

Test 11 cont'd ☛

C Identify what property has been applied.

c - commutative   **d - distributive**

d ① $2(3 + 3) = 12$
$(2 \times 3) + (2 \times 3) = 12$

___ ② $40 \times 3 = 120$
$3 \times 40 = 120$

___ ③ $712 \times 10 = 7{,}120$
$10 \times 712 = 7{,}120$

___ ④ $12(1 + 8) = 108$
$(12 \times 1) + (12 \times 8) = 108$

___ ⑤ $7(4 + 11) = 105$
$(7 \cdot \times 4) + (7 \times 11) = 105$

___ ⑥ $90 \times 91 = 8{,}190$
$91 \times 90 = 8{,}190$

___ ⑦ $20(4 + 6) = 200$
$(20 \times 4) + (20 \times 6) = 200$

___ ⑧ $100 \times 7 = 700$
$7 \times 100 = 700$

___ ⑨ $2(3 + 5) = 16$
$(2 \times 3) + (2 \times 5) = 16$

___ ⑩ $12(4 + 1) = 60$
$(12 \times 4) + (12 \times 1) = 60$

___ ⑪ $6(7 + 9) = 96$
$(6 \times 7) + (6 \times 9) = 96$

___ ⑫ $10 \times 32 = 320$
$32 \times 10 = 320$

___ ⑬ $700 \times 4 = 2{,}800$
$4 \times 700 = 2{,}800$

___ ⑭ $3(4 + 7) = 33$
$(3 \times 4) + (3 \times 7) = 33$

___ ⑮ $99 \times 1 = 99$
$1 \times 99 = 99$

D Find the products.

① $4 \times 18 = $ **72**

② $17 \times 10 = $

③ $12 \times 6 = $

④ $30 \times 7 = $

⑤ $9 \times 11 = $

⑥ $56 \times 2 = $

⑦ $41 \times 6 = $

⑧ $5 \times 100 = $

⑨ $3 \times 25 = $

⑩ $72 \times 11 = $

⑪ $50 \times 20 = $

⑫ $49 \times 30 = $

⑬ $29 \times 12 = $

⑭ $10 \times 4 = $

⑮ $4 \times 104 = $

⑯ $8 \times 61 = $

⑰ $91 \times 42 = $

⑱ $38 \times 3 = $

⑲ $13 \times 13 = $

⑳ $81 \times 43 = $

㉑ $150 \times 5 = $

㉒ $120 \times 6 = $

㉓ $1 \times 999 = $

㉔ $121 \times 11 = $

Write a paragraph explaining the distributive property of multiplication.

_____

_____

_____

_____

_____

_____

_____

Multiplication Practice

Learning Objective: *We will practice multiplying.*

Multiplication is a shortcut for adding a number to itself.

EXAMPLE: When we multiply, we
sometimes carry.

$$\begin{array}{r} 83 \\ \times\,76 \\ \hline 498 \\ 581 \\ \hline 6,308 \end{array}$$

A Multiply.

① $\begin{array}{r} 66 \\ \times\,81 \\ \hline 66 \\ 528 \\ \hline 5,346 \end{array}$

② $\begin{array}{r} 94 \\ \times\,28 \end{array}$

③ $\begin{array}{r} 47 \\ \times\,55 \end{array}$

④ $\begin{array}{r} 81 \\ \times\,36 \end{array}$

⑤ $\begin{array}{r} 79 \\ \times\,47 \end{array}$

⑥ $\begin{array}{r} 98 \\ \times\,11 \end{array}$

⑦ $\begin{array}{r} 65 \\ \times\,33 \end{array}$

⑧ $\begin{array}{r} 42 \\ \times\,71 \end{array}$

⑨ $\begin{array}{r} 342 \\ \times\,861 \end{array}$

⑩ $\begin{array}{r} 972 \\ \times\,436 \end{array}$

⑪ $\begin{array}{r} 689 \\ \times\,328 \end{array}$

⑫ $\begin{array}{r} 765 \\ \times\,117 \end{array}$

⑬ $\begin{array}{r} 602 \\ \times\,514 \end{array}$

⑭ $\begin{array}{r} 486 \\ \times\,711 \end{array}$

⑮ $\begin{array}{r} 814 \\ \times\,786 \end{array}$

⑯ $\begin{array}{r} 437 \\ \times\,226 \end{array}$

⑰ $\begin{array}{r} 861 \\ \times\,281 \end{array}$

⑱ $\begin{array}{r} 365 \\ \times\,287 \end{array}$

⑲ $\begin{array}{r} 492 \\ \times\,396 \end{array}$

⑳ $\begin{array}{r} 648 \\ \times\,113 \end{array}$

㉑ $\begin{array}{r} 4,962 \\ \times\,8,172 \end{array}$

㉒ $\begin{array}{r} 8,117 \\ \times\,4,320 \end{array}$

㉓ $\begin{array}{r} 6,920 \\ \times\,3,217 \end{array}$

㉔ $\begin{array}{r} 8,163 \\ \times\,4,794 \end{array}$

REMINDER: Write the definition of multiplication.

_____

_____

Unit 56 cont'd 🖝

B Match each problem with its answer.

_a_ ① 333
    × 111

—— ② 22
    × 46

—— ③ 91
    × 31

—— ④ 213
    × 609

—— ⑤ 474
    × 699

—— ⑥ 572
    × 836

—— ⑦ 986
    × 517

—— ⑧ 361
    × 899

—— ⑨ 46
    × 73

—— ⑩ 91
    × 60

—— ⑪ 1,056
    × 356

—— ⑫ 9,642
    × 617

—— ⑬ 4,637
    × 837

—— ⑭ 9,001
    × 402

—— ⑮ 1,000
    × 1,000

—— ⑯ 5,682
    × 9,654

—— ⑰ 4,201
    × 1,689

—— ⑱ 4,405
    × 9,999

a.	36,963	g.	2,821	m.	3,618,402
b.	478,192	h.	509,762	n.	44,045,595
c.	7,095,489	i.	5,460	o.	1,012
d.	3,881,169	j.	375,936	p.	1,000,000
e.	331,326	k.	3,358	q.	5,949,114
f.	324,539	l.	129,717	r.	54,854,028

C Read each problem and find the product.

① At her brother's graduation, Carmen saw 26 rows of white-dressed Marines. There were 11 in each row. How many Marines did she see?

$$\begin{array}{r} 26 \\ \times\ 11 \\ \hline 26 \\ 26 \\ \hline 286 \end{array}$$

② At a bargain sale, Marilyn bought 462 packages of gum. Each package had 12 sticks in it. How many sticks of gum did she buy?

③ Four hundred sixteen flowers were planted in each of 92 plots at Gainesville's City Hall. How many flowers were planted?

④ With only hours away from the deadline, Robin completed her book. Each page had 629 words. She had 423 pages. How many words had she written altogether?

⑤ Kathleen bought 9 packages of cookies for the picnic. Each package contained 36 cookies. How many cookies were there?

⑥ Chelsey ordered 12 boxes of typing paper for the office. Each box contained 2,500 sheets. How many sheets were in the 12 boxes?

Simple Division

Learning Objective: *We will learn to divide by one-digit numbers.*

Division is the method by which we determine how many times one number contains another.

EXAMPLE: To divide 200 by 4, first determine how many 4's are in 20. From the multiplication tables, we know $4 \times 5 = 20$. Subtract 20 from 20. The answer is 0. Bring the last number of the dividend down and divide 0 by 4. The answer is 0. There are 50 4's in 200. $200 \div 4 = 50$

$$\begin{array}{r} 50 \\ 4\overline{)200} \\ \underline{20} \\ 0 \\ \underline{0} \end{array}$$

A Divide.

① $3\overline{)9}$ $\underline{9}$ with quotient **3**

② $4\overline{)8}$

③ $2\overline{)6}$

④ $3\overline{)6}$

⑤ $1\overline{)7}$

⑥ $8\overline{)64}$

⑦ $4\overline{)44}$

⑧ $2\overline{)36}$

⑨ $2\overline{)4}$

⑩ $1\overline{)1}$

⑪ $3\overline{)3}$

⑫ $2\overline{)4}$

⑬ $1\overline{)6}$

⑭ $5\overline{)20}$

⑮ $6\overline{)12}$

⑯ $9\overline{)36}$

⑰ $7\overline{)21}$

⑱ $2\overline{)34}$

⑲ $6\overline{)48}$

⑳ $3\overline{)72}$

㉑ $7\overline{)49}$

㉒ $1\overline{)83}$

㉓ $3\overline{)99}$

㉔ $8\overline{)72}$

㉕ $5\overline{)50}$

㉖ $2\overline{)66}$

㉗ $9\overline{)63}$

㉘ $7\overline{)42}$

㉙ $6\overline{)54}$

㉚ $8\overline{)48}$

㉛ $3\overline{)69}$

㉜ $5\overline{)70}$

㉝ $2\overline{)42}$

㉞ $8\overline{)64}$

㉟ $4\overline{)84}$

㊱ $9\overline{)63}$

㊲ $6\overline{)42}$

㊳ $3\overline{)84}$

㊴ $2\overline{)82}$

㊵ $3\overline{)27}$

REMINDER: Write the definition of division.

_____

_____

Unit 57 cont'd ☛

B Divide by these one-digit numbers.

① 18 ÷ 6 = **3**   ② 40 ÷ 8 =   ③ 45 ÷ 5 =   ④ 56 ÷ 8 =

⑤ 16 ÷ 2 =   ⑥ 32 ÷ 4 =   ⑦ 10 ÷ 2 =   ⑧ 25 ÷ 5 =

⑨ 92 ÷ 2 =   ⑩ 93 ÷ 3 =   ⑪ 28 ÷ 2 =   ⑫ 67 ÷ 1 =

⑬ 75 ÷ 5 =   ⑭ 36 ÷ 6 =   ⑮ 30 ÷ 2 =   ⑯ 34 ÷ 2 =

⑰ 80 ÷ 4 =   ⑱ 99 ÷ 9 =   ⑲ 21 ÷ 7 =   ⑳ 35 ÷ 5 =

㉑ 56 ÷ 2 =   ㉒ 42 ÷ 2 =   ㉓ 72 ÷ 4 =   ㉔ 28 ÷ 4 =

㉕ 66 ÷ 3 =   ㉖ 76 ÷ 1 =   ㉗ 32 ÷ 8 =   ㉘ 81 ÷ 9 =

㉙ 66 ÷ 2 =   ㉚ 70 ÷ 7 =   ㉛ 72 ÷ 2 =   ㉜ 40 ÷ 1 =

C Read each problem and write the answer.

① Marma, a six-year-old golden retriever, had nine puppies. Three people came and bought all the puppies. If each person took the same number of puppies, how many puppies did each person take?

② Mr. and Mrs. Bartlett ordered 21 slipcovers for the furniture in their house. If they put an equal number of covers in each of their seven rooms, how many slipcovers were in each room?

③ Mr. Harden had 72 chickens on his egg farm. He had four houses for his chickens. How many chickens were in each house?

④ While on a walk through the park, Don and June saw 6 mother swans paddling in the water. Behind the mothers followed 48 cygnets. If each mother had the same number of babies, how many cygnets did each mother swan have?

Long Division

Learning
Objective: *We will learn to use long division.*

Division is the method by which we determine how many times one number contains another.

EXAMPLE: To divide 1,125 by 25, first determine how many 25's are in 112. $25 \times 4 = 100$. Subtract 100 from 112. The remainder is 12. Bring down the next number of the dividend. Divide 125 by 25. $25 \times 5 = 125$.

$$1,125 \div 25 = 45$$

$$\begin{array}{r} 45 \\ 25\overline{)1,125} \\ \underline{100} \\ 125 \\ \underline{125} \end{array}$$

A Use long division to find the answers.

① $\begin{array}{r} 68 \\ 45\overline{)3,060} \\ \underline{270} \\ 360 \\ \underline{360} \end{array}$

② $96\overline{)1,344}$

③ $72\overline{)3,456}$

④ $63\overline{)3,528}$

⑤ $25\overline{)2,125}$

⑥ $26\overline{)1,924}$

⑦ $51\overline{)1,326}$

⑧ $31\overline{)1,457}$

⑨ $88\overline{)4,400}$

⑩ $38\overline{)1,178}$

⑪ $54\overline{)4,158}$

⑫ $68\overline{)4,284}$

⑬ $46\overline{)4,508}$

⑭ $49\overline{)1,078}$

⑮ $69\overline{)1,311}$

⑯ $29\overline{)2,755}$

⑰ $84\overline{)6,804}$

⑱ $96\overline{)8,832}$

⑲ $24\overline{)1,368}$

⑳ $43\overline{)2,537}$

REMINDER: Write the definition of division.

Unit 58 cont'd ☞

B Divide.

①
```
      43
86 ) 3,698
    344
    258
    258
```

② 67) 2,211

③ 55) 1,265

④ 37) 3,219

⑤ 44) 2,992

⑥ 57) 5,016

⑦ 36) 2,592

⑧ 46) 4,094

⑨ 65) 4,810

⑩ 80) 7,920

⑪ 73) 2,774

⑫ 37) 3,552

C Read each problem and divide.

① In New York harbor there are 5,589 yachts. If there are 27 docks, how many boats are in each dock?

```
      207
27 ) 5,589
    54
    189
    189
```

② There are 5,450 flowers in bloom at Wentworth Gardens. If each of 50 flower beds has the same number of blooms in it, how many flowers are in each bed?

③ Twenty-six people donated turkeys. If 78 were collected, how many turkeys did each person give?

④ Icey-Time's warehouse holds 3,696 fudge bars. If 56 bars will fit in a box, how many boxes are there?

⑤ There are 1,200 children at Kings Cross Elementary School. If each of 48 classrooms has the same number of students, how many students are in each classroom?

⑥ There are 72 ears of corn in a field. If there are 40,608 kernels, how many kernels are on each ear of corn?

142

Dividing by Three Digits   Unit 59

Learning Objective: *We will learn to divide by three-digit numbers.*

A three-digit number has digits in the ones' place, the tens' place, and the hundreds' place.

EXAMPLE: When we divide with a three-digit number, we usually move to the hundreds' place to put the answer. Sometimes we must go lower than the hundreds' place.

$$
\begin{array}{r}
101 \\
500 \overline{)50,500} \\
\underline{500} \\
500 \\
\underline{500} \\
\end{array}
\qquad
\begin{array}{r}
400 \\
300 \overline{)120,000} \\
\underline{1200} \\
00 \\
\underline{00} \\
\end{array}
$$

A Divide.

①
$$
\begin{array}{r}
27 \\
365 \overline{)9,855} \\
\underline{730} \\
2555 \\
\underline{2555} \\
\end{array}
$$

② $417 \overline{)35,862}$

③ $653 \overline{)31,997}$

④ $216 \overline{)14,040}$

⑤ $866 \overline{)45,032}$

⑥ $918 \overline{)67,932}$

⑦ $217 \overline{)4,557}$

⑧ $300 \overline{)18,000}$

⑨ $399 \overline{)37,905}$

⑩ $355 \overline{)30,885}$

⑪ $498 \overline{)23,406}$

⑫ $467 \overline{)13,543}$

⑬ $376 \overline{)19,552}$

⑭ $800 \overline{)50,400}$

⑮ $427 \overline{)30,744}$

⑯ $361 \overline{)9,747}$

REMINDER: Write the definition of a three-digit number.

_____

_____

Unit 59 cont'd ☞

B Divide by three-digit numbers.

① 42,189 ÷ 861 = **49**

② 20,176 ÷ 776 =

③ 8,076 ÷ 673 =

④ 8,076 ÷ 673 =

⑤ 5,016 ÷ 264 =

⑥ 6,250 ÷ 250 =

⑦ 8,094 ÷ 213 =

⑧ 44,631 ÷ 513 =

⑨ 65,484 ÷ 963 =

⑩ 4,884 ÷ 111 =

⑪ 48,024 ÷ 696 =

⑫ 21,996 ÷ 423 =

⑬ 12,636 ÷ 486 =

⑭ 54,513 ÷ 673 =

⑮ 55,593 ÷ 639 =

⑯ 42,228 ÷ 918 =

⑰ 64,998 ÷ 942 =

⑱ 8,921 ÷ 811 =

⑲ 20,304 ÷ 432 =

⑳ 33,583 ÷ 781 =

㉑ 60,710 ÷ 934 =

㉒ 7,968 ÷ 498 =

㉓ 46,176 ÷ 962 =

㉔ 42,840 ÷ 630 =

㉕ 41,976 ÷ 583 =

㉖ 22,537 ÷ 727 =

㉗ 16,770 ÷ 215 =

C Read each paragraph and work each long division problem in the space provided.

① A rock star sold $18,460 worth of tickets for her upcoming concert. If the auditorium held only 710 people, how much was each ticket?

② In a factory warehouse, there are 9,970 boxes of candy bars. If the boxes are stacked in 997 rows, how many boxes high was each stack?

③ On Valentine's Day, a flower shop sold 6,504 roses. The owner gathered the roses into 542 bunches. How many roses were in each bunch?

④ A space shuttle can travel to a satellite in 879 days. The distance between the earth and the satellite is 29,007 miles. How many miles per day will the shuttle travel?

Dividing by Four Digits

Learning
Objective: *We will learn to divide by four-digit numbers.*

A four-digit number has digits in the ones' place, the tens' place, the hundreds' place, and the thousands' place.

EXAMPLE: When we divide with a four-digit number, we usually move to the hundreds' place to put the answer. Sometimes we must go lower than the hundreds' place.

$$2{,}211 \overline{)\,121{,}605} \qquad \begin{array}{r} 55 \end{array}$$
$$\underline{11055}$$
$$11055$$
$$\underline{11055}$$

$$9{,}879 \overline{)\,69{,}153} \qquad \begin{array}{r} 7 \end{array}$$
$$\underline{69153}$$

A Divide.

①
$$7{,}654 \overline{)\,887{,}864} \qquad \begin{array}{r} 116 \end{array}$$
$$\underline{7654}$$
$$12246$$
$$\underline{7654}$$
$$45924$$
$$\underline{45924}$$

② $6{,}532 \overline{)\,5{,}676{,}308}$

③ $5{,}032 \overline{)\,4{,}720{,}016}$

④ $5{,}474 \overline{)\,990{,}794}$

⑤ $3{,}060 \overline{)\,1{,}220{,}940}$

⑥ $4{,}992 \overline{)\,2{,}755{,}584}$

⑦ $3{,}327 \overline{)\,2{,}308{,}938}$

⑧ $7{,}487 \overline{)\,1{,}197{,}920}$

⑨ $2{,}340 \overline{)\,332{,}280}$

REMINDER: *Write the definition of a four-digit number.*

Unit 60 cont'd ☞

B Divide by four-digit numbers.

① $2,694,848 \div 4,264 = \textbf{632}$

② $4,221,644 \div 5,831 =$

③ $2,448,080 \div 3,448 =$

④ $7,940,520 \div 9,864 =$

⑤ $4,829,804 \div 6,671 =$

⑥ $749,737 \div 2,987 =$

⑦ $2,327,500 \div 4,655 =$

⑧ $9,560,952 \div 9,918 =$

⑨ $3,679,030 \div 9,314 =$

⑩ $5,831,265 \div 9,735 =$

⑪ $4,204,608 \div 8,616 =$

⑫ $246,642 \div 2,222 =$

⑬ $4,420,920 \div 5,540 =$

⑭ $2,852,421 \div 4,251 =$

⑮ $1,768,302 \div 6,338 =$

⑯ $1,134,063 \div 2,681 =$

⑰ $3,660,111 \div 4,251 =$

⑱ $1,386,524 \div 5,524 =$

C Read each paragraph and work the problem.

① Mr. Owens owns a catalog distribution center. In May he mailed 128,232 catalogs to his customers. If each state in his mailing had 4,932 customers, how many states were involved in this mailing?

② There are 362,375 words in Bennett's history book. If there are 1,115 pages and each page has the same number of words, how many words are on each page?

③ Shelly picked 1,117,770 berries. She froze 2,014 quarts of the berries. How many berries were in each quart?

④ Pelham Maddick had 870,565 tropical fish in his pet shop. If the fish are equally divided into 1,109 different tanks, how many tropical fish are in each tank?

Comprehension Check

A Multiply.

① 298
×37
2086
894
11,026

② 303
×90

③ 461
×38

④ 909
×60

⑤ 309
×21

⑥ 778
×25

⑦ 555
×32

⑧ 399
×466

⑨ 100
×958

⑩ 588
×421

⑪ 121
×235

⑫ 712
×217

⑬ 318
×444

⑭ 900
×346

⑮ 5,608
×2,192

⑯ 6,161
×3,222

⑰ 5,221
×1,692

⑱ 8,910
×2,432

⑲ 3,240
×1,400

⑳ 7,432
×2,409

B Divide.

①
5)20 quotient 4
20

② 6)36

③ 8)72

④ 9)81

⑤ 5)35

⑥ 4)28

⑦ 6)42

⑧ 5)40

⑨ 10)100

⑩ 2)48

⑪ 12)24

⑫ 30)60

C Divide using long division.

① 25)8,050

② 36)9,216

③ 57)1,881

④ 61)5,978

Test 12 cont'd

D Divide.

① 685) 18,495
$$\begin{array}{r} 27 \\ 685) \overline{18,495} \\ 1370 \\ \hline 4795 \\ 4795 \\ \hline \end{array}$$

② 486) 14,094

③ 596) 49,468

④ 737) 65,593

⑤ 831) 45,705

⑥ 369) 27,675

⑦ 412) 39,552

⑧ 259) 9,583

⑨ 4,182) 359,652

⑩ 3,446) 334,262

⑪ 6,750) 546,750

⑫ 2,766) 143,832

⑬ 5,227) 245,669

⑭ 7,459) 462,458

⑮ 8,640) 267,840

⑯ 9,926) 833,784

⑰ 5,336) 346,840

⑱ 9,352) 205,744

⑲ 8,966) 484,164

⑳ 7,268) 123,556

㉑ 6,432) 559,584

㉒ 4,886) 454,398

㉓ 2,207) 64,003

㉔ 3,984) 306,768

Define.

① multiplication _____

_____

② division _____

_____

③ three-digit number _____

_____

④ four-digit number _____

_____

Checking Division Problems

Learning Objective: *We will learn to check division problems.*

Checking is the process of proving correctness.

EXAMPLE:

To check a division problem, simply multiply the quotient by the divisor. Your answer should be the dividend.

$$\begin{array}{r} 37 \\ 9\overline{)333} \\ 27 \\ \hline 63 \\ 63 \\ \hline \end{array} \qquad \begin{array}{r} 37 \\ \times\ 9 \\ \hline 333 \end{array}$$

A Divide. Use the blank space to check your answers.

① $\begin{array}{r} 38 \\ 26\overline{)988} \\ 78 \\ \hline 208 \\ 208 \\ \hline \end{array}$ $\begin{array}{r} 38 \\ \times\ 26 \\ \hline 228 \\ 76 \\ \hline 988 \end{array}$

② $69\overline{)3,243}$

③ $89\overline{)5,607}$

④ $41\overline{)2,911}$

⑤ $56\overline{)5,488}$

⑥ $35\overline{)1,225}$

⑦ $685\overline{)50,005}$

⑧ $205\overline{)9,430}$

⑨ $969\overline{)84,303}$

⑩ $421\overline{)23,155}$

⑪ $547\overline{)19,145}$

⑫ $748\overline{)69,564}$

REMINDER: Write the definition of checking

_____

_____

Unit 61 cont'd ☞

B Check each problem with multiplication. If the problem is correct, place a check (✓) in the blank.

✓ ① 12)‾5‾6‾,‾3‾1‾6‾   4,693

___ ② 29)‾1‾8‾8‾,‾2‾9‾7‾   6,493

___ ③ 43)‾1‾6‾1‾,‾7‾6‾6‾   3,761

___ ④ 67)‾3‾2‾2‾,‾3‾3‾7‾   4,811

$$
\begin{array}{r}
4,693 \\
\times\ 12 \\
\hline
9386 \\
4693 \\
\hline
56,316
\end{array}
$$

___ ⑤ 70)‾6‾7‾4‾,‾2‾4‾0‾   9,632

___ ⑥ 51)‾2‾1‾,‾5‾7‾3‾   423

___ ⑦ 87)‾5‾5‾8‾,‾8‾7‾2‾   6,419

___ ⑧ 34)‾1‾9‾5‾,‾9‾4‾2‾   5,763

C Check the division problems.

① Around Lee's neighborhood, 27 children collected 1,242 items items of clothing to give to charity. If each child collected the same amount, how many items of clothing did each child collect?

$$
\begin{array}{r}
46 \\
27)\overline{1,242} \\
108 \\
\hline
162 \\
162 \\
\hline
\end{array}
$$

② Sixteen workers put in 10,048 hours of labor. If each put in the same number of hours, how long did each work?

$$
\begin{array}{r}
628 \\
16)\overline{10,048} \\
96 \\
\hline
44 \\
32 \\
\hline
128 \\
128 \\
\hline
\end{array}
$$

③ During a snowball fight, one team had 1,652 snowballs ready to throw. If there were 28 people on that team, how many balls did each throw?

$$
\begin{array}{r}
59 \\
28)\overline{1,652} \\
140 \\
\hline
252 \\
252 \\
\hline
\end{array}
$$

④ In a candle shop there are 19,596 fragrant candles in 92 bunches. How many candles are in each bunch?

$$
\begin{array}{r}
213 \\
92)\overline{19,596} \\
184 \\
\hline
119 \\
92 \\
\hline
276 \\
276 \\
\hline
\end{array}
$$

Having Remainders   Unit 62

A remainder is the final undivided part of a division problem.

EXAMPLE:

A remainder is always less than
the divisor. After dividing 69 by 4,
there is a remainder of 1.

$$\begin{array}{r} 17\ R1 \\ 4\overline{)69} \\ \underline{4} \\ 29 \\ \underline{28} \\ 1 \end{array}$$

$$69 \div 4 = 17\ R1$$

A Divide and find the remainders.

① $\begin{array}{r} 2\ R2 \\ 3\overline{)8} \\ \underline{6} \\ 2 \end{array}$ ② $2\overline{)7}$ ③ $5\overline{)6}$ ④ $3\overline{)5}$ ⑤ $2\overline{)9}$

⑥ $4\overline{)9}$ ⑦ $2\overline{)5}$ ⑧ $6\overline{)7}$ ⑨ $4\overline{)5}$ ⑩ $5\overline{)9}$

⑪ $11\overline{)456}$ ⑫ $32\overline{)147}$ ⑬ $41\overline{)851}$ ⑭ $13\overline{)751}$ ⑮ $11\overline{)404}$

⑯ $15\overline{)252}$ ⑰ $12\overline{)789}$ ⑱ $21\overline{)345}$ ⑲ $19\overline{)217}$ ⑳ $41\overline{)608}$

㉑ $25\overline{)4,251}$ ㉒ $10\overline{)4,073}$ ㉓ $60\overline{)2,120}$ ㉔ $14\overline{)3,271}$ ㉕ $35\overline{)7,036}$

REMINDER: Write the definition of a remainder.

_____

_____

B Divide.

① 302 R1
$24 \overline{)7{,}249}$
$\underline{72}$
49
$\underline{48}$
1

② $31 \overline{)6{,}234}$

③ $70 \overline{)1{,}052}$

④ $75 \overline{)1{,}806}$

⑤ $15 \overline{)3{,}068}$

⑥ $101 \overline{)5{,}051}$

⑦ $612 \overline{)2{,}449}$

⑧ $736 \overline{)2{,}946}$

⑨ $403 \overline{)8{,}079}$

⑩ $502 \overline{)2{,}009}$

⑪ $212 \overline{)214{,}190}$

⑫ $401 \overline{)810{,}046}$

⑬ $204 \overline{)409{,}346}$

⑭ $819 \overline{)328{,}641}$

C Read the paragraphs, work the problems, and find the remainders.

① Mr. Crawford's Pizza Shop made 26 pizzas on Friday. He sold an equal number of them to each of 5 customers that night. How many were left over?

_____

② Lula picked 46 flowers. She made six arrangements and gave them to her friends. How many flowers were left if each arrangement had the same number of flowers?

_____

③ There are 47 library books in Mrs. Collins' classroom. If each of her 15 students takes the same number of books back to the library, how many will remain?

_____

④ Laurie had 388 recipe index cards. If she put an equal number of cards in each of 15 index card boxes, how many were left over?

_____

Remainders as Fractions

Unit 63

Learning Objective: *We will learn to write fractions as the remainders of division problems.*

A remainder is the final undivided part of a division problem.

EXAMPLE:

The fraction 1/3 may also be read 1 divided by 3. Remember that the remainder is always less than the divisor; we may write the remainder as a fraction.

$$\begin{array}{r} 7 \\ 3\overline{)22} \\ 21 \\ \hline 1 \end{array}$$

$$22 \div 3 = 7\ 1/3$$

A Divide and write the remainders as fractions.

① $\begin{array}{r} 4\ 3/4 \\ 4\overline{)19} \\ 16 \\ \hline 3 \end{array}$

② $6\overline{)38}$

③ $5\overline{)27}$

④ $9\overline{)86}$

⑤ $7\overline{)65}$

⑥ $3\overline{)26}$

⑦ $8\overline{)35}$

⑧ $2\overline{)17}$

⑨ $11\overline{)255}$

⑩ $36\overline{)910}$

⑪ $49\overline{)690}$

⑫ $23\overline{)967}$

⑬ $53\overline{)651}$

⑭ $72\overline{)999}$

⑮ $64\overline{)986}$

⑯ $88\overline{)972}$

⑰ $643\overline{)17,363}$

⑱ $434\overline{)29,950}$

⑲ $718\overline{)20,107}$

⑳ $357\overline{)33,920}$

REMINDER: *Write the definition of a remainder.*

_____

_____

Unit 63 cont'd ☛

B Divide.

① $22 \div 7 = $ **3 1/7**   ② $58 \div 9 = $ ③ $49 \div 6 = $

④ $39 \div 4 = $ ⑤ $14 \div 3 = $ ⑥ $20 \div 8 = $

⑦ $690 \div 53 = $ ⑧ $840 \div 27 = $ ⑨ $2,215 \div 33 = $

⑩ $1,262 \div 45 = $ ⑪ $1,726 \div 78 = $ ⑫ $3,675 \div 68 = $

⑬ $4,421 \div 67 = $ ⑭ $1,306 \div 51 = $ ⑮ $37 \div 5 = $

⑯ $43 \div 2 = $ ⑰ $3,613 \div 20 = $ ⑱ $6,770 \div 40 = $

⑲ $445 \div 15 = $ ⑳ $360 \div 13 = $ ㉑ $3,211 \div 25 = $

㉒ $698 \div 75 = $ ㉓ $900 \div 31 = $ ㉔ $6,555 \div 25 = $

㉕ $560 \div 33 = $ ㉖ $555 \div 16 = $ ㉗ $6,000 \div 59 = $

C Read the paragraphs, work the problems, and write the remainders as fractions.

① If there were 49,405 apples to be canned and each gallon can could contain 99 apples, how many gallon cans would it take to can the apples?

```
        499 4/99
   99)49,405
       396
       980
       891
       895
       891
         4
```

② The cafeteria made 1,076 cupcakes for 533 students. How many cupcakes could each student have?

③ At Bill's party there were 400 finger sandwiches. If each of his 26 guests ate the same number of sandwiches, how many could each have?

④ Each of 56 yards in a neighborhood shares 27,600 man hours of labor a year from Lawn-Care. How many hours a year of yard work does each yard receive?

⑤ Over the Thanksgiving holiday, Illinois state police gave out 536 traffic tickets. If there were 15 officers on duty, how many tickets did each issue?

⑥ Tom and his father caught 37 fish. Each said he caught the same number of fish as the other. How many did each catch?

Quotients

Learning
Objective: *We will learn to find quotients.*

A quotient is the answer to a division problem.

EXAMPLES: 3 is the quotient of 9 ÷ 3.
12 is the quotient of 24 ÷ 2.
100 is the quotient of 10,000 ÷ 1,000.

A Find the quotients. Express all remainders as numbers.

①
```
      33
104)3,432
    312
    312
    312
```

② 678)66,444

③ 118)10,856

④ 928)46,400

⑤ 778)48,300

⑥ 985)84,710

⑦ 728)62,600

⑧ 664)43,824

⑨ 4,617)1,463,589

⑩ 2,356)2,174,589

⑪ 7,356)1,588,896

⑫ 5,121)2,913,844

⑬ 6,978)6,670,968

⑭ 5,794)2,282,831

REMINDER: Write the definition of a quotient.

_____

_____

Unit 64 cont'd

B Divide and find the quotients.

① $16{,}056 \div 892 = \textbf{18}$ ② $18{,}879 \div 651 =$ ③ $35{,}999 \div 439 =$

④ $63{,}756 \div 924 =$ ⑤ $35{,}880 \div 690 =$ ⑥ $28{,}119 \div 721 =$

⑦ $49{,}972 \div 617 =$ ⑧ $12{,}083 \div 281 =$ ⑨ $41{,}280 \div 480 =$

⑩ $16{,}080 \div 240 =$ ⑪ $8{,}519 \div 120 =$ ⑫ $26{,}286 \div 848 =$

⑬ $1{,}844{,}964 \div 6{,}212 =$ ⑭ $648{,}788 \div 1{,}363 =$

⑮ $3{,}473{,}472 \div 5{,}496 =$ ⑯ $6{,}102{,}140 \div 8{,}235 =$

⑰ $2{,}406{,}840 \div 7{,}764 =$ ⑱ $841{,}806 \div 6{,}426 =$

⑲ $5{,}053{,}779 \div 6{,}942 =$ ⑳ $1{,}062{,}550 \div 2{,}579 =$

㉑ $2{,}339{,}187 \div 8{,}761 =$ ㉒ $4{,}117{,}300 \div 4{,}925 =$

C Match each quotient to its problem.

c ① John Brother's Pizza sold 3,850 pieces of pizza at lunch. If each of 350 people bought the same number of pieces, how many pieces did each buy?

____ ④ The Charity League baked 1,140 pies for 285 needy families at Christmas. How many pies did each family receive?

     a. 7 R21

     b. 60

     c. 11

     d. 750

     e. 4

____ ② Myra's Bakery made 5,660 doughnuts for a company party. If 566 attended, how many doughnuts could each have?

____ ⑤ The Joneston Sun delivers 562,500 papers to 750 neighborhoods. How many papers are needed in each neighborhood?

     f. 10

____ ③ John caught 5,299 minnows. He divided them into groups of 754 and sold them to fishing stores. How many stores did he sell them to?

____ ⑥ Grandma's Cookie Shop sold an equal number of cookies to 120 customers on Friday. If the total number sold to those customers was 7,200 cookies, how many cookies did each buy?

Division Practice

Learning Objective: *We will practice dividing.*

Division is a method by which we determine how many times one number contains another.

EXAMPLES:

$555 \div 5 = 111$

$2,376 \div 3 = 792$

$$\begin{array}{r} 89 \\ 34\overline{)3,026} \\ 272 \\ \hline 306 \\ 306 \\ \hline \end{array}$$

$$\begin{array}{r} 12\ 37/46 \\ 46\overline{)589} \\ 46 \\ \hline 129 \\ 92 \\ \hline 37 \end{array}$$

A Divide and write all remainders as fractions.

① $5\overline{)20}$ quotient 4, $\frac{20}{}$

② $6\overline{)48}$

③ $9\overline{)83}$

④ $7\overline{)56}$

⑤ $8\overline{)66}$

⑥ $3\overline{)24}$

⑦ $4\overline{)32}$

⑧ $2\overline{)15}$

⑨ $16\overline{)1,314}$

⑩ $47\overline{)2,867}$

⑪ $56\overline{)4,875}$

⑫ $72\overline{)6,626}$

⑬ $37\overline{)2,997}$

⑭ $22\overline{)1,386}$

⑮ $74\overline{)3,626}$

⑯ $63\overline{)3,654}$

⑰ $265\overline{)5,035}$

⑱ $861\overline{)67,160}$

⑲ $426\overline{)22,155}$

⑳ $364\overline{)14,560}$

REMINDER: Write the definition of division.

Unit 65 cont'd ☞

B Divide.

① $$\begin{array}{r} 56\ 1/654 \\ 654\overline{)36{,}625} \\ \underline{3270} \\ 3925 \\ \underline{3924} \\ 1 \end{array}$$

② $729\overline{)28{,}435}$

③ $534\overline{)47{,}529}$

④ $851\overline{)39{,}148}$

⑤ $234\overline{)23{,}169}$

⑥ $941\overline{)583{,}424}$

⑦ $395\overline{)34{,}369}$

⑧ $499\overline{)49{,}405}$

C Work these division problems.

① There are 63,437 records in Tom's Record Shop. The store has 73 shelves to keep the records on. If each shelf has the same number of records on it, how many are on each shelf?

② The Army's cooks baked 7,194 pieces of pizza for dinner on Tuesday. If each of 654 enlisted men eat all the pizza they want, how many pieces could each have?

③ Jeremy's Copy Shop printed 46,940 sheets. If it printed an equal number of sheets each day for 63 days, how many sheets a day did it print?

④ Robin's Deli made 3,283 sandwiches for the class of 1981 five-year reunion. If 469 people attended the reunion, how many sandwiches could each have?

158

Comprehension Check

A Check each division problem with multiplication. If it is wrong, place a ✓ in the blank.

✓ ① $2,150 \div 86 = 26$ ___ ② $4,464 \div 72 = 62$ ✓ ③ $1,090 \div 35 = 60$

$$\begin{array}{r} 86 \\ \times\ 26 \\ \hline 516 \\ 172\ \ \\ \hline 2,236 \end{array}$$

___ ④ $4,620 \div 84 = 55$ ✓ ⑤ $65,803 \div 14 = 36$ ___ ⑥ $1,376 \div 43 = 32$

✓ ⑦ $8,956 \div 89 = 40$ ___ ⑧ $3,782 \div 61 = 62$ ✓ ⑨ $7,681 \div 45 = 64$

B Match each problem with its quotient.

_d_ ① $6 \div 2$	___ ⑨ $1 \div 1$	___ ⑰ $312 \div 12$	a. 28	i. 58	q. 1
___ ② $18 \div 3$	___ ⑩ $80 \div 4$	___ ⑱ $364 \div 26$	b. 9	j. 2	r. 32
___ ③ $30 \div 2$	___ ⑪ $16 \div 2$	___ ⑲ $1,584 \div 44$	c. 11	k. 20	s. 10
___ ④ $28 \div 14$	___ ⑫ $81 \div 9$	___ ⑳ $754 \div 13$	d. 3	l. 12	t. 50
___ ⑤ $64 \div 2$	___ ⑬ $28 \div 7$	___ ㉑ $100 \div 2$	e. 26	m. 5	u. 24
___ ⑥ $39 \div 3$	___ ⑭ $816 \div 51$	___ ㉒ $28 \div 1$	f. 36	n. 15	v. 8
___ ⑦ $48 \div 4$	___ ⑮ $160 \div 16$	___ ㉓ $49 \div 7$	g. 6	o. 13	w. 7
___ ⑧ $10 \div 2$	___ ⑯ $517 \div 47$	___ ㉔ $1,944 \div 81$	h. 14	p. 4	x. 16

Test 13 cont'd ☞

C Divide. Express all remainders as numbers.

①
```
      87 R3
65)5,658
    520
    ───
    458
    455
    ───
      3
```

② 47)4,233

③ 81)3,160

④ 61)3,665

⑤ 21)1,702

⑥ 78)3,279

⑦ 49)1,479

⑧ 93)1,025

D Divide. Express all remainders as fractions.

①
```
    58 2/41
41)2,380
   205
   ───
   330
   328
   ───
     2
```

② 24)1,899

③ 89)6,498

④ 77)2,005

⑤ 33)2,480

⑥ 19)840

⑦ 22)1,895

⑧ 59)945

⑨ 314)20,412

⑩ 768)19,200

⑪ 981)56,898

⑫ 677)67,025

Define.

① checking _____

_____

② remainder _____

_____

③ quotient _____

_____

④ division _____

_____

Multiply or Divide?

Learning
Objective: *We will learn to determine if a problem calls for multiplication or division.*

Division is the method by which we determine how many times one number contains another. Multiplication is a shortcut for adding a number to itself.

EXAMPLES: In problem a, the quotient of 1,375 divided by 25 is 55. In problem b, the product of 275 times 5 is 1,375.

$$\text{a. } 1,375 \div 25 = 55 \qquad \text{b. } 275 \times 5 = 1,375$$

A Multiply or divide.

①
```
   69
  ×54
  276
  345
 3,726
```

② $32 \overline{)2,432}$

③
```
  45
 ×38
```

④ $28 \overline{)392}$

⑤
```
  64
 ×78
```

⑥ $33 \overline{)2,343}$

⑦
```
  79
 ×57
```

⑧ $87 \overline{)1,392}$

⑨
```
  23
 ×85
```

⑩ $45 \overline{)2,745}$

⑪
```
  697
  ×53
```

⑫ $450 \overline{)7,200}$

⑬
```
  342
  ×71
```

⑭ $614 \overline{)46,664}$

⑮
```
  173
  ×52
```

⑯ $317 \overline{)27,262}$

⑰
```
  643
  ×45
```

⑱ $325 \overline{)22,100}$

⑲
```
  957
  ×67
```

⑳ $759 \overline{)37,191}$

REMINDER: Write the definitions of multiplication and division.

_____

_____

Unit 66 cont'd 🖝

B Supply a × or ÷ sign for the operations that produced the results.

① 3 __×__ 6 = 18

② 23 ____ 51 = 1,173

③ 489 ____ 352 = 172,128

④ 8,557 ____ 701 = 5,998,457

⑤ 6 ____ 3 = 2

⑥ 75 ____ 14 = 1,050

⑦ 158 ____ 330 = 52,140

⑧ 21,180,222 ____ 642 = 32,991

⑨ 9 ____ 3 = 27

⑩ 88 ____ 11 = 8

⑪ 241 ____ 557 = 134,237

⑫ 1,170 ____ 483 = 565,110

⑬ 8 ____ 4 = 2

⑭ 42 ____ 69 = 2,898

⑮ 14,366 ____ 22 = 653

⑯ 5,306,301 ____ 589 = 9,009

⑰ 8 ____ 3 = 24

⑱ 36 ____ 12 = 3

⑲ 3,204 ____ 36 = 89

⑳ 8,628 ____ 535 = 4,615,980

㉑ 10 ____ 5 = 2

㉒ 74 ____ 82 = 6,068

㉓ 11,368 ____ 56 = 203

㉔ 4,986,480 ____ 632 = 7,890

㉕ 8 ____ 8 = 64

㉖ 54 ____ 46 = 2,484

㉗ 607 ____ 829 = 503,203

㉘ 1,563 ____ 128 = 200,064

㉙ 3 ____ 7 = 21

㉚ 75 ____ 25 = 3

C Write the answers.

① Seventy-one times ninety-four equals ___*six thousand, six hundred seventy-four*___

_____ .

② Two thousand, nine hundred ninety-two divided by thirty-four equals _____

_____ .

③ Five hundred sixty-five times eight hundred seventy-three equals _____

_____ .

④ Forty-three thousand, nine hundred sixty-eight divided by nine hundred sixteen equals _____ .

⑤ Three thousand, eight hundred forty-five times four hundred eighty-nine equals

_____ .

⑥ Forty-three thousand, three hundred seventy-seven divided by seven hundred sixty-one equals _____ .

⑦ Six thousand, eighty-seven times eight thousand, one hundred fifteen equals _____

_____ .

⑧ Two hundred eighty-nine thousand, five hundred sixty-two divided by four hundred eighty-one equals _____ .

Fractions

Learning Objective: *We will learn to identify fractions.*

A fraction is a numerical representation of some portion of a whole.

EXAMPLES: The shaded area on each box represents a portion of the whole.

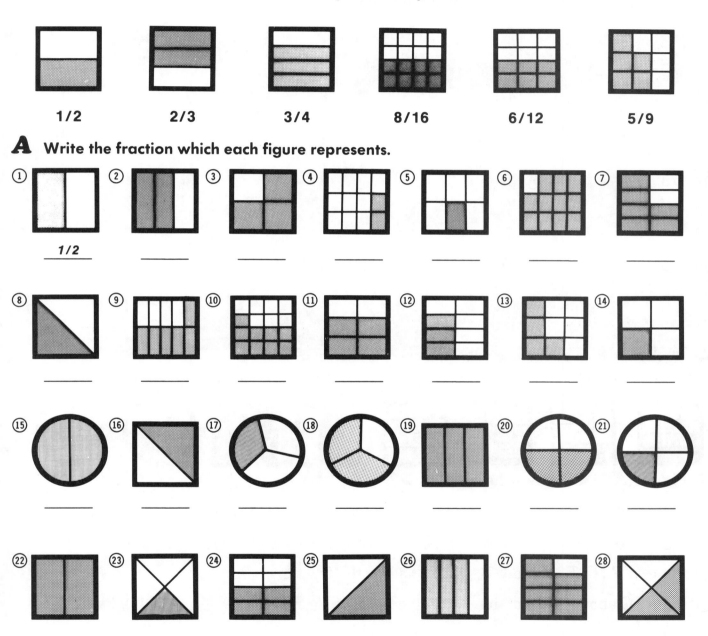

| 1/2 | 2/3 | 3/4 | 8/16 | 6/12 | 5/9 |

A Write the fraction which each figure represents.

① 1/2

REMINDER: Write the definition of a fraction.

_____

_____

Unit 67 cont'd ☞

B **Draw a picture that represents each fraction.**

① 1/2 　　② 2/3　　③ 1/3　　④ 1/4

⑤ 2/5　　⑥ 2/4　　⑦ 3/5　　⑧ 3/4

⑨ 1/5　　⑩ 4/5　　⑪ 5/8　　⑫ 1/6

⑬ 3/8　　⑭ 3/6　　⑮ 1/8　　⑯ 2/6

⑰ 2/8　　⑱ 4/6　　⑲ 4/8　　⑳ 5/6

C **Study the figures and underline the correct answers.**

A　B　C　D　E　F　G　H

    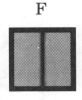 

① Figure (A, <u>B</u>, C) shows the fraction 3/9.

② Figure (A, C, H) shows the fraction 6/12.

③ Figures (A, B, C, D) and (E, F, G, H) show the fraction 1/4.

④ Figures (A, C, E, H) and (B, D, F, G) show the fraction 1/3.

⑤ Figure C shows the fraction (7/12, 5/12, 6/12).

⑥ Figure F shows the fraction (1/2, 2/2, 4/4).

⑦ Figure D shows (3/4, 2/4, 1/4) unshaded.

⑧ Figure B shows (6/9, 7/9, 3/9) unshaded.

⑨ Figure H shows (1/4, 2/4, 3/4) unshaded.

164

Reducing Fractions

Learning Objective: *We will learn to reduce fractions to the lowest terms.*

Reducing a fraction to lowest terms is finding an equivalent, lower fraction until 1 is the only number by which both the numerator and the denominator are divisible.

EXAMPLE: As shown on the number line, 3/12 and 1/4 are equivalent fractions. To find the lowest terms of 3/12, divide the numerator and the denominator by the same number until 1 is the only number by which both may be divided.

$$\frac{3}{12} = \frac{3 \div 3}{12 \div 3} = \frac{1}{4}$$

A Study the number line and find the lowest term for each fraction.

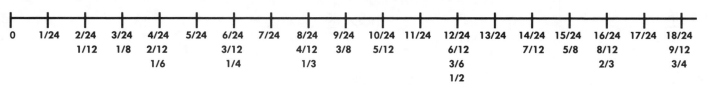

① $2/24 = 1/12$ ② $3/24 =$ ③ $4/24 =$ ④ $5/24 =$ ⑤ $6/24 =$

⑥ $8/24 =$ ⑦ $9/24 =$ ⑧ $10/24 =$ ⑨ $11/24 =$ ⑩ $12/24 =$

⑪ $15/24 =$ ⑫ $16/24 =$ ⑬ $18/24 =$ ⑭ $4/12 =$ ⑮ $6/12 =$

⑯ $2/12 =$ ⑰ $3/12 =$ ⑱ $8/12 =$ ⑲ $3/6 =$ ⑳ $17/24 =$

B Find the lowest terms of each fraction by dividing numerator and demoninator by the number by which both are divisible.

① $\dfrac{2}{4} = \dfrac{2 \div 2}{4 \div 2} = \dfrac{1}{2}$ ② $\dfrac{3}{9} =$ ③ $\dfrac{4}{12} =$

④ $\dfrac{5}{25} =$ ⑤ $\dfrac{15}{48} =$ ⑥ $\dfrac{7}{49} =$

⑦ $\dfrac{38}{56} =$ ⑧ $\dfrac{9}{18} =$ ⑨ $\dfrac{14}{24} =$

⑩ $\dfrac{49}{63} =$ ⑪ $\dfrac{5}{15} =$ ⑫ $\dfrac{4}{6} =$

REMINDER: Write the definition of reducing fractions.

_____

_____

Unit 68 cont'd ☞

C Reduce each fraction to lowest terms.

① $\dfrac{12}{48} = \dfrac{12 \div 12}{48 \div 12} = \dfrac{1}{4}$

② $\dfrac{45}{60} =$

③ $\dfrac{15}{60} =$

④ $\dfrac{35}{85} =$

⑤ $\dfrac{16}{76} =$

⑥ $\dfrac{72}{80} =$

⑦ $\dfrac{24}{100} =$

⑧ $\dfrac{90}{100} =$

⑨ $\dfrac{25}{75} =$

⑩ $\dfrac{26}{78} =$

⑪ $\dfrac{36}{60} =$

⑫ $\dfrac{56}{92} =$

D Underline the correct answers.

① Three-fifths is the lowest term for (2/12, 1/3, 6/10).

② Nine-eighteenths stated in lowest terms is (3/6, 1/2, 2/5).

③ Four-eighths stated in lowest terms is (1/2, 2/6, 4/8).

④ Five-twenty-fifths stated in lowest terms is (1/6, 1/5, 3/5).

⑤ Sixteen-thirtieths stated in lowest terms is (8/10, 8/15, 9/15).

⑥ Eight-twentieths stated in lowest terms is (4/10, 1/8, 2/5).

⑦ One-half is the lowest term for (3/6, 6/8, 9/12).

⑧ Two-thirds is the lowest term for (6/12, 8/12, 10/12).

⑨ Four-fifths is the lowest term for (20/25, 21/25, 10/25).

⑩ Nine-tenths is the lowest term for (27/30, 29/30, 12/30).

Common Denominators   Unit 69

Learning Objective: We will learn to recognize common denominators, to identify multiples of given numbers, and to find the least common denominator of two or more fractions.

The least common denominator of two or more fractions is the least common multiple of the fractions' denominators.

EXAMPLE: The fractions 2/3, 1/3, and 1/6 share a common denominator of six. To express 2/3 and 1/3 with the common denominator of 6, multiply the denominator by 2 ($2 \times 3 = 6$), and multiply the numerators by the same number ($2 \times 2 = 4$, $2 \times 1 = 2$). Thus 2/3 = 4/6 and 1/3 = 2/6. The fractions 4/6, 2/6, and 1/6 are now expressed with least common denominators.

A   In each group of fractions, underline those with common denominators.

① 1/2, 2/2, 3/4, 9/6   ② 4/6, 3/9, 4/5, 5/9   ③ 2/3, 1/6, 5/9, 2/6
④ 2/3, 1/5, 6/10, 4/5   ⑤ 1/3, 2/3, 4/6, 7/8   ⑥ 1/5, 5/6, 2/4, 1/4
⑦ 6/7, 5/6, 5/7, 7/8   ⑧ 7/8, 5/8, 5/7, 7/9   ⑨ 3/10, 4/9, 4/10, 3/4
⑩ 4/5, 3/5, 3/4, 5/6   ⑪ 7/8, 9/10, 6/7, 3/8   ⑫ 1/2, 2/3, 3/9, 5/9
⑬ 6/9, 7/10, 5/9, 3/7   ⑭ 2/7, 3/8, 4/9, 5/7   ⑮ 2/3, 4/7, 6/8, 5/7

B   Underline each number that has, as a multiple, the number indicated.

① multiple 4   ② multiple 22   ③ multiple 8
  1, 2, 3, 4   2, 7, 9, 11   2, 4, 6, 8
④ multiple 16   ⑤ multiple 5   ⑥ multiple 12
  3, 5, 2, 8   1, 2, 3, 5   2, 3, 4, 6
⑦ multiple 18   ⑧ multiple 14   ⑨ multiple 6
  2, 9, 11, 15   2, 7, 10, 12   2, 3, 4, 6
⑩ multiple 24   ⑪ multiple 20   ⑫ multiple 10
  2, 3, 4, 8   2, 4, 5, 10   2, 5, 7, 9
⑬ multiple 36   ⑭ multiple 7   ⑮ multiple 9
  6, 9, 12, 20   2, 3, 5, 7   3, 6, 8, 9

C   Find the least common denominator for each group of fractions.

_8_ ① 1/2, 2/4, 3/4, 1/8   ___ ② 3/9, 1/5, 10/45, 6/9   ___ ③ 1/2, 12/23, 20/23, 2/46
___ ④ 2/3, 1/6, 2/4, 1/12   ___ ⑤ 1/7, 2/5, 6/7, 12/35   ___ ⑥ 7/10, 5/14, 3/7, 4/7
___ ⑦ 2/10, 5/60, 6/12, 1/6 ___ ⑧ 2/5, 4/5, 12/25, 21/25 ___ ⑨ 3/9, 1/3, 2/6, 2/3
___ ⑩ 7/15, 2/3, 5/10, 4/6   ___ ⑪ 1/2, 7/11, 3/22, 2/2   ___ ⑫ 1/7, 1/3, 1/21, 4/7

REMINDER: *Write the definition of a least common denominator.*

_____

_____

The least common denominator of 2/4 and 3/6 is 12. To express both fractions with least common denominators, multiply each numerator by the number that, when multiplied with the denominator, results in 12.

$$\frac{2\times3}{4\times3}=\frac{6}{12} \qquad \frac{3\times2}{6\times2}=\frac{6}{12}$$

D Express each set of fractions with least common denominators.

① $\dfrac{1}{4}, \dfrac{2}{3}$: $\dfrac{1\times3}{4\times3}=\dfrac{3}{12}$ $\dfrac{2\times4}{3\times4}=\dfrac{8}{12}$

② $\dfrac{7}{11}, \dfrac{5}{55}$:

③ $\dfrac{3}{6}, \dfrac{4}{8}$:

④ $\dfrac{3}{10}, \dfrac{7}{30}$:

⑤ $\dfrac{9}{10}, \dfrac{5}{15}$:

⑥ $\dfrac{1}{4}, \dfrac{3}{9}$:

⑦ $\dfrac{3}{6}, \dfrac{2}{12}$:

⑧ $\dfrac{6}{15}, \dfrac{7}{8}$:

⑨ $\dfrac{4}{20}, \dfrac{3}{5}$:

⑩ $\dfrac{4}{7}, \dfrac{3}{12}$:

E Underline the correct answers.

① Twenty-four is a multiple of each of (<u>2</u>, <u>4</u>, <u>6</u>, <u>8</u>, 9, <u>12</u>, 14, 16, 18).

② Twelve is a (multiple, common denominator, numerator) of 1, 2, 3, 4, 6, and 12.

③ The fractions 1/2, 2/4, 4/8, and 8/16 all could share (24, 16, 4) as the lowest common denominator.

④ The fractions 5/12, 7/12, 3/12, and 6/12 share a (multiple, common numerator, common denominator).

⑤ The fractions 3/16, 3/15, 3/12, and 3/9 share a (multiple, common denominator, common numerator).

⑥ To express 1/12 and 3/8 as fractions with common denominators, one would use (two, twelve, twenty-four) as the denominator.

⑦ To express 2/3 and 4/5 as fractions with common denominators, one would use (ten, fifteen, twenty-five) as the denominator.

⑧ (Three, Four, Five) of these fractions have common denominators: 1/12, 3/12, 4/24, 5/6, 8/12, and 6/6.

Adding Fractions   Unit 70

Learning
Objective: *We will learn to add fractions that have common denominators as well as those that do not.*

A common denominator is one that is shared by two or more fractions.

EXAMPLE:

To add fractions that have common denominators, simply add the numerators and write the sum above the common denominator.

$$2/3 + 1/3 = 3/3$$

To add fractions that do not have common denominators, express each fraction with the least common denominator and add.

$$2/3 + 1/4 = 8/12 + 3/12 = 11/12$$

A Add these fractions which have common denominators. Express each answer in lowest terms.

① $1/3 + 1/3 = $ **2/3**   ② $4/5 + 1/5 = $ ③ $3/9 + 4/9 = $

④ $2/6 + 4/6 = $ ⑤ $1/2 + 1/2 = $ ⑥ $3/4 + 1/4 = $

⑦ $3/7 + 2/7 = $ ⑧ $1/8 + 3/8 = $ ⑨ $2/10 + 4/10 = $

⑩ $6/11 + 3/11 = $ ⑪ $4/12 + 2/12 = $ ⑫ $10/13 + 1/13 = $

⑬ $7/14 + 2/14 = $ ⑭ $9/15 + 3/15 = $ ⑮ $6/16 + 2/16 = $

⑯ $7/18 + 8/18 = $ ⑰ $9/19 + 10/19 = $ ⑱ $1/20 + 6/20 = $

⑲ $7/21 + 3/21 = $ ⑳ $5/25 + 3/25 = $ ㉑ $2/24 + 7/24 = $

B Add these fractions which do not have common denominators. Express each answer in lowest terms.

① $1/3 + 2/6 = $ **2/6 + 2/6 = 4/6 = 2/3**   ② $3/6 + 2/12 = $

③ $3/9 + 2/6 = $ ④ $4/9 + 3/24 = $

⑤ $9/12 + 1/4 = $ ⑥ $5/15 + 3/30 = $

⑦ $5/7 + 2/14 = $ ⑧ $8/12 + 6/36 = $

⑨ $7/8 + 1/9 = $ ⑩ $5/8 + 1/6 = $

⑪ $3/10 + 9/20 = $ ⑫ $6/17 + 1/2 = $

⑬ $5/8 + 1/18 = $ ⑭ $7/21 + 9/42 = $

REMINDER: Write the definition of a common denominator.

169   **Unit 70 cont'd** ☛

C Add these fractions. Reduce each answer to lowest terms.

① 2/5 + 1/5 + 1/5 = **4/5**

② 1/2 + 1/5 + 1/10 =

③ 1/8 + 1/24 + 2/12 =

④ 2/8 + 1/8 + 1/24 =

⑤ 1/3 + 1/5 + 1/15 =

⑥ 3/4 + 1/8 + 1/12 =

⑦ 1/4 + 1/4 + 1/16 =

⑧ 5/10 + 1/10 + 30/100 =

⑨ 2/8 + 2/8 + 1/4 =

⑩ 3/8 + 4/12 + 5/24 =

⑪ 3/9 + 1/9 + 1/18 =

⑫ 3/12 + 1/12 + 1/24 =

⑬ 1/12 + 1/12 + 1/24 =

⑭ 3/4 + 1/16 + 1/24 =

⑮ 3/10 + 2/10 + 1/5 =

⑯ 3/5 + 2/10 + 1/15 =

⑰ 2/11 + 1/11 + 1/22 =

⑱ 1/2 + 2/6 + 1/9 =

D Solve the problems. Reduce all answers to lowest terms.

① Shelly had 1/3 of a cherry pie, 2/4 of an apple pie, and 1/8 of a pumpkin pie left after her guests finished eating on Thanksgiving. How much pie remained?

② Tom had 1/4 tank of gas in his blue car. He also had 2/4 tank of gas in his red car and 1/4 tank of gas in his tractor. How much of a tank of gas did Tom have altogether?

③ One-tenth of Miss Wilson's class made A's on the final exam. Another 2/5 of the class made passing grades. Still another 1/10 of the class failed the exam. The rest of the students in the class never showed up to take the test. What was the total of the students in the class who took the test?

④ Robin bought 1/3 of her groceries in specialty shops and 2/6 of her groceries from farmers' markets. What portion of her groceries were not bought in a grocery store?

⑤ One-fifth of Janet's salary pays her household bills. Another 3/10 of her salary makes her car payment. The rest is used for fun. How much of her salary does she pay bills with?

Comprehension Check

A Multiply or divide.

①
$$\begin{array}{r} 2{,}345 \\ \times 63 \\ \hline 7035 \\ 14070 \\ \hline 147{,}735 \end{array}$$

② $75\,\overline{)\,17{,}625}$

③
$$\begin{array}{r} 1{,}235 \\ \times 25 \\ \hline \end{array}$$

④ $26\,\overline{)\,6{,}500}$

⑤
$$\begin{array}{r} 4{,}567 \\ \times 301 \\ \hline \end{array}$$

⑥ $130\,\overline{)\,7{,}020}$

⑦
$$\begin{array}{r} 8{,}931 \\ \times 265 \\ \hline \end{array}$$

⑧ $268\,\overline{)\,11{,}524}$

⑨
$$\begin{array}{r} 5{,}267 \\ \times 3{,}212 \\ \hline \end{array}$$

⑩ $210\,\overline{)\,12{,}180}$

⑪
$$\begin{array}{r} 3{,}497 \\ \times 2{,}156 \\ \hline \end{array}$$

⑫ $497\,\overline{)\,226{,}632}$

B Write each fraction that represents each figure.

①   1/4

② _____

③ _____

④ _____

⑤ _____

⑥ _____

⑦ _____

⑧ _____

⑨ _____

⑩ _____

⑪ _____

⑫ _____

⑬ _____

⑭ _____

⑮ _____

171

Test 14 cont'd ☞

C Reduce each fraction to lowest terms.

① $\dfrac{5}{25} = \dfrac{5 \div 5}{25 \div 5} = \dfrac{1}{5}$ ② $\dfrac{3}{6} =$ ③ $\dfrac{16}{64} =$

④ $\dfrac{9}{36} =$ ⑤ $\dfrac{7}{21} =$ ⑥ $\dfrac{22}{42} =$

⑦ $\dfrac{12}{28} =$ ⑧ $\dfrac{32}{98} =$ ⑨ $\dfrac{18}{36} =$

D Underline the fractions which have common denominators.

① 1/2, 2/4, <u>3/6</u>, <u>5/6</u> ② 9/10, 11/12, 6/12, 3/12 ③ 5/6, 3/6, 2/6, 1/6

④ 2/10, 3/10, 7/11, 8/41 ⑤ 3/17, 4/16, 7/17, 8/17 ⑥ 8/10, 9/11, 3/10, 4/9

⑦ 9/12, 3/13, 4/14, 5/13 ⑧ 6/18, 5/19, 3/20, 1/18 ⑨ 1/22, 2/22, 3/22, 4/22

E Add each problem. Reduce each answer to lowest terms.

① 2/3 + 1/3 = **3/3 = 1** ② 5/7 + 1/7 = ③ 3/6 + 2/6 =

④ 9/10 + 1/10 = ⑤ 2/8 + 3/8 = ⑥ 3/11 + 4/11 =

⑦ 2/3 + 1/6 = ⑧ 1/2 + 1/6 =

⑨ 4/12 + 2/24 = ⑩ 3/9 + 3/18 =

⑪ 2/15 + 3/30 = ⑫ 4/10 + 1/20 =

⑬ 1/3 + 1/3 + 1/6 = ⑭ 1/9 + 2/9 + 3/9 =

⑮ 1/2 + 1/5 + 3/10 =

⑯ 1/20 + 2/20 + 11/60 =

Define.

① multiplication _____

② division _____

③ fraction _____

④ denominator _____

⑤ numerator _____

⑥ common denominator _____

Subtracting Fractions   **Unit 71**

Learning
Objective: *We will learn to subtract fractions that have common denominators as well as those that do not.*

A common denominator is one that is shared by two or more fractions.

EXAMPLE:

To subtract fractions that have common denominators, simply subtract the numerators and write the answer above the common denominator. $3/4 - 1/4 = 2/4$

To subtract fractions that do not have common denominators, express each fraction with the least common denominator and subtract. $2/4 - 1/8 = 4/8 - 1/8 = 7/8$

A Subtract these fractions which have common denominators. Reduce each answer to lowest terms.

① $5/6 - 3/6 = $ ***2/6 = 1/3***   ② $3/7 - 2/7 = $

③ $2/2 - 1/2 = $ ④ $8/10 - 2/10 = $

⑤ $5/9 - 4/9 = $ ⑥ $12/30 - 6/30 = $

⑦ $3/6 - 1/6 = $ ⑧ $9/17 - 7/17 = $

⑨ $6/15 - 4/15 = $ ⑩ $4/5 - 3/5 = $

⑪ $60/72 - 32/72 = $ ⑫ $9/21 - 7/21 = $

⑬ $2/8 - 1/8 = $ ⑭ $3/6 - 2/6 = $

⑮ $9/18 - 1/18 = $ ⑯ $9/11 - 3/11 = $

⑰ $3/20 - 1/20 = $ ⑱ $17/36 - 15/36 = $

⑲ $7/12 - 3/12 = $ ⑳ $2/14 - 1/14 = $

㉑ $21/42 - 18/42 = $ ㉒ $9/20 - 8/20 = $

㉓ $17/17 - 3/17 = $ ㉔ $19/63 - 15/63 = $

㉕ $3/16 - 1/16 = $ ㉖ $6/26 - 2/26 = $

㉗ $31/75 - 25/75 = $ ㉘ $5/10 - 1/10 = $

㉙ $2/10 - 1/10 = $ ㉚ $3/16 - 2/16 = $

㉛ $3/34 - 1/34 = $ ㉜ $7/23 - 4/23 = $

㉝ $41/80 - 40/80 = $ ㉞ $20/64 - 19/64 = $

㉟ $5/27 - 3/27 = $ ㊱ $6/49 - 2/49 = $

㊲ $18/30 - 15/30 = $ ㊳ $20/54 - 17/54 = $

㊴ $19/50 - 15/50 = $ ㊵ $24/60 - 14/60 = $

㊶ $31/70 - 30/70 = $ ㊷ $71/80 - 63/80 = $

㊸ $33/50 - 20/50 = $ ㊹ $24/60 - 22/60 = $

REMINDER: Write the definition of a common denominator.

_____

_____

B Subtract these fractions which do not have common denominators. Reduce the answers to lowest terms.

① 3/12 − 1/4 = *3/12 − 3/12 = 0*

② 5/7 − 3/6 =

③ 9/11 − 3/7 =

④ 3/9 − 1/3 =

⑤ 8/12 − 3/10 =

⑥ 3/5 − 1/4 =

⑦ 5/10 − 1/15 =

⑧ 6/11 − 3/22 =

⑨ 9/20 − 2/8 =

⑩ 9/20 − 3/10 =

⑪ 6/7 − 4/5 =

⑫ 9/11 − 4/5 =

⑬ 16/18 − 5/9 =

⑭ 6/9 − 3/8 =

⑮ 4/8 − 3/7 =

⑯ 3/6 − 1/3 =

⑰ 10/15 − 3/20 =

⑱ 5/6 − 1/7 =

⑲ 2/4 − 1/3 =

⑳ 4/8 − 1/11 =

㉑ 8/20 − 1/15 =

㉒ 3/5 − 1/4 =

㉓ 3/8 − 1/7 =

㉔ 3/8 − 1/12 =

㉕ 8/12 − 3/24 =

㉖ 4/12 − 3/16 =

C Underline the correct answers.

① Four-fifths minus three-fourths equals (1/20, 2/20, 3/18).

② Three-fifths minus one-half equals (1/10, 3/9, 6/18).

③ Seven-twelfths minus three-tenths equals (17/60, 20/31, 9/18).

④ Four-ninths minus two-fifths equals (18/45, 8/35, 2/45).

⑤ Five-eighteenths minus one-sixth equals (5/18, 10/40, 1/9).

⑥ Three-tenths minus one-twentieth equals (6/20, 4/18, 1/4).

⑦ Seven-eighths minus five-sixths equals (2/12, 1/24, 3/8).

⑧ Five-ninths minus four-twelfths equals (2/9, 3/6, 2/8).

⑨ One-third minus one-eighth equals (5/24, 6/24, 6/12).

⑩ Five-sixths minus three-sevenths equals (17/42, 18/42, 19/53).

⑪ One third minus three-tenths equals (1/30, 2/61, 5/79).

Multiplying Fractions

Learning Objective: *We will learn to multiply fractions.*

A fraction is a numerical representation of some portion of the whole.

EXAMPLE: To multiply fractions, simply multiply the two numerators and the two denominators. Reduce the products to lowest terms. $1/3 \times 2/4 = 2/12 = 1/6$

A Multiply the numerators and the denominators. Reduce the answers to lowest terms.

① $1/3 \times 2/5 =$ **2/15**

② $2/4 \times 2/4 =$

③ $1/4 \times 2/6 =$

④ $2/5 \times 3/8 =$

⑤ $4/6 \times 3/9 =$

⑥ $5/8 \times 2/6 =$

⑦ $1/3 \times 6/8 =$

⑧ $5/6 \times 1/4 =$

⑨ $1/4 \times 3/6 =$

⑩ $3/4 \times 1/8 =$

⑪ $3/5 \times 1/4 =$

⑫ $9/11 \times 1/3 =$

⑬ $2/3 \times 1/4 =$

⑭ $2/8 \times 1/6 =$

⑮ $4/5 \times 1/6 =$

⑯ $1/3 \times 5/9 =$

⑰ $2/4 \times 1/7 =$

⑱ $4/9 \times 4/5 =$

⑲ $8/10 \times 2/6 =$

⑳ $2/5 \times 1/9 =$

㉑ $8/9 \times 1/7 =$

㉒ $3/4 \times 1/5 =$

㉓ $3/6 \times 2/10 =$

㉔ $4/8 \times 1/4 =$

㉕ $2/8 \times 2/8 =$

㉖ $3/14 \times 1/2 =$

㉗ $3/5 \times 1/8 =$

㉘ $2/7 \times 2/7 =$

㉙ $7/9 \times 3/9 =$

㉚ $2/9 \times 2/6 =$

㉛ $2/10 \times 2/5 =$

㉜ $3/7 \times 1/4 =$

㉝ $2/4 \times 6/8 =$

㉞ $5/10 \times 2/5 =$

㉟ $2/4 \times 2/4 =$

㊱ $2/8 \times 1/7 =$

㊲ $2/4 \times 7/8 =$

㊳ $2/6 \times 4/5 =$

㊴ $2/15 \times 3/4 =$

㊵ $7/8 \times 1/4 =$

㊶ $2/6 \times 2/8 =$

㊷ $4/7 \times 1/5 =$

REMINDER: Write the definition of a fraction.

_____

_____

Unit 72 cont'd ☞

A shortcut to multiplying fractions is called cancellation. The numerator of the fraction 2/3 may be divided by the same number as the denominator of the fraction 1/4.

$$1/\overset{1}{\cancel{4}} \times \overset{1}{\cancel{2}}/3 = 1/6$$

B Multiply using cancellation.

① $1/\overset{2}{\cancel{3}} \times \underset{1}{\cancel{6}}/9 = \textbf{2/9}$ ② $2/3 \times 1/4 =$ ③ $2/7 \times 3/8 =$

④ $4/9 \times 3/7 =$ ⑤ $5/6 \times 2/3 =$ ⑥ $4/6 \times 2/9 =$

⑦ $4/10 \times 2/3 =$ ⑧ $6/7 \times 1/2 =$ ⑨ $4/5 \times 1/20 =$

⑩ $2/3 \times 3/8 =$ ⑪ $2/7 \times 1/6 =$ ⑫ $2/9 \times 3/6 =$

⑬ $1/10 \times 5/6 =$ ⑭ $2/5 \times 1/6 =$ ⑮ $7/9 \times 3/4 =$

⑯ $6/9 \times 3/12 =$ ⑰ $2/8 \times 2/4 =$ ⑱ $2/16 \times 4/8 =$

⑲ $8/40 \times 2/16 =$ ⑳ $4/10 \times 5/8 =$ ㉑ $2/4 \times 8/10 =$

C Underline the correct answers.

① One-fourth times three-fourths equals (<u>three-sixteenths</u>, four-sixteenths, two-sixteenths).

② Eight-tenths times one-ninth equals (four-forty-fifths , six-thirteenths, twelve-twentieths).

③ One-sixth times three-ninths equals (one-eighteenth, two-twentieths, nine-eighteenths).

④ Two-sixths times one-sixth equals (three-fourths, one-eighteenth , three-sixths).

⑤ Six-sevenths times two-fourths equals (twelve-sixteenths, three-sevenths , four-sixths).

⑥ Two-tenths times three-sevenths equals (three-thirty-fifths, five-twelfths, ten-elevenths).

⑦ Two-eighths times two-ninths equals (four-fifths, two-sixths, one-eighteenth).

Dividing Fractions

Learning Objective: *We will learn to find reciprocals and to divide fractions.*

A reciprocal is a fraction that, when multiplied with another fraction, results in the product of one.

EXAMPLE:
The reciprocal of 3/4 is 4/3 (3/4 × 4/3 = 1). To divide fractions, multiply the dividend by the reciprocal of the divisor.

$$2/6 \div 1/2 = 2/6 \times 2/1 = 4/6 = 2/3$$

A Find each reciprocal.

① 3/6 × _6/3_ = 1　② 4/8 × ____ = 1　③ 2/6 × ____ = 1　④ 1/5 × ____ = 1

⑤ 2/8 × ____ = 1　⑥ 4/5 × ____ = 1　⑦ 6/7 × ____ = 1　⑧ 5/8 × ____ = 1

⑨ 9/16 × ____ = 1　⑩ 3/4 × ____ = 1　⑪ 5/10 × ____ = 1　⑫ 3/8 × ____ = 1

⑬ 2/9 × ____ = 1　⑭ 5/11 × ____ = 1　⑮ 3/5 × ____ = 1　⑯ 2/7 × ____ = 1

⑰ 5/9 × ____ = 1　⑱ 3/7 × ____ = 1　⑲ 4/9 × ____ = 1　⑳ 2/5 × ____ = 1

B Divide. Express all answers in lowest terms.

① 1/3 ÷ 3/4 = *1/3 × 4/3 = 4/9*

② 1/4 ÷ 2/3 =

③ 4/8 ÷ 2/3 =

④ 1/5 ÷ 2/3 =

⑤ 3/4 ÷ 6/7 =

⑥ 1/6 ÷ 2/7 =

⑦ 3/5 ÷ 6/8 =

⑧ 1/4 ÷ 2 =

⑨ 3/7 ÷ 5/9 =

⑩ 1/2 ÷ 6/7 =

⑪ 2/9 ÷ 3/8 =

⑫ 1/3 ÷ 2/3 =

⑬ 1/9 ÷ 7/8 =

⑭ 1/5 ÷ 4/6 =

⑮ 2/6 ÷ 7/9 =

⑯ 1/9 ÷ 3/7 =

⑰ 2/3 ÷ 2 =

⑱ 2/5 ÷ 1/2 =

REMINDER: Write the definition of a reciprocal.

_____

_____

Unit 73 cont'd ☞

C Divide using cancellation. Express each answer in lowest terms.

① 2/5 ÷ 4/6 = 2̸/5 × 6̸/4̸ = 6/10 = 3/5

② 1/15 ÷ 1/5 =

③ 2/9 ÷ 2/3 =

④ 4/12 ÷ 3/4 =

⑤ 2/4 ÷ 1/2 =

⑥ 3/8 ÷ 3/4 =

⑦ 3/9 ÷ 2/3 =

⑧ 6/11 ÷ 3/22 =

⑨ 8/10 ÷ 2/5 =

⑩ 1/9 ÷ 1/3 =

⑪ 2/6 ÷ 2/3 =

⑫ 2/3 ÷ 8/9 =

D Underline the correct answers.

① Six-thirty-sixths divided by four-ninths equals (<u>three-eighths</u>, two-thirds, five-sixths).

② Six-twenty-fourths divided by three-eighths equals (one-third, two-thirds, two-fourths).

③ Five-twenty-fifths divided by ten-fifteenths equals (four-eighths, three-tenths, two-tenths).

④ Two-twelfths divided by four-sixths equals (one-third, nine-tenths, one-fourth).

⑤ Six-twenty-eighths divided by four-sevenths equals (one-fifth, three-eighths, two-eighths).

⑥ Two-twenty-seconds divided by six-elevenths equals (one-sixth, two-sixths, three-sixths).

⑦ Two-ninths divided by six-eighteenths equals (one-third, two-thirds, three-thirds).

Mixed Numbers   Unit 74

Learning Objective: *We will learn to write improper fractions as mixed numbers and to add and subtract mixed numbers.*

A mixed number is made of both a whole number and a fraction.

EXAMPLE:

An improper fraction has a numerator that is greater than the denominator. By dividing the numerator by the denominator, we may write an improper fraction as a mixed number.

$$6/4 = 6 \div 4 = 1\ 2/4 \text{ or } 1\ 1/2$$

To convert a mixed number to an improper fraction, multiply the denominator by the whole number ($3 \times 1 = 3$) and add this product to the numerator ($3 + 2 = 5$). Write this sum above the original denominator.

$$1\ 2/3 = 5/3$$

A Write these improper fractions as mixed numbers. Express each fraction in lowest terms.

① $6/5 = 6 \div 5 = 1\ 1/5$ ② $17/14 =$ ③ $9/6 =$

④ $7/4 =$ ⑤ $6/4 =$ ⑥ $18/4 =$

⑦ $8/3 =$ ⑧ $11/9 =$ ⑨ $7/2 =$

⑩ $12/5 =$ ⑪ $16/3 =$ ⑫ $5/2 =$

⑬ $14/6 =$ ⑭ $11/4 =$ ⑮ $3/2 =$

⑯ $20/9 =$ ⑰ $13/9 =$ ⑱ $5/4 =$

⑲ $13/8 =$ ⑳ $42/5 =$ ㉑ $10/6 =$

B Add these mixed numbers. Express each fraction in lowest terms.

① $5\ 2/3 + 4\ 3/5 =$ ② $6\ 7/8 + 2\ 3/4 =$

     $17/3 + 23/5 =$
     $85/15 + 69/15 = 154/15 = 10\ 4/15$

③ $4\ 2/9 + 3\ 5/6 =$ ④ $2\ 4/5 + 5\ 1/10 =$

⑤ $5\ 2/3 + 4\ 6/7 =$ ⑥ $4\ 6/10 + 3\ 2/5 =$

REMINDER: Write the definition of a mixed number.

_____

_____

C Subtract these mixed numbers. Express each fraction in lowest terms.

① 5 6/8 − 3 2/4 =
    46/8 − 14/4 =
    46/8 − 28/8 = 18/8 = 2 2/8 = 2 1/4

② 7 3/4 − 5 2/5 =

③ 9 1/10 − 6 4/5 =

④ 4 3/8 − 2 6/12 =

⑤ 2 3/5 − 1 1/10 =

⑥ 6 1/4 − 4 2/8 =

⑦ 7 3/6 − 5 2/12 =

⑧ 8 1/3 − 6 4/9 =

D Underline the correct answers.

① The improper fraction 22/3 is written (<u>7 1/3</u>, 8 3/4, 9 6/7) as a mixed number.

② The improper fraction 19/6 is written (4 2/6, 3 1/6, 5 8/9) as a mixed number.

③ The improper fraction 26/8 is written (3 2/8, 3 6/8, 4 3/8) as a mixed number.

④ The improper fraction 25/4 is written (6 1/4, 6 5/6, 6 2/4) as a mixed number.

⑤ The improper fraction 12/11 is written (1 1/11, 2 1/11, 1 3/11) as a mixed number.

⑥ The improper fraction 14/5 is written (3 4/5, 4 4/5, 2 4/5) as a mixed number.

⑦ Eight and one-third plus two and one-fourth equals (10 7/12, 9, 11 2/5).

⑧ Six and two-ninths minus four and two-thirds equals (1 5/9, 2 7/8, 3 1/3).

⑨ Five and two-eighths plus six and two-fourths equals (12, 11 3/4, 13 1/3).

⑩ Three and five-eighths minus two and five-sixths equals (19/24, 12/24, 3 1/8).

Whole Numbers Unit 75

Learning Objective: *We will learn to work problems with whole numbers.*

The set of whole numbers begins with zero and continues indefinitely. A whole number is not a fraction, a percent, or a decimal.

EXAMPLE:

We use whole numbers every day to add, subtract, multiply, and divide.

$$
\begin{array}{r} 123 \\ + 103 \\ \hline 226 \end{array}
\qquad
\begin{array}{r} 345 \\ - 201 \\ \hline 144 \end{array}
\qquad
\begin{array}{r} 406 \\ \times 7 \\ \hline 2{,}842 \end{array}
\qquad
\begin{array}{r} 99 \\ 8\overline{)792} \\ 72 \\ \hline 72 \\ 72 \\ \hline \end{array}
$$

A Add these whole numbers.

① 7 + 0 = **7** ② 7 + 8 = ③ 3 + 4 = ④ 5 + 11 = ⑤ 9 + 21 = ⑥ 70 + 7 =

⑦ $\begin{array}{r} 89 \\ + 71 \\ \hline \end{array}$ ⑧ $\begin{array}{r} 10 \\ + 9 \\ \hline \end{array}$ ⑨ $\begin{array}{r} 21 \\ + 34 \\ \hline \end{array}$ ⑩ $\begin{array}{r} 36 \\ + 89 \\ \hline \end{array}$ ⑪ $\begin{array}{r} 73 \\ + 46 \\ \hline \end{array}$ ⑫ $\begin{array}{r} 35 \\ + 53 \\ \hline \end{array}$ ⑬ $\begin{array}{r} 19 \\ + 87 \\ \hline \end{array}$

⑭ $\begin{array}{r} 1{,}023 \\ + 309 \\ \hline \end{array}$ ⑮ $\begin{array}{r} 6{,}606 \\ + 23 \\ \hline \end{array}$ ⑯ $\begin{array}{r} 7{,}891 \\ + 312 \\ \hline \end{array}$ ⑰ $\begin{array}{r} 7{,}989 \\ + 3{,}121 \\ \hline \end{array}$ ⑱ $\begin{array}{r} 3{,}211 \\ + 1{,}576 \\ \hline \end{array}$ ⑲ $\begin{array}{r} 60{,}717 \\ + 34{,}022 \\ \hline \end{array}$

B Subtract these whole numbers.

① 10 − 5 = **5** ② 12 − 6 = ③ 4 − 2 = ④ 23 − 17 = ⑤ 15 − 7 = ⑥ 60 − 4 =

⑦ $\begin{array}{r} 53 \\ - 21 \\ \hline \end{array}$ ⑧ $\begin{array}{r} 99 \\ - 70 \\ \hline \end{array}$ ⑨ $\begin{array}{r} 76 \\ - 54 \\ \hline \end{array}$ ⑩ $\begin{array}{r} 11 \\ - 7 \\ \hline \end{array}$ ⑪ $\begin{array}{r} 46 \\ - 39 \\ \hline \end{array}$ ⑫ $\begin{array}{r} 54 \\ - 16 \\ \hline \end{array}$ ⑬ $\begin{array}{r} 87 \\ - 19 \\ \hline \end{array}$

⑭ $\begin{array}{r} 2{,}031 \\ - 201 \\ \hline \end{array}$ ⑮ $\begin{array}{r} 7{,}819 \\ - 245 \\ \hline \end{array}$ ⑯ $\begin{array}{r} 7{,}891 \\ - 6{,}115 \\ \hline \end{array}$ ⑰ $\begin{array}{r} 4{,}897 \\ - 391 \\ \hline \end{array}$ ⑱ $\begin{array}{r} 56{,}917 \\ - 40{,}132 \\ \hline \end{array}$ ⑲ $\begin{array}{r} 71{,}224 \\ - 36{,}718 \\ \hline \end{array}$

C Multiply these whole numbers.

① 5 × 7 = **35** ② 3 × 6 = ③ 4 × 8 = ④ 9 × 10 = ⑤ 6 × 8 = ⑥ 7 × 3 =

⑦ $\begin{array}{r} 23 \\ \times 14 \\ \hline \end{array}$ ⑧ $\begin{array}{r} 913 \\ \times 10 \\ \hline \end{array}$ ⑨ $\begin{array}{r} 461 \\ \times 123 \\ \hline \end{array}$ ⑩ $\begin{array}{r} 4{,}983 \\ \times 23 \\ \hline \end{array}$ ⑪ $\begin{array}{r} 5{,}361 \\ \times 301 \\ \hline \end{array}$ ⑫ $\begin{array}{r} 4{,}569 \\ \times 1{,}093 \\ \hline \end{array}$

REMINDER: Write the definition of the set of whole numbers.

_____

_____

Unit 75 cont'd ☞

D Divide these whole numbers.

① $21 \div 7 = 3$ ② $34 \div 2 =$ ③ $50 \div 10 =$ ④ $45 \div 15 =$ ⑤ $60 \div 3 =$

⑥ $15 \div 5 =$ ⑦ $81 \div 9 =$ ⑧ $46 \div 0 =$ ⑨ $10 \div 2 =$ ⑩ $49 \div 7 =$

⑪ $12\overline{)516}$ ⑫ $24\overline{)13,464}$ ⑬ $53\overline{)21,730}$ ⑭ $61\overline{)33,855}$

⑮ $131\overline{)7,336}$ ⑯ $245\overline{)73,745}$ ⑰ $568\overline{)236,288}$ ⑱ $614\overline{)243,758}$

E Underline the correct answers.

① Seven plus eleven equals (<u>eighteen</u>, eight, seventy-one).

② Twenty-one plus forty equals (sixteen, sixty-one, two hundred forty).

③ Nineteen minus seven equals (twelve, two, twenty-one).

④ Three hundred fifty minus two hundred ninety-nine equals (fifteen, five, fifty-one).

⑤ Sixteen times eight equals (one hundred twenty-eight, twenty-eight, one hundred twenty-four).

⑥ Five times four equals (thirty, twenty, nine).

⑦ Ten divided by two equals (eight, twenty, five).

⑧ Thirty-six divided by six equals (seven, sixteen, six).

⑨ Five thousand, three hundred fifty-five divided by eighty-five equals (sixty-three, seventy-five, fifty-five).

⑩ Seven thousand, three hundred eighty-three divided by three hundred twenty-one equals (twenty-one, twenty-two, twenty-three).

Comprehension Check

A Subtract these fractions. Reduce each answer to lowest terms.

① 2/3 − 1/3 = **1/3**   ② 7/8 − 1/8 =   ③ 9/12 − 3/12 =

④ 10/15 − 5/15 =   ⑤ 9/10 − 1/10 =   ⑥ 3/6 − 1/6 =

⑦ 3/21 − 1/21 =   ⑧ 7/30 − 4/30 =   ⑨ 10/12 − 9/12 =

⑩ 11/20 − 1/5 =   ⑪ 2/3 − 1/5 =

⑫ 12/30 − 2/15 =   ⑬ 5/6 − 1/4 =

B Multiply these fractions. Reduce each answer to lowest terms. Use cancellation when possible.

① 2/3 × 1/7 = **2/21**   ② 1/3 × 3/9 =   ③ 1/6 × 2/5 =

④ 6/8 × 1/10 =   ⑤ 5/8 × 1/3 =   ⑥ 2/4 × 1/2 =

⑦ 9/10 × 11/13 =   ⑧ 1/4 × 2/8 =   ⑨ 1/9 × 3/6 =

⑩ 3/9 × 1/12 =   ⑪ 4/10 × 11/12 =   ⑫ 3/9 × 2/5 =

⑬ 6/7 × 1/8 =   ⑭ 3/6 × 3/6 =   ⑮ 6/9 × 1/6 =

C Find the reciprocals.

① 1/3 × **3/1** = 1   ② 2/3 × ____ = 1   ③ 5/6 × ____ = 1   ④ 3/2 × ____ = 1   ⑤ 4/7 × ____ = 1

⑥ 6/8 × ____ = 1   ⑦ 1/10 × ____ = 1   ⑧ 2/10 × ____ = 1   ⑨ 5/7 × ____ = 1   ⑩ 6/10 × ____ = 1

⑪ 3/6 × ____ = 1   ⑫ 1/15 × ____ = 1   ⑬ 1/8 × ____ = 1   ⑭ 3/8 × ____ = 1   ⑮ 1/9 × ____ = 1

D Divide these fractions. Reduce each answer to lowest terms. Use cancellation when possible.

① 2/3 ÷ 1/3 = **2/3 × 3/1 = 2**   ② 2/12 ÷ 1/3 =

③ 1/5 ÷ 1/4 =   ④ 5/20 ÷ 1/4 =

⑤ 2/8 ÷ 2/3 =   ⑥ 2/16 ÷ 3/8 =

⑦ 7/12 ÷ 5/6 =   ⑧ 4/20 ÷ 1/5 =

Test 15 cont'd ☞

E Write these improper fractions as mixed numbers. Reduce.

① $6/5 = 6 \div 5 = 1\ 1/5$　　② $4/3 =$　　③ $9/5 =$

④ $8/7 =$　　⑤ $3/2 =$　　⑥ $11/7 =$

⑦ $16/5 =$　　⑧ $9/2 =$　　⑨ $7/4 =$

⑩ $13/3 =$　　⑪ $24/7 =$　　⑫ $25/6 =$

F Add or subtract these mixed numbers. Reduce answers.

① $5\ 1/4 + 2\ 2/3 = 21/4 + 8/3 =$
$63/12 + 32/12 = 95/12 = 7\ 11/12$

② $3\ 2/3 + 4\ 1/4 =$

③ $9\ 1/4 + 3\ 6/8 =$

④ $4\ 1/3 - 2\ 1/4 =$

⑤ $6\ 1/8 - 2\ 2/3 =$

⑥ $9\ 2/3 - 6\ 1/3 =$

G Add, subtract, multiply, or divide these whole numbers.

①
```
  390
 +172
  ───
  562
```
②
```
  889
 -422
```
③
```
  633
 +122
```
④
```
  5,051
 -1,562
```

⑤
```
  6,193
 +1,050
```
⑥
```
  25,701
 -21,171
```
⑦
```
   23
  ×14
```
⑧
```
  302
  ×24
```

⑨
```
  468
 ×508
```
⑩ $23\overline{)1,035}$

⑪ $45\overline{)10,395}$

⑫ $369\overline{)167,895}$

Define.

① common denominator _____

② fraction _____

③ reciprocal _____

④ mixed number _____

⑤ improper fraction _____

⑥ whole numbers _____

Properties of Whole Numbers

Learning Objective: *We will learn to identify a number as belonging to a certain property.*

The set of whole numbers begins with zero and goes on indefinitely.

EXAMPLE: There are four properties of whole numbers. They delineate if a whole number is 1) negative or positive; 2) odd or even; 3) composite, prime, or zero; and 4) cardinal, ordinal, or Roman.

A Property Number One
Write "n" beside each number if it is negative or "p" if it is positive.

n ① -1	___ ② 61	___ ③ -71	___ ④ 499	___ ⑤ -506	___ ⑥ 192
___ ⑦ 2	___ ⑧ 62	___ ⑨ 89	___ ⑩ 398	___ ⑪ -589	___ ⑫ 902
___ ⑬ -3	___ ⑭ 63	___ ⑮ -14	___ ⑯ -16	___ ⑰ -18	___ ⑱ -40
___ ⑲ 4	___ ⑳ -12	___ ㉑ 93	___ ㉒ -123	___ ㉓ -600	___ ㉔ 900
___ ㉕ 5	___ ㉖ -10	___ ㉗ -99	___ ㉘ -109	___ ㉙ -20	___ ㉚ 999
___ ㉛ -6	___ ㉜ 8	___ ㉝ 96	___ ㉞ -106	___ ㉟ -701	___ ㊱ 800

B Property Number Two
Write "o" beside each number if it is odd or "e" if it is even.

e ① 52	___ ② 780	___ ③ 108	___ ④ 180	___ ⑤ 107	___ ⑥ 447
___ ⑦ 3	___ ⑧ 54	___ ⑨ 102	___ ⑩ 186	___ ⑪ 125	___ ⑫ 79
___ ⑬ 5	___ ⑭ 57	___ ⑮ 56	___ ⑯ 87	___ ⑰ 187	___ ⑱ 663
___ ⑲ 7	___ ⑳ 156	___ ㉑ 32	___ ㉒ 62	___ ㉓ 78	___ ㉔ 80
___ ㉕ 9	___ ㉖ 69	___ ㉗ 42	___ ㉘ 134	___ ㉙ 199	___ ㉚ 689
___ ㉛ 11	___ ㉜ 168	___ ㉝ 15	___ ㉞ 132	___ ㉟ 299	___ ㊱ 82
___ ㊲ 13	___ ㊳ 77	___ ㊴ 27	___ ㊵ 93	___ ㊶ 399	___ ㊷ 84

REMINDER: Write the definition of the set of whole numbers.

_____

_____

Unit 76 cont'd 👉

C Property Number Three
Write "c" beside each number if it is composite, "p" if it is prime, or "z" if it is zero.

_c_ ① 60	___ ② 31	___ ③ 50	___ ④ 61	___ ⑤ 89	___ ⑥ 106
___ ⑦ 19	___ ⑧ 12	___ ⑨ 25	___ ⑩ 97	___ ⑪ 67	___ ⑫ 47
___ ⑬ 0	___ ⑭ 41	___ ⑮ 137	___ ⑯ 107	___ ⑰ 103	___ ⑱ 204
___ ⑲ 139	___ ⑳ 32	___ ㉑ 0	___ ㉒ 113	___ ㉓ 73	___ ㉔ 888

D Property Number Four
Write "c" beside each number if it is cardinal, "o" if it is ordinal, or "r" if it is Roman.

_r_ ① L	___ ② 3rd	___ ③ 32	___ ④ 1st	___ ⑤ 401	___ ⑥ 77
___ ⑦ C	___ ⑧ 11th	___ ⑨ 32nd	___ ⑩ LV	___ ⑪ 61	___ ⑫ 111
___ ⑬ 3	___ ⑭ X	___ ⑮ IV	___ ⑯ 10	___ ⑰ CC	___ ⑱ D
___ ⑲ 7	___ ⑳ 8	___ ㉑ 2nd	___ ㉒ 21	___ ㉓ 5th	___ ㉔ 81st

E Underline the correct answers.

① Six is a (negative, <u>positive</u>, odd, <u>even</u>, <u>composite</u>, prime, <u>cardinal</u>, ordinal, Roman) number.

② Seventeen is a (negative, positive, odd, even, composite, prime, cardinal, ordinal, Roman) number.

③ XXXII is a (negative, positive, odd, even, composite, prime, cardinal, ordinal, Roman) number.

④ The number -703rd is a (negative, positive, odd, even, composite, prime, cardinal, ordinal, Roman) number.

⑤ The number -D is a (negative, positive, odd, even, composite, prime, cardinal, ordinal, Roman) number.

⑥ Four hundred ninety-eight is a (negative, positive, odd, even, composite, prime, cardinal, ordinal, Roman) number.

⑦ Six thousand, three is a (negative, positive, odd, even, composite, prime, cardinal, ordinal, Roman) number.

Properties of Numbers

Learning Objective: *We will learn to identify a number as belonging to a certain property.*

The set of all numbers, if zero is assumed to be the middle point, goes on indefinitely both negatively and positively.

EXAMPLE: There are five properties of all numbers. They delineate if a number is 1) whole, mixed, or fractional; 2) negative or positive; 3) odd or even; 4) composite, prime, or zero; and 5) cardinal, ordinal, or Roman.

A Property Number One
Write "w" beside each number if it is whole, "m" if it is mixed, or "f" if it is fractional.

w ① 2	___ ② 1/2	___ ③ 5 1/3	___ ④ 6	___ ⑤ 7	___ ⑥ 3/4
___ ⑦ 7 1/3	___ ⑧ 91	___ ⑨ 10 1/2	___ ⑩ 87	___ ⑪ 3 1/6	___ ⑫ 8 1/9
___ ⑬ 897	___ ⑭ 21/30	___ ⑮ 73	___ ⑯ 41/50	___ ⑰ 64	___ ⑱ 42/60
___ ⑲ 11/15	___ ⑳ 8 1/9	___ ㉑ 1 1/3	___ ㉒ 900	___ ㉓ 7 2/6	___ ㉔ 3 3/4

B Property Number Two
Write "n" beside each number if it is negative or "p" if it is positive.

n ① -3	___ ② 4	___ ③ -8	___ ④ 16	___ ⑤ -32	___ ⑥ 56
___ ⑦ 201	___ ⑧ -30	___ ⑨ -36	___ ⑩ -78	___ ⑪ -54	___ ⑫ -63
___ ⑬ 7	___ ⑭ 1	___ ⑮ -3	___ ⑯ -24	___ ⑰ 26	___ ⑱ -13
___ ⑲ 63	___ ⑳ 66	___ ㉑ 71	___ ㉒ -72	___ ㉓ -86	___ ㉔ -81

C Property Number Three
Write "o" beside each number if it is odd or "e" if it is even.

o ① 1	___ ② 2	___ ③ 3	___ ④ 4	___ ⑤ 5	___ ⑥ 6
___ ⑦ 10	___ ⑧ 14	___ ⑨ 18	___ ⑩ 20	___ ⑪ 26	___ ⑫ 29
___ ⑬ 56	___ ⑭ 71	___ ⑮ 88	___ ⑯ 92	___ ⑰ 103	___ ⑱ 121
___ ⑲ 55	___ ⑳ 57	___ ㉑ 81	___ ㉒ 107	___ ㉓ 189	___ ㉔ 200

REMINDER: Write the definition of the set of all numbers.

_____

_____

Unit 77 cont'd ☞

D Property Number Four
Write "c" beside each number if it is composite, "p" if it is prime, or "z" if it is zero.

_p_ ① 3   ___ ② 100   ___ ③ 98   ___ ④ 0   ___ ⑤ 51   ___ ⑥ 75

___ ⑦ 60   ___ ⑧ 5   ___ ⑨ 54   ___ ⑩ 7   ___ ⑪ 0   ___ ⑫ 43

___ ⑬ 36   ___ ⑭ 0   ___ ⑮ 32   ___ ⑯ 42   ___ ⑰ 41   ___ ⑱ 25

___ ⑲ 83   ___ ⑳ 131   ___ ㉑ 2   ___ ㉒ 113   ___ ㉓ 55   ___ ㉔ 141

E Property Number Five
Write "c" beside each number if it is cardinal, "o" if it is ordinal, or "r" if it is Roman.

_o_ ① 1st   ___ ② CI   ___ ③ III   ___ ④ 88   ___ ⑤ 55th   ___ ⑥ 3

___ ⑦ L   ___ ⑧ 31st   ___ ⑨ 44th   ___ ⑩ CC   ___ ⑪ 61st   ___ ⑫ IV

___ ⑬ 2nd   ___ ⑭ C   ___ ⑮ 4th   ___ ⑯ 91   ___ ⑰ XX   ___ ⑱ 63

___ ⑲ 3rd   ___ ⑳ 7   ___ ㉑ XV   ___ ㉒ 72   ___ ㉓ 33rd   ___ ㉔ 93

F Underline the correct answers.

① The number -6 1/4 is (whole, <u>mixed</u>, fraction, <u>negative</u>, positive, odd, <u>even</u>, <u>composite</u>, prime, zero, <u>cardinal</u>, ordinal, Roman).

② The number 3 1/9 is (whole, mixed, fraction, negative, positive, odd, even, composite, prime, zero, cardinal, ordinal, Roman).

③ Seventy-four thousand is (whole, mixed, fraction, negative, positive, odd, even, composite, prime, zero, cardinal, ordinal, Roman).

④ CCCIII is (whole, mixed, fraction, negative, positive, odd, even, composite, prime, zero, cardinal, ordinal, Roman).

⑤ The number 2/6 is (whole, mixed, fraction, negative, positive, odd, even, composite, prime, zero, cardinal, ordinal, Roman).

⑥ The number -71 is (whole, mixed, fraction, negative, positive, odd, even, composite, prime, zero, cardinal, ordinal, Roman).

⑦ The number -9 1/9 is (whole, mixed, fraction, negative, positive, odd, even, composite, prime, zero, cardinal, ordinal, Roman).

Percents

Learning Objective: **We will learn to convert to and from percents.**

A percent is a way of writing a fraction that has 100 as a denominator.

EXAMPLES: To write 1/10 as a percent, write it first as a hundredth.

$$\frac{1}{10} = \frac{1 \times 10}{10 \times 10} = \frac{10}{100} = 10\%$$

To write 10% as a fraction, multiply 10 times 1/100.

$$10\% = \overset{1}{\cancel{10}}/1 \times 1/\underset{10}{\cancel{100}} = 1/10$$

A   Convert these fractions to percents.

① $\frac{2}{5} = \frac{2 \times 20}{5 \times 20} = \frac{40}{100} = 40\%$ ② $\frac{3}{50} =$ ③ $\frac{3}{4} =$

④ $\frac{1}{2} =$ ⑤ $\frac{8}{10} =$ ⑥ $\frac{9}{20} =$

⑦ $\frac{7}{25} =$ ⑧ $\frac{4}{20} =$ ⑨ $\frac{6}{10} =$

⑩ $\frac{3}{5} =$ ⑪ $\frac{2}{25} =$ ⑫ $\frac{10}{20} =$

⑬ $\frac{4}{50} =$ ⑭ $\frac{1}{5} =$ ⑮ $\frac{7}{20} =$

B   Convert percents to fractions.

① $6\% = \overset{3}{\cancel{6}}/1 \times 1/\underset{50}{\cancel{100}} = 3/50$ ② $12\% =$ ③ $16\% =$

④ $21\% =$ ⑤ $25\% =$ ⑥ $31\% =$

⑦ $42\% =$ ⑧ $63\% =$ ⑨ $50\% =$

⑩ $35\% =$ ⑪ $49\% =$ ⑫ $72\% =$

⑬ $69\% =$ ⑭ $85\% =$ ⑮ $99\% =$

REMINDER: Write the definition of a percent.

_____

_____

Whole numbers and mixed numbers may be expressed as percents.

$1 = 100\% \left(\dfrac{1 \times 100}{1 \times 100} = \dfrac{100}{100}\right)$ or $(1 \times 100 = 100)$

$1\,1/2 = 150\% \left(\dfrac{3 \times 50}{2 \times 50} = \dfrac{150}{100}\right)$
$3/2 = 150\%$

C Convert to percents.

① $2\,3/5 = \dfrac{13 \times 20}{5 \times 20} = \dfrac{260}{100} = 260\%$

② $8\,3/4 =$

③ $56/20 =$

④ $6\,7/10 =$

⑤ $4 =$

⑥ $9\,8/10 =$

D Convert to whole or mixed numbers.

① $115\% = \overset{23}{\cancel{115}}/1 \times 1/\underset{20}{\cancel{100}} = 23/20 = 1\,3/20$

② $227\% =$

③ $310\% =$

④ $742\% =$

⑤ $456\% =$

⑥ $900\% =$

E Underline the correct answers.

① If thirty percent was expressed as two different fractions, they would be (6/20, 3/100, 3/10) and 30/100.

② Four-tenths is also equal to (four percent, four hundredths, forty percent).

③ In the fraction eighty-one hundredths, (81, 80, 100) would occupy the position of the numerator.

④ Forty-eight percent is equal to (16/20, 12/25, 4/100).

⑤ Fifty-three percent is equal to (100/53, 53/10, 53/100).

⑥ Eleven-twentieths can also be expressed as (20/11, 55/100, 65/100).

⑦ Nine-fiftieths can also be expressed as (19%, 20%, 18%).

⑧ Six percent can also be expressed as (3/50, 6/100, 4/8).

⑨ Five-twenty-fifths can also be expressed as (5/100, 20%, 50/100).

Decimals

Learning Objective: *We will learn to convert to and from decimals.*

A decimal is a way of writing a fraction that has 10; 100; 1,000; 10,000; or another power of 10 as a denominator.

EXAMPLE: To write 1/10 as a decimal, divide the numerator by the denominator.

$$10 \overline{)1.0} \quad \begin{array}{r} .1 \\ \underline{10} \end{array}$$

To write .1 as a fraction, simply write the equivalent common fraction and reduce to lowest terms.

$$.1 = \frac{1}{10} = \frac{1 \div 1}{10 \div 1} = \frac{1}{10}$$

A Convert fractions to decimals.

① 1/5 = **.2**   ② 3/5 =   ③ 4/20 =   ④ 3/6 =   ⑤ 2/4 =

$$5 \overline{)1.0} \quad \begin{array}{r} .2 \end{array}$$

⑥ 1/4 =   ⑦ 3/12 =   ⑧ 3/4 =   ⑨ 8/16 =   ⑩ 6/8 =

B Convert decimals to fractions. Reduce.

① .7 = $\frac{7}{10}$ ② .4 =

③ .64 =   ④ .722 =

⑤ .008 =   ⑥ .90 =

⑦ .0652 =   ⑧ .25 =

⑨ .6 =   ⑩ .48 =

REMINDER: Write the definition of a decimal.

_____

_____

Rounding off is the process of approximating a number to a specific place value. For instance, .153 rounded to the nearest tenth would be .2. To round a number to a certain place value, look at the digit immediately to the right of that place. If the digit is 5 or more, round the number upward. If the digit is less than 5, simply drop that digit as well as all others that follow.

C Convert these fractions to decimals. Round off all answers to the nearest hundredth.

① 6/9 =   ② 2/7 =   ③ 13/21 =   ④ 3/11 =

D Underline the correct answers.

① Written as a decimal, forty-eight thousandths is (.48, .0048, <u>.048</u>).

② Written as a fraction, sixty-one hundredths is (61/100, 61/10, 100/61).

③ The result of .05698 rounded to the nearest ten-thousandth is (.0570, .1660, .1670).

④ When converting a fraction to a decimal, you may add as many (zeroes, tens, ones) to the (left, right) of the decimal point without changing the value of that number.

⑤ In the conversion of a fraction to a decimal, the decimal point in the (dividend, quotient, divisor) should be directly above the decimal point in the (divisor, quotient, dividend).

⑥ Written as a decimal, ninety-nine hundredths is (.99, .099, 9.90).

⑦ Written as a decimal, sixty-five thousandths is (.065, .65, .0065).

⑧ Written as a fraction, four-hundredths is (4/10, 4/100, 4/1,000).

⑨ Written as a fraction, fifty-hundredths is (50/100, 100/50, .050).

⑩ Written as a decimal, thirty-six thousandths is (.36, .036, 3.06).

Percents and Decimals

Learning Objective: *We will learn to convert percents to decimals and decimals to percents.*

A percent is a way of writing a fraction that has 100 as a denominator. A decimal is a way of writing a fraction that has any power of 10 as a denominator.

EXAMPLE: To convert a percent to a decimal, simply drop the percent sign and move the decimal point two places to the left.

$$99\% = .99$$

To convert a decimal to a percent, move the decimal point two places to the right and add a percent sign.

$$.99 = 99\%$$

A Convert these decimals to percents.

① .962 = **96.2%**   ② 2.81 =   ③ .902 =   ④ 6.1 =

⑤ .40 =   ⑥ .604 =   ⑦ 9.005 =   ⑧ 2.85 =

⑨ .635 =   ⑩ .041 =   ⑪ 6.071 =   ⑫ .761 =

⑬ .0961 =   ⑭ .735 =   ⑮ 8.4210 =   ⑯ 4.8 =

⑰ .25 =   ⑱ .3351 =   ⑲ .521 =   ⑳ .864 =

㉑ 1.67 =   ㉒ .0776 =   ㉓ 2.2 =   ㉔ .001 =

B Convert these percents to decimals.

① 86% = **.86**   ② .2% =   ③ 92% =   ④ .005% =

⑤ 927% =   ⑥ .63% =   ⑦ 33.65% =   ⑧ .625% =

⑨ 11.06% =   ⑩ 1.75% =   ⑪ 20% =   ⑫ 1.007% =

⑬ 9.8% =   ⑭ 621.5% =   ⑮ 35% =   ⑯ 92.01% =

⑰ 60.51% =   ⑱ 29.5% =   ⑲ 4.25% =   ⑳ 68.74% =

㉑ .46% =   ㉒ 6.59% =   ㉓ 67.3% =   ㉔ .206% =

㉕ .39% =   ㉖ .84% =   ㉗ 9.99% =   ㉘ .007% =

REMINDER: Write the definition of a percent and a decimal.

_____

_____

Unit 80 cont'd ☞

C Round off each decimal to the nearest hundredth and convert to percent.

① .416 = .42 = 42%

② .0078 =

③ 65.02 =

④ .214 =

⑤ .617 =

⑥ .065 =

⑦ .316 =

⑧ 1.05 =

⑨ .814 =

⑩ .083 =

⑪ .215 =

⑫ .65 =

⑬ .659 =

⑭ 1.67 =

⑮ 6.721 =

⑯ 8.42 =

⑰ .892 =

⑱ 7.025 =

⑲ 8.101 =

⑳ .72 =

㉑ .046 =

㉒ .2821 =

㉓ .0567 =

㉔ 3.63 =

D Underline the correct answers.

① The (fractional, mixed numeral, decimal) equivalent for 25% is 1/4.

② Fractions can be written in forms of (zeroes and prime numbers, percents and decimals, percents and prime numbers).

③ In Hendrikson County, it was reported that .765 of the registered voters actually used the privilege of voting. Rounded to the nearest hundredth, the correct figure of the people voting in Hendrikson County would be (.87, .77, .76) or (77%, 87%, 76%).

④ If 37.4% is converted to a decimal and rounded to the nearest tenth, its fractional equivalent would be (37/100, 4/10, 4/100).

⑤ It was recorded in Hendrikson County that .256% of the households and businesses had smoke alarms. Rounded to the nearest hundredth, the correct figure representing the total amount of smoke alarms in Hendrikson County would be (.35, .45, .26) or (45%, 35%, 26%).

Comprehension Check

Test 16

A Identify each number as being whole (w), mixed (m), fractional (f), negative (n), positive (p), odd (o), or even (e).

_w, p, e_ ① 398   _____ ② 4 1/2   _____ ③ -2/3   _____ ④ 47   _____ ⑤ -93

_____ ⑥ -3 3/9   _____ ⑦ 52 17/18   _____ ⑧ -60   _____ ⑨ -75   _____ ⑩ -80 1/2

_____ ⑪ 7/8   _____ ⑫ 480   _____ ⑬ 9/10   _____ ⑭ -3/5   _____ ⑮ 92 1/8

B Identify each number as being composite (c), prime (p), zero (z), cardinal (k), ordinal (o), or Roman (r).

_p, o_ ① 5th   _____ ② 8th   _____ ③ D   _____ ④ CII   _____ ⑤ 76

_____ ⑥ CC   _____ ⑦ II   _____ ⑧ VI   _____ ⑨ 17th   _____ ⑩ 92

_____ ⑪ 26   _____ ⑫ 201   _____ ⑬ 43rd   _____ ⑭ CVI   _____ ⑮ L

C Convert fractions to percents.

① $\dfrac{3}{5} = \dfrac{3 \times 20}{5 \times 20} = \dfrac{60}{100} = 60\%$ ② $\dfrac{4}{50} =$ ③ $\dfrac{6}{25} =$

④ $\dfrac{1}{2} =$ ⑤ $\dfrac{3}{4} =$ ⑥ $\dfrac{1}{5} =$

D Convert percents to fractions.

① $12\% = \overset{3}{\cancel{12}}/1 \times 1/\underset{25}{\cancel{100}} = 3/25$ ② $68\% =$ ③ $44\% =$

④ $15\% =$ ⑤ $30\% =$ ⑥ $55\% =$

E Convert mixed numbers to percents.

① $5\ 3/4 = \dfrac{23 \times 25}{4 \times 25} = \dfrac{575}{100} = 575\%$ ② $4\ 2/20 =$ ③ $1\ 2/5 =$

④ $7\ 1/10 =$ ⑤ $3\ 6/10 =$ ⑥ $2\ 1/5 =$

F Convert to whole or mixed numbers.

① $116\% = \overset{29}{\cancel{116}}/1 \times 1/\underset{25}{\cancel{100}} = 29/25 = 1\ 4/25$ ② $130\% =$

③ $200\% =$ ④ $360\% =$

⑤ $250\% =$ ⑥ $420\% =$

Test 16 cont'd ☞

G Convert decimals to fractions.

① $.075 = \dfrac{75}{1,000} = \dfrac{75 \div 25}{1,000 \div 25} = \dfrac{3}{40}$

② $.654 =$

③ $.82 =$

④ $.64 =$

⑤ $.4 =$

⑥ $.70 =$

H Convert decimals to percents.

① $1.23 = 123\%$　　② $0.12 =$　　③ $.001 =$　　④ $.051 =$

⑤ $79.3 =$　　⑥ $86.12 =$　　⑦ $2.001 =$　　⑧ $2.012 =$

I Convert percents to decimals.

① $50\% = .5$　　② $72\% =$　　③ $31.3\% =$　　④ $5.09\% =$

⑤ $201\% =$　　⑥ $3.19\% =$　　⑦ $100\% =$　　⑧ $1\% =$

J Round off each decimal to the nearest hundredth and convert to a percent.

① $.516 = .52 = 52\%$　　② $1.99 =$　　③ $.78 =$

④ $.479 =$　　⑤ $.39 =$　　⑥ $.89 =$

Define.

① whole numbers _____

② mixed number _____

③ fraction _____

④ negative or positive number _____
_____

⑤ odd or even number _____
_____

⑥ composite number _____

⑦ prime number _____

⑧ cardinal number _____

⑨ ordinal number _____

⑩ Roman number _____

⑪ decimal _____

⑫ percent _____

Factors

Learning Objective: *We will learn to find factors.*

A factor is a multiplier that, when multiplied with another factor, forms a product.

EXAMPLES: Factors must be whole numbers.
2, 4, 5, and 10 are factors of 20.
Factors of 20 also include
20 and 1.

A Study each factor tree and list all factors of a given number. Do not forget the number and 1 as factors.

①   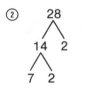

18: *1, 2, 3, 6,*
    9, 18

②

28: _____
_____

③

30: _____
_____

④

36: _____
_____

⑤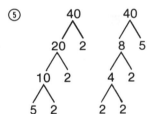

40: _____
_____

⑥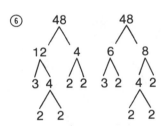

48: _____
_____

⑦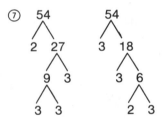

54: _____
_____

⑧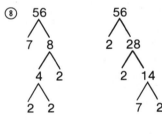

56: _____
_____

⑨

12: _____
_____

⑩

20: _____
_____

⑪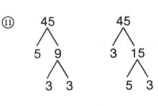

45: _____
_____

⑫

50: _____
_____

REMINDER: *Write the definition of a factor.*

_____
_____

   Unit 81 cont'd

B Complete each factor tree and list all the prime factors of a given number.

①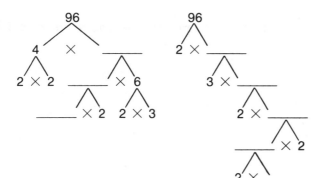

24: **2, 3** _____

②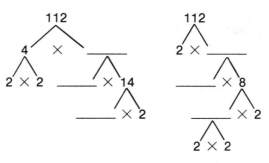

140: _____

③

96: _____

④

112: _____

⑤

64: _____

⑥

80: _____

C Underline the correct answers.

① The prime factors of (70, 35, 8) are 2, 5, and 7.

② The prime factors of 76 are (2, 19 ; 3, 13; 5, 15).

③ The prime factors of (28, 46, 73) are 2 and 7.

④ The prime factors of 88 are (2, 11 ; 3, 7; 3, 11).

⑤ The prime factors of (50, 26, 78) are 2 and 5.

⑥ The prime factors of 42 are (2, 3, 7 ; 2, 5, 7; 2, 11, 13).

⑦ The prime factors of (99, 109, 119) are 3 and 11.

⑧ The prime factors of 315 are (5, 11; 9, 13; 3, 5, 7).

⑨ The prime factors of (45, 65, 75) are 3 and 5.

⑩ The prime factors of 99 are (2, 5; 3, 11 ; 3, 5, 7).

Prime Factors   Unit 82

Learning
Objective: *We will learn to write prime factorizations.*

A prime factorization shows a number as the product of its prime factors.

EXAMPLE:
The prime factors of 20 are 2, 5.

$$\begin{array}{r} 10 \\ 2\overline{)20} \end{array} \qquad \begin{array}{r} ⑤ \\ 2\overline{)10} \end{array}$$

The prime factorization of 20 is $20 = 5 \times 2 \times 2$.

A Write a prime factorization of each number.

① 62: 2×31 _____   ② 25: _____   ③ 84: _____   ④ 57: _____

$$\begin{array}{r} 31 \\ 2\overline{)62} \end{array}$$

⑤ 21: _____   ⑥ 62: _____   ⑦ 11: _____   ⑧ 34: _____

⑨ 42: _____   ⑩ 78: _____   ⑪ 99: _____   ⑫ 95: _____

⑬ 107: _____   ⑭ 182: _____   ⑮ 164: _____   ⑯ 155: _____

⑰ 218: _____   ⑱ 220: _____   ⑲ 248: _____   ⑳ 278: _____

㉑ 315: _____   ㉒ 345: _____   ㉓ 783: _____   ㉔ 390: _____

REMINDER: Write the definition of a prime factorization.

_____

_____

B Write a factor tree for each problem. Write the prime factorizations.

① 64: _2 × 2 × 2 ×_   ② 76: _____   ③ 100: _____   ④ 150: _____

_2 × 2 × 2_   _____   _____   _____

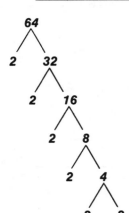

⑤ 84: _____   ⑥ 95: _____   ⑦ 220: _____   ⑧ 108: _____

_____   _____   _____   _____

C True or False

___t___ ① The prime factors of 171 are 3, 3, and 19.   _____ ⑥ The prime factors of 205 are 5 and 41.

_____ ② The prime factors of 16 are 2, 2, 2, and 2.   _____ ⑦ The prime factors of 92 are 2, 2, and 23.

_____ ③ The prime factors of 68 are 2, 2, 2, and 17.   _____ ⑧ The prime factors of 153 are 3, 3, 17, and 17.

_____ ④ The prime factors of 81 are 3, 3, and 3.   _____ ⑨ The prime factors of 335 are 5 and 67.

_____ ⑤ The prime factors of 45 are 3 and 5.   _____ ⑩ The prime factors of 189 are 3, 3, 3, and 7.

Common Factors

Learning Objective: *We will learn to find common factors.*

The largest common factor that is shared by two or more numbers is called the greatest common factor, or GCF.

EXAMPLES:
The common factors of 15 and 30 are 15, 5, 3, and 1. The greatest common factor of 15 and 30 is 15.

  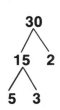 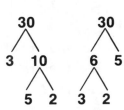

A Study each factor tree, and list all the factors of a given number. Circle the common factors of a and b and draw a square around the GCF.

(a)	(b)	(a)	(b)

①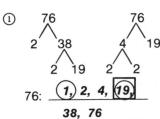
76: ①, 2, 4, ⑲, 38, 76

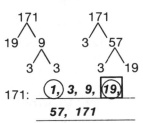
171: ①, 3, 9, ⑲, 57, 171

②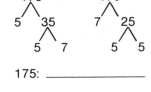
98: _____

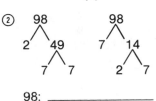
175: _____

(a)	(b)	(a)	(b)

③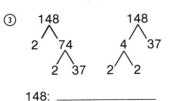
148: _____

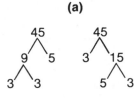
124: _____

④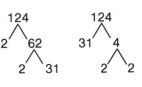
45: _____

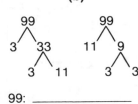
99: _____

(a)	(b)	(a)	(b)

⑤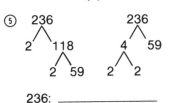
236: _____

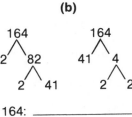
164: _____

⑥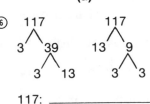
117: _____

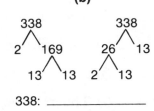
338: _____

REMINDER: Write the definition of the greatest common factor.

_____

_____

Unit 83 cont'd ☛

B List the common factors. Circle the GCF.

① A = factors of 18
B = factors of 24
A = {1, 2, 3, 6, 9, 18}
B = {1, 2, 3, 4, 6, 8, 12, 24}
A ∩ B = _1, 2, 3,⑥_____

② A = factors of 42
B = factors of 36
A = {1, 2, 3, 6, 7, 14, 21, 42}
B = {1, 2, 3, 4, 6, 9, 12, 18, 36}
A ∩ B = _____

③ A = factors of 64
B = factors of 32
A = {1, 2, 4, 8, 16, 32, 64}
B = {1, 2, 4, 8, 16, 32}
A ∩ B = _____

④ A = factors of 45
B = factors of 63
A = {1, 3, 5, 9, 15, 45}
B = {1, 3, 7, 9, 21, 63}
A ∩ B = _____

⑤ A = factors of 28
B = factors of 72
A = {1, 2, 4, 7, 14, 28}
B = {1, 2, 3, 4, 6, 8, 9, 12, 18, 24, 72}
A ∩ B = _____

⑥ A = factors of 30
B = factors of 150
A = {1, 2, 3, 5, 6, 10, 15, 30}
B = {1, 2, 3, 5, 6, 10, 15, 25, 30, 50, 75, 150}
A ∩ B = _____

⑦ A = factors of 54
B = factors of 81
A = {1, 2, 3, 6, 9, 18, 27, 54}
B = {1, 3, 9, 27, 81}
A ∩ B = _____

⑧ A = factors of 10
B = factors of 35
A = {1, 2, 5, 10}
B = {1, 5, 7, 35}
A ∩ B = _____

C True or False

__f__ ① All even numbers share at least one and three as common factors.

_____ ② Both prime and composite numbers share one as a common factor.

_____ ③ Factor trees show only prime numbers of a given number.

_____ ④ There are at least two prime numbers in all factor trees.

_____ ⑤ All multiples of nine share one and nine as common factors.

_____ ⑥ Any factor that is divisible only by one and itself is prime.

_____ ⑦ The greatest common factor of 325 and 245 is 7.

_____ ⑧ The greatest common factor of 148 and 175 is 1.

_____ ⑨ The greatest common factor of 12 and 18 is 6.

_____ ⑩ The greatest common factor of 49 and 77 is 7.

_____ ⑪ The greatest common factor of 35 and 33 is 1.

Finding Missing Factors

Learning Objective: *We will learn to find missing factors.*

A factor is a multiplier that, when multiplied with another factor, forms a product.

EXAMPLE:

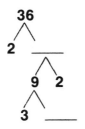

36
2 / ___
9 2
3 ___

There are two missing factors on this factor tree. To find the missing factors, divide 36 by 2. The answer is 18. To find the other missing factor, divide 9 by 3. The answer is 3.

A Find each of the missing factors.

① 49
7 7

7) 49
  7

② 50
5 ___
   5 2

③ 64
8   ___
2 4   2 4
   2 2 2 2

④ 144
2 ___
  2 ___
    ___ 6
   3 2 3 2

⑤ 368
2 184
  2 ___
    2 ___
      ___ 2

⑥ 788
2 ___
  2 ___

⑦ 565
5 ___

⑧ 705
5 ___
  3 ___

⑨ 666

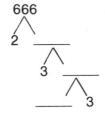

2 ___
  3 ___
    ___ 3

REMINDER: Write the definition of a factor.

_____

_____

Unit 84 cont'd ☞

B Find each missing factor and write a prime factorization.

① 1,000

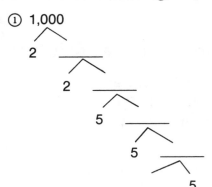

② 368

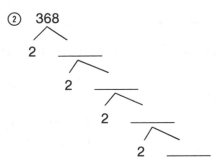

1,000: _____

368: _____

③ 664

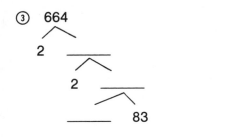

④ 560

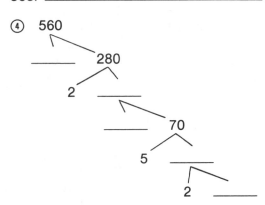

664: _____

560: _____

C Find the missing factors.

① Seven times _____*two*_____ equals fourteen, _____ times five equals seventy, seventy times _____ equals one hundred forty, and one hundred forty times five equals _____ . The number being factored is
_____ .

② The number _____ is being factored. _____ times two equals _____ , six times two equals _____ , twelve times _____ equals _____ .

③ _____ divided by seventy-two equals _____ , seventy-two divided by _____ equals eight, twelve divided by _____ equals six, eight divided by _____ equals two, nine divided by _____ equals three, six divided by _____ equals two. The number being factored is _____ .

④ The number _____ is being factored. Eight hundred eighty-two divided by _____ equals twenty-one. Twenty-one divided by seven equals _____ . _____ divided by six equals seven. _____ divided by three equals two.

Factoring

Learning Objective: *We will learn to find prime factors.*

Factoring is the process of finding the prime factors of a number.

EXAMPLE:

To factor a number, divide by the smallest prime factor. Divide this quotient by its smallest prime factor. Repeat this process until the quotient obtained is a prime number. The prime factors of 60 are 2, 3, and 5.

$$3 \overline{)60} \quad \overset{20}{} \qquad 2 \overline{)20} \quad \overset{10}{} \qquad 2 \overline{)10} \quad \overset{5}{}$$

Three clues to easier factoring are ① 2 is the smallest prime factor of all even numbers; ② if the sum of an odd number's digits is divisible by 3, then 3 is the smallest prime factor of that number; and ③ if the number ends with the digit 5 and is not a multiple of 3, then 5 is the smallest prime factor of that number.

A Using repeated division, factor the following numbers. List the prime factors beside each number.

① 42: __2, 3, 7__   ② 74: _____   ③ 63: _____   ④ 70: _____

$$2 \overline{)42} \quad \overset{21}{} \qquad 3 \overline{)21} \quad \overset{7}{}$$

⑤ 10: _____   ⑥ 24: _____   ⑦ 28: _____   ⑧ 26: _____

⑨ 129: _____   ⑩ 35: _____   ⑪ 54: _____   ⑫ 102: _____

⑬ 18: _____   ⑭ 84: _____   ⑮ 132: _____   ⑯ 38: _____

The 10 smallest prime factors are 2, 3, 5, 7, 11, 13, 17, 19, 23, and 29.

REMINDER: Write the definition of factoring.

_____

_____

Unit 85 cont'd ☞

B Determine the smallest prime factor for each of the following numbers.

_2_ ① 36   _____ ⑯ 652   _____ ㉛ 136   _____ ㊻ 265

_____ ② 363   _____ ⑰ 345   _____ ㉜ 705   _____ ㊼ 65

_____ ③ 623   _____ ⑱ 161   _____ ㉝ 375   _____ ㊽ 933

_____ ④ 407   _____ ⑲ 566   _____ ㉞ 46   _____ ㊾ 112

_____ ⑤ 856   _____ ⑳ 444   _____ ㉟ 253   _____ ㊿ 168

_____ ⑥ 742   _____ ㉑ 52   _____ ㊱ 486   _____ ⑤ 399

_____ ⑦ 205   _____ ㉒ 534   _____ ㊲ 287   _____ ⑤ 679

_____ ⑧ 55   _____ ㉓ 148   _____ ㊳ 478   _____ ⑤ 200

_____ ⑨ 247   _____ ㉔ 143   _____ ㊴ 35   _____ ⑤ 69

_____ ⑩ 485   _____ ㉕ 788   _____ ㊵ 435   _____ ⑤ 678

_____ ⑪ 855   _____ ㉖ 915   _____ ㊶ 74   _____ ⑤ 342

_____ ⑫ 198   _____ ㉗ 895   _____ ㊷ 665   _____ ⑤ 741

_____ ⑬ 391   _____ ㉘ 82   _____ ㊸ 415   _____ ⑤ 325

_____ ⑭ 261   _____ ㉙ 968   _____ ㊹ 261   _____ ⑤ 979

_____ ⑮ 187   _____ ㉚ 722   _____ ㊺ 314   _____ ⑥ 777

C True or False

_t_ ① The prime factors of 70 are 2, 5, and 7.   _____ ⑥ The prime factors of 342 are 2, 3, and 5.

_____ ② The prime factors of 68 are 2 and 17.   _____ ⑦ The prime factors of 620 are 2, 5, and 31.

_____ ③ The prime factors of 86 are 2 and 43.   _____ ⑧ The prime factors of 448 are 2 and 7.

_____ ④ The prime factors of 124 are 2 and 31.   _____ ⑨ The prime factors of 584 are 2 and 37.

_____ ⑤ The prime factors of 74 are 2 and 37.   _____ ⑩ The prime factors of 385 are 5, 7, and 11.

A Study the factor trees and list all the factors of a given number.

① 45
5 9
3 3

② 64
8   8
4 2   2 4
2 2   2 2

③ 120
2 60
2 30
2 15

④ 105
3 35
5 7

⑤ 210
2 105
5 21
3 7

45: **1, 3, 5,**
    9, 45

64: _____

120: _____

105: _____

210: _____

⑥ 50
5 10
2 5

⑦ 46
2 23

⑧ 95
5 19

⑨ 25
5 5

⑩ 36
2 18
9 2
3 3

50: _____

46: _____

95: _____

25: _____

36: _____

B Write a prime factorization of each number.

① 34
2 17

② 38
2 19

③ 142
71 2

④ 102
2 51

⑤ 131
1 131

⑥ 62
31 2

34: **2 × 17**

38: _____

142: _____

102: _____

131: _____

62: _____

⑦ 66
2 33
3 11

⑧ 75
5 15
3 5

⑨ 158
2 79

⑩ 92
2 46
2 23

⑪ 130
2 65
5 13

⑫ 68
2 34
2 17

66: _____

75: _____

158: _____

92: _____

130: _____

68: _____

C Find the missing factors.

① 56
2 _____
    2 _____
        2 _____

② 78
2 _____
    3 _____

Test 17 cont'd

D Study each factor tree and list all factors of a given number. Circle the common factors of a and b and draw a square around the GCF.

(a)

①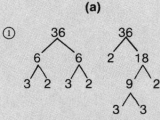

36: ①, ②, ③, 6,
9, 18, 36

(b)

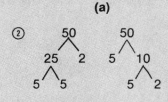

42: _____

_____

(a)

②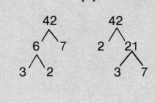

50: _____

(b)

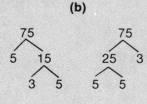

75: _____

_____

(a)

③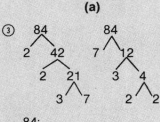

84: _____

_____

(b)

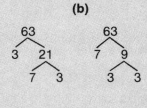

63: _____

_____

(a)

④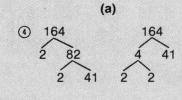

164: _____

_____

(b)

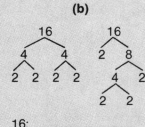

16: _____

_____

E Find the prime factors of each number.

① 45: _3, 5, 9_

$$5\overline{)45} \quad \overset{9}{} \qquad 3\overline{)9} \quad \overset{3}{}$$

② 73: _____

③ 102: _____

④ 56: _____

⑤ 38: _____

⑥ 123: _____

⑦ 12: _____

⑧ 47: _____

Define.

① prime factorization _____

_____

② greatest common factor _____

_____

③ factor _____

_____

④ factoring _____

_____

Writing Equations

Learning Objective: *We will learn to write and solve simple equations of addition and subtraction.*

An equation is a mathematical sentence. Both sides of an equation are equal.

EXAMPLE:

$x = 10$

In math, letters represent unknown numbers. Here the letter "x" represents the number 10.

$10 = 10$

$a = 2$

Here the letter "a" represents the number 2.

$2 = 2$

A Show how both sides of an equation are equal.

① $x = 11$ ② $b = 7$ ③ $y = 20$ ④ $d = 1$ ⑤ $c = 30$

$11 = 11$

⑥ $a = 18$ ⑦ $z = 99$ ⑧ $n = 5$ ⑨ $r = 25$ ⑩ $x = 50$

$x + 2 = 10$ How do you solve for x?

To solve this equation, remember that you must do the same to each side of the equation. If we subtract 2 from each side, we leave the x on the left.

$x + 2 - 2 = 10 - 2$

$x = 8$

To check the problem, substitute 8 for x. $8 + 2 = 10$

B Solve for x. Then check each problem.

① $x + 1 = 7$ ② $x + 10 = 15$ ③ $x + 0 = 11$ ④ $x + 3 = 9$

$x + 1 - 1 = 7 - 1$

$x = 6$

$6 + 1 = 7$

⑤ $x + 20 = 25$ ⑥ $x + 2 = 12$ ⑦ $x + 6 = 19$ ⑧ $x + 50 = 100$

REMINDER: Write the definition of an equation.

_____

_____

Unit 86 cont'd ☞

$$x - 3 = 11 \qquad \text{How do you solve for x?}$$

To solve this equation, remember that you must do the same to each side of the equation. If we add 3 to each side, we leave the x on the left.

$$x - 3 + 3 = 11 + 3$$
$$x = 14$$

To check the problem, substitute 14 for x. $14 - 3 = 11$

C Solve for x. Then check each problem.

① $x - 4 = 3$
  $x - 4 + 4 = 3 + 4$
  $x = 7$

  $7 - 4 = 3$

② $x - 2 = 8$

③ $x - 6 = 6$

④ $x - 10 = 1$

⑤ $x - 5 = 10$

⑥ $x - 1 = 17$

⑦ $x - 0 = 2$

⑧ $x - 7 = 14$

D Work the problems.

① Kate and Alex sold 22 magazine subscriptions. Kate sold 12. How many did Alex sell?

② There are 19 cars on Phil's Car Lot. Twelve of them are blue. The others are white. How many white cars are on the lot?

③ Warren works 40 hours per week. Fourteen hours are spent at the car wash. The rest are spent at Giant Food Market. How many hours does Warren work at the market?

④ David collected 47 stamps. Twenty of them were from Europe. How many stamps were from places other than Europe?

Solving Equations

Learning Objective: *We will learn to write and solve simple equations of multiplication and division.*

An equation is a mathematical sentence. Both sides of an equation are equal.

$2x = 10$ How do you solve for x?

To solve this equation, first remember that when a number is written beside a letter, the operation is multiplication. Here 2x means "two times x."

In order to solve the equation, we must divide each side of the equation by 2. This leaves x on the left.

$$\frac{2x}{2} = \frac{10}{2}$$

$$x = 5$$

To check the problem, substitute 5 for x. $2 \times 5 = 10$

A Solve for x. Then check each problem.

① $3x = 9$ ② $5x = 20$ ③ $2x = 14$ ④ $6x = 30$

$$\frac{3x}{3} = \frac{9}{3}$$
$$x = 3$$

$3 \times 3 = 9$

⑤ $1x = 11$ ⑥ $4x = 28$ ⑦ $8x = 16$ ⑧ $10x = 40$

⑨ $7x = 49$ ⑩ $12x = 144$ ⑪ $9x = 45$ ⑫ $13x = 26$

REMINDER: *Write the definition of an equation.*

Unit 87 cont'd ☛

$$\frac{x}{2} = 12 \qquad \text{How do you solve for x?}$$

This equation states that x divided by 2 equals 12. To solve for x, we must multiply each side of the equation by 2. This leaves x on the left.

$$2 \cdot \frac{x}{2} = 12 \cdot 2$$

$$x = 24$$

To check the problem, substitute 24 for x. $\qquad 24 \div 2 = 12$

B Solve for x. Then check each problem.

① $\dfrac{x}{3} = 3$ ② $\dfrac{x}{5} = 4$ ③ $\dfrac{x}{4} = 7$ ④ $\dfrac{x}{2} = 10$

$$3 \cdot \frac{x}{3} = 3 \cdot 3$$

$$x = 9$$

$$\frac{9}{3} = 3$$

⑤ $\dfrac{x}{10} = 5$ ⑥ $\dfrac{x}{6} = 8$ ⑦ $\dfrac{x}{3} = 9$ ⑧ $\dfrac{x}{7} = 7$

C Work the problems.

① Fran and Jill sold 20 boxes of candy. Fran sold half of the total. How many boxes did Jill sell?

② John must deliver 25 crates of oranges in 5 weeks. If he delivers an equal number per week, how many does he deliver in a week?

③ Five people each must bring 6 pencils. How many pencils will all five bring?

④ Nine students each worked 3 days in March. How many days did all 9 work?

Parentheses and Brackets Unit 88

Learning Objective: *We will learn how parentheses and brackets are used in equations.*

Parentheses ( ) and brackets [ ] enclose quantities. You should work the operations inside the parentheses or brackets first.

$$2 + (6 + 3) = 11$$
First add 6 plus 3. Then add the 9 to 2.
$$2 + 9 = 11$$

$$x + (4 + 1) = 14$$
First add 4 plus 1. Then solve for x.
$$x + 5 = 14$$
$$x + 5 - 5 = 14 - 5$$
$$x = 9$$

A Solve each equation.

① $3 + (5 + 2) = 10$
  $3 + 7 = 10$
  $10 = 10$

② $x + (2 + 8) = 15$

③ $x + (1 + 7) = 13$

④ $10 + (4 + 4) = 18$

⑤ $x + (7 - 4) = 9$

⑥ $x - (6 + 1) = 2$

⑦ $[3 + 5] + 2 = 10$

⑧ $12 - [6 - 1] = 7$

⑨ $x - (11 - 4) = 8$

⑩ $x - (20 - 10) = 3$

⑪ $x + (9 - 1) = 11$

⑫ $x + (4 + 2) = 26$

When both parentheses and brackets are used in the same problem, work the inside of the problem first.

$$1 + [6 + (4 + 6)] = 17 \qquad 1 + [6 + 10] = 17 \qquad 1 + 16 = 17$$

B Work the problems.

① $x + [2 + (3 + 5)] = 12$

② $x - [17 - (6 - 4)] = 5$

③ $x + [20 - (1 + 4)] = 30$

REMINDER: Write the definitions of parentheses and brackets.

_____

_____

Unit 88 cont'd ☛

C Work the problems. Check your answers.

① $x + [11 + (7 + 2)] = 50$
$x + [11 + 9] = 50$
$x + 20 = 50$
$x + 20 - 20 = 50 - 20$
$x = 30$

$30 + [11 + (7 + 2)] = 50$
$30 + [11 + 9] = 50$
$30 + 20 = 50$
$50 = 50$

② $x - [9 + (12 - 10)] = 6$

③ $x + [30 - (8 + 1)] = 31$

④ $x(6 + 6) = 24$

⑤ $\dfrac{(9 + 21)}{5} = 6$

⑥ $\dfrac{(x + 4)}{2} = 7$

⑦ $x + [13 - (6 - 0)] = 20$

⑧ $x - [14 + (5 + 3)] = 8$

⑨ $x(14 - 11) = 39$

⑩ $\dfrac{(x - 10)}{5} = 4$

⑪ $x(21 - 17) = 28$

Four Basic Operations   Unit 89

Learning Objective: *We will learn to solve equations.*

Addition, subtraction, multiplication, and division are the four basic operations.

EXAMPLE:

a.
$$x + 1 = 4$$
$$x + 1 - 1 = 4 - 1$$
$$x = 3$$

b.
$$x - 2 = 4$$
$$x - 2 + 2 = 4 + 2$$
$$x = 6$$

c.
$$\frac{3x}{3} = \frac{30}{3}$$
$$x = 10$$

d.
$$\frac{x}{2} = 11$$
$$2 \cdot \frac{x}{2} = 11 \cdot 2$$
$$x = 22$$

A Solve these equations.

① $x + 10 = 67$
$$x + 10 - 10 = 67 - 10$$
$$x = 57$$

② $x - 19 = 10$

③ $4x = 36$

④ $\dfrac{x}{4} = 3$

⑤ $x + 9 = 17$

⑥ $x - 8 = 4$

⑦ $5x = 75$

⑧ $\dfrac{x}{10} = 10$

⑨ $x + 23 = 40$

⑩ $x - 16 = 39$

⑪ $7x = 77$

⑫ $\dfrac{x}{3} = 33$

⑬ $x + 30 = 70$

⑭ $x - 6 = 42$

⑮ $14x = 56$

⑯ $\dfrac{x}{8} = 64$

⑰ $x + 13 = 51$

⑱ $x - 24 = 50$

⑲ $12x = 60$

⑳ $\dfrac{x}{2} = 500$

REMINDER: What are the four basic operations?

_____

_____

215   **Unit 89 cont'd** 👉

B Solve for x.

① $x + 12 = 20$

$x + 12 - 12 = 20 - 12$

$x = 8$

② $x - 40 = 10$

③ $2x = 28$

④ $\dfrac{x}{4} = 4$

⑤ $x + 18 = 22$

⑥ $x - 15 = 14$

⑦ $5x = 100$

⑧ $\dfrac{x}{2} = 13$

⑨ $x + 31 = 60$

⑩ $x - 3 = 40$

⑪ $3x = 90$

⑫ $\dfrac{x}{5} = 12$

⑬ $x + 16 = 29$

⑭ $x - 1 = 50$

⑮ $10x = 70$

⑯ $\dfrac{x}{3} = 10$

C Work the problems.

① Cassie turned in 12 pages of notes. She and Jeff had a total of 25 pages. How many pages did Jeff turn in?

② Rita collected 10 cans of food. Ann collected food too for a total of 31 cans. How many cans did Ann collect?

③ Susan read 15 books last year. She and Blakely read 27 books together. How many books did Blakely read last year?

④ Ted's group took 16 minutes for the poetry presentation. Ms. Owens took the remainder of the 30 minutes for questions. How long did Ms. Owens talk?

Practice with Equations

Learning Objective: *We will practice solving equations.*

An equation is a mathematical sentence. Both sides of an equation are equal.

EXAMPLE: Study these two mathematical sentences in which x equals two.

$$\text{(a)} \quad x + 6 = 8 \qquad \text{(b)} \quad x + 8 = 9$$

Statement a is an equation because, if x equals two, two plus six equals 8. Statement b is not an equation because, if x equals two, two plus eight does not equal nine.

A Place a check (✓) beside each equation. Let x equal five.

✓ ① $x + 6 = 11$ ___ ② $x + 9 = 12$ ___ ③ $x + 5 = 10$ ___ ④ $x + 11 = 16$
    5 + 6 = 11
      11 = 11

___ ⑤ $x - 0 = 4$ ___ ⑥ $x - 1 = 4$ ___ ⑦ $x - 4 = 1$ ___ ⑧ $x - 7 = 3$

___ ⑨ $2x = 10$ ___ ⑩ $3x = 20$ ___ ⑪ $10x = 50$ ___ ⑫ $7x = 35$

___ ⑬ $\dfrac{x}{1} = 5$ ___ ⑭ $\dfrac{x}{2} = 2.5$ ___ ⑮ $\dfrac{x}{3} = 6$ ___ ⑯ $\dfrac{x}{10} = 2$

___ ⑰ $x + 20 = 25$ ___ ⑱ $x + 7 = 12$ ___ ⑲ $x - 5 = 0$ ___ ⑳ $x - 2 = 3$

___ ㉑ $x + 95 = 100$ ___ ㉒ $11x = 55$ ___ ㉓ $x + 13 = 20$ ___ ㉔ $x + 42 = 47$

REMINDER: Write the definition of an equation.

_____

_____

Unit 90 cont'd ☞

B Solve these equations.

① $x + 8 = 17$
$x + 8 - 8 = 17 - 8$
$x = 9$

② $x - 30 = 40$

③ $3x = 42$

④ $\dfrac{x}{2} = 90$

⑤ $x + 70 = 100$

⑥ $x - 10 = 55$

⑦ $4x = 44$

⑧ $\dfrac{x}{5} = 25$

⑨ $x + 12 = 31$

⑩ $x - 6 = 48$

⑪ $5x = 90$

⑫ $\dfrac{x}{10} = 10$

⑬ $x + 29 = 50$

⑭ $x - 18 = 63$

⑮ $10x = 1{,}000$

⑯ $\dfrac{x}{4} = 3$

C Solve these equations. Remember to work problems inside parentheses and brackets first.

① $x + [7 + 8] = 41$
$x + 15 = 41$
$x + 15 - 15 = 41 - 15$
$x = 26$

② $x - (32 + 8) = 60$

③ $x + [25 - 10] = 17$

④ $x + [2 + (1 + 8)] = 30$

⑤ $x - [21 - (8 - 6)] = 60$

⑥ $x + [12 + (6 - 1)] = 24$

⑦ $x(100 - 50) = 450$

⑧ $x(17 + 1) = 90$

⑨ $x(10 + 2) = 24$

Comprehension Check

A Solve these addition equations.

① $x + 10 = 13$

$x + 10 - 10 = 13 - 10$

$x = 3$

② $x + 7 = 15$

③ $x + 3 = 10$

④ $x + 9 = 20$

⑤ $x + 6 = 26$

⑥ $x + 2 = 18$

⑦ $x + 1 = 30$

⑧ $x + 17 = 22$

⑨ $x + 21 = 50$

⑩ $x + 12 = 24$

⑪ $x + 50 = 60$

⑫ $x + 4 = 34$

B Solve these subtraction equations.

① $x - 6 = 13$

$x - 6 + 6 = 13 + 6$

$x = 19$

② $x - 10 = 25$

③ $x - 20 = 5$

④ $x - 19 = 1$

⑤ $x - 2 = 28$

⑥ $x - 12 = 13$

⑦ $x - 36 = 70$

⑧ $x - 41 = 59$

⑨ $x - 29 = 10$

⑩ $x - 3 = 40$

⑪ $x - 14 = 4$

⑫ $x - 99 = 2$

C Solve the multiplication equations.

① $\dfrac{6x}{6} = \dfrac{30}{6}$

$x = 5$

② $\dfrac{5x}{} = \dfrac{100}{}$

③ $\dfrac{2x}{} = \dfrac{42}{}$

④ $\dfrac{7x}{} = \dfrac{56}{}$

⑤ $\dfrac{10x}{} = \dfrac{80}{}$

⑥ $\dfrac{8x}{} = \dfrac{72}{}$

⑦ $\dfrac{12x}{} = \dfrac{36}{}$

⑧ $\dfrac{3x}{} = \dfrac{66}{}$

⑨ $\dfrac{4x}{} = \dfrac{100}{}$

⑩ $\dfrac{100x}{} = \dfrac{500}{}$

⑪ $\dfrac{50x}{} = \dfrac{150}{}$

⑫ $\dfrac{15x}{} = \dfrac{75}{}$

Test 18 cont'd ☞

D Solve these division equations.

① $\dfrac{x}{3} = 10$ 　　② $\dfrac{x}{2} = 50$ 　　③ $\dfrac{x}{5} = 1$ 　　④ $\dfrac{x}{3} = 9$

$3 \cdot \dfrac{x}{3} = 10 \cdot 3$

$x = 30$

⑤ $\dfrac{x}{7} = 63$ 　　⑥ $\dfrac{x}{9} = 81$ 　　⑦ $\dfrac{x}{4} = 3$ 　　⑧ $\dfrac{x}{6} = 5$

⑨ $\dfrac{x}{5} = 10$ 　　⑩ $\dfrac{x}{10} = 9$ 　　⑪ $\dfrac{x}{2} = 14$ 　　⑫ $\dfrac{x}{11} = 6$

E Place a check (✓) beside each equation. Let x equal 10.

✓ ① $x + 5 = 15$ 　　___ ② $x - 2 = 8$ 　　___ ③ $5x = 40$ 　　___ ④ $\dfrac{x}{5} = 2$

$10 + 5 = 15$

$15 = 15$

___ ⑤ $x + 1 = 12$ 　　___ ⑥ $x - 1 = 9$ 　　___ ⑦ $10x = 100$ 　　___ ⑧ $\dfrac{x}{1} = 10$

Write a short paragraph which defines an equation as a mathematical sentence.

_____

_____

_____

_____

_____

_____

Measuring Time

Learning Objective: *We will learn to measure time.*

Time may be a second, minute, hour, day, week, month, year, decade, or century. Time may be measured by a clock or calendar.

EXAMPLES: Clocks measure the seconds, minutes, and hours that occur within 12-hour periods known as a.m. (ante meridian) and p.m. (post meridian).

Calendars measure the days, weeks, and months that are required for the earth to complete a revolution around the sun (1 year).

A Sixty seconds equal one minute, sixty minutes equal one hour, and twenty-four hours equal one day. Study the problems below and match the periods of time that are equal.

① 1 day, 1 hour, and 1 minute   four hundred thirty minutes and thirty-six seconds

② 1,440 minutes   twenty-five hours and sixty seconds

③ 7 hours, 10 minutes, and 36 seconds   twenty-four hours

④ 270 minutes   eight hours

⑤ 5 hours and 10,800 seconds   four hours and thirty minutes

⑥ 7,380 minutes   six hours and ten seconds

⑦ 1,920 seconds   thirty-two minutes

⑧ 360 minutes and 10 seconds   five days and three hours

B Ante meridian (a.m.) begins at midnight and lasts until noon. Post meridian (p.m.) begins at noon and lasts until midnight. A beginning time is circled on each pair of clocks. Add the number of hours specified and circle the ending time on the appropriate a.m. or p.m. clock.

①   **a.m.**   **p.m.**   ②   **a.m.**   **p.m.**   ③   **a.m.**   **p.m.**

 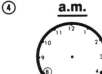   

    10 a.m. + 3 hours   9 a.m. + 3 hours   6 a.m. + 12 hours

④   **a.m.**   **p.m.**   ⑤   **a.m.**   **p.m.**   ⑥   **a.m.**   **p.m.**

 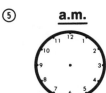   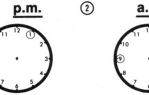

    8 a.m. + 24 hours   12 p.m. + 10 hours   7 a.m. + 18 hours

REMINDER: How is time measured?

_____

_____

Unit 91 cont'd ☞

C Shown here is a calendar for the first three months of 1985. Study the calendar and answer the questions.

1985

January

S	M	T	W	T	F	S
		1	2	3	4	5
6	7	8	9	10	11	12
13	14	15	16	17	18	19
20	21	22	23	24	25	26
27	28	29	30	31		

February

S	M	T	W	T	F	S
					1	2
3	4	5	6	7	8	9
10	11	12	13	14	15	16
17	18	19	20	21	22	23
24	25	26	27	28		

March

S	M	T	W	T	F	S
					1	2
3	4	5	6	7	8	9
10	11	12	13	14	15	16
17	18	19	20	21	22	23
24 31	25	26	27	28	29	30

① On which day of the week does January first fall? ___*Tuesday*___

② On which day of the week does the last day of January fall? _____

③ On which day of the week does February first fall? _____

④ What is the name of the third month? _____

⑤ How many seven-day or calendar weeks are there in January? _____

⑥ Which two months begin on Friday? _____

⑦ What is the name of the day that begins each calendar week? _____

D Underline the correct answers.

① One hour equals (sixty seconds, <u>sixty minutes</u>, sixty days).

② (Ante meridian, Post meridian) is that period of time between noon and midnight.

③ A clock measures (seconds, days), (minutes, weeks), and (years, hours).

④ A calendar measures the time required for the earth to complete a revolution around the (moon, sun, planet Jupiter).

⑤ If a person's workday lasts (480 minutes, 840 minutes, 260 minutes), then that person works eight hours.

⑥ A minute is (1/60, 1/20, 1/120) of an hour.

⑦ A second is (1/24, 1/160, 1/60) of a minute.

⑧ There are (24, 60, 120) hours in a day.

⑨ A calendar for a year would contain (24, 60, 12) months.

⑩ A (calendar, week, day, hour) is the measurement of 7 days.

Time-Related Problems

Learning Objective: **We will learn to calculate time.**

Time may be a second, minute, hour, day, week, month, year, decade, or century. Time may be measured by a clock or calendar.

EXAMPLES:

The long hand on a clock measures minutes. The short hand on a clock measures hours. This clock shows 9:10, or 10 minutes after nine.

A calendar measures time in days, months, and years. A month is 1/12 of a year.

			July			
S	M	T	W	Th	F	S
	1	2	3	4	5	6
7	8	9	10	11	12	13
14	15	16	17	18	19	20
21	22	23	24	25	26	27
28	29	30	31			

A Draw clock hands to show the indicated time.

①  seven o'clock

② five o'clock

③ three o'clock

④ noon

⑤ nine o'clock

⑥ one o'clock

⑦ 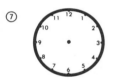 fifteen minutes after three o'clock

⑧ 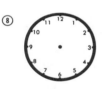 forty minutes after seven o'clock

⑨ ten minutes after five o'clock

⑩  fifty minutes after six o'clock

⑪ eleven minutes after nine o'clock

⑫ twenty-five minutes after four o'clock

A digital clock shows time without hands like a clock. A colon separates the hour on the left from the minutes on the right. A.M. and P.M. are designated on the clock face. This clock shows fifteen minutes after three, post meridian.

p.m. 3:15

B How would you read these digital times?

① 2:45 a.m. _____

② 3:16 p.m. _____

③ 6:50 a.m. _____

④ 8:30 a.m. _____

⑤ 7:25 a.m. _____

REMINDER: Write the definition of time.

_____

_____

Unit 92 cont'd ☞

One month is 1/12 of a year. One year is 1/10 of a decade. Ten decades equal one century. One hundred years equal one century.

C Match the periods of time that are equal.

_b_ ① 1/12 of a year   _____ ⑨ one hundred years   a. seven days   i. the ninth month

_____ ② January   _____ ⑩ September   b. one month   j. one century

_____ ③ the fourth month   _____ ⑪ the eighth month   c. the first month   k. five decades

_____ ④ a week   _____ ⑫ fifty years   d. April   l. August

_____ ⑤ February   _____ ⑬ six hundred years   e. the second month   m. the eleventh month

_____ ⑥ the fifth month   _____ ⑭ November   f. the third month   n. six centuries

_____ ⑦ a decade   _____ ⑮ the last month   g. May   o. three decades

_____ ⑧ March   _____ ⑯ thirty years   h. ten years   p. December

D Underline the correct answers.

① The long hand on a clock measures (seconds, <u>minutes</u>, hours).

② The short hand on a clock measures (seconds, minutes, hours).

③ Twenty-five minutes until five o'clock is written (5:25, 25:5, 4:35).

④ Post meridian is time between (Monday and Wednesday, noon and midnight, midnight and noon).

⑤ A calendar measures (hours, weeks, seconds).

⑥ A clock measures time in (hours, days, years).

⑦ A month measures (days and weeks, seconds and hours, years and centuries).

⑧ A digital clock measures time with (a colon, two hands, a week).

⑨ Fifteen minutes after two o'clock is written (15:2, 2:15, 1:45).

⑩ Twenty minutes until four o'clock is written (20:4, 4:20, 3:40).

⑪ (Twelve, Sixty, Twenty-four) months equal one year.

⑫ (Ten, One hundred, Sixty) years equal one decade.

⑬ (Sixty, Twelve, Twenty-four) seconds equal one minute.

⑭ (Sixty, Ten, Twenty-four) hours equal one day.

⑮ (Seven, Sixty, Twelve) days make one week.

Money Recognition

Learning Objective: *We will learn to recognize and calculate U.S. coins and paper money.*

A coin is a piece of metal that is issued by the government as money. A bill is a piece of paper that is issued by the government as money.

EXAMPLE: **Coins**

Bills

A Identify the value of each coin or bill. Total the values.

①

$ ____**1**____ + $ ____**1**____ + $ ____**5**____ + $ ____**10**____ +
$ ____**20**____ = $ ____**37**____

②

____ ¢ + ____ ¢ + ____ ¢ = ____ ¢

③

____ ¢ + ____ ¢ + ____ ¢ + ____ ¢ +
____ ¢ = ____ ¢

④

____ ¢ + ____ ¢ + ____ ¢ + ____ ¢
____ ¢ + ____ ¢ + ____ ¢ = ____ ¢

⑤

$ ____ + $ ____ + $ ____ + $ ____ +
$ ____ = $ ____

⑥

$ ____ + $ ____ + $ ____ + $ ____ +
$ ____ + $ ____ = $ ____

REMINDER: Write the definitions of a coin and a bill.

_____

_____

Unit 93 cont'd ☛

Bills and coins are separated by a decimal (.) when they are written together.

 = **$22.36**

B Match the bills and coins with the numbers that represent them.

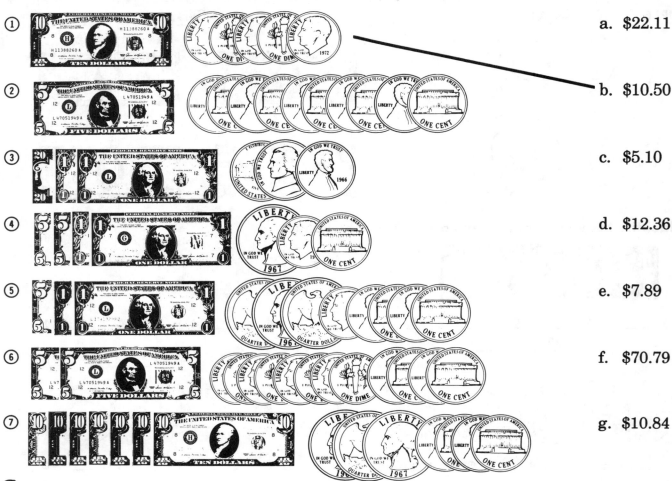

a. $22.11

b. $10.50

c. $5.10

d. $12.36

e. $7.89

f. $70.79

g. $10.84

C True or False

<u>_true_</u> ① Four quarters are equal to one dollar.

_____ ② Two ten dollar bills and three quarters are written $210.75.

_____ ③ George Washington is pictured on a twenty-dollar bill.

_____ ④ Four twenty-dollar bills equal one hundred dollars.

_____ ⑤ Three dimes and three dollars equal $3.30.

_____ ⑥ Coins and bills are issued by the government as money.

_____ ⑦ Jimmy Carter is pictured on a five-dollar bill.

_____ ⑧ Five one-dollar bills equal one hundred twenty-five quarters.

_____ ⑨ A $ sign means coins and a ¢ sign means bills.

_____ ⑩ One hundred pennies equal one dollar.

Buying Skills

Learning Objective: **We will learn to determine what is a good bargain.**

A good bargain is buying a product at a fair price.

EXAMPLE: **The Hunters need a new mattress. They can buy one for $250 that has a 10-year warranty, or they can buy the same size mattress for $75 that has no warranty. The mattress for $250 is the better bargain because it has a warranty which suggests the mattress is of good quality and will last longer than the cheaper one which, because of its price, was obviously made from lower quality material.**

A Check the items that would be a better bargain. Tell why.

① _____ a. a recliner for $70 with no warranty
   ✓ b. a recliner for $120 with a 10-year warranty

For $50 more you get a 10-year warranty.

② _____ a. a used car for $500 with a 5-year warranty
   _____ b. a used car for $700 with no warranty

③ _____ a. a used washer for $400 with a 10-year warranty
   _____ b. a new washer for $600 with no warranty

④ _____ a. a large pizza with one topping for $10
   _____ b. a medium pizza with three toppings for $8

⑤ _____ a. a 32-ounce soda for 90¢
   _____ b. a 16-ounce soda for 50¢

⑥ _____ a. a new English textbook for $8
   _____ b. a good, used English textbook for $5

⑦ _____ a. a new 3-bedroom house for $75,000
   _____ b. an older but similar 3-bedroom house for $55,000

⑧ _____ a. a new color t.v. with a 32-inch screen and 5-year warranty for $500
   _____ b. a used color t.v. with a 32-inch screen and 3-year warranty for $400

⑨ _____ a. ten gallons of gas for $8
   _____ b. five gallons of gas for $5

REMINDER: Write the definition of a good bargain.

_____

_____

Unit 94 cont'd ☛

B Match the bargains with a better bargain.

① 4 tires for $200

② 1-liter soda for $1.50

③ hair dryer for $12 with a
2-year warranty

④ used car with 20,000 miles for
$5,000 with no warranty

⑤ used stove for $150 with
no warranty

⑥ used car with 20,000 miles for
$5,000 and five-year warranty

⑦ new stove for $200 with
no warranty

⑧ 1 year of insurance
for $250

⑨ 1 64-ounce loaf of bread
for $1.50

a. 2-liter soda for $2

b. 4 tires for $200 with a five-
year warranty

c. new car for $5,000 with
no warranty

d. used stove for $175 with two-
year warranty

e. hair dryer for $15 with a five-
year warranty

f. new stove for $200 with one-
year warranty

g. 3 years of insurance for $600

h. used car with 10,000 miles for
$6,000 and no warranty

i. 3 22-ounce loaves of bread
for $1.00

C Tell which bargains are the best.

① Robin needs a new car. She has $7,500. She can buy a new car for $6,000 and have a 10-year
warranty, or she can buy a used car with 25,000 miles and no warranty for $5,000. She is
considering a different used car for $5,000. It has only 2,000 miles and a 9-year warranty.
Which one should she buy and why?

_____

_____

_____

② Cassie's mother sent her to the store to buy a bottle of soda and a loaf of bread. Her mother
gave Cassie three $1 bills. Cassie can buy 1 liter of soda for 75¢, 2 liters of soda for $1.50, or 3
liters of soda for $2. She can also buy an 8-ounce loaf of bread for 50¢, a 16-ounce loaf for 75¢,
or a 32-ounce loaf of bread for $2. Which should Cassie buy and why?

_____

_____

_____

③ Robert needed a new clothes dryer. He could buy a new one with a 10-year warranty for $300,
a used one with a 5-year warranty for $250, or a used one with no warranty for $100. Robert
has $350 to spend on a dryer. Which one should he buy and why?

_____

_____

_____

228

Making Change   Unit 95

We will learn to make change.

Change is the money that is returned when the amount paid is more than the amount due.

EXAMPLE:

Change in coins and bills may be made by adding to the amount due.

Amount Due	+	Change	=	Amount Paid
$4	+	$1	=	$5

When making change, state the amount due and add the necessary change until the amount paid is reached. For example, if the amount due is 57¢ and the amount paid is $1, say "57," give three pennies in change saying "58, 59, 60," give one nickel saying "65," give one dime saying "75," and then give one quarter saying "$1."

A For each problem, identify the change that would be given and how it would be counted.

___*b*___ ① $\frac{\text{Amount}}{\text{Due}} + \frac{}{\text{Change}} = \frac{\text{Amount}}{\text{Paid}}$
         29¢ +   71¢ = $1

a. 2 quarters, 1 nickel, 2 pennies
   43, 44, 45, 50, 75, 1

_____ ② $\frac{\text{Amount}}{\text{Due}} + \frac{}{\text{Change}} = \frac{\text{Amount}}{\text{Paid}}$
       $1.28 +   22¢ = $1.50

b. 2 quarters, 2 dimes, 1 penny
   29, 30, 40, 50, 75, 1

_____ ③ $\frac{\text{Amount}}{\text{Due}} + \frac{}{\text{Change}} = \frac{\text{Amount}}{\text{Paid}}$
       $1.67 +   33¢ = $2

c. 2 dimes, 2 pennies
   128, 29, 30, 40, 150

_____ ④ $\frac{\text{Amount}}{\text{Due}} + \frac{}{\text{Change}} = \frac{\text{Amount}}{\text{Paid}}$
        43¢ +   57¢ = $1

d. $1 bill, 1 quarter, 2 dimes, 1 penny
   354, 55, 65, 75, 4, 5

_____ ⑤ $\frac{\text{Amount}}{\text{Due}} + \frac{}{\text{Change}} = \frac{\text{Amount}}{\text{Paid}}$
       $3.54 + $1.46 = $5

e. 2 dimes, 1 penny
   654, 55, 65, 75

_____ ⑥ $\frac{\text{Amount}}{\text{Due}} + \frac{}{\text{Change}} = \frac{\text{Amount}}{\text{Paid}}$
       $6.54 +   21¢ = $6.75

f. 1 quarter, 1 nickel, 3 pennies
   167, 68, 69, 70, 75, 2

REMINDER: Write the definition of change.

_____

_____

B In each problem match the change due with the way it would be counted.

		Amount Paid	+	Amount Due	=	Change	
_b_	①	$1	+	91¢	=	9¢	a. 125, 50, 75, 2, 3, 4, 5
___	②	$5	+	$4.86	=	14¢	b. 91, 92, 93, 94, 95, 1
___	③	$5	+	$1.25	=	$3.75	c. 486, 87, 88, 89, 90, 5
___	④	$7	+	$6.07	=	93¢	d. 914, 15, 25, 50, 75, 10
___	⑤	$10	+	$9.14	=	86¢	e. 607, 8, 9, 10, 15, 25, 50, 75, 7
___	⑥	$10	+	$5.54	=	$4.46	f. 1442, 43, 44, 45, 50, 75, 15, 20
___	⑦	$20	+	$8.59	=	$11.41	g. 554, 55, 65, 75, 6, 7, 8, 9, 10
___	⑧	$20	+	$14.42	=	$5.58	h. 859, 60, 65, 75, 9, 10, 20
___	⑨	$5	+	$2.43	=	$2.57	i. 826, 27, 28, 29, 30, 40, 50, 75, 9
___	⑩	$9	+	$8.26	=	74¢	j. 243, 44, 45, 50, 75, 3, 4, 5
___	⑪	$10	+	$4.77	=	$5.23	k. 253, 54, 55, 65, 75, 3, 4, 5, 10
___	⑫	$10	+	$8.64	=	$1.36	l. 477, 78, 79, 80, 90, 5, 10
___	⑬	$10	+	$2.53	=	$7.47	m. 864, 65, 75, 9, 10
___	⑭	$12	+	$11.50	=	50¢	n. 1150, 75, 12
___	⑮	$15	+	$10.84	=	$4.16	o. 1276, 77, 78, 79, 80, 90, 13, 14, 15, 20
___	⑯	$20	+	$12.76	=	$7.24	p. 1084, 85, 90, 11, 12, 13, 14, 15

C Read each paragraph and write how the change would be counted.

① Lisa bought a hot dog, an order of French fries, and a large soda. The amount due was $3.65 and she paid with a ten-dollar bill. The cashier gave her back $6.35. How was it counted?

365, 75, 4, 5, 10

_____

② Mrs. Smith paid her water bill of $13.13 with a ten- and a five-dollar bill. How was her change of $1.87 counted back?

_____

_____

③ Alex bought a bottle of perfume for his wife. It cost $5.43. He paid for it with a twenty-dollar bill and received $14.57 in change. How was it counted?

_____

_____

④ Valerie filled her car with $7.65 worth of gas. She paid for it with a ten-dollar bill. How was her change of $2.35 counted back to her?

_____

_____

⑤ Maryann bought a pair of tennis shoes for $15.87 and paid the cashier with a twenty-dollar bill. Maryann received $4.13 in change. How was it counted?

_____

_____

⑥ Robert paid for a bunch of daisies that cost $2.78 with a twenty-dollar bill. He received $17.22 in change. How was his change counted back to him?

_____

_____

Comprehension Check

A Study the problems below and match the periods of time that are equal.

__c__ ① 720 seconds   ____ ⑦ 1 month   a. three days   g. 1/12 year

____ ② 72 hours   ____ ⑧ 6 decades   b. one minute, ten seconds   h. 1/2 year

____ ③ 70 seconds   ____ ⑨ 6 months   c. twelve minutes   i. sixty years

____ ④ 86,400 seconds   ____ ⑩ 100 years   d. ten minutes, two seconds   j. seven days

____ ⑤ 360 minutes   ____ ⑪ 1 week   e. twenty-four hours   k. a century

____ ⑥ 602 seconds   ____ ⑫ Friday   f. 6 hours   l. 1/7 week

B Draw the time specified under each clock.

① two o'clock

② ten minutes until four o'clock

③ fifteen minutes after eight o'clock

④ noon

⑤ twenty minutes after six o'clock

⑥ midnight

C Write the time specified under each clock. Underline either a.m. or p.m.

① a.m. / p.m. **2:50**
ten minutes until three o'clock, ante meridian

② a.m. / p.m.
midnight

③ a.m. / p.m.
twenty minutes until nine o'clock, post meridian

④ a.m. / p.m.
one o'clock, ante meridian

⑤ a.m. / p.m.
noon

⑥ a.m. / p.m.
twenty-five minutes after five o'clock, post meridian

D Identify the value of each coin or bill and total the values.

①

____ ¢ + ____ ¢ + ____ ¢ + ____ ¢ + ____ ¢ = ____ ¢

②

$ ____ + $ ____ + $ ____ + $ ____ = $ ____

③

$ ____ + ____ ¢ + ____ ¢ + ____ ¢ = $ ____

④

$ ____ + $ ____ + $ ____ + ____ ¢ + ____ ¢ + ____ ¢ + ____ ¢ = $ ____

231

Test 19 cont'd

E Check the items that would be a better bargain. Tell why.

① _____ a. two 10-ounce steak dinners for $10   _____

    _____ b. two 10-ounce steak dinners for $8   _____

② _____ a. four quarts of oil for $2.00   _____

    _____ b. three quarts of oil for $1.20   _____

③ _____ a. a new lawn mower for $200 and   _____
             a 10-year warranty   _____

    _____ b. a used lawn mower for $50
             and a 7-year warranty

④ _____ a. a new stereo system for $300 and a   _____
             5-year warranty   _____

    _____ b. a 6-year-old stereo system for $100
             and no warranty

F For each problem identify the change that would be given and how it would be counted.

		Amount Due	+	Change	=	Amount Paid

_____ ① $1.97 + $8.03 = $10   a. 1 five-dollar bill, 3 one-dollar bills, 3 pennies
                                           197, 98, 99, 2, 3, 4, 5, 10

_____ ② $3.88 + $6.12 = $10   b. 1 ten-dollar bill, 1 five-dollar bill, 2 one-dollar
                                           bills, 2 dimes, 2 pennies
                                           278, 79, 80, 90, 3, 4, 5, 10, 20

_____ ③ $2.78 + $17.22 = $20   c. 1 five-dollar bill, 1 one-dollar bill,
                                           1 dime, 2 pennies
                                           388, 89, 90, 4, 5, 10

_____ ④ $18.05 + $1.95 = $20   d. 5 quarters
                                           875, 9, 925, 950, 975, 10

_____ ⑤ $8.75 + $1.25 = $10   e. 1 one-dollar bill, 3 quarters, 2 dimes
                                           1805, 15, 25, 50, 75, 19, 20

Define.

① clock _____

② calendar _____

③ week _____

④ month _____

⑤ century _____

⑥ decade _____

⑦ post meridian _____

⑧ ante meridian _____

Adding Money

Learning Objective: **We will learn to add money.**

Adding money is combining two values to find a sum.

EXAMPLE:	Money is added like decimal numerals.	$34.77 + 5.11	34 dollars, 77 cents + 5 dollars, 11 cents
		$39.88	39 dollars, 88 cents

A Add dollars and cents. Check your addition as shown above.

① $ 2.71   **2 dollars, 71 cents**
  + 3.22   **+ 3 dollars, 22 cents**
  $ 5.93   **5 dollars, 93 cents**

② $ 2.03
  + 1.74

③ $ 1.47
  + 2.11

④ $ 8.98
  + 1.00

⑤ $ 5.57
  + 2.12

⑥ $ 3.61
  + 7.12

⑦ $ 8.14
  + 9.82

⑧ $ 2.06
  + 1.12

⑨ $ 4.01
  + 2.05

⑩ $14.54
  + 3.10

⑪ $15.60
  + 4.31

⑫ $61.54
  + 33.21

⑬ $12.10
  + 6.14

⑭ $20.76
  + 66.10

⑮ $54.61
  + 14.38

⑯ $31.72
  + 51.11

⑰ $25.42
  + 13.03

⑱ $14.36
  + 5.23

⑲ $10.21
  + 13.75

⑳ $28.90
  + 11.01

㉑ $11.32
  + 17.55

REMINDER: Write the definition of adding money.

Unit 96 cont'd ☞

B Work each problem. Match the total of each amount to its written answer.

_a_ ① $14.90
   + 13.75
   $28.65

___ ⑤ $27.75
   + 27.75

a. twenty-eight dollars, sixty-five cents

b. fifty-five dollars, fifty cents

c. fifty-two dollars, sixty three cents

___ ② $52.27
   + 11.84

___ ⑥ $12.62
   + 18.60

d. sixty-two dollars, forty cents

e. thirty-five dollars, fifty cents

___ ③ $19.80
   + 15.70

___ ⑦ $14.69
   + 37.94

f. sixty-four dollars, eleven cents

g. thirty dollars, twelve cents

h. thirty-one dollars, twenty-two cents

___ ④ $13.40
   + 16.72

___ ⑧ $41.51
   + 20.89

C Underline the correct answers.

① Fifty-four dollars, twenty-three cents plus twenty-three dollars, sixty-six cents equals (seventy-seven dollars, eighty-nine cents ; seventy-six dollars, eighty-nine cents; sixty-seven dollars, eighty-five cents).

② Fifty-six dollars, fifty-five cents plus twenty-three dollars, eleven cents equals (seventy-eight dollars, fifty-five cents; seventy-nine dollars, sixty-six cents ; sixty-nine dollars, sixty-nine cents).

③ Forty-five dollars, thirty-six cents, plus eleven dollars, fifty-five cents equals (fifty-six dollars, ninety-one cents; sixty-five dollars, twenty-nine cents; twenty-nine dollars, ninety-two cents).

④ Seventy-eight dollars, twelve cents plus ten dollars, fifty-five cents equals (eighty-one dollars, sixty-seven cents; eighty-five dollars, sixty-seven cents; eighty-eight dollars, sixty-seven cents).

⑤ Forty-five dollars, twenty-five cents plus twelve dollars, eighty-nine cents equals (fifty-six dollars, fourteen cents; fifty-seven dollars, fourteen cents; fifty-eight dollars, fourteen cents).

Subtracting Money

Learning Objective: *We will learn to subtract money.*

Subtraction is finding the difference between two values.

EXAMPLE: Dollars and cents are subtracted as decimal numerals.

$$\begin{array}{r} \$4.50 \\ -\ 2.25 \\ \hline \$2.25 \end{array}$$

4 dollars, 50 cents
$$\begin{array}{r} -\ 2\ \text{dollars, 25 cents} \\ \hline 2\ \text{dollars, 25 cents} \end{array}$$

A Subtract dollars and cents. Check your subtraction as shown above.

① $\begin{array}{r} \$85.79 \\ -\ 45.14 \\ \hline \$40.65 \end{array}$ *85 dollars, 79 cents* *− 45 dollars, 14 cents* *40 dollars, 65 cents*

② $\begin{array}{r} \$66.13 \\ -\ 16.02 \\ \hline \end{array}$

③ $\begin{array}{r} \$19.99 \\ -\ 8.37 \\ \hline \end{array}$

④ $\begin{array}{r} \$92.63 \\ -\ 31.43 \\ \hline \end{array}$

⑤ $\begin{array}{r} \$33.15 \\ -\ 22.04 \\ \hline \end{array}$

⑥ $\begin{array}{r} \$17.98 \\ -\ 5.66 \\ \hline \end{array}$

⑦ $\begin{array}{r} \$79.99 \\ -\ 60.79 \\ \hline \end{array}$

⑧ $\begin{array}{r} \$95.04 \\ -\ 81.04 \\ \hline \end{array}$

⑨ $\begin{array}{r} \$37.76 \\ -\ 22.45 \\ \hline \end{array}$

⑩ $\begin{array}{r} \$75.27 \\ -\ 1.22 \\ \hline \end{array}$

⑪ $\begin{array}{r} \$69.30 \\ -\ 9.20 \\ \hline \end{array}$

⑫ $\begin{array}{r} \$82.82 \\ -\ 11.61 \\ \hline \end{array}$

⑬ $\begin{array}{r} \$97.70 \\ -\ 63.40 \\ \hline \end{array}$

⑭ $\begin{array}{r} \$30.79 \\ -\ 10.46 \\ \hline \end{array}$

⑮ $\begin{array}{r} \$86.22 \\ -\ 35.10 \\ \hline \end{array}$

⑯ $\begin{array}{r} \$43.80 \\ -\ 10.10 \\ \hline \end{array}$

⑰ $\begin{array}{r} \$38.91 \\ -\ 7.11 \\ \hline \end{array}$

⑱ $\begin{array}{r} \$56.03 \\ -\ 13.00 \\ \hline \end{array}$

⑲ $\begin{array}{r} \$69.79 \\ -\ 39.29 \\ \hline \end{array}$

⑳ $\begin{array}{r} \$79.95 \\ -\ 15.73 \\ \hline \end{array}$

㉑ $\begin{array}{r} \$76.76 \\ -\ 44.25 \\ \hline \end{array}$

REMINDER: Write the definition of subtraction.

Unit 97 cont'd ☛

B Work each problem. Match the total amount to its written answer.

_a_ ① $60.00   ___ ⑤ $70.06   a. twenty-eight dollars, one cent
   − 31.99   − 5.73
   $28.01   b. seventy-five cents

___ ② $66.76   ___ ⑥ $33.33   c. nineteen dollars, twenty-nine cents
   − 34.88   − 17.92
                                 d. twenty-four dollars, seventy-one cents

___ ③ $50.00   ___ ⑦ $33.07   e. twenty-two dollars, ninety-three cents
   − 30.71   − 8.36
                                 f. thirty-one dollars, eighty-eight cents

___ ④ $44.06   ___ ⑧ $47.16   g. fifteen dollars, forty-one cents
   − 21.13   − 46.41
                                 h. sixty-four dollars, thirty-three cents

C Underline the correct answers.

① Eighteen dollars, twelve cents minus three dollars, seventy cents equals (fifteen dollars, sixty-two cents; <u>fourteen dollars, forty-two cents</u>; fourteen dollars, eighty-two cents).

② Fifty-five dollars minus forty dollars, seven cents equals (fourteen dollars, ninety-three cents; fourteen dollars, sixty-seven cents; fifteen dollars, ninety-three cents).

③ Ninety-one dollars, nine cents minus eighty dollars, twenty-six cents equals (eleven dollars, eighteen cents; eleven dollars, eighty-three cents; ten dollars, eighty-three cents).

④ Seventeen dollars, sixty-five cents minus fourteen dollars, twenty-three cents equals (three dollars, thirty-two cents; three dollars, forty-two cents; three dollars, forty-three cents).

⑤ Thirty-six dollars, forty-five cents minus twenty-one dollars, eleven cents equals (twenty-five dollars, eleven cents; fifteen dollars, thirty-six cents; fifteen dollars, thirty-four cents).

⑥ Twenty-five dollars, forty-three cents minus fourteen dollars, twenty-two cents equals (eleven dollars, twenty-one cents; ten dollars, five cents; nine dollars, sixty-five cents).

⑦ Ten dollars, thirty-six cents minus seven dollars, fifty-five cents equals (four dollars, eighty-one cents; two dollars, eighty-one cents; one dollar, eighteen cents).

⑧ Sixty-four dollars, twenty-two cents minus thirty-three dollars, thirty-three cents equals (thirty dollars, seventy-nine cents; thirty-one dollars, sixty-eight cents; thirty dollars, eighty-nine cents).

Multiplying Money

Learning Objective: *We will learn to multiply money.*

Multiplication is a shortcut for adding a number to itself.

EXAMPLE: Dollars and cents are multiplied as decimal numerals. The decimal point is placed the same number of places from the right as there are decimal places in both the multiplier and multiplicand.

$$
\begin{array}{r}
\$2.00 \\
\times\ 3 \\
\hline
\$6.00
\end{array}
\left.\begin{array}{l}
\\
\\
\end{array}\right\}
\begin{array}{l}
2\ \text{decimal places} \\
+\ 0\ \text{decimal places} \\
\hline
2\ \text{decimal places}
\end{array}
$$

A Multiply.

① $43.19 × 3 = **$129.57**

② $88.33 × 9

③ $7.99 × 5

④ $611.05 × 8

⑤ $72.53 × 6

⑥ $30.11 × 4

⑦ $9.66 × 2

⑧ $72.74 × 7

⑨ $18.00 × 5

⑩ $321.48 × 9

⑪ $19.41 × 8

⑫ $8.79 × 4

⑬ $62.58 × 56

⑭ $22.70 × 41

⑮ $797.06 × 51

⑯ $84.96 × 96

⑰ $9.03 × 61

⑱ $408.56 × 14

⑲ $55.25 × 29

⑳ $43.81 × 52

㉑ $11.38 × 71

㉒ $886.10 × 64

㉓ $51.63 × 87

㉔ $6.33 × 42

㉕ $18.27 × 551

㉖ $348.56 × 292

㉗ $50.00 × 724

㉘ $7.83 × 552

㉙ $822.66 × 211

㉚ $52.74 × 729

REMINDER: Write the definition of multiplication.

Unit 98 cont'd ☞

When multiplying by a power of ten (i.e., 10; 100; 1,000; etc.), count the number of zeroes in the multiplier and move the decimal point that many places to the right.
$1.25 × 10 = $12.50

B Multiply.

① $78.21 × 10 = **$782.10**

② $81.15 × 100 =

③ $78.50 × 1,000 =

④ $56.07 × 10 =

⑤ $66.39 × 100 =

⑥ $20.13 × 1,000 =

⑦ $16.86 × 10 =

⑧ $44.22 × 100 =

⑨ $39.77 × 1,000 =

⑩ $34.93 × 10 =

⑪ $17.87 × 100 =

⑫ $11.97 × 1,000 =

⑬ $228.00 × 10 =

⑭ $863.93 × 100 =

⑮ $700.00 × 1,000 =

⑯ $131.04 × 10 =

⑰ $109.12 × 100 =

⑱ $819.81 × 1,000 =

⑲ $591.11 × 10 =

⑳ $722.81 × 100 =

㉑ $118.12 × 1,000 =

㉒ $333.00 × 10 =

㉓ $555.23 × 100 =

㉔ $122.89 × 1,000 =

㉕ $564.30 × 10 =

㉖ $663.78 × 100 =

㉗ $971.36 × 1,000 =

㉘ $411.56 × 10 =

㉙ $111.89 × 100 =

㉚ $565.56 × 1,000 =

C Read each paragraph and multiply.

① Whitehead University charges in-district students $561.82 per semester. If there are 76 students enrolled, how much will the university receive?

② At Kirby High School, each band student needed to raise $94.99 to go to the Rose Bowl Parade. If there are 88 band students, how much will be raised?

③ The local churches sold Christmas candy to raise money for an orphanage. They sold 913 boxes of candy at $33.10 a box. How much money did the church raise from the sale of Christmas candy?

④ At a national choir meeting, it was announced that each member must buy his own robe. Each choir robe costs $172.95. There were 400 choir members at the national meeting. How much was needed for the choir robes?

Dividing Money

Learning Objective: *We will learn to divide money.*

Division is the method by which we determine how many times one number contains another.

EXAMPLE: Dollars and cents are divided as decimal numerals. The decimal in the quotient is placed directly above the decimal in the dividend.

$$
\begin{array}{r}
\$\ .36 \\
15\overline{)\ \$5.40} \\
45 \\
\hline
90 \\
90 \\
\hline
\end{array}
$$

A Divide. Round quotients to nearest cent.

① $\dfrac{\$2.335}{2\overline{)\$4.670}} = \$2.34$

$$
\begin{array}{r}
4 \\
\hline
6 \\
6 \\
\hline
7 \\
6 \\
\hline
10 \\
10 \\
\hline
\end{array}
$$

② $5\overline{)\$8.61}$

③ $4\overline{)\$2.39}$

④ $3\overline{)\$8.24}$

⑤ $7\overline{)\$21.16}$

⑥ $23\overline{)\$68.91}$

⑦ $43\overline{)\$61.74}$

⑧ $29\overline{)\$58.34}$

⑨ $26\overline{)\$18.49}$

⑩ $71\overline{)\$64.83}$

⑪ $59\overline{)\$53.87}$

⑫ $47\overline{)\$49.21}$

REMINDER: Write the definition of division.

Unit 99 cont'd ☞

When dividing by a power of 10, count the number of zeroes in the divisor and move the decimal point that many places to the left.

B Divide. Round quotients to nearest cent.

① $60.70 ÷ 10 = **$6.07** ② $54.00 ÷ 10 = ③ $49.00 ÷ 10 =

④ $86.00 ÷ 10 = ⑤ $80.00 ÷ 100 = ⑥ $70.00 ÷ 100 =

⑦ $30.00 ÷ 100 = ⑧ $50.00 ÷ 100 = ⑨ $150.00 ÷ 100 =

⑩ $325.00 ÷ 100 = ⑪ $575.00 ÷ 100 = ⑫ $225.00 ÷ 100 =

⑬ $225.00 ÷ 10 = ⑭ $125.00 ÷ 10 = ⑮ $525.00 ÷ 10 =

⑯ $300.00 ÷ 100 = ⑰ $70.00 ÷ 1,000 = ⑱ $90.00 ÷ 1,000 =

⑲ $30.00 ÷ 10 = ⑳ $40.00 ÷ 10 = ㉑ $120.00 ÷ 1,000 =

㉒ $450.00 ÷ 100 = ㉓ $76.00 ÷ 10 = ㉔ $10.00 ÷ 1,000 =

㉕ $155.00 ÷ 10 = ㉖ $175.00 ÷ 100 = ㉗ $245.00 ÷ 100 =

㉘ $350.00 ÷ 1,000 = ㉙ $720.00 ÷ 10 = ㉚ $40.00 ÷ 100 =

C Divide. Round quotients to nearest cent.

① James Baker has $61.20 that he wants to put into four different kinds of savings accounts. If he puts an equal amount into each account, how much will go into each account?

② A woman won $135,000 in a lottery spin-off. She divided the money equally among her three sons. How much did each son receive?

③ Mrs. Williams spent $168 during a shopping spree on Saturday. She visited three stores. If she spent the same amount of money in each store, how much did she spend?

④ At Tom's Fishhouse three employees earned a total of $375 over a busy holiday. If each worker earned the same amount, how much did each employee get paid?

Working as a Cashier

We will learn to count change as a cashier.

A cashier is a person who receives and gives money when a product is bought.

EXAMPLE: Robin bought a soda for 78¢. She paid with a dollar bill and the cashier gave her 22¢ in change.

Robin's change would be in the form of 2 dimes and 2 pennies. It would be counted "78, 79, 80, 90, 1."

A Determine how the change would be counted in each of these problems.

① Sally bought a book for $6.33. She gave the cashier $10.00. The cashier gave her $3.67 in change.

3 $1 bills, 2 quarters, 1 dime, 1 nickel, 2 pennies

633, 34, 35, 40, 50, 75, 7, 8, 9, 10

_____

② Margie paid for her lunch with a $5 bill. Her lunch cost $4.88. The cashier gave her 12¢ in change.

_____

_____

_____

③ Matt bought a greeting card for his wife's birthday. The card cost 74¢. He gave a $1 bill to the cashier. She gave him 26¢ in return.

_____

_____

_____

④ Magan bought some groceries for her dinner. The total came to $9.45. She gave the cashier $10. The cashier gave her 55¢ in change.

_____

_____

_____

⑤ Bradley paid $13.56 for a flower bouquet for his sick mother. He gave the cashier $15. She paid him $1.44 in change.

_____

_____

_____

⑥ A ticket to the opera cost $16.25. Mrs. Lewis gave a $20 bill to the cashier. The cashier gave her $3.75 in change.

_____

_____

_____

⑦ Mr. Larabee took his family out to dinner. It cost him $21.06. He gave the cashier $22. She gave him 94¢ in change.

_____

_____

_____

⑧ Sarah bought a winter sweater on sale for $23.50. She gave the cashier $25. The cashier gave her $1.50 in change.

_____

_____

_____

REMINDER: Write the definition of cashier.

_____

_____

Unit 100 cont'd ☞

B Match the change due with the way it would be counted.

	Amount Paid	−	Amount Due	=	Change			Amount Paid	−	Amount Due	=	Change
_a_ ①	$13	−	$12.72	=	$ .28		⑨	$25	−	$21.11	=	$ 3.89
②	$ 7	−	$ 6.65	=	$ .35		⑩	$28	−	$27.33	=	$ .67
③	$ 9	−	$ 8.37	=	$ .63		⑪	$20	−	$ 4.69	=	$15.31
④	$20	−	$17.23	=	$ 2.77		⑫	$80	−	$72.56	=	$ 7.44
⑤	$18.50	−	$18.31	=	$ .19		⑬	$90	−	$86.90	=	$ 3.10
⑥	$20	−	$13.84	=	$ 6.16		⑭	$95	−	$91.05	=	$ 3.95
⑦	$15	−	$12.36	=	$ 2.64		⑮	$30	−	$25.62	=	$ 4.38
⑧	$20	−	$ 6.42	=	$13.58		⑯	$30	−	$22	=	$ 8

a. 1272, 73, 74, 75, 13
b. 837, 38, 39, 40, 50, 75, 9
c. 1384, 85, 90, 14, 15, 20
d. 1236, 37, 38, 39, 40, 50, 75, 13, 14, 15
e. 665, 75, 7
f. 1723, 24, 25, 50, 75, 18, 19, 20
g. 1831, 32, 33, 34, 35, 40, 50
h. 642, 43, 44, 45, 50, 75, 7, 8, 9, 10, 20

i. 469, 70, 75, 5, 10, 20
j. 7256, 57, 58, 59, 60, 65, 75, 73, 74, 75, 80
k. 9105, 15, 25, 50, 75, 92, 93, 94, 95
l. 22, 23, 24, 25, 30
m. 2562, 63, 64, 65, 75, 26, 27, 28, 29, 30
n. 2733, 34, 35, 40, 50, 75, 28
o. 8690, 87, 88, 89, 90
p. 2111, 12, 13, 14, 15, 25, 50, 75, 22, 23, 24, 25

C Work these problems.

① Karen paid $32.85 for a new telephone installation. She gave the phone company $40. They gave her $7.15 as change. How was it counted?

3285, 90, 95, 33, 34, 35, 40

② Mardi paid for some groceries at Food Mart. They cost $43.03. Mardi gave the cashier $44. The cashier gave her $.97 in change. How was it counted?

③ Tyler bought some typewriter ribbon for $4.46. He gave the cashier a $50 bill. She counted the change and gave him $45.54. How was it counted?

④ Rosemary bought a new blouse for $22.81. She gave the cashier $25. The cashier gave Rosemary $2.19. How was it counted?

⑤ Mrs. Simpson paid her electricity bill with $40. The bill was $38.25. The cashier gave her $1.75 in change. How was it counted?

⑥ Jim bought two large pizzas for himself and his two brothers. The pizzas cost $21.75. Jim gave the delivery boy $25. The boy gave Jim $3.25 in change. How was it counted?

Comprehension Check

A Add money.

① $ 26.42   **26 dollars, 42 cents**   ② $ 37.59   ③ $ 36.01
  + 11.19 **+ 11 dollars, 19 cents**   + 92.67   + 74.12

  $ 37.61   37 dollars, 61 cents

④ $ 56.23   ⑤ $ 47.63   ⑥ $ 78.22
  + 82.46   + 92.07   + 6.33

B Subtract money.

① $ 85.42   **85 dollars, 42 cents**   ② $ 45.66   ③ $ 55.75
  − 63.31 **− 63 dollars, 31 cents**   − 34.53   − 31.50

  $ 22.11   22 dollars, 11 cents

④ $ 67.24   ⑤ $ 78.94   ⑥ $ 87.49
  − 16.13   − 43.43   − 52.18

C Multiply money.

① $26.42   ② $54.76   ③ $63.41   ④ $39.25   ⑤ $46.27   ⑥ $71.49
  × 8   × 7   × 5   × 9   × 8   × 7

$211.36

⑦ $36.42   ⑧ $87.43   ⑨ $67.72   ⑩ $97.61   ⑪ $57.92   ⑫ $28.61
  × 11   × 58   × 47   × 64   × 81   × 45

D Divide money. Round quotients to nearest cent.

① 7) $6.78   ② 8) $9.74   ③ 8) $7.59   ④ 5) $.62

Test 20 cont'd ☛

E **Read each paragraph and write out how the change would be returned and counted.**

① Robin bought a bag of candy for $.67. She paid the cashier $1. The cashier gave her $.33 in change.

1 quarter, 1 nickel, 3 pennies

67, 68, 69, 70, 75, 1

② Sheila paid $3.59 for a summer hat. She gave the cashier $5. The cashier gave her $1.41 in change.

③ A box of water paints cost $1.27. Bob paid the cashier $5. The change he received was $3.73.

④ Dale paid $7.14 for a pair of gloves. He gave the cashier $10. She gave him $2.86 in change.

⑤ Sue bought $6.89 of school supplies. She received $3.11 out of $10.

⑥ Max paid $12.04 for a large pizza. He gave the delivery boy $15. The boy gave Max $2.96 in change.

⑦ George paid $4.86 for medicine. He gave the druggist $20. The druggist gave him $15.14 in change.

⑧ Jeremy paid $17.69 for books he needed for school. He gave the cashier $20. She gave him $2.31 in change.

Define.

① money _____
② addition _____
③ subtraction _____
④ multiplication _____
⑤ division _____
⑥ change _____
⑦ amount due _____
⑧ amount paid _____

Making a Budget

Learning Objective: *We will learn to make a budget.*

A budget is a projection of expenses for a certain period.

EXAMPLE:
Larry made a budget for the month.

projected	
house payment	$300.00
car payment	145.00
electric bill	75.00
phone bill	40.00
	$560.00

These were the actual bills.

bills	
house payment	$300.00
car payment	145.00
electric bill	70.00
phone bill	25.00
	$540.00

Larry allocated $20.00 more than was needed. $560.00 − 540.00 = $20.00

A Read each budget, add the columns, and place a check (✓) if enough money was allocated.

		projected	bills
✓	① rent	$200.00	$200.00
	phone bill	50.00	58.00
	grocery bill	70.00	50.00
	electric bill	70.00	56.00
	car payment	150.00	150.00
		$540.00	$514.00

		projected	bills
___	② car payment	$212.00	$212.00
	rent	250.00	250.00
	grocery bill	127.00	140.00
	phone bill	65.00	70.00
	water bill	15.00	20.00

		projected	bills
___	③ house payment	$350.00	$350.00
	grocery bill	160.00	140.00
	electric bill	126.00	150.00
	phone bill	73.00	75.00
	car insurance	650.00	650.00

		projected	bills
___	④ truck payment	$145.00	$145.00
	house payment	250.00	250.00
	truck insurance	135.00	135.00
	grocery bill	206.00	200.00
	electric bill	117.00	70.00

		projected	bills
___	⑤ rent	$250.00	$250.00
	car payment	175.00	175.00
	grocery bill	100.00	70.00
	stereo payment	30.00	30.00
	trash service	20.00	20.00

		projected	bills
___	⑥ rent	$175.00	$175.00
	grocery bill	145.00	140.00
	electric bill	80.00	65.00
	trash service	15.00	15.00
	phone bill	60.00	70.00

REMINDER: *Write the definition of a budget.*

_____

_____

B Add the budgets. Match the budgets with the amounts needed to pay them.

a. $890.00   b. $650.00   c. $500.00   d. $870.00   e. $470.00   f. $922.00

__c__ ① gas bill $79.00
      rent $200.00
      car payment $115.00
      grocery bill $70.00
      trash service $25.00
                         $489.00

_____ ② house payment $200.00
      car payment $150.00
      electric bill $195.00
      grocery bill $176.00
      insurance $200.00

_____ ③ rent $150.00
      car payment $200.00
      grocery bill $65.00
      gas bill $35.00
      water bill $17.00

_____ ④ rent $250.00
      car payment $175.00
      gas bill $75.00
      grocery bill $95.00
      phone bill $35.00

_____ ⑤ stereo payment $50.00
      car payment $200.00
      insurance $150.00
      rent $360.00
      gas bill $80.00

_____ ⑥ car payment $125.00
      rent $400.00
      grocery bill $265.00
      phone bill $12.00
      water bill $76.00

C Write "y" for yes, or "n" for no to answer each question.

__y__ ① Steve projected $210 for a $170 car repair bill. Can he pay it?

_____ ② Will the $200 Laurie projected cover her rent of $200 for May?

_____ ③ Can Shelia pay a $175 phone bill with the $165 she projected?

_____ ④ Cindy projected $300 to pay her credit card account in full. Will she be able to pay the bill of $276?

_____ ⑤ Victoria projected $75 for a trip to the dentist. The bill was $67. Can she pay it?

_____ ⑥ Chris projected $32 for two tanks of gas. The bill came to $35. Can he pay the gas bill?

_____ ⑦ Will the $59 Sherry projected for a new outfit cover the bill of $54?

_____ ⑧ Can Sharon buy a bus ticket to Chicago for $112 with the $100 she projected?

_____ ⑨ Denise received a phone bill of $76. Will the $80 she projected cover it?

_____ ⑩ Will the $60 Robin projected to buy a calculator cover the bill of $89?

Wages

Learning Objective: *We will learn to calculate wages.*

A wage is the hourly amount of money one receives for working. Wages are the total amount of money paid during a pay period.

EXAMPLE: If Lezli works 40 hours a week for $3 an hour, she makes $120 a week.

$$\begin{array}{r} \$3 \\ \times\ 40 \\ \hline \$120 \end{array}$$

A Find the total amount of wages each person makes.

① Cathy gets paid $4.50 an hour. She works 35 hours a week.

$$\begin{array}{r} \$4.50 \\ \times\ 35 \\ \hline 2250 \\ 1350 \\ \hline \$157.50 \end{array}$$

② Trey works 35 hours a week for $3.50 an hour.

③ Gerald works 12 hours for $8.25 an hour.

④ Jerry works for $6.65 an hour. He works 40 hours a week.

⑤ Margie earns $4.25 an hour and works 18 hours.

⑥ Mitch earns $7.75 an hour and works 34 hours.

⑦ Jacob works 25 hours a week at the rate of $5.50 an hour.

⑧ Elsie works 20 hours a week for $4.00 an hour.

⑨ David receives $3.35 an hour for 38 hours.

⑩ Ray receives $2.65 an hour for a 36-hour work week.

⑪ Brian works 42 hours a week and earns $11 an hour.

⑫ Bob works 40 hours for $7.85 an hour.

⑬ Kim works 40 hours a week and earns $5.75 an hour.

⑭ Tommy earns $7.50 an hour for a 37-hour workweek.

⑮ James works 27 hours a week and earns $12 an hour.

REMINDER: *Write the definition of wage and wages.*

_____

_____

Unit 102 cont'd ☞

The federal and state governments take money from all paychecks at the end of every pay period. Federal income tax, state income tax, and social security tax are taken out. The amount made before taxes are taken out is called "gross earnings." The amount made after taxes is called "net earnings."

B Study the chart and answer the questions.

① Joe grossed $800. How much did he net?
   $624
   _____

② John grossed $200. How much state tax did
   he pay? _____

③ Marie netted $390. How much did she gross?
   _____

④ Rocky netted $975. How much social security tax
   did he pay? _____
   Federal tax? _____

⑤ Robin paid $40 social security. How much did
   she gross? _____

⑥ Sue grossed $500. How much state tax did
   she pay? _____

⑦ Carry paid $10 in federal tax. How much did he
   pay in state tax? _____
   Social security? _____

WEEKLY DOLLAR TOTALS

Gross Earnings	State Tax	Federal Tax	Social Security Tax	Net Earnings
$2,000	$140	$200	$100	$1,560
$1,500	$105	$150	$75	$1,170
$1,250	$87.50	$125	$62.50	$975
$1,000	$70	$100	$50	$780
$900	$63	$90	$45	$702
$800	$56	$80	$40	$624
$700	$49	$70	$35	$546
$500	$35	$50	$25	$390
$400	$28	$40	$20	$312
$300	$21	$30	$15	$234
$200	$14	$20	$10	$156
$100	$7	$10	$5	$78

⑧ Allen grossed $800. How much social security did he pay? _____
   Federal tax? _____ State tax? _____

⑨ Barry paid $10 in social security tax. How much did he gross? _____ Net? _____

C True or False

true ① Dean earns $4.75 an hour and works 40 work hours a week. He grosses $190.

_____ ② Earl works 45 hours a week, earns $22 an hour, and grosses $990 a week.

_____ ③ Norma earns $2.75 an hour and works 40 hours a week. She grosses $110.

_____ ④ Dana earns $4.45 an hour and is working 36 hours a week. She grosses $160.20.

_____ ⑤ Walter worked 39 hours a week and was paid $5 an hour. He grossed $185.

_____ ⑥ Marilyn works 40 hours a week for $10 an hour. She grosses $300 a week.

_____ ⑦ Cindy is paid $3.75 an hour for a 20-hour work week. She grosses $75 a week.

_____ ⑧ Gayla works for $33 an hour for 4 hours a week. She grosses $132.

_____ ⑨ Nathan works 60 hours a week for $8 an hour. He grosses $480 a week.

_____ ⑩ Amy works 22 hours a week and makes $3.50 an hour. She grosses $79.

Writing Checks   Unit 103

Learning Objective: *We will learn to write checks.*

A check is a draft written to a place or person substituting for bills and coins.

EXAMPLE: When we write a check, we must fill <u>in</u> this information.

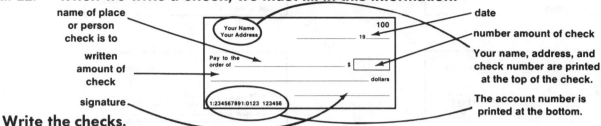

name of place or person check is to

written amount of check

signature

date

number amount of check

Your name, address, and check number are printed at the top of the check.

The account number is printed at the bottom.

A Write the checks.

① Tommy Shaw paid City Water and Light $93.03 on July 2, 1980.

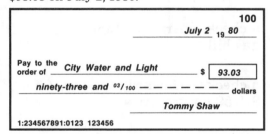

```
                                            100
                    ____ July 2  19 80 ____

Pay to the
order of ___ City Water and Light ___ $ [ 93.03 ]

  ___ ninety-three and 03/100 — — — — — — ___ dollars
                    Tommy Shaw
1:234567891:0123  123456
```

② Phillip's Repair received a check from Sue Lewis for $20.89 on August 1, 1981.

```
                                            100
                    _____ 19 ____

Pay to the
order of _____ $ [      ]

  _____ dollars

1:234567891:0123  123456
```

③ Cindy Williams paid Stereo Shak $208.78 on September 1, 1985.

```
                                            100
                    _____ 19 ____

Pay to the
order of _____ $ [      ]

  _____ dollars

1:234567891:0123  123456
```

④ Lillian Murray paid Marvel Bakery $100 on June 1, 1985 for a wedding cake.

```
                                            100
                    _____ 19 ____

Pay to the
order of _____ $ [      ]

  _____ dollars

1:234567891:0123  123456
```

⑤ On December 1, 1980, Roger Dennis paid Appliance World $28.91 for a blender.

```
                                            100
                    _____ 19 ____

Pay to the
order of _____ $ [      ]

  _____ dollars

1:234567891:0123  123456
```

⑥ Martha Long paid $26.00 to Jean World on November 8, 1983.

```
                                            100
                    _____ 19 ____

Pay to the
order of _____ $ [      ]

  _____ dollars

1:234567891:0123  123456
```

REMINDER: Write the definition of a check.

_____

_____

B Match each description with its check.

a.

```
                                              100
                            6/1  19 80
Pay to the
order of   Charles Albright        $ 200.00
      two hundred and ⁿᵒ/100 — — — — —  dollars
                      Henry Lamb
1:234567891:0123  123456
```

b.

```
                                              100
                            6/2  19 80
Pay to the
order of   Sam's Auto              $ 36.00
      thirty-six and ⁿᵒ/100 — — — — —  dollars
                      Henry Lamb
1:234567891:0123  123456
```

c.

```
                                              100
                            6/5  19 80
Pay to the
order of   Argo                    $ 12.00
      twelve and ⁿᵒ/100 — — — — — —  dollars
                      Henry Lamb
1:234567891:0123  123456
```

d.

```
                                              100
                            6/6  19 80
Pay to the
order of   Howard's                $ 19.59
      nineteen and ⁵⁹/100 — — — — — —  dollars
                      Henry Lamb
1:234567891:0123  123456
```

Henry Lamb wrote these checks in one week during 1980.

_____ ① a check to his landlord Charles Albright for June's rent on the first of June, for $200

_____ ② a check to Argo on June 5 for a $12 gas bill

_____ ③ a check to Sam's Auto on June 2 for $36 for car repairs

_____ ④ a check to Howard's on June 6 for $19.59 for groceries

C Read each check and determine if it is complete. Write t if it is complete or f if it is not.

__t__ ①

```
                                              100
                           12/1  19 80
Pay to the
order of   Food-Mart               $ 12.65
      twelve and ⁶⁵/100 — — — — — —  dollars
                      Joe Willis
1:234567891:0123  123456
```

_____ ②

```
                                              100
                            6/8  19 85
Pay to the
order of   Pat Kinzer              $ 25.00
      twenty-five and ⁿᵒ/100 — — — — —  dollars
                      Howard Kinzer
1:234567891:0123  123456
```

_____ ③

```
                                              100
                            2/3  19 80
Pay to the
order of   Pat's Pet Shop          $
      fifty-eight and ⁿᵒ/100 — — — — —  dollars
                      Larry Ball
1:234567891:0123  123456
```

_____ ④

```
                                              100
                                 19
Pay to the
order of   Carr's Gas Stop         $ 10.00
      ten                                dollars
                      Richard Crenning
1:234567891:0123  123456
```

_____ ⑤

```
                                              100
                          March 7  19 81
Pay to the
order of   Hamburger Heaven        $ 7.50
      seven and ⁵⁰/100 — — — — —  dollars
                      Terry Hollis
1:234567891:0123  123456
```

_____ ⑥

```
                                              100
                          Dec. 24  19 79
Pay to the
order of   Christmas Land           $ 60.10
      sixty and ¹⁰/100 — — — — — —  dollars

1:234567891:0123  123456
```

Keeping a Checkbook

Learning Objective: **We will learn to keep a checkbook.**

A checkbook is an account of all the checks one writes. It is used to keep track of money in the checking account.

EXAMPLE:

When we keep a checkbook, we enter all deposits to the account and add them to the balance. We enter all checks written and subtract them from the balance.

check #	date	check issued to	amount of check	deposit	balance
					100.00
1001	7/1	Banarie's	20.00		80.00
1002	7/1	Big Save	12.00		68.00
	7/3			50.00	118.00

A Fill in the checkbooks.

① John Jacobson wrote a check to Snider's on June 21 for $170, to Ronald's 66 Gas on June 21 for $78, to the Melville Star on June 23 for $360, and to Southtown Drug Store on June 26 for $15.75. On June 22 he deposited $450. His first check was number 78 and his beginning balance was $600.

check #	date	check issued to	amount of check	deposit	balance
					600.00
78	6/21	Snider's	170.00		430.00

② Linda McEvans had a balance of $700. On July 2 she wrote check number 51 to Kid's Bakery for $21.65, check number 52 to Peg's Cleaners for $4.76, and the next check on the same day to Roger's Shop for $136.42. The next day she made a house payment to People's Bank for $400 and deposited $200.

check #	date	check issued to	amount of check	deposit	balance

③ Alex Ball wrote check number 201 to Harry's Books on September 5 for $26. On September 6 he wrote checks to Stan's Shoes for $17.45 and to T.V. World for $22.14. The next day he made a car payment to Smithton Bank for $150. On September 10, he paid Dr. Kassidee $77. His beginning balance was $450.

check #	date	check issued to	amount of check	deposit	balance

REMINDER: Write the definition of a checkbook.

_____

_____

Unit 104 cont'd ☞

B Fill in the checkbooks.

① Janet Thomas had a balance of $170 on August 14. On that day she wrote check number 333 to City Water for $155.70. The next day she deposited $150 and wrote a check to Becky Evans for $14. On August 16 she wrote a check to Sam's Auto Repair for $28.

check #	date	check issued to	amount of check	deposit	balance
					170.00

② Dennis Ramsey wrote five checks, beginning with number 781, in five consecutive days. His beginning balance was $200. On October 1 he wrote one to Harry's for $188. The next were to Tom's Fish for $37.41, to Ann's Flowers for $68, to City Water for $25, and to Valco Gas for $30. On October 2 he deposited $1,000.

check #	date	check issued to	amount of check	deposit	balance
					200.00

C True or False

true ① An entry dated October second, nineteen eighty-one would read 10/2/81.

_____ ② A deposit of $200 added to a balance of $156.87 would equal $356.87.

_____ ③ The name of the place or person to whom the check is issued is written in the "check issued to" column.

_____ ④ A deposit of $550 added to a balance of $387.53 would equal $937.53.

_____ ⑤ Deposits are not recorded.

_____ ⑥ Only checks issued over $100 are written in a checkbook.

_____ ⑦ The number of the check written is put in the "check number" column.

_____ ⑧ The date of the check written does not matter.

_____ ⑨ The balance is how much money is in the account.

_____ ⑩ The name of the place or person to whom the check is issued is not written.

_____ ⑪ The checkbook balance is the total amount of money in the account.

_____ ⑫ A checkbook is a personal record of a checking account.

A Savings Account

Learning Objective: *We will learn to keep a savings account record.*

A savings account is an account where one puts money to accumulate and draw interest. Interest is what the bank pays you for using your money.

EXAMPLE:

Robert opened a savings account on February 9 and deposited $100. On March 9 he deposited $100. On April 1 the bank paid him $5 interest and on April 9 he deposited $100. His balance is $305.

Date	Interest	Withdrawals	Deposits	Balance
2/9			100.00	100.00
3/9			100.00	200.00
4/1	5.00			205.00
4/9			100.00	305.00

A Fill in the savings account records.

① On July 16 Jerry deposited $500 which made his account balance $1,500. On July 25 he withdrew $200. On August 5 he deposited $150. On August 11 he withdrew $600. On August 15 the bank paid him $5 interest. On August 29 he withdrew $750. On September 15 the bank paid him $1 interest. On September 21, Jerry deposited $345.

Date	Interest	Withdrawals	Deposits	Balance
7/16			500.00	1,500.00

② During the month of April, the Hamilton's savings account was very active. At the end of March they had a balance of $200. On the first of April the bank paid them $5 interest and they deposited $600. On the second they withdrew $50, and on the fourth they withdrew $600. On the seventh they deposited $1,000. On the tenth they withdrew $600. They also withdrew $400 on the thirteenth, and $60 on the twentieth. On the twenty-ninth they deposited $250.

Date	Interest	Withdrawals	Deposits	Balance

REMINDER: Write the definition of a savings account.

Unit 105 cont'd

B Fill in the savings account record.

Liz had a balance of $600 in her savings account on March 2. On that day she deposited $450. Three days later the bank paid her interest of $5 and she deposited $600. On the ninth she deposited $100, on the twentieth $470, and on the twenty-eighth $500. On April 5 the bank paid her $10 interest and on April 15 she deposited $787. On the twenty-first she withdrew $3,000. On May 5, the bank paid $7 interest to the account. On May 6 she deposited $700 and on May 15 withdrew $878.

Date	Interest	Withdrawals	Deposits	Balance
3/2				600.00

C True or False

true   ① A savings account pays interest.

_____ ② A savings account helps people save money.

_____ ③ A balance of $600 and a withdrawal of $500 equals $100.

_____ ④ One can write checks on a savings account.

_____ ⑤ A balance of $322 and a deposit of $45 equals $367.

_____ ⑥ A balance of $563.63 and a withdrawal of $563.63 equals $563.63.

_____ ⑦ A balance of $500 and a deposit of $500 equals $1,000.

_____ ⑧ Anyone can withdraw money from anyone else's savings account.

_____ ⑨ A balance of $777 and a withdrawal of $334 equals $1,111.

_____ ⑩ A balance of $640 and a deposit of $100.50 equals $740.50.

_____ ⑪ One must make deposits daily.

_____ ⑫ One must write in the savings account book what a withdrawal is used for.

Comprehension Check

A Read the paragraphs, study the projected budgets, fill in the actual bills, and determine if enough money was projected.

① Mrs. Hamilton's bills for the month of August were as follows: loan payment - $540, grocery bill - $363.63, phone bill - $58.93, electric bill - $63, and gas bill - $43.92. did she project enough money?

	projected	bills
loan payment	$540	
grocery bill	$400	
phone bill	$60	
electric bill	$60	
gas bill	$60	

_____

② During her first semester at college, Robin's bills were as follows: gas -$500, food - $840, school supplies -$200, textbooks - $163.84, personal items - $273.85, and phone bill - $258.90. Did she project enough money?

	projected	bills
gas	$460	
food	$700	
school supplies	$250	
textbooks	$150	
personal items	$250	
phone bill	$300	

_____

B Find how much money each person brings home per week before taxes.

① Bob works 40 hours per week for $3.35 an hour.

② Robert works 35 hours per week for $5.60 an hour.

③ Janet works 40 hours per week for $4.75 an hour.

C Read the paragraph and write the checks.

Mr. James Hancock gave his son check number 100, signed but blank, on August 30, 1983 to take to school to pay for a school shirt. On August 31, Mr. Hancock paid Western Phone $30 with check number 101. On September 1, Mr. Hancock's son made out his blank check to the high school for ten dollars. On September 3, Mr. Hancock wrote check number 102 to Big Save for $36.

```
                                        101
                      _____ 19____
Pay to the
order of _____  $ [      ]
_____  dollars
                      _____
1:234567891:0123  123456
```

```
                                        100
                      _____ 19____
Pay to the
order of _____  $ [      ]
_____  dollars
                      _____
1:234567891:0123  123456
```

```
                                        102
                      _____ 19____
Pay to the
order of _____  $ [      ]
_____  dollars
                      _____
1:234567891:0123  123456
```

Test 21 cont'd

D Read the paragraph and fill in the checkbook and savings account book. Find the balances.

On July 1, 1983, Bob and Mary Milton's checkbook had a balance of $350.63. Their savings account balance was $600. On July 5, their bank paid $20 interest to their savings account, and Mary wrote two checks: 101 to Big Save for $70.63 and 102 to Gas-Mart for $24. On July 12, Bob deposited $350 into savings and $200 into checking. On July 28, Mary withdrew $700 from savings, deposited it into checking, and wrote the next three checks. She wrote one to Appliance World for $250, one to Perfume, Ltd. for $175, and one to Roland's Clothes for $370. On August 5, their bank paid the Milton's $10 interest. On August 7, Bob wrote the next check to Honda Car Repair for $280.63, and on August 18 he deposited $350 into their savings account.

Milton's Checkbook

Check #	Date	Check issued to	Amount of Check	Amount of Deposit	Balance 350.63
101	7/5	Big Save	70.63		280.00
102	7/5				
	7/12				
	7/28				
103	7/28				
104	7/28				
105	7/28				
106	8/7				

Milton's Savings Account Book

Date	Interest	Withdrawal	Deposit	Balance
7/1				600.00
7/5				
7/12				
7/28				
8/5				
8/18				

Define.

① budget _____

② wage _____

③ check _____

④ checking account _____

⑤ savings account _____

⑥ interest _____

Profit or Loss? Unit 106

Learning Objective: *We will learn to determine profit and loss.*

A profit is made when one makes more money than one has invested in a project. A loss is made when one loses more money than one has invested in a project.

EXAMPLE:

Stan bought a used car for $750. He spent $200 repairing it. He sold the car for $1,000.	money received = $1,000.00 money invested = −$950.00 ($750 + $200) profit $50.00

Stan made a profit of $50.

A Read each paragraph and work each problem. Is there a profit or a loss?

① Connie bought a new stove for $345. She sold the stove for $150. Did she make a profit or a loss? **_loss_**

$345
−$150
$195

② Darren sold his motorcycle for $700. Three years earlier he had paid only $500 for it. Did he make a profit or a loss? _____

③ Mike paid $250 for his stereo. When he went away to school, he sold the stereo for $200. Did he make a profit or a loss? _____

④ Larry paid $400 for a horse. Five years later he sold the horse for $575. Did he make a profit or a loss?

_____

⑤ Sue sold her aquarium for $100. She had paid $59 for it. Did she make a profit or a loss?

_____

⑥ Mrs. Simmons bought $600 worth of yarn. She made afghans with the yarn and sold them all for $1200. Did she make a profit or a loss?

_____

⑦ Francis bought a piece of antique cookware for $5 and resold it for $300. Did she make a profit or a loss? _____

⑧ Karen bought a coat for $120. She sold it to a friend for $150. Did she make a profit or a loss?

_____

REMINDER: Write the definitions of profit and loss.

_____

_____

Unit 106 cont'd ☞

B Write "p" for profit or "l" for loss.

_l_ ① Danny bought a used car for $600. He wrecked it and sold the car for $36 to the junk yard.

_____ ② Gary invested $1500 in a business. It went bankrupt one year later.

_____ ③ Harold bought stock in Tasty-Cola company for $80. The market fell and his stock was only worth $36.

_____ ④ Mr. Sims opened a bookstore for $5,000. Years later he sold his store for $650,000.

_____ ⑤ Corey bought two old bikes for $20. After he repaired them he sold them for $45.

_____ ⑥ Mr. Clanahan sold his car for $6,000. Twenty-five years earlier he had paid only $2,300 for it.

_____ ⑦ Tracy invested $250 in a set of books. She sold them later for $600.

_____ ⑧ Mary bought an outfit for $55. She later sold it in a yard sale for $16.

_____ ⑨ Lucy bought a puppy for $45. She later sold the dog for $150.

C Read each paragraph and work each problem. Is there a profit or loss?

① Karen spent $300 on craft material. She sold all the creations for $175. Did she make a profit or a loss? _____

② Becky invested $1700 in a used car. After a week of problems, she sold the car to the junk yard for $300. Did she make a profit or a loss? _____

③ Lilian bought an album for $50. A collector bought the album for $225. Did Lilian make a profit or a loss? _____

④ Alex invested $45 in a boat motor. He later sold it to a friend for $75. Did he make a profit or a loss?

_____

Inches and Centimeters Unit 107

An inch is an English unit of measure equaling 1/12 of a foot or 1/36 of a yard.

12 inches = 1 foot   **36 inches = 1 yard**

A centimeter is a metric unit of measure equaling 10 millimeters or 1/100 of one meter.

10 millimeters = 1 centimeter   **100 centimeters = 1 meter**

A Perform the indicated operations. Will the answers be in inches or centimeters?

①   72 inches
   +19 inches
   91 inches

②   100 inches
   −50 inches

③   21 inches
   ×7 inches

④   3 inches $\overline{)360 \text{ inches}}$

⑤   418 inches
   −263 inches

⑥   97 inches
   +36 inches

⑦   20 inches $\overline{)750.0 \text{ inches}}$

⑧   510 inches
   ×12 inches

⑨   331 centimeters
   +147 centimeters

⑩   71 centimeters
   −11 centimeters

⑪   186 centimeters
   ×5 centimeters

⑫   2 cm $\overline{)18 \text{ cm}}$

⑬   709 centimeters
   −518 centimeters

⑭   10 cm $\overline{)44.80 \text{ cm}}$

⑮   687 centimeters
   ×12 centimeters

⑯ 710 centimeters
  105 centimeters
  +31 centimeters

⑰   9 cm × 2 cm =

⑱   11 in. + 13 in. =

⑲   72 cm ÷ 8 cm =

⑳   45 in. − 41 in. =

REMINDER: Write the definitions of an inch and a centimeter.

_____

_____

Unit 107 cont'd ☞

1 inch = 2.54 centimeters   **1 centimeter = .3937 inch**

B Convert inches to centimeters and centimeters to inches.

① 4 inches

$4 \times 2.54 = 10.16$ cm

② 7 centimeters

③ 10 inches

④ 11 centimeters

⑤ 5 centimeters

⑥ 12 inches

⑦ 100 centimeters

⑧ 20 inches

⑨ 8 inches

⑩ 42 inches

⑪ 19 centimeters

⑫ 50 inches

C Work the problems.

① Anthony needs 4 boards measuring 64 centimeters. If he saws one board into the four needed, how long will the one board need to be?

    64 cm
    $\times$4 boards
    256 cm

② Chris needs 250 inches of string. If the string comes on rolls of 50 inches each, how many rolls will he need?

③ Karen's younger sister is 92 centimeters tall. Karen is 160 centimeters tall. How much taller is she than her sister?

④ Melanie bought 121 inches of felt. She returned later and bought another 84 inches. How much felt did she buy?

⑤ Leonard bought curtains that were 84 inches long. He needed curtains that were 52 inches long. How much would he have to cut off the new curtains to make them fit?

⑥ Anna cut 12 ribbons at 10 inches each. How much ribbon did she cut?

Feet

Learning Objective: *We will learn to measure with the English unit of feet.*

A foot is an English unit of measure equaling 12 inches or 1/3 of a yard.

EXAMPLE:
    a. To convert feet to inches, multiply by 12.
        1 foot = 12 inches   **3 feet = 36 inches**
    b. To convert feet to yards, divide by 3.
        3 feet = 1 yard   **12 feet = 4 yards**

A Convert feet to inches.

1. 1 ft. = *12 in.*
2. 2 ft. =
3. 3 ft. =
4. 4 ft. =
5. 5 ft. =
6. 1/2 ft. =
7. 10 ft. =
8. 12 ft. =
9. 1 1/2 ft. =
10. 1/3 ft. =
11. 1/12 ft. =
12. 8 ft. =
13. 1/6 ft. =
14. 11 ft. =
15. 1/4 ft. =
16. 5 1/12 ft. =
17. 100 ft. =
18. 2 1/4 ft. =
19. 1 1/6 ft. =
20. 6 1/3 ft. =

B Convert feet to yards.

1. 3 ft. = *1 yd.*
2. 6 ft. =
3. 9 ft. =
4. 12 ft. =
5. 1 ft. =
6. 27 ft. =
7. 2 ft. =
8. 36 ft. =
9. 18 ft. =
10. 15 ft. =
11. 4 ft. =
12. 21 ft. =
13. 33 ft. =
14. 11 ft. =
15. 8 ft. =
16. 5 ft. =
17. 7 ft. =
18. 20 ft. =
19. 10 ft. =
20. 99 ft. =

C Fill in the blanks.

1. One foot equals _____ inches.
2. Twelve inches equal _____ foot.
3. Three feet equal _____ yard.
4. One yard equals _____ feet.

REMINDER: Write the definition of a foot.

_____

_____

       Unit 108 cont'd 👉

To convert inches to feet, divide by 12. To convert yards to feet, multiply by 3.

D **Convert these measures to feet.**

① 2 yds. = **6 ft.**　　② 12 in. =　　③ 1 yd. =　　④ 6 in. =

⑤ 8 yds. =　　⑥ 1 in. =　　⑦ 40 yds. =　　⑧ 1/3 yd. =

⑨ 10 yds. =　　⑩ 60 in. =　　⑪ 30 in. =　　⑫ 24 in. =

⑬ 16 in. =　　⑭ 1/2 yd. =　　⑮ 4 in. =　　⑯ 33 yds. =

⑰ 48 in. =　　⑱ 5 yds. =　　⑲ 36 in. =　　⑳ 9 in. =

㉑ 7 yds. =　　㉒ 50 yds. =　　㉓ 13 in. =　　㉔ 11 yds. =

㉕ 42 in. =　　㉖ 2 in. =　　㉗ 3 yds. =　　㉘ 72 in. =

㉙ 2/3 yd. =　　㉚ 18 in. =　　㉛ 20 yds. =　　㉜ 14 yds. =

㉝ 3 in. =　　㉞ 100 yds. =　　㉟ 84 in. =　　㊱ 25 yds. =

E **Work the problems.**

① Jerry needs a string that is 2 1/2 feet long. Bill will give him one that is 25 inches long. Is Bill's string long enough?

No, Bill's string is only 2 1/12 feet long.

_____

_____

② Eric wants to hang blinds on his bedroom window. His window measures 3 feet across. The blinds measure 36 inches. Will the blinds fit?

_____

_____

_____

③ Lydia needs 3 1/2 yards of material to make a dress. On the remnant table, she finds a piece of cotton that is 11 feet long. Is it enough for the dress?

_____

_____

_____

④ Chris is 5 feet, 6 inches tall. His sister is 62 inches tall. Who is taller?

_____

_____

_____

⑤ Jan bought a rug that was 72 inches long. She wants to put it in the foyer. The foyer is 5 feet long. Will the rug fit?

_____

_____

_____

⑥ Diane bought 25 yards of lace. It took 15 feet of lace to finish the pillows she made for her aunt. Did Diane have any lace left over?

_____

_____

_____

Yards and Meters

Learning Objective: **We will learn to measure with yards and meters.**

A yard is an English unit of measure equaling 36 inches or 3 feet.
A meter is a metric unit of measure equaling 100 centimeters or 1,000 millimeters.

EXAMPLES:

a. **To convert yards to inches, multiply by 36. To convert inches to yards, divide by 36.**

   1 yard = 36 inches   2 yards = 72 inches   108 inches = 3 yards

b. **To convert yards to feet, multiply by 3. To convert feet to yards, divide by 3.**

   2 yards = 6 feet   12 feet = 4 yards   36 feet = 12 yards

A **Fill in the blanks with equivalent measures.**

① yd. ___8___   ② yd. ___1___   ③ yd. _____   ④ yd. ___5___
   ft. ___24___   ft. _____   ft. _____   ft. _____
   in. ___288___   in. _____   in. ___72___   in. _____

⑤ yd. _____   ⑥ yd. _____   ⑦ yd. ___12___   ⑧ yd. _____
   ft. ___27___   ft. _____   ft. _____   ft. ___9___
   in. _____   in. ___360___   in. _____   in. _____

EXAMPLES:

a. **To convert meters to centimeters, multiply by 100. To convert centimeters to meters, divide by 100.**

   1 m = 100 cm   2 m = 200 cm   300 cm = 3 m

b. **To convert meters to millimeters, multiply by 1,000. To convert millimeters to meters, divide by 1,000.**

   1 m = 1,000 mm   2,000 mm = 2 m   3,000 mm = 3 m

B **Fill in the blanks with equivalent measures.**

① m ___1___   ② m ___5___   ③ m _____   ④ m _____
   cm ___100___   cm _____   cm ___1,000___   cm _____
   mm ___1,000___   mm _____   mm _____   mm ___7,000___

⑤ m ___20___   ⑥ m _____   ⑦ m _____   ⑧ m ___15___
   cm _____   cm ___200___   cm _____   cm _____
   mm _____   mm _____   mm ___9,000___   mm _____

REMINDER: Write the definitions of a yard and a meter.

_____

_____

Unit 109 cont'd 👉

Multiply by .9 when converting yards to meters.
Multiply by 1.1 when converting meters to yards.

C Convert yards to meters.

① 2 yds. = **1.8 m**   ② 1 yd. =   ③ 3 yds. =   ④ 4 yds. =

⑤ 10 yds. =   ⑥ 20 yds. =   ⑦ 6 yds. =   ⑧ 50 yds. =

⑨ 5 yds. =   ⑩ 100 yds. =   ⑪ 9 yds. =   ⑫ 11 yds. =

⑬ 12 yds. =   ⑭ 7 yds. =   ⑮ 15 yds. =   ⑯ 8 yds. =

D Convert meters to yards.

① 5 m = **5.5 yds.**   ② 2 m =   ③ 1 m =   ④ 6 m =

⑤ 12 m =   ⑥ 8 m =   ⑦ 50 m =   ⑧ 3 m =

⑨ 10 m =   ⑩ 15 m =   ⑪ 4 m =   ⑫ 21 m =

⑬ 100 m =   ⑭ 25 m =   ⑮ 11 m =   ⑯ 40 m =

E Work the problems.

① June bought 12 yards of cotton and 15 meters of polyester. Of which material did she buy more?

_____**polyester**_____

② Luigi has both a yardstick and a meterstick. Which stick is shorter?

_____

③ Carla needs 21 yards of yarn. Lisa needs 20 meters of yarn. Who needs more yarn?

_____

④ A project requires 50 yards of yellow string and 40 meters of red string. Which string will be longer?

_____

⑤ Bennett dug a trench 6 meters long. Adam dug one beside it 7 yards long. Which trench was longer?

_____

⑥ The line outside the ticket office was 10 yards long. The line outside the theatre was 10 meters long. Which line was shorter?

_____

⑦ Martha needs 12 meters of lace to finish a skirt. She has 14 yards of lace. Does she have enough?

_____

⑧ Pam's tablecloth is 3 yards long. Her table is 4 meters long. Will the cloth cover the table?

_____

⑨ Karen bought a rope 50 yards long. She had one at home that was 100 meters long. Which rope was longer?

_____

264

Miles and Kilometers   Unit 110

We will learn to measure with miles and kilometers.

A mile is an English unit of measure equaling 5,280 feet or 1,760 yards.
A kilometer is a metric unit of measure equaling 1,000 meters or 100,000 centimeters.

EXAMPLE:

a. **To convert miles to feet, multiply by 5,280. To convert feet to miles, divide by 5,280.**

b. **To convert miles to yards, multiply by 1,760. To convert yards to miles, divide by 1,760.**

A Complete the tables.

1 mile =	**5,280 feet**	1 mile =	**1,760 yards**	3,520 yards =	**2 miles**
2 miles =		2 miles =		21,120 feet =	
3 miles =		3 miles =		1,760 yards =	
4 miles =		4 miles =		15,840 feet =	
5 miles =		5 miles =		8,800 yards =	
6 miles =		6 miles =		31,680 feet =	
7 miles =		7 miles =		19,360 yards =	
8 miles =		8 miles =		5,280 feet =	
9 miles =		9 miles =		35,200 yards =	
10 miles =		10 miles =		132,000 feet =	

EXAMPLE:

a. **To convert kilometers to meters, multiply by 1,000. To convert meters to kilometers, divide by 1,000.**

b. **To convert kilometers to centimeters, multiply by 100,000. To convert centimeters to kilometers, divide by 100,000.**

B Complete the tables.

1 km =	**1,000 m**	1 km =	**100,000 cm**	6,000 m =	**6 km**
2 km =		2 km =		100,000 cm =	
3 km =		3 km =		10,000 m =	
4 km =		4 km =		700,000 cm =	
5 km =		5 km =		5,000 m =	
6 km =		6 km =		800,000 cm =	
7 km =		7 km =		2,000 m =	
8 km =		8 km =		300,000 cm =	
9 km =		9 km =		1,000 m =	
10 km =		10 km =		500,000 cm =	

REMINDER: Write the definitions of a mile and a kilometer.

Unit 110 cont'd ☞

Multiply by 1.6 when converting miles to kilometers.
Multiply by .6 when converting kilometers to miles.

C Convert miles to kilometers.

① 1 mi. = **1.6 km**   ② 2 mi. =   ③ 3 mi. =   ④ 5 mi. =

⑤ 10 mi. =   ⑥ 21 mi. =   ⑦ 25 mi. =   ⑧ 100 mi. =

⑨ 50 mi. =   ⑩ 8 mi. =   ⑪ 11 mi. =   ⑫ 4 mi. =

⑬ 12 mi. =   ⑭ 7 mi. =   ⑮ 75 mi. =   ⑯ 16 mi. =

D Convert kilometers to miles.

① 2 km = **1.2 mi.**   ② 5 km =   ③ 18 km =   ④ 1 km =

⑤ 10 km =   ⑥ 25 km =   ⑦ 100 km =   ⑧ 30 km =

⑨ 12 km =   ⑩ 125 km =   ⑪ 42 km =   ⑫ 14 km =

⑬ 50 km =   ⑭ 200 km =   ⑮ 75 km =   ⑯ 1,000 km =

E Work the problems.

① Harrison traveled 200 miles. Collier traveled 150 kilometers. Who traveled farther?

Harrison
_____

② Highway 14 is 900 kilometers long. Highway 21 is 750 miles long. Which highway is longer?

_____

③ Carrie jogs 15 miles per week. Sandi jogs 28 kilometers per week. Who jogs more?

_____

④ Andrea drove 412 miles on Monday. On Tuesday she drove 500 kilometers. On which day did she drive farther?

_____

⑤ Bob lives 2 miles from school. Rick lives 4 kilometers from school. Who lives closer?

_____

⑥ Dr. North walks 8 kilometers each day. Mrs. North walks 4 miles each day. Who walks more?

_____

⑦ Nina lives 18 kilometers from Linnville and 14 miles from Turman. Which town is closer?

_____

⑧ Stuart rode his bicycle 5 miles on Thursday and 6 kilometers on Friday. On which day did he ride more?

_____

⑨ The nearest exit is 32 miles. The nearest rest stop is 36 kilometers. Which place is closer?

_____

Comprehension Check

Test 22

A Fill in the blanks.

① An _____*inch*_____ is an English unit of measure equaling 1/12 of a foot.

② A _____ is a metric unit of measure equaling 10 millimeters.

③ A _____ is an English unit of measure equaling 12 inches or 1/3 of a yard.

④ A _____ is an English unit of measure equaling 36 inches or 3 feet.

⑤ A _____ is a metric unit of measure equaling 100 centimeters or 1,000 millimeters.

⑥ A _____ is an English unit of measure equaling 5,280 feet or 1,760 yards.

⑦ A _____ is a metric unit of measure equaling 1,000 meters or 100,000 centimeters.

⑧ Inches, feet, yards, and miles are _____ units of measure.

⑨ Centimeters, meters, and kilometers are _____ units of measure.

⑩ One foot equals _____ inches. Three feet equal _____ yard. Five thousand, two hundred eighty feet equal one _____.

B Match the equivalent measures.

① 12 inches	1 yard	⑩ 36 inches	1 yard
② 10 millimeters	1 meter	⑪ 6 inches	10 centimeters
③ 3 feet	1 foot	⑫ 100 millimeters	1 kilometer
④ 100 centimeters	1 centimeter	⑬ 100,000 centimeters	1 mile
⑤ 10,000 millimeters	3 yards	⑭ 1,760 yards	1/3 yard
⑥ 5,280 feet	1 mile	⑮ 1 foot	1/2 foot
⑦ 1,000 meters	10 meters	⑯ 1,000 millimeters	1/12 foot
⑧ 9 feet	2 miles	⑰ 1 inch	2 miles
⑨ 3,520 yards	1 kilometer	⑱ 10,560 feet	1 meter

Test 22 cont'd ☛

1 inch = 1/12 foot	1 yard = 36 inches	100 centimeters = 1 meter
12 inches = 1 foot	5,280 feet = 1 mile	1,000 millimeters = 1 meter
1 foot = 1/3 yard	1,760 yards = 1 mile	1,000 meters = 1 kilometer
3 feet = 1 yard	1 centimeter= 10 millimeters	100,000 centimeters = 1 kilometer

C Fill in the equivalent measures.

① in. __12__
  ft. __*1*__
  yd. __*1/3*__

② mm _____
  cm __100__
  m _____

③ in. __36__
  ft. _____
  yd. _____

④ mm _____
  cm _____
  m __5__

⑤ ft. _____
  yd. _____
  mi. __4__

⑥ cm __100,000__
  m _____
  km _____

⑦ cm _____
  m __4,000__
  km _____

⑧ ft. __5,280__
  yd. _____
  mi. _____

⑨ mm __12,000__
  cm _____
  m _____

⑩ in. _____
  ft. _____
  yd. __10__

⑪ in. _____
  ft. __18__
  yd. _____

⑫ ft. _____
  yd. __17,600__
  mi. _____

⑬ cm _____
  m _____
  km __22__

⑭ mm _____
  cm __900__
  m _____

⑮ ft. __15,840__
  yd. _____
  mi. _____

⑯ in. _____
  ft. __300__
  yd. _____

⑰ in. _____
  ft. _____
  yd. __12__

⑱ cm _____
  m __14,000__
  km _____

⑲ mm _____
  cm __1,500__
  m _____

⑳ cm _____
  m _____
  km __100__

㉑ ft. _____
  yd. _____
  mi. __25__

㉒ mm _____
  cm _____
  m __7__

㉓ ft. __2,640__
  yd. _____
  mi. _____

㉔ in. _____
  ft. _____
  yd. __1,000__

Write a paragraph describing a business transaction in which there is a profit.

_____
_____
_____
_____
_____
_____
_____

English Units of Length

Learning Objective: *We will learn to measure with English units of length.*

Inches, feet, yards, and miles are English units of length.

EXAMPLE:

1 inch = 1/12 foot	3 feet = 1 yard	5,280 feet = 1 mile
12 inches = 1 foot	1 inch = 1/36 yard	1,760 yards = 1 mile
1 foot = 1/3 yard	36 inches = 1 yard	

A Match the equivalent measures.

① 12 inches	2 yards	⑪ 5,280 feet	2 miles
② 36 inches	1 foot	⑫ 3,520 yards	1 mile
③ 2 feet	24 inches	⑬ 360 inches	10 yards
④ 6 feet	20 yards	⑭ 5 miles	270 feet
⑤ 1 inch	1 yard	⑮ 100 feet	1/2 mile
⑥ 18 inches	30 feet	⑯ 90 yards	1,200 inches
⑦ 60 feet	1/2 yard	⑰ 2,640 feet	26,400 feet
⑧ 10 yards	1/36 yard	⑱ 440 yards	63,360 inches
⑨ 10 feet	144 inches	⑲ 1 mile	12,320 yards
⑩ 12 feet	120 inches	⑳ 7 miles	1/4 mile

B Fill in the blanks.

① An ____inch____ is a unit of length equaling 1/12 foot.

② A _____ is a unit of length equaling 12 inches.

③ A _____ is a unit of length equaling 36 inches.

④ A _____ is a unit of length equaling 5,280 feet.

⑤ In this lesson, the shortest unit of length is the _____ .

⑥ In this lesson, the longest unit of length is the _____ .

⑦ Compared to inches, a foot is _____ .

⑧ A yard is _____ than a mile.

⑨ A mile is _____ than a foot.

⑩ Two yards _____ six feet.

REMINDER: Name four English units of length.

_____

_____

C Which unit of length is usually used to measure these distances?

inch ① the length of a curtain

_____ ② the distance to the next town

_____ ③ the length of a long piece of material

_____ ④ the length of a trailer

_____ ⑤ the length of a road

_____ ⑥ the length of a long table

_____ ⑦ the length of a photograph

_____ ⑧ the height of a person

_____ ⑨ the length of thread on a spool

_____ ⑩ the width of a door

_____ ⑪ the length of a roll of lace

_____ ⑫ the distance from home to school

_____ ⑬ the length of a telephone cord

_____ ⑭ the size of a picture frame

_____ ⑮ the length of an interstate

_____ ⑯ the height of a mountain

D Work the problems.

① David is 5 feet, 10 inches tall. His sister Kay is 5 feet, 2 inches tall. How much taller is David than Kay?

② Wendell drove 300 miles on Tuesday, 250 miles on Wednesday, and 312 miles on Thursday. How far did Wendell drive in the three days?

③ Sarah wants to cut 36 yards of trim into 6 equal pieces. How long will each piece be?

④ Washington jogs 6 miles per day. How far does he jog in 30 days?

Metric Units of Length

Learning Objective: *We will learn to measure with metric units of length.*

Millimeters, centimeters, meters, and kilometers are metric units of length.

EXAMPLE:

1 centimeter = 10 millimeters	1,000 meters = 1 kilometer
100 centimeters = 1 meter	100,000 centimeters = 1 kilometer
1,000 millimeters = 1 meter	

A Match the equivalent measures.

① 1 centimeter   1 meter
② 10 centimeter   10 millimeters
③ 100 centimeters   10 meters
④ 1,000 centimeter   100 millimeters
⑤ 40 centimeters   2 meters
⑥ 2,000 millimeter   1 kilometer
⑦ 1,000 meters   8,000 meters
⑧ 8 kilometers   400 millimeters
⑨ 90 millimeters   4 kilometers
⑩ 400,000 centimeters   9 centimeters

⑪ 700,000 centimeters   10 meters
⑫ 500 centimeters   7 kilometers
⑬ 1,000 millimeters   1 meter
⑭ 1 centimeter   1/100 meter
⑮ 10,000 millimeters   5 meters
⑯ 1 millimeter   1/1,000 meter
⑰ 11,000 meters   9 kilometers
⑱ 900,000 centimeters   13,000 meters
⑲ 13 kilometers   11 kilometers
⑳ 1 meter   1/1,000 kilometer

B Fill in the blanks.

① A _____ is a metric unit of length equaling 10 millimeters.

② A _____ is a metric unit of length equaling 100 centimeters.

③ A _____ is a metric unit of length equaling 1,000 meters.

④ In this lesson, the _____ is the shortest unit of length.

⑤ In this lesson, the _____ is the longest unit of length.

REMINDER: Name four metric units of length.

_____

_____

Unit 112 cont'd ☞

C Underline the longer lengths.

① <u>10 meters</u>
900 centimeters

② 2 kilometers
3,000 meters

③ 100,000 centimeters
1/2 kilometer

④ 10,000 millimeters
100 centimeter

⑤ 1 centimeter
5 millimeters

⑥ 5 meters
5 kilometers

⑦ 70 millimeters
7 meters

⑧ 600 centimeters
30 millimeters

⑨ 20 kilometers
200 meters

⑩ 22 centimeters
200 millimeters

⑪ 1/100 meter
10 centimeters

⑫ 1/1,000 kilometer
100 meters

⑬ 700,000 centimeters
10 kilometers

⑭ 80 kilometers
8,000 meters

⑮ 65 millimeters
7 centimeters

⑯ 80,000 meters
8 millimeters

⑰ 45 millimeters
5 centimeters

⑱ 1,900,000 centimeters
190 kilometers

⑲ 2,000 millimeters
1 kilometer

⑳ 1,000,000 millimeters
100 meters

㉑ 80 kilometers
8,500 meters

㉒ 1/10 centimeter
1/2 millimeter

㉓ 1/10 centimeter
1/10 millimeter

㉔ 1 kilometer
1,000 millimeter

D Work the problems.

① From Beachport to Melville is 60 kilometers. From Melville to Canyon Bluff is 126 kilometers. From Canyon Bluff to Riverside is 111 kilometers. How far is it from Beachport to Riverside?

② Highway A is 47 kilometers long. Highway B is 83 kilometers long. How much longer is Highway B than Highway A?

③ Jena bought 12 meters of linen to make napkins. If a set of napkins takes 2 meters, how many sets can Jena make?

④ Mr. Delaney has four tables. Each table is 50 centimeters long. If he puts the tables end to end, how long will the tables be?

Ounces and Grams   Unit 113

We will learn to measure with ounces and grams.

An ounce is an English unit of measure equaling 1/16 of a pound.
A gram is a metric unit of measure equaling .001 kilogram.

EXAMPLE:

1 oz. = 1/16 lb.	8 oz. = 1/2 lb.	1 g = .001 kg	50 g = .05 kg
2 oz. = 1/8 lb.	12 oz. = 3/4 lb.	2 g = .002 kg	500 g = .5 kg
4 oz. = 1/4 lb.	16 oz. = 1 lb.	5 g = .005 kg	1,000 g = 1 kg

A Complete the tables.

1 ounce = *1/16 pound*	32 ounces = *2 pounds*	1 pound = *16 ounces*
2 ounces =	48 ounces =	2 pounds =
3 ounces =	64 ounces =	3 pounds =
4 ounces =	80 ounces =	4 pounds =
5 ounces =	96 ounces =	5 pounds =
6 ounces =	112 ounces =	10 pounds =
7 ounces =	128 ounces =	15 pounds =
8 ounces =	144 ounces =	20 pounds =
9 ounces =	160 ounces =	25 pounds =
10 ounces =	176 ounces =	50 pounds =
11 ounces =	192 ounces =	75 pounds =
12 ounces =	208 ounces =	100 pounds =
13 ounces =	224 ounces =	500 pounds =
14 ounces =	240 ounces =	1,000 pounds =
15 ounces =	256 ounces =	2,000 pounds =
16 ounces =	272 ounces =	5,000 pounds =

1 gram = *.001 kilogram*	100 grams = *.1 kilogram*	1,500 grams = *1.5 kilograms*
2 grams =	200 grams =	2,000 grams =
3 grams =	300 grams =	2,500 grams =
4 grams =	400 grams =	3,000 grams =
5 grams =	500 grams =	5,000 grams =
6 grams =	600 grams =	7,500 grams =
7 grams =	700 grams =	10,000 grams =
8 grams =	800 grams =	100,000 grams =
9 grams =	900 grams =	150,000 grams =
10 grams =	1,000 grams =	500,000 grams =

REMINDER: Write the definitions of an ounce and a gram.

_____

_____

Unit 113 cont'd

Multiply by 28 when converting ounces to grams.
Multiply by .035 when converting grams to ounces.

B Convert ounces to grams.

① 1 oz. = **28 g**   ② 2 oz. =   ③ 4 oz. =   ④ 8 oz. =

⑤ 14 oz. =   ⑥ 16 oz. =   ⑦ 20 oz. =   ⑧ 12 oz. =

⑨ 25 oz. =   ⑩ 50 oz. =   ⑪ 75 oz. =   ⑫ 100 oz. =

⑬ 200 oz. =   ⑭ 250 oz. =   ⑮ 500 oz. =   ⑯ 1,000 oz. =

C Convert grams to ounces.

① 28 g = **.98 oz.**   ② 56 g =   ③ 84 g =   ④ 112 g =

⑤ 140 g =   ⑥ 14 g =   ⑦ 2 g =   ⑧ 1 g =

⑨ 500 g =   ⑩ 1,000 g =   ⑪ 2,500 g =   ⑫ 5,000 g =

⑬ 1,250 g =   ⑭ 75 g =   ⑮ 450 g =   ⑯ 10,000 g =

D Work the problems.

① Connie needs 16 ounces of green beans. The package contains 450 grams. Will one package be enough?

_____**yes**_____

② Robin used 200 grams of rice cereal. The recipe called for 6-8 ounces. Did she use the right amount?

_____

③ Kevin read that a package of flour weighed 2,240 grams. Is this more or less than a 10-pound bag?

_____

④ Lucy divided the fudge into one-ounce squares. Does each square weigh more or less than a gram?

_____

⑤ Joe used 224 grams of noodles. The package contained 8 ounces. How much of the package did he use?

_____

⑥ Andy's math book weighs 560 grams. His history book weighs 32 ounces. Which book is heavier?

_____

⑦ A loaf of bread weighed 32 ounces. A package of hamburger buns weighed 784 grams. Which weighed more?

_____

⑧ How many grams are in one ounce?

_____

⑨ If Ed ate 400 grams of cereal and Jean ate 10 ounces of cereal, who ate more?

_____

Pounds and Kilograms

Learning Objective: *We will learn to measure with pounds and kilograms.*

A pound is an English unit of measure equaling 16 ounces or 1/2,000 ton.
A kilogram is a metric unit of measure equaling 1,000 grams or .001 metric ton.

EXAMPLE:

1 pound = 16 ounces	1 kilogram = 1,000 grams
1 pound = 1/2,000 ton	1 kilogram = .001 metric ton
2,000 pounds = 1 ton	1,000 kilograms = 1 metric ton

A Complete the tables.

1 pound = *16 ounces*	1 pound = *1/2,000 ton*	16 ounces = *1 pound*
2 pounds =	500 pounds =	32 ounces =
3 pounds =	1,000 pounds =	80 ounces =
4 pounds =	1,500 pounds =	160 ounces =
5 pounds =	2,000 pounds =	400 ounces =
6 pounds =	4,000 pounds =	800 ounces =
7 pounds =	6,000 pounds =	1,600 ounces =
8 pounds =	8,000 pounds =	1 ton = *2,000 pounds*
9 pounds =	10,000 pounds =	2 tons =
10 pounds =	12,000 pounds =	10 tons =
11 pounds =	20,000 pounds =	25 tons =
12 pounds =	24,000 pounds =	50 tons =

1 kilogram = *1,000 grams*	1 kilogram = *.001 metric ton*	1,000 grams = *1 kilogram*
2 kilograms =	5 kilograms =	5,000 grams =
3 kilograms =	10 kilograms =	10,000 grams =
4 kilograms =	25 kilograms =	50,000 grams =
5 kilograms =	50 kilograms =	100,000 grams =
6 kilograms =	100 kilograms =	1 metric ton = *1,000 kilograms*
7 kilograms =	500 kilograms =	2 metric tons =
8 kilograms =	1,000 kilograms = *1 metric ton*	5 metric tons =
9 kilograms =	2,000 kilograms =	10 metric tons =
10 kilograms =	5,000 kilograms =	50 metric tons =
11 kilograms =	10,000 kilograms =	100 metric tons =
12 kilograms =	50,000 kilograms =	1,000 metric tons =

REMINDER: Write the definitions of an ounce and a kilogram.

_____

_____

Multiply by .45 when converting pounds to kilograms.
Multiply by 2.2 when converting kilograms to pounds.

B Convert pounds to kilograms.

① 1 lb. = *.45 kg*　　② 2 lbs. =　　③ 3 lbs. =　　④ 4 lbs. =

⑤ 5 lbs. =　　⑥ 10 lbs. =　　⑦ 12 lbs. =　　⑧ 15 lbs. =

⑨ 25 lbs. =　　⑩ 50 lbs. =　　⑪ 100 lbs. =　　⑫ 250 lbs. =

⑬ 500 lbs. =　　⑭ 1,000 lbs. =　　⑮ 2,000 lbs. =　　⑯ 4,000 lbs. =

C Convert kilograms to pounds.

① 1 kg = *2.2 lbs.*　　② 2 kg =　　③ 5 kg =　　④ 10 kg =

⑤ 50 kg =　　⑥ 100 kg =　　⑦ 200 kg =　　⑧ 500 kg =

⑨ 700 kg =　　⑩ 1,000 kg =　　⑪ 1,500 kg =　　⑫ 2,000 kg =

⑬ 76 kg =　　⑭ 42 kg =　　⑮ 85 kg =　　⑯ 5,000 kg =

D Work the problems.

① Kelly weighs 105 pounds. Her twin sister Kelsey weighs 50 kilograms. Who weighs more?
　　Kelsey
　　_____

② George weighs 75 kilograms. Benson weighs 195 pounds. Who weighs more?
　　_____

③ Marcus received a box of candy that weighed 4 1/2 kilograms. If he ate half of it, how many pounds were left?
　　_____

④ Donna bought a 5-pound bag of sugar. She also bought a 7-kilogram bag of flour. Did she buy more sugar or flour?
　　_____

⑤ Calvin weighs 140 pounds. Alex weighs 60 kilograms. Who weighs less?
　　_____

⑥ Which is heavier, a 25-pound bag of sand or a 15-kilogram bag of grass seed?
　　_____

⑦ Henry's birthday present weighed 60 pounds. He hoped he was getting weights. The weights would weigh 27 kilograms. Could the present be the weights?
　　_____

⑧ Mindy weighs 100 pounds. Jill weighs 55 kilograms. Who weighs more?
　　_____

⑨ Which is lighter, a 5-kilogram box of sawdust or a 5-pound box of potting soil?
　　_____

English Units of Weight   Unit 115

Learning Objective: *We will learn to measure with English units of weight.*

Ounces and pounds are English units of weight.

EXAMPLE:

1 oz. = 1/16 lb.	12 oz. = 3/4 lb.	1 lb. = 16 oz.
4 oz. = 1/4 lb.	16 oz. = 1 lb.	1 lb. = 1/2,000 T.
8 oz. = 1/2 lb.	32 oz. = 2 lbs.	2,000 lbs. = 1 T.

A Match the equivalent measures.

① 16 ounces	1 pound		⑪ 1,000 pounds	1 ton
② 8 ounces	1/4 pound		⑫ 500 pounds	1/2 ton
③ 4 ounces	10 pounds		⑬ 1,500 pounds	1/4 ton
④ 64 ounces	128 ounces		⑭ 2,000 pounds	3/4 ton
⑤ 160 ounces	1/2 pound		⑮ 4,000 pounds	60,000 pounds
⑥ 112 ounces	400 pounds		⑯ 10,000 pounds	2 tons
⑦ 8 pounds	4 pounds		⑰ 1 pound	1/2,000 ton
⑧ 6,400 ounces	640 ounces		⑱ 30 tons	5 tons
⑨ 25 pounds	7 pounds		⑲ 96,000 ounces	3 tons
⑩ 40 pounds	400 ounces		⑳ 50 tons	100,000 pounds

B Fill in the blanks.

① An _____ is an English unit of weight equaling 1/16 pound.

② A _____ is an English unit of weight equaling 16 ounces.

③ Ounces are _____ than pounds.

④ Pounds are _____ than ounces.

⑤ Ounces and pounds are _____ units of weight.

REMINDER: Name two English units of weight.

_____

_____

Unit 115 cont'd ☛

C Underline the heavier weights.

1. 16 ounces
   <u>16 pounds</u>

2. 32 ounces
   3 pounds

3. 1/2 pound
   10 ounces

4. 100 pounds
   1,000 ounces

5. 1/4 pound
   2 ounces

6. 1 pound
   15 ounces

7. 30 ounces
   2 pounds

8. 5 pounds
   75 ounces

9. 21 ounces
   2 pounds

10. 160 ounces
    11 pounds

11. 17 pounds
    200 ounces

12. 11 ounces
    3/4 pound

13. 12 ounces
    1/3 pound

14. 9 pounds
    76 ounces

15. 1 pound
    1 ounce

16. 16 pounds
    1 ounce

17. 1 pound
    18 ounces

18. 50 ounces
    5 pounds

19. 15 pounds
    250 ounces

20. 64 pounds
    64 ounces

21. 99 ounces
    7 pounds

22. 42 ounces
    4 pounds

23. 49 ounces
    3 pounds

24. 1/2 ounce
    1/2 pound

D Work the problems.

1. Edna bought a ham that weighed 14 pounds. She cut it into 7 equal portions. How much did each portion weigh?

2. Nancy's suitcase weighed 9 pounds empty. She packed it for her vacation, and the suitcase weighed 46 pounds. How much did Nancy pack?

3. Kenneth bought 16 ounces of green beans, 10 ounces of spinach, 18 ounces of cauliflower, and 22 ounces of brussel sprouts. How much did the groceries weigh?

4. Walt has 8 boxes of candy. Each box weighs 10 pounds. How much candy does Walt have?

Comprehension Check

A Fill in the blanks.

① Inches, feet, yards, and miles are __English__ units of length.

② Millimeters, centimeters, meters, and kilometers are _____ units of length.

③ Ounces and pounds are _____ units of weight.

④ Grams and kilograms are _____ units of weight.

⑤ An _____ is an English unit of measure equaling 1/16 pound.

⑥ A _____ is a metric unit of measure equaling .001 kilogram.

⑦ A _____ is an English unit of measure equaling 16 ounces.

⑧ A _____ is a metric unit of measure equaling 1,000 grams.

⑨ An ounce is _____ than a pound.

⑩ A gram is _____ than a kilogram.

⑪ A pound is _____ than an ounce.

⑫ A kilogram is _____ than a gram.

B Match the equivalent measures.

① 8 ounces	1 pound		⑧ 1 kilogram	1,000 grams
② 16 ounces	160 ounces		⑨ 1 gram	50,000 grams
③ 2,000 pounds	1 ton		⑩ 1,000 kilograms	1 metric ton
④ 1 ounce	1/2 pound		⑪ 50 kilograms	.001 kilogram
⑤ 10 pounds	1/16 pound		⑫ 2,000 grams	.006 kilogram
⑥ 2 pounds	80 ounces		⑬ 6 grams	.1 kilogram
⑦ 5 pounds	32 ounces		⑭ 100 grams	2 kilograms

Test 23 cont'd ☞

1 ounce = 1/16 pound	1/2 ton 1,000 pounds	100 grams = .1 kilogram
8 ounces = 1/2 pound	1 ton = 2,000 pounds	1,000 grams = 1 kilogram
16 ounces = 1 pound	1 gram = .001 kilogram	1 kilogram = .001 metric ton
1 pound = 1/2,000 ton	10 grams = .01 kilogram	1,000 kilograms = 1 metric ton

C Fill in the equivalent measures.

① oz. 8
   lb. *1/2*

② g 1,000
   kg

③ oz. 16
   lb.

④ g 200
   kg

⑤ lb.
   T. 1/2

⑥ lb. 10,000
   T.

⑦ kg 5,000
   t

⑧ kg
   t 7

⑨ oz. 32
   lb.

⑩ lb. 500
   T.

⑪ kg
   t 10

⑫ g 900
   kg

⑬ g 1,100
   kg

⑭ lb. 100,000
   T.

⑮ kg
   t .001

⑯ oz.
   lb. 8

⑰ oz.
   lb.
   T. 1

⑱ oz.
   lb.. 6,000
   T.

⑲ g
   kg
   t 5

⑳ g
   kg
   t 80

㉑ oz.
   lb.
   T. 1/4

㉒ oz. 128,000
   lb.
   T.

㉓ g
   kg 1,200
   t

㉔ g 25,000,000
   kg
   t

㉕ oz. 320,000
   lb.
   T.

㉖ oz.
   lb. 110,000
   T.

㉗ g 1,000,000
   kg
   t

㉘ g
   kg 13,000
   t

Write a list of 10 items usually measured in ounces and grams and 10 items measured in pounds and kilograms.

        ounces and grams   **pounds and kilograms**

_____ _____   _____ _____

_____ _____   _____ _____

_____ _____   _____ _____

_____ _____   _____ _____

_____ _____   _____ _____

Metric Units of Weight

Unit 116

Learning Objective: *We will learn to measure with metric units of weight.*

Grams and kilograms are metric units of weight.

EXAMPLE:	1 g = .001 kg	50 g = .05 kg	1 kg = 1,000 g
	2 g = .002 kg	500 g = .5 kg	1 kg = .001 t
	5 g = .005 kg	1,000 g = 1 kg	1,000 kg = 1 t

A Match the equivalent measures.

① .01 kilogram	.1 kilogram	⑪ 1,000 kilograms	.007 metric ton
② 100 grams	10 grams	⑫ 1,000 grams	1 kilogram
③ 4,000 grams	4 kilograms	⑬ 7 kilograms	90 grams
④ 400 grams	.04 kilogram	⑭ 8,000 grams	1 metric ton
⑤ 40 grams	4 metric tons	⑮ .009 metric ton	9 kilograms
⑥ 4 grams	.4 kilogram	⑯ .09 kilograms	19 kilograms
⑦ 4 kilograms	.004 metric ton	⑰ .9 kilograms	8 kilograms
⑧ 4,000 kilograms	400 metric tons	⑱ 19,000 grams	9 metric tons
⑨ 40,000 grams	.004 kilograms	⑲ 9,000 kilograms	.001 kilogram
⑩ 400,000 kilograms	40 kilograms	⑳ 1 gram	900 grams

B Fill in the blanks.

① A _____ is a metric unit of weight equaling .001 kilogram.

② A _____ is a metric unit of weight equaling 1,000 grams.

③ A gram is _____ than a kilogram.

④ A kilogram is _____ than a gram.

⑤ Grams and kilograms are _____ units of weight.

REMINDER: Name two metric units of weight.

_____

_____

Unit 116 cont'd ☞

C Underline the heavier weights.

① 1 gram
<u>1 kilogram</u>

② .003 kilograms
.03 grams

③ 6,000 grams
8 kilograms

④ 50 grams
.005 kilograms

⑤ 10 grams
.1 kilogram

⑥ 10 kilograms
1,000 grams

⑦ 100 grams
1.1 kilograms

⑧ 100 grams
100 kilograms

⑨ .05 kilograms
500 grams

⑩ 7.7 kilograms
8,000 grams

⑪ 2,000 grams
4 kilograms

⑫ 1/2 kilogram
650 grams

⑬ 22,000 grams
23 kilograms

⑭ 900 grams
9 kilograms

⑮ 60 grams
.05 kilograms

⑯ 100 kilograms
1,000 grams

⑰ 1,000 grams
1/2 kilogram

⑱ 1/2 kilogram
1/2 gram

⑲ .5 kilogram
.5 gram

⑳ 17,000 grams
170 kilograms

㉑ 25 kilograms
2.5 grams

㉒ 750 kilograms
7,700 grams

㉓ 1.5 grams
1.5 kilograms

㉔ .002 kilograms
1 gram

D Work the problems.

① Robert weighs 84 kilograms. Cameron weighs 72 kilograms. Donald weighs 90 kilograms. How much do the three weigh together?

② Bradley weighs 91 kilograms. Edith weighs 52 kilograms. How much heavier is Bradley than Edith?

③ Ted bought 6 boxes of cereal. Each box weighed 896 grams. How much did the 6 boxes weigh?

④ Felix bought 25 kilograms of beef. He had the butcher wrap it in 5 equal packages. How much did each package weigh?

Cups, Pints, and Quarts   Unit 117

Learning
Objective: *We will learn to measure with cups, pints, and quarts.*

A cup is an English unit of measure equaling 8 ounces.
A pint is an English unit of measure equaling 2 cups.
A quart is an English unit of measure equaling 2 pints.

EXAMPLE:	1 cup = 8 ounces	1 pint = 2 cups	1 quart = 2 pints
	2 cups = 16 ounces	2 pints = 4 cups	1 quart = 4 cups

A Complete the tables.

1 ounce = *1/8 cup*	1 pint = *2 cups*	1 quart =
2 ounces =	2 pints =	2 quarts =
3 ounces =	3 pints =	3 quarts =
4 ounces =	4 pints =	4 quarts =
5 ounces =	5 pints =	5 quarts =
6 ounces =	6 pints =	6 quarts =
7 ounces =	7 pints =	7 quarts =
8 ounces =	8 pints =	8 quarts =
1 cup = *8 ounces*	9 pints =	1 quart = *4 cups*
2 cups =	10 pints =	2 quarts =
3 cups =	11 pints =	3 quarts =
4 cups =	12 pints =	4 quarts =
5 cups =	13 pints =	5 quarts =

B Match the equivalent measures.

① 1 pint	1 cup	⑥ 12 pints		40 cups
② 1/2 pint	4 cups	⑦ 10 quarts		24 cups
③ 1 quart	2 cups	⑧ 100 cups		50 pints
④ 160 ounces	20 cups	⑨ 70 cups		80 cups
⑤ 24 ounces	3 cups	⑩ 20 quarts		35 pints

REMINDER: Write the definitions of cups, pints, and quarts.

C Fill in the equivalent measures.

① c. _____**80**_____   ② c. _____18_____   ③ c. _____   ④ c. _____16_____

   pt. _____40_____   pt. _____   pt. _____   pt. _____

   qt. _____**20**_____   qt. _____   qt. _____2_____   qt. _____

⑤ c. _____   ⑥ c. _____160_____   ⑦ c. _____   ⑧ c. _____

   pt. _____   pt. _____   pt. _____   pt. _____1,000_____

   qt. _____11_____   qt. _____   qt. _____5_____   qt. _____

⑨ c. _____   ⑩ c. _____300_____   ⑪ c. _____   ⑫ c. _____

   pt. _____1,500_____   pt. _____   pt. _____   pt. _____

   qt. _____   qt. _____   qt. _____16_____   qt. _____1/2_____

⑬ c. _____   ⑭ c. _____100_____   ⑮ c. _____   ⑯ c. _____10_____

   pt. _____42_____   pt. _____   pt. _____   pt. _____

   qt. _____   qt. _____   qt. _____50_____   qt. _____

D Work the problems.

① In one week, Lester drank 2 quarts of milk, 2 pints of tea, and 320 ounces of water. Of which liquid did he drink most?

_____*water*_____

② Marty needs 4 cups of milk to make pudding. She has one quart of milk. Does she have enough?

_____

③ Pamela canned 10 quarts of tomato juice. She also canned 30 pints of peaches. Which did she can more of?

_____

④ Tim canned 18 pints of peas. He canned 10 quarts of beans. Which did he can more of?

_____

⑤ Fred picked 41 pints of blueberries. Zeke picked 20 quarts of blueberries. Who picked more?

_____

⑥ Elizabeth drinks 448 ounces of water per week. Carolyn drinks 35 cups of water per week. Who drinks more water?

_____

Gallons and Liters

Learning Objective: *We will learn to measure with gallons and liters.*

A gallon is an English unit of measure equaling 4 quarts.
A liter is a metric unit of measure equaling approximately 1 quart.

EXAMPLE:

1 gallon = 4 quarts	1 liter = 1.06 quarts	
1 gallon = 8 pints	1 liter = 2.1 pints	
1 gallon = 16 cups	1 liter = 100 centiliters	
1 gallon = 128 ounces	1 liter = 1,000 milliliters	
	1 liter = .26 gallon	

A Complete the tables.

1 gallon = *128 ounces*	1 gallon = *8 pints*	1 gallon = *4 quarts*
2 gallons =	2 gallons =	2 gallons =
3 gallons =	3 gallons =	3 gallons =
4 gallons =	4 gallons =	4 gallons =
5 gallons =	5 gallons =	5 gallons =
6 gallons =	6 gallons =	6 gallons =
7 gallons =	7 gallons =	7 gallons =
8 gallons =	8 gallons =	8 gallons =
9 gallons =	9 gallons =	9 gallons =
10 gallons =	10 gallons =	10 gallons =
1 gallon = *16 cups*	11 gallons =	11 gallons =
2 gallons =	12 gallons =	12 gallons =
3 gallons =	13 gallons =	13 gallons =
4 gallons =	14 gallons =	14 gallons =
5 gallons =	15 gallons =	15 gallons =

1 liter = *100 centiliters*	1 liter = *1.06 quarts*	1 liter = *2.1 pints*
2 liters =	2 liters =	2 liters =
3 liters =	3 liters =	3 liters =
4 liters =	4 liters =	4 liters =
5 liters =	5 liters =	5 liters =
1 liter = *1,000 milliliters*	6 liters =	1 liter = *.26 gallon*
2 liters =	7 liters =	2 liters =
3 liters =	8 liters =	3 liters =
4 liters =	9 liters =	4 liters =
5 liters =	10 liters =	5 liters =

REMINDER: Write the definitions of a gallon and a liter.

B Underline the larger measures.

① <u>1 gallon</u>   ② 1/2 gallon   ③ 1/4 gallon   ④ 2 gallons
  1 liter   1 liter   1 liter   10 liters

⑤ 1 gallon   ⑥ 1 gallon   ⑦ 1 gallon   ⑧ 1 gallon
  5 quarts   7 pints   130 ounces   18 cups

⑨ 1 liter   ⑩ 1 liter   ⑪ 1 liter   ⑫ 1 liter
  500 centiliters   500 milliliters   2 quarts   1.1 pints

C Fill in the equivalent measures.

① oz. __256__   ② oz. _____   ③ oz. _____   ④ oz. _____
  c. __32__   c. __64__   c. _____   c. _____
  pt. __16__   pt. _____   pt. __80__   pt. _____
  qt. __8__   qt. _____   qt. _____   qt. _____
  gal. __2__   gal. _____   gal. _____   gal. __5__

⑤ ml _____   ⑥ ml _____   ⑦ ml __6,000__   ⑧ ml _____
  cl _____   cl __500__   cl _____   cl _____
  l __10__   l _____   l _____   l __8__

D Work the problems.

① Darrell made 6 gallons of iced tea for the picnic. Wanda made 8 liters of punch. Was there more tea or punch?

_____ *tea* _____

② Rhonda buys 2 liters of milk each week. Phil buys 1 gallon of milk each week. Who buys more milk?

_____

③ Hannah buys gas at $1 per gallon. If she could buy it at 50 cents per liter, would the gas be cheaper?

_____

④ Louise made 4 liters of lemonade. Did she make more or less than a gallon?

_____

⑤ Steve has 13 liters of cola. He has 4 gallons of fruit drink. Does he have more cola than fruit drink?

_____

⑥ Winston has 2 gallons of root beer. He has 6 liters of ginger ale. Does he have more root beer than ginger ale?

_____

English Units of Volume

Learning Objective: *We will learn to measure with English units of volume.*

Ounces, cups, pints, quarts, and gallons are English units of volume.

EXAMPLE:	1/2 cup = 4 ounces	2 pints = 4 cups	1 gallon = 4 quarts
	1 cup = 8 ounces	1 quart = 2 pints	1 gallon = 8 pints
	2 cups = 16 ounces	1 quart = 4 cups	1 gallon = 16 cups
	1 pint = 2 cups	1 quart = 32 ounces	1 gallon = 128 ounces

A Match the equivalent measures.

① 1 cup   2 cups   ⑪ 64 ounces   1/4 cup

② 1 pint   4 quarts   ⑫ 2 ounces   1/2 gallon

③ 1 quart   8 ounces   ⑬ 1/2 quart   2 cups

④ 1 gallon   256 ounces   ⑭ 18 pints   1 cup

⑤ 2 gallons   2 pints   ⑮ 180 cups   32 ounces

⑥ 6 quarts   1 1/2 gallons   ⑯ 1/2 pint   45 quarts

⑦ 1 ounce   20 cups   ⑰ 1 quart   9 quarts

⑧ 10 pints   32 ounces   ⑱ 10 cups   20 pints

⑨ 5 gallons   1/8 cup   ⑲ 10 quarts   5 pints

⑩ 1 quart   20 quarts   ⑳ 1 1/4 quarts   5 cups

B Fill in the blanks.

① One ounce equals ___1/8___ cup.

② One cup equals _____ ounces.

③ Two cups equal _____ pint.

④ One pint equals _____ ounces.

⑤ One pint equals _____ quart.

⑥ One quart equals _____ pints.

⑦ One quart equals _____ cups.

⑧ One quart equals _____ ounces.

⑨ One gallon equals _____ quarts.

⑩ One gallon equals _____ pints.

REMINDER: Name five English units of volume.

_____

_____

Unit 119 cont'd ☞

C Fill in the equivalent measures.

① oz. ____16____
  c. ____2____
  pt. ____1____
  qt. ____1/2____
  gal. ____1/8____

② oz. ____64____
  c. _____
  pt. _____
  qt. _____
  gal. _____

③ oz. _____
  c. _____
  pt. _____
  qt. _____
  gal. ____1____

④ oz. _____
  c. _____
  pt. ____10____
  qt. _____
  gal. _____

⑤ oz. _____
  c. _____
  pt. ____36____
  qt. _____
  gal. _____

⑥ oz. _____
  c. _____
  pt. _____
  qt. ____8____
  gal. _____

⑦ oz. _____
  c. _____
  pt. _____
  qt. _____
  gal. ____10____

⑧ oz. _____
  c. ____200____
  pt. _____
  qt. _____
  gal. _____

⑨ oz. ____640____
  c. _____
  pt. _____
  qt. _____
  gal. _____

⑩ oz. _____
  c. ____100____
  pt. _____
  qt. _____
  gal. _____

⑪ oz. ____1____
  c. _____
  pt. _____
  qt. _____
  gal. _____

⑫ oz. _____
  c. _____
  pt. _____
  qt. _____
  gal. ____100____

D Work the problems.

① Louis made 16 quarts of punch for the class reunion. He also made 12 quarts of tea and 8 quarts of lemonade. How many gallons of beverages did Louis make?

② Carrie canned 30 pints of carrots, 24 pints of beets, 32 pints of green beans, and 15 pints of peas. How many cups of vegetables did she can?

③ Mr. Hawkins bought 12 cups of frozen cauliflower, 8 cups of frozen beans, and 10 cups of frozen spinach. How many ounces of vegetables did he buy?

④ Tammy drinks 64 ounces of water each day. How many quarts of water does she drink in a week?

Metric Units of Volume

Learning Objective: *We will learn to measure with metric units of volume.*

Milliliters, centiliters, and liters are metric units of volume.

EXAMPLE:
1,000 milliliters = 1 liter
100 centiliters = 1 liter
1 centiliter = 10 milliliters

A Match the equivalent measures.

① 1 liter ———————— 1,000 milliliters		⑨ 5 liters	4,000 milliliters	
② 2 liters	10 milliliters	⑩ 50 liters	50,000 milliliters	
③ 1 centiliter	1,100 milliliters	⑪ 4 liters	500 centiliters	
④ 110 centiliters	200 centiliters	⑫ 400 liters	40,000 centiliters	
⑤ 5,000 centiliters	3 liters	⑬ 50 milliliters	5 centiliters	
⑥ 400 centiliters	4 liters	⑭ 50 centiliters	2 liters	
⑦ 3,000 milliliters	50 liters	⑮ 200 centiliters	20 liters	
⑧ 500 centiliters	5 liters	⑯ 20,000 milliliters	1/2 liter	

B Underline the larger volumes.

① 1 centiliter
1 milliliter

② 300 centiliters
300 milliliters

③ 4 liters
4,500 milliliters

④ 2,000 centiliters
21 liters

⑤ 1 liter
1,000 centiliters

⑥ 10 liters
5,000 milliliters

⑦ 10 centiliters
50 milliliters

⑧ 1 centiliter
1 liter

⑨ 100 liters
110,000 milliliters

⑩ 500 centiliters
50 liters

⑪ 50 centiliters
3/4 liter

⑫ 1,000 milliliters
150 centiliters

REMINDER: Name three metric units of volume.

_____

_____

Unit 120 cont'd ☞

C Fill in the equivalent measures.

① ml ___1,000___
  cl ___**100**___
  l ___**1**___

② ml _____
  cl ___200___
  l _____

③ ml _____
  cl _____
  l ___8___

④ ml _____
  cl ___500___
  l _____

⑤ ml ___3,500___
  cl _____
  l _____

⑥ ml _____
  cl _____
  l ___16___

⑦ ml _____
  cl ___150___
  l _____

⑧ ml ___7,000___
  cl _____
  l _____

⑨ ml ___20,000___
  cl _____
  l _____

⑩ ml _____
  cl _____
  l ___4 1/2___

⑪ ml _____
  cl ___600___
  l _____

⑫ ml _____
  cl ___950___
  l _____

⑬ ml _____
  cl _____
  l ___1/2___

⑭ ml ___25,000___
  cl _____
  l _____

⑮ ml _____
  cl ___5,000___
  l _____

⑯ ml ___100,000___
  cl _____
  l _____

⑰ ml _____
  cl ___1,300___
  l _____

⑱ ml _____
  cl _____
  l ___1/4___

⑲ ml _____
  cl _____
  l ___11___

⑳ ml ___80,000___
  cl _____
  l _____

D Work the problems.

① Jeffrey bought a container of milk and poured it equally into four 100-centiliter containers. What size container did Jeffrey buy?

② Dwight has 150 centiliters of tea, 300 centiliters of milk, and 175 centiliters of juice. How much liquid does Dwight have?

③ Sylvia poured a 1,500-milliliter container of milk into 8 equal glasses. How much did she pour in each glass?

④ Paul bought a 450-centiliter container of orange juice. In one week he had drunk 220 centiliters of juice. How much juice was left?

Comprehension Check

A Answer the questions.

① What are five English units of volume? _ounce, cup, pint, quart, and gallon_ _____

   Put them in order of smallest to largest. _____

② What are three metric units of volume? _____

   Put them in order of smallest to largest. _____

③ Which metric unit is closest to the quart? _____

④ Which English unit equals 128 ounces? _____

⑤ Which English unit equals 2 cups? _____

⑥ How many quarts are in a gallon? _____

⑦ Is a gallon larger than a liter? _____

⑧ How many milliliters are in one centiliter? _____

⑨ How many centiliters are in one liter? _____

⑩ Which is larger, a quart or a liter? _____

B Match the equivalent measures.

① 100 centiliters	6 quarts	⑬ 1.06 quarts	1 liter
② 10 milliliters	1 centiliter	⑭ 10 liters	50 pints
③ 12 pints	1 liter	⑮ 100 liters	200 pints
④ 12 cups	6 pints	⑯ 100 pints	200 cups
⑤ 12 ounces	48 quarts	⑰ 100 quarts	10,000 centiliters
⑥ 12 gallons	3 gallons	⑱ 100 gallons	10,000 milliliters
⑦ 12 quarts	3/4 cup	⑲ 100 cups	400 quarts
⑧ 2 gallons	.52 gallon	⑳ 20 cups	160 ounces
⑨ 2 liters	256 ounces	㉑ 100 milliliters	1/10 liter
⑩ 12 liters	120,000 milliliters	㉒ 110 centiliters	1/2 liter
⑪ 120 liters	1,200 centiliters	㉓ 50 centiliters	50 milliliters
⑫ 4 liters	8.4 pints	㉔ 5 centiliters	1,100 milliliters

Test 24 cont'd 👉

1 cup = 8 ounces	10 milliliters = 1 centiliter	1 liter = 1.06 quarts
1 pint = 2 cups	100 centiliters = 1 liter	1 liter = 2.1 pints
1 quart = 2 pints	1,000 milliliters = 1 liter	1 liter = .26 gallon
1 gallon = 4 quarts		

C Fill in the equivalent measures.

① oz. ___40___   ② ml _____   ③ l ___5___   ④ l _____
c. ___5___   cl ___10___   ml _____   gal. ___1.04___

⑤ pt. ___1___   ⑥ c. ___1___   ⑦ qt. _____   ⑧ l ___100___
qt. _____   pt. _____   gal. ___5___   qt. _____

⑨ ml _____   ⑩ cl _____   ⑪ l ___10___   ⑫ gal. ___2___
l ___40___   l ___7___   pt. _____   qt. _____

⑬ ml ___10___   ⑭ l ___1___   ⑮ c. _____   ⑯ pt. ___16___
cl _____   qt. _____   pt. ___10___   qt. _____

⑰ l _____   ⑱ oz. ___16___   ⑲ ml ___10,000___   ⑳ oz. ___32___
pt. ___10 1/2___   pt. _____   l _____   c. _____

D Are these units of volume or units of weight?

① pound ___*weight*___   ⑤ gram _____   ⑨ quart _____
② liter _____   ⑥ pint _____   ⑩ kilogram _____
③ cup _____   ⑦ milliliter _____   ⑪ gallon _____
④ centiliter _____   ⑧ ounce _____

Write a paragraph which tells how to prepare your favorite food. Do you use English or metric measures?

_____
_____
_____
_____
_____
_____

Conversion — Length

Learning Objective: *We will learn to convert English and metric units of length.*

From English to Metric
inches $\times$ 25 $\longrightarrow$ millimeters
inches $\times$ 250 $\longrightarrow$ centimeters
feet $\times$ 30 $\longrightarrow$ centimeters
yards $\times$ .9 $\longrightarrow$ meters
miles $\times$ 1.6 $\longrightarrow$ kilometers

From Metric to English
millimeters $\times$ .04 $\longrightarrow$ inches
centimeters $\times$ .4 $\longrightarrow$ inches
meters $\times$ 1.1 $\longrightarrow$ yards
kilometers $\times$ .6 $\longrightarrow$ miles

Measures are approximate.

A Convert inches to millimeters.

① 10 inches $\times$ __25__ = __250__ millimeters

② 126 inches $\times$ _____ = _____ millimeters

③ 1 inch $\times$ _____ = _____ millimeters

④ 72 inches $\times$ _____ = _____ millimeters

⑤ 37 inches $\times$ _____ = _____ millimeters

⑥ 108 inches $\times$ _____ = _____ millimeters

B Convert inches to centimeters.

① 5 inches $\times$ __250__ = __1,250__ centimeters

② 1 inch $\times$ _____ = _____ centimeters

③ 28 inches $\times$ _____ = _____ centimeters

④ 9 inches $\times$ _____ = _____ centimeters

⑤ 17 inches $\times$ _____ = _____ centimeters

⑥ 60 inches $\times$ _____ = _____ centimeters

C Convert feet to centimeters.

① 3 feet $\times$ __30__ = __90__ centimeters

② 12 feet $\times$ _____ = _____ centimeters

③ 10 feet $\times$ _____ = _____ centimeters

④ 1/2 foot $\times$ _____ = _____ centimeters

⑤ 1 foot $\times$ _____ = _____ centimeters

⑥ 5 feet $\times$ _____ = _____ centimeters

D Convert yards to meters.

① 7 yards $\times$ __.9__ = __6.3__ meters

② 6 yards $\times$ _____ = _____ meters

③ 1 yard $\times$ _____ = _____ meters

④ 26 yards $\times$ _____ = _____ meters

⑤ 10 yards $\times$ _____ = _____ meters

⑥ 1,000 yards $\times$ _____ = _____ meters

REMINDER: List 4 English measures of length and 4 metric measures of length.

_____

_____

Unit 121 cont'd ☞

E Convert miles to kilometers.

① 50 miles × ___1.6___ = ___80___ kilometers   ② 121 miles × _____ = _____ kilometers

③ 12 miles × _____ = _____ kilometers   ④ 500 miles × _____ = _____ kilometers

⑤ 1 mile × _____ = _____ kilometers   ⑥ 712 miles × _____ = _____ kilometers

F Convert millimeters to inches.

① 100 millimeters × ___.04___ = ___4___ inches   ② 1,200 millimeters × _____ = _____ inches

③ 78 millimeters × _____ = _____ inches   ④ 502 millimeters × _____ = _____ inches

⑤ 145 millimeters × _____ = _____ inches   ⑥ 1 millimeter × _____ = _____ inches

G Convert centimeters to inches.

① 20 centimeters × ___.4___ = ___8___ inches   ② 415 centimeters × _____ = _____ inches

③ 88 centimeters × _____ = _____ inches   ④ 196 centimeters × _____ = _____ inches

⑤ 1 centimeter × _____ = _____ inch   ⑥ 11 centimeters × _____ = _____ inches

H Convert meters to yards.

① 6 meters × ___1.1___ = ___6.6___ yards   ② 101 meters × _____ = _____ yards

③ 12 meters × _____ = _____ yards   ④ 50 meters × _____ = _____ yards

⑤ 34 meters × _____ = _____ yards   ⑥ 1 meter × _____ = _____ yards

I Convert kilometers to miles.

① 8 kilometers × ___.6___ = ___4.8___ miles   ② 13 kilometers × _____ = _____ miles

③ 40 kilometers × _____ = _____ miles   ④ 138 kilometers × _____ = _____ miles

⑤ 1 kilometer × _____ = _____ mile   ⑥ 375 kilometers × _____ = _____ miles

Conversion — Weight

Learning Objective: *We will learn to convert English and metric units of weight.*

From English to Metric
ounces $\times$ 28 $\longrightarrow$ grams
pounds $\times$ .45 $\longrightarrow$ kilograms
tons $\times$ .9 $\longrightarrow$ metric tons

From Metric to English
grams $\times$ .035 $\longrightarrow$ ounces
kilograms $\times$ 2.2 $\longrightarrow$ pounds
metric tons $\times$ 1.1 $\longrightarrow$ tons

Measures are approximate.

A Convert ounces to grams.

① 1 ounce $\times$ __28__ = __28__ grams

② 15 ounces $\times$ _____ = _____ grams

③ 5 ounces $\times$ _____ = _____ grams

④ 16 ounces $\times$ _____ = _____ grams

⑤ 10 ounces $\times$ _____ = _____ grams

⑥ 25 ounces $\times$ _____ = _____ grams

⑦ 12 ounces $\times$ _____ = _____ grams

⑧ 50 ounces $\times$ _____ = _____ grams

B Convert pounds to kilograms.

① 3 pounds $\times$ __.45__ = __1.35__ kilograms

② 1 pound $\times$ _____ = _____ kilogram

③ 10 pounds $\times$ _____ = _____ kilograms

④ 50 pounds $\times$ _____ = _____ kilograms

⑤ 65 pounds $\times$ _____ = _____ kilograms

⑥ 100 pounds $\times$ _____ = _____ kilograms

⑦ 150 pounds $\times$ _____ = _____ kilograms

⑧ 175 pounds $\times$ _____ = _____ kilograms

C Convert tons to metric tons.

① 1 ton $\times$ __.9__ = __.9__ metric ton

② 5 tons $\times$ _____ = _____ metric tons

③ 12 tons $\times$ _____ = _____ metric tons

④ 10 tons $\times$ _____ = _____ metric tons

⑤ 20 tons $\times$ _____ = _____ metric tons

⑥ 6 tons $\times$ _____ = _____ metric tons

⑦ 100 tons $\times$ _____ = _____ metric tons

⑥ 2 tons $\times$ _____ = _____ metric tons

REMINDER: List 3 English measures of weight and 3 metric measures of weight.

_____

_____

Unit 122 cont'd ☛

D Convert grams to ounces.

① 1,000 grams × __.035__ = __35__ ounces
② 100 grams × _____ = _____ ounces

③ 250 grams × _____ = _____ ounces
④ 705 grams × _____ = _____ ounces

⑤ 1 gram × _____ = _____ ounces
⑥ 336 grams × _____ = _____ ounces

⑦ 500 grams × _____ = _____ ounces
⑧ 1,482 grams × _____ = _____ ounces

E Convert kilograms to pounds.

① 10 kilograms × __2.2__ = __22__ pounds
② 1 kilogram × _____ = _____ pounds

③ 62 kilograms × _____ = _____ pounds
④ 18 kilograms × _____ = _____ pounds

⑤ 47 kilograms × _____ = _____ pounds
⑥ 150 kilograms × _____ = _____ pounds

⑦ 22 kilograms × _____ = _____ pounds
⑧ 39 kilograms × _____ = _____ pounds

F Convert metric tons to tons.

① 1 metric ton × __1.1__ = __1.1__ tons
② 4 metric tons × _____ = _____ tons

③ 11 metric tons × _____ = _____ tons
④ 20 metric tons × _____ = _____ tons

⑤ 9 metric tons × _____ = _____ tons
⑥ 55 metric tons × _____ = _____ tons

⑦ 100 metric tons × _____ = _____ tons
⑧ 32 metric tons × _____ = _____ tons

G Match the units of measure with the things they usually measure.

a. grams and ounces

b. pounds and kilograms

c. tons and metric tons

① the weight of a car

② the weight of a person

③ the weight of a box of cereal

④ the weight of a bag of apples

⑤ the weight of a can of tuna

⑥ the weight of a truck

⑦ the weight of a box of candy

⑧ the weight of an earthworm

⑨ the weight of an elephant

⑩ the weight of a dog

Conversion — Volume

Learning Objective: *We will learn to convert English and metric units of volume.*

From English to Metric
ounces $\times$ 30 $\longrightarrow$ milliliters
pints $\times$ .47 $\longrightarrow$ liters
quarts $\times$ .95 $\longrightarrow$ liters
gallons $\times$ 1.14 $\longrightarrow$ liters

From Metric to English
milliliters $\times$ .034 $\longrightarrow$ ounces
liters $\times$ 2.1 $\longrightarrow$ pints
liters $\times$ 1.06 $\longrightarrow$ quarts
liters $\times$ .26 $\longrightarrow$ gallons

Measures are approximate.

A Convert ounces to milliliters.

① 10 ounces $\times$ __30__ = __300__ milliliters   ② 6 ounces $\times$ _____ = _____ milliliters

③ 25 ounces $\times$ _____ = _____ milliliters   ④ 50 ounces $\times$ _____ = _____ milliliters

⑤ 5 ounces $\times$ _____ = _____ milliliters   ⑥ 1 ounce $\times$ _____ = _____ milliliters

B Convert pints to liters.

① 5 pints $\times$ __.47__ = __2.35__ liters   ② 12 pints $\times$ _____ = _____ liters

③ 8 pints $\times$ _____ = _____ liters   ④ 60 pints $\times$ _____ = _____ liters

⑤ 21 pints $\times$ _____ = _____ liters   ⑥ 1 pint $\times$ _____ = _____ liters

C Convert quarts to liters.

① 2 quarts $\times$ __.95__ = __1.9__ liters   ② 30 quarts $\times$ _____ = _____ liters

③ 18 quarts $\times$ _____ = _____ liters   ④ 1 quart $\times$ _____ = _____ liter

⑤ 7 quarts $\times$ _____ = _____ liters   ⑥ 10 quarts $\times$ _____ = _____ liters

D Convert gallons to liters.

① 4 gallons $\times$ __1.14__ = __4.56__ liters   ② 1 gallon $\times$ _____ = _____ liters

③ 100 gallons $\times$ _____ = _____ liters   ④ 42 gallons $\times$ _____ = _____ liters

⑤ 12 gallons $\times$ _____ = _____ liters   ⑥ 10 gallons $\times$ _____ = _____ liters

REMINDER: List 4 English measures of volume and 2 metric measures of volume.

_____

_____

Unit 123 cont'd ☞

E Convert milliliters to ounces.

① 20 milliliters × __.034__ = __.68__ ounce

② 19 milliliters × _____ = _____ ounce

③ 10 milliliters × _____ = _____ ounce

④ 1 milliliter × _____ = _____ ounce

⑤ 200 milliliters × _____ = _____ ounces

⑥ 600 milliliters × _____ = _____ ounces

F Convert liters to pints.

① 12 liters × __2.1__ = __25.2__ pints

② 10 liters × _____ = _____ pints

③ 1 liter × _____ = _____ pints

④ 46 liters × _____ = _____ pints

⑤ 30 liters × _____ = _____ pints

⑥ 18 liters × _____ = _____ pints

G Convert liters to quarts.

① 11 liters × __1.06__ = __11.66__ quarts

② 34 liters × _____ = _____ quarts

③ 5 liters × _____ = _____ quarts

④ 25 liters × _____ = _____ quarts

⑤ 1 liter × _____ = _____ quarts

⑥ 8 liters × _____ = _____ quarts

H Convert liters to gallons.

① 2 liter × __.26__ = __.52__ gallon

② 1 liter × _____ = _____ gallon

③ 10 liters × _____ = _____ gallons

④ 16 liters × _____ = _____ gallons

⑤ 50 liters × _____ = _____ gallons

⑥ 27 liters × _____ = _____ gallons

I Match the units of measure with the things they usually measure.

a. ounces and milliliters

b. quarts and liters

c. gallons

① oil for your car

② water in a glass

③ orange juice in a can

④ soft drink in a bottle

⑤ shampoo in a bottle

⑥ gasoline in your car

⑦ water in a swimming pool

⑧ iced tea in a large pitcher

⑨ milk in a large container

⑩ ketchup in a bottle

Measuring by the Dozen

Unit 124

Learning Objective: **We will learn to measure by the dozen.**

A dozen is made up of twelve.

EXAMPLE:

$1 \times 12 = 12 = 1$ dozen $\qquad 4 \times 12 = 48 = 4$ dozen

$2 \times 12 = 24 = 2$ dozen $\qquad 5 \times 12 = 60 = 5$ dozen

$3 \times 12 = 36 = 3$ dozen $\qquad 6 \times 12 = 72 = 6$ dozen

A How many are in each dozen?

① 1 dozen = ___12___   ② 2 dozen = _____   ③ 10 dozen = _____

④ 6 dozen = _____   ⑤ 3 dozen = _____   ⑥ 12 dozen = _____

⑦ 20 dozen = _____   ⑧ 8 dozen = _____   ⑨ 15 dozen = _____

⑩ 4 dozen = _____   ⑪ 50 dozen = _____   ⑫ 13 dozen = _____

⑬ 11 dozen = _____   ⑭ 5 dozen = _____   ⑮ 60 dozen = _____

⑯ 100 dozen = _____   ⑰ 9 dozen = _____   ⑱ 25 dozen = _____

B How many dozen are in these numbers?

① 12 = ___1 dozen___   ② 24 = _____   ③ 36 = _____

④ 48 = _____   ⑤ 60 = _____   ⑥ 72 = _____

⑦ 108 = _____   ⑧ 120 = _____   ⑨ 1,200 = _____

⑩ 300 = _____   ⑪ 384 = _____   ⑫ 840 = _____

⑬ 180 = _____   ⑭ 144 = _____   ⑮ 6 = _____

⑯ 480 = _____   ⑰ 600 = _____   ⑱ 204 = _____

REMINDER: Write the definition of a dozen.

_____

_____

Unit 124 cont'd 👉

C Match the equivalent amounts.

① 1/12 dozen ————————————— 3 eggs

② 1/6 dozen ——————————— 1 egg

③ 1/4 dozen   2 eggs

④ 1/3 dozen   6 eggs

⑤ 5/12 dozen   5 eggs

⑥ 1/2 dozen   4 eggs

⑦ 7/12 dozen   7 eggs

⑧ 2/3 dozen   10 eggs

⑨ 3/4 dozen   11 eggs

⑩ 5/6 dozen   8 eggs

⑪ 11/12 dozen   9 eggs

⑫ 1 dozen   12 eggs

D Work the problems.

① Lisa bought 2 dozen doughnuts. If each person in her office ate 2 doughnuts and all the doughnuts were eaten, how many people work in Lisa's office?

$2 \times 12 = 24$ *doughnuts*

$24 \div 2 = 12$ *people*

② Jim's family colored eggs for Easter. They colored 6 blue ones, 6 green ones, 10 yellow ones, 7 pink ones, and 7 orange ones. How many dozen eggs did they color?

③ Chris baked a cake that required 1/3 dozen eggs. How many eggs were in the cake?

④ Mr. and Mrs. Williams have 6 dozen great-grandchildren. How many great-grandchildren do they have?

⑤ Mary bought 8 packages of hot dog buns. If each package contains a dozen, how many hot dog buns did Mary buy?

⑥ Apples sell for $2.40 per dozen. How much does one apple cost?

⑦ Candace decorated 5 dozen cupcakes for the party at school. How many cupcakes did she decorate?

⑧ The bakery made 30 dozen doughnuts. If half of them were chocolate, how many were not?

Temperature

Learning Objective: *We will learn to measure in Fahrenheit and Celsius degrees.*

Temperature is the degree of hot and cold. It may be measured in Fahrenheit or Celsius degrees.

EXAMPLE: a. To convert from Fahrenheit to Celsius, subtract 32 and then multiply by 5/9.
b. To convert from Celsius to Fahrenheit, multiply by 9/5 and then add 32.

A Convert these Fahrenheit temperatures to Celsius.

① 70° F

② 50° F

③ 100° F

$70 - 32 = 38$

$38 \times 5/9 = 190/9 = 21.1° \ C$

④ 25° F

⑤ 80° F

⑥ 98° F

⑦ 212° F

⑧ 48° F

⑨ -5° F

⑩ 66° F

⑪ 120° F

⑫ 81° F

⑬ 37° F

⑭ 0° F

⑮ 150° F

REMINDER: What two ways do we measure temperature?

_____

_____

Unit 125 cont'd

B Convert these Celsius temperatures to Fahrenheit.

① 35° C

② 80° C

③ 100° C

$35 \times 9/5 = 315/5 = 63$

$63 + 32 = 95° F$

④ 10° C

⑤ 36° C

⑥ 77° C

⑦ 65° C

⑧ 41° C

⑨ 162° C

⑩ 22° C

⑪ 1° C

⑫ 50° C

⑬ 97° C

⑭ 140° C

⑮ -10° C

C Work the problems.

① Arlette listened to the weather report before dressing for school. The report predicted a high of 32°F. Should Arlette wear cool or warm clothes?

_____

_____

② Daniel read that the average July temperature in Washington D.C., is 26° C. Would it be necessary to take a coat when visiting there in July?

_____

_____

③ Water boils at 212° F. At what temperature does it boil on the Celsius scale?

_____

_____

④ Water freezes at 0° C. At what temperature does it freeze on the Fahrenheit scale?

_____

_____

Comprehension Check

A Identify each unit of measure as English (E) or metric (m).

___m___ ① millimeters   _____ ⑦ gallons   _____ ⑬ kilograms

_____ ② grams   _____ ⑧ ounces   _____ ⑭ meters

_____ ③ miles   _____ ⑨ tons   _____ ⑮ pints

_____ ④ metric tons   _____ ⑩ centimeters   _____ ⑯ quarts

_____ ⑤ inches   _____ ⑪ pounds   _____ ⑰ liters

_____ ⑥ kilometers   _____ ⑫ yards   _____ ⑱ milliliters

B Identify each unit of measure as a unit of weight (w), length (l), or volume (v).

___v___ ① quarts   _____ ⑦ centimeters   _____ ⑬ grams

_____ ② kilometers   _____ ⑧ tons   _____ ⑭ ounces

_____ ③ milliliters   _____ ⑨ liters   _____ ⑮ inches

_____ ④ millimeters   _____ ⑩ miles   _____ ⑯ kilograms

_____ ⑤ pounds   _____ ⑪ gallons   _____ ⑰ meters

_____ ⑥ metric tons   _____ ⑫ yards   _____ ⑱ pints

C Match the equivalent measures.

① 1 mile	25 millimeters	⑦ 1 ounce	28 grams
② 1 inch	1.1 yards	⑧ 1 kilogram	1.06 quarts
③ 1 meter	30 milliliters	⑨ 1 milliliter	2.2 pounds
④ 1 liter	1.6 kilometers	⑩ 1 liter	1.1 tons
⑤ 1 ounce	1.14 liters	⑪ 1 inch	250 centimeters
⑥ 1 gallon	2.1 pints	⑫ 1 metric ton	.034 ounce

303

Test 25 cont'd ☞

D Fill in the blanks.

① 1 dozen = _____12_____   ⑥ 6 dozen = _____   ⑪ 11 dozen = _____

② 2 dozen = _____   ⑦ 7 dozen = _____   ⑫ 12 dozen = _____

③ 3 dozen = _____   ⑧ 8 dozen = _____   ⑬ 13 dozen = _____

④ 4 dozen = _____   ⑨ 9 dozen = _____   ⑭ 14 dozen= _____

⑤ 5 dozen = _____   ⑩ 10 dozen = _____   ⑮ 15 dozen = _____

E Convert these temperatures.

From Fahrenheit to Celsius: subtract 32 multiply by 5/9	From Celsius to Fahrenheit: multiply by 9/5 add 32

① 85° F   ② 30° C   ③ 10° C

$85 - 32 = 53$

$53 \times 5/9 = 265/9 = 29.4° C$

④ 50° F   ⑤ 70° C   ⑥ 210° F

⑦ 32° F   ⑧ 100° C   ⑨ 72° F

Write a paragraph about whether or not the United States should change from the English system to the metric system. Give two reasons for your choice.

_____

_____

_____

_____

_____

_____

_____

Lines

Learning Objective: *We will learn to recognize straight and curved lines.*

A line is the path traced by a moving point. A line may be either straight or curved.

EXAMPLES:

_____

The line at the left is a straight line. It has no bends or curves.

⌒

The line at the left is a curved line. It continuously bends.

A Identify the straight and curved lines.

① _____ straight

② _____

③ _____

④ _____

⑤ _____

⑥ _____

⑦ _____

⑧ _____

B Fill in the blanks.

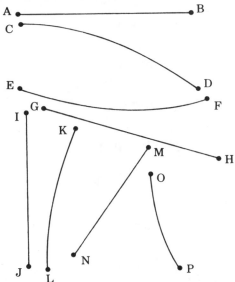

① Segment AB is a _____ *straight* _____ line.

② Segment GH is a _____ line.

③ Segment EF is a _____ line.

④ Segment MN is not a _____ line.

⑤ Segments CD and OP are both _____ .

⑥ Segments IJ and AB are both _____ .

⑦ A straight line has no _____ .

⑧ A _____ line continuously bends.

REMINDER: Write the definition of a line.

_____

_____

Unit 126 cont'd ☞

C Draw a line just like each given line.

D Match the exact shapes.

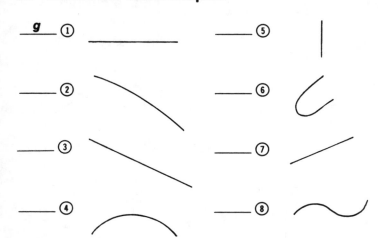

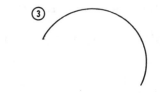

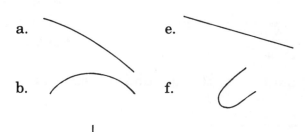

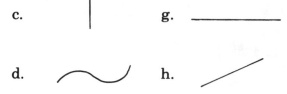

_g_ ① _____   ⑤ _____   a.   e.

② _____   ⑥ _____   b.   f.

③ _____   ⑦ _____   c.   g. _____

④ _____   ⑧ _____   d.   h.

E Underline the objects which consist mainly of straight lines.

① <u>ruler</u>   ⑪ newspaper
② picture frame   ⑫ box
③ triangle   ⑬ room
④ circle   ⑭ book
⑤ refrigerator   ⑮ roof
⑥ vase   ⑯ window
⑦ sidewalk   ⑰ fan
⑧ postcard   ⑱ door
⑨ album cover   ⑲ light bulb
⑩ flower   ⑳ towel

F Underline the objects which consist mainly of curved lines.

① <u>log</u>   ⑪ pearl
② penny   ⑫ wheel
③ spider web   ⑬ moon
④ glass   ⑭ apple
⑤ stairs   ⑮ stamp
⑥ eyes   ⑯ doorknob
⑦ spoon   ⑰ can
⑧ key   ⑱ button
⑨ flower pot   ⑲ hat
⑩ smile   ⑳ faucet

Intersecting Lines

Learning Objective: *We will learn to determine if two lines intersect.*

A line is the path traced by a moving point. Two lines intersect when they pass through or cut across each other and have one or more points in common.

EXAMPLE: Segment AD intersects segment BC at point E.

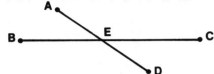

A Place a check (✓) beside each set of lines which intersect.

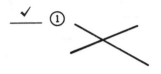 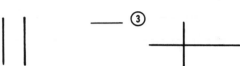 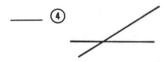 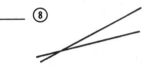

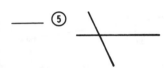 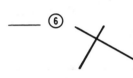 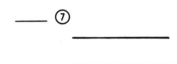 

B Draw a line that intersects each line.

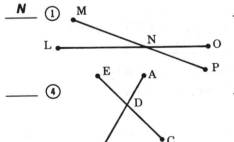  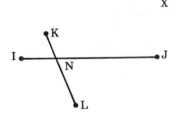 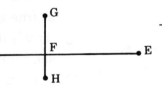

C What is the point of intersection?

REMINDER: When do two lines intersect?

_____

_____

Unit 127 cont'd 🖎

D Describe how each set of lines intersects.

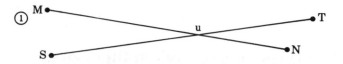

①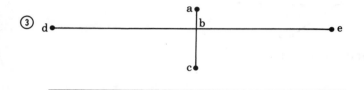

Segment MN intersects segment ST at point u.

_____

②

_____

_____

③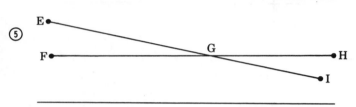

_____

_____

④

_____

_____

⑤

_____

_____

⑥

_____

_____

E Answer the questions.

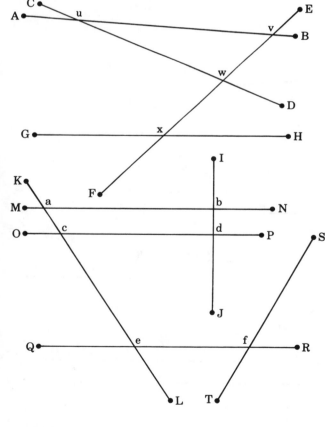

① Which lines intersect segment AB? _____
   segments CD and EF

② Which lines intersect segment EF? _____

   _____

③ Which line intersects segment GH? _____

   _____

④ Does segment MN intersect segment OP? _____

⑤ At what point does segment KL intersect segment QR? _____

⑥ At what point does segment ST intersect segment QR? _____

⑦ If segments KL and ST were extended downward on the page, would they eventually intersect? _____

⑧ Which lines intersect segment KL? _____

   _____

⑨ How many segments intersect segment IJ? ____

   _____

⑩ At what point does segment OP intersect segment KL? _____

308

Parallel Lines

Learning
Objective: *We will learn to determine if two lines are parallel.*

A line is the path traced by a moving point. Two lines are parallel if they extend alongside each other at an equal distance apart. Parallel lines never meet.

EXAMPLE: **Segment AB is parallel to segment CD.**

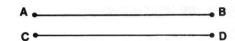

A Place a check (✓) beside each set of lines which are parallel.

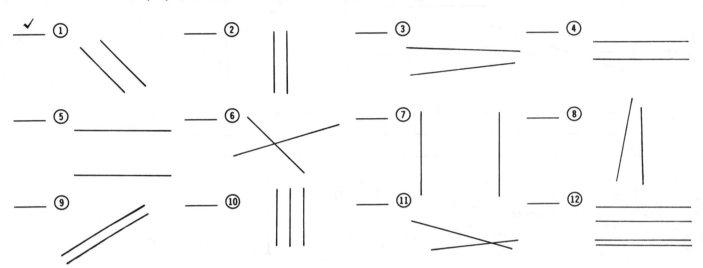

① ✓   ②   ③   ④

⑤   ⑥   ⑦   ⑧

⑨   ⑩   ⑪   ⑫

B Draw a line that is parallel to each given line.

① _____   ②   ③   ④

⑤   ⑥   ⑦   ⑧

⑨   ⑩   ⑪   ⑫

REMINDER: When are two lines parallel?

_____

_____

Unit 128 cont'd 👉

C Are these lines parallel? If yes, identify the parallel line segments. If no, explain why.

① A •————————————• C
B •————————————• D

Yes, segment AC is parallel with segment BD.

_____

_____

_____

② M •————————————• N
O •————————————• P

_____

_____

_____

③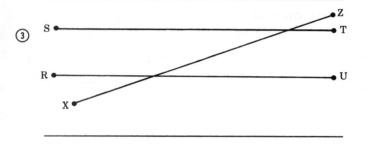

_____

_____

_____

④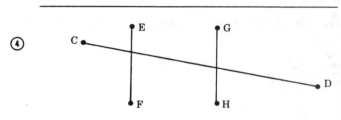

_____

_____

_____

⑤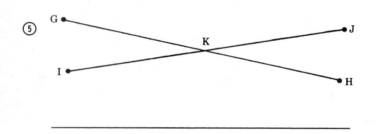

_____

_____

_____

⑥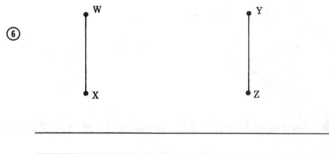

_____

_____

_____

E Underline the examples of parallel lines.

① <u>two roads that run exactly north and south</u>

② the four legs of a dining table

③ the wings of an airplane

④ the sides of an 8″ x 10″ picture frame

⑤ the north and west boundaries of a property line

⑥ the sides of a box

⑦ the edges of a wood saw

⑧ the ceiling and floor of a room

⑨ the top and bottom edges of a dollar bill

⑩ the outside edge of an ice cream cone

⑪ the edges of a book

⑫ the straight edges of a ruler

⑬ the top edge of a protractor

⑭ the east and west walls of a kitchen

310

Oblique Lines

Learning
Objective: *We will learn to identify an oblique line.*

A line is the path traced by a moving point. An oblique line is a slanting line. It is
neither straight up and down nor straight across.

EXAMPLES: **Segments AB and GH are oblique
because they slant.
Segment CD is not oblique; it
runs straight up and down.
Segment EF is not oblique; it runs
straight across.**

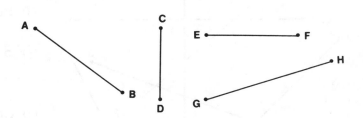

A Place a check (✓) beside each oblique line.

B Is each line an oblique line? If no, explain why.

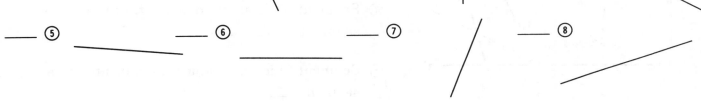

① *Yes, it is an
oblique line.*

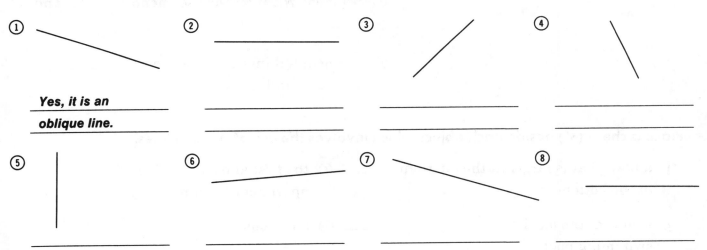

REMINDER: What is an oblique line?

311   Unit 129 cont'd ☛

C Fill in the blanks.

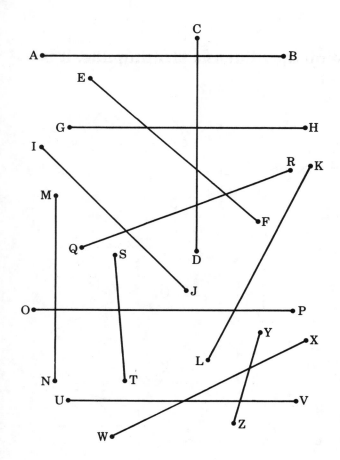

① Segment AB runs straight _____*across*_____ .

② Segment CD runs straight _____ _____ .

③ Segment EF is an _____ line.

④ Segments _____ , _____ , _____ , and _____ run straight across.

⑤ Segments _____ and _____ run straight up and down.

⑥ Segments _____ , _____ , _____ , _____ , _____ , _____ , and _____ are oblique lines.

⑦ Segment ST is an oblique line that intersects segment _____ .

⑧ Segment IJ is an oblique line that intersects segment _____ .

⑨ Segment WX intersects segments _____ and _____ .

⑩ Segment QR intersects segments _____ , _____ , and _____ .

D Place a check (✓) beside each object which involves the use of oblique lines.

__✓__ ① a bowl that is larger at the top than at the bottom

____ ② a slide at the local swimming pool

____ ③ a reclining lounge chair

____ ④ the roof of a house

____ ⑤ the seesaw on a child's playground

____ ⑥ the first and second floors in an apartment building

____ ⑦ a flagpole

____ ⑧ a triangular-shaped flower bed

____ ⑨ the lines on a sheet of notebook paper

____ ⑩ the slope of a mountain

312

Perpendicular Lines **Unit 130**

Learning Objective: *We will learn to recognize perpendicular lines.*

A line is the path traced by a moving point. A line is perpendicular to another line when it makes a 90° angle with it.

EXAMPLE: **Segment CD is perpendicular to segment AB. Their meeting forms a 90° angle.**

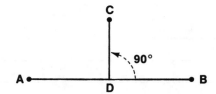

A Place a check (✓) beside each set of perpendicular lines.

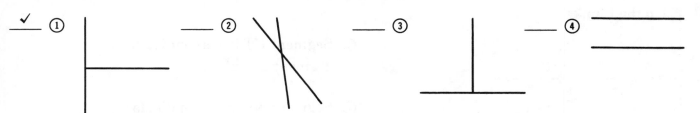

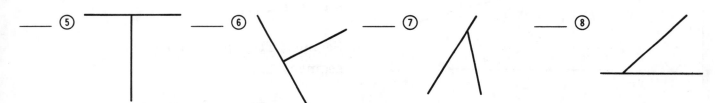

B Draw a line perpendicular to each of these lines.

REMINDER: When are two lines perpendicular?

_____

_____

Unit 130 cont'd ☞

C What makes these lines perpendicular?

①
B
A ——— C ——— D (with B above C)

②
E
G ——— H (with E above G, F below G)
F

③
I ——— K ——— J (with L below K)
L

④
M
N (with O below, P to the right)
O   P

_____   _____   _____   _____
_____   _____   _____   _____
_____   _____   _____   _____
_____   _____   _____   _____

D Fill in the blanks.

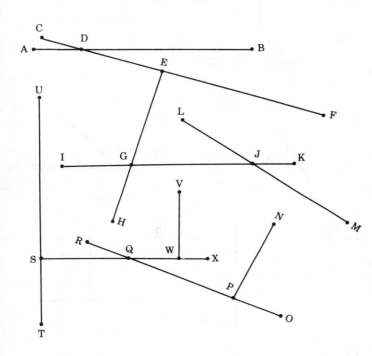

① Segment UT is perpendicular to segment _____*SX*_____ .

② Segment NP is perpendicular to segment _____ .

③ Segment EH is perpendicular to segment _____ .

④ Segment VW is perpendicular to segment _____ .

⑤ Segments RO and SX _____ perpendicular.

⑥ Segments LM and IK _____ perpendicular.

E Underline the objects which involve the use of perpendicular lines.

① <u>the place where a wall and ceiling meet</u>

② the position of a tree with the ground

③ the corner of a picture frame

④ the top and bottom of a box

⑤ a person standing on a sidewalk

⑥ a road that runs beside a river

⑦ the joining of two stairs

⑧ a clock's hands at three o'clock

Comprehension Check

A Fill in the blanks.

① A _____*line*_____ is the path traced by a moving point.

② A line may be either _____ or _____ .

③ A _____ line has no bends or curves.

④ A _____ line continuously bends.

⑤ Two lines _____ when they pass through or cut across each other.

⑥ Two lines are _____ if they extend alongside each other at an equal distance apart.

⑦ Parallel lines _____ meet.

⑧ An oblique line is a _____ line.

⑨ An _____ line is neither straight up and down nor straight across.

⑩ A line is perpendicular to another line when it makes a _____ with it.

B Identify these lines as either straight (s) or curved (c).

C Identify these lines as either intersecting (i), parallel (p), oblique (o), or perpendicular (pp).

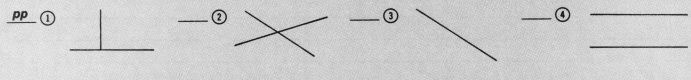

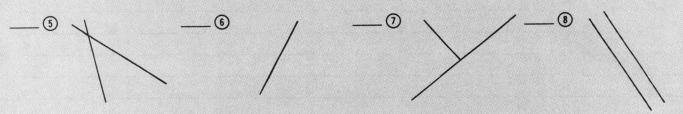

Test 26 cont'd ☛

D Fill in the blanks.

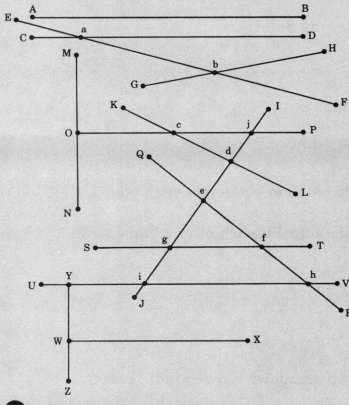

① Segments AB and CD are ____*parallel*____ .

② Segment MN is perpendicular to _____ .

③ Segment GH intersects EF at point _____ .

④ Segment KL is an _____ line.

⑤ There are no _____ lines in this exercise.

⑥ Segments ST and QR _____ .

⑦ Segments YZ and WX are _____ .

⑧ Segments ST and UV are _____ .

⑨ Segment IJ intersects segments _____ , _____ , _____ , _____ , and _____ .

⑩ All of the lines in this exercise are _____ .

E Match the lines described with their names.

① the floor and the wall meet at a 90° angle

② two roads run exactly east and west

③ the slope of the roof on a house

④ a road running north and south crosses one running east and west

a. parallel lines

b. oblique lines

c. intersecting lines

d. perpendicular lines

Write a paragraph describing the kinds of lines found in your room.

_____

_____

_____

_____

_____

_____

_____

Geometric Shapes

Unit 131

Learning Objective: *We will learn to recognize various geometric shapes.*

A geometric shape is a distinct form that is made up of curved or straight lines.

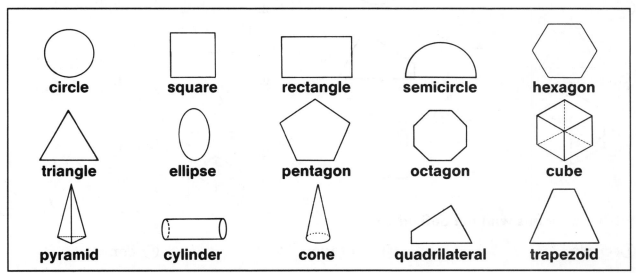

circle　square　rectangle　semicircle　hexagon

triangle　ellipse　pentagon　octagon　cube

pyramid　cylinder　cone　quadrilateral　trapezoid

A Study the geometric shapes in the box above. Then identify each of these shapes.

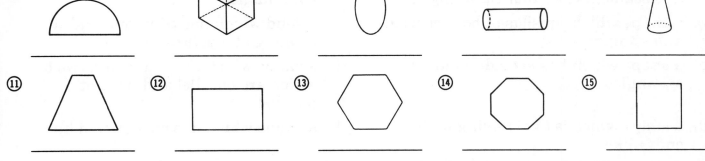

① *triangle*

② _____

③ _____

④ _____

⑤ _____

⑥ _____

⑦ _____

⑧ _____

⑨ _____

⑩ _____

⑪ _____

⑫ _____

⑬ _____

⑭ _____

⑮ _____

⑯ _____

⑰ _____

⑱ _____

⑲ _____

⑳ _____

REMINDER: Write the definition of a geometric shape.

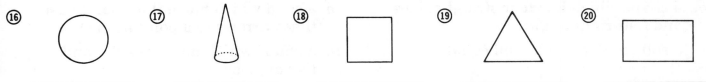

_____

_____

B Match the shapes.

_f_ ①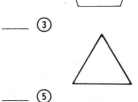

—— ③

—— ⑤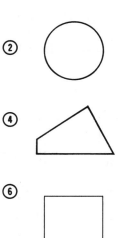

—— ②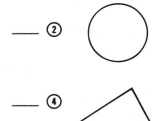

—— ④

—— ⑥

a. 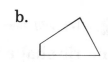   b.

c.   d.

e.    f.

g.   h.

C Match the shapes with the definitions.

_l_ ① circle   —— ⑥ pentagon   —— ⑪ cone

—— ② triangle   —— ⑦ hexagon   —— ⑫ pyramid

—— ③ semicircle   —— ⑧ ellipse   —— ⑬ cylinder

—— ④ rectangle   —— ⑨ octagon   —— ⑭ quadrilateral

—— ⑤ square   —— ⑩ cube   —— ⑮ trapezoid

a. a shape which has four equal straight line segments and four right angles

b. a shape which consists of both curved and straight lines

c. a shape which has six sides and six angles

d. a shape which is oval having both ends alike

e. a shape which has four straight sides and four right angles

f. a solid with six sides, all equal

g. a solid with two parallel circles connected by straight lines

h. a shape which has three sides and three angles

i. a shape which has eight sides and eight angles

j. a solid which has triangular sides meeting at a point

k. a shape which has four sides, two of which are parallel and two not parallel

l. a shape which has only curved lines

m. a solid which has a flat, round base that narrows to a point at the top

n. a shape which has five sides and five angles

o. a shape which has four sides and four angles

Rectangles

Learning Objective: *We will learn to identify the rectangle as a distinct geometric shape.*

A rectangle consists of four straight line segments and four right angles. Its opposite sides are equal and parallel.

EXAMPLE:

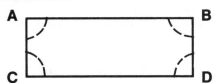

Segment AB is parallel and equal to segment CD.
Segment AC is parallel and equal to segment BD.
Angles A, B, C, and D are right angles.

A List 3 sentences that explain why each of these shapes is considered a rectangle.

① M   N
   O   P

Segment MN is parallel and equal to segment OP.
Segment MO is parallel and equal to segment NP.
Angles M, N, O, and P are right angles.

② L   M
   N   O

_____

_____

_____

③ C   D
   E   F

_____

_____

_____

④ U   V
   W   X

_____

_____

_____

⑤ A   B
   C   D

_____

_____

_____

⑥ W   X
   Y   Z

_____

_____

_____

REMINDER: Write the definition of a rectangle.

_____

_____

       Unit 132 cont'd ☛

Area is the amount of a surface. To measure the area of a rectangle, we use the formula A = LW. The answer is expressed in square units.

B Find the areas of rectangles with the following dimensions.

① length = 10 cm
width = 8 cm

$A = LW$
$A = 10 \times 8$
$A = 80$ sq. cm

② length = 12 ft.
width = 12 ft.

③ length = 5 yds.
width = 7 yds.

④ length = 30 in.
width = 10 in.

⑤ length = 100 in.
width = 50 in.

⑥ length = 16 mi.
width = 12 mi.

⑦ length = 42 cm
width = 9 cm

⑧ length = 11 m
width = 6 m

⑨ length = 1/2 yd.
width = 1/4 yd.

⑩ length = 2.3 m
width = 1.3 m

⑪ length = 15 ft.
width = 14 ft.

⑫ length = 22 in.
width = 11 in.

Perimeter is the measure around. To measure the perimeter of a rectangle, use the formula P = 2 (L + W).

C Find the perimeters of rectangles with the following dimensions.

① length = 4 ft.
width = 2 ft.

$P = 2 (L + W)$
$P = 2 (4 + 2)$
$P = 2(6)$
$P = 12$ ft.

② length = 40 m
width = 36 m

③ length = 99 in.
width = 49 in.

④ length = 100 yds.
width = 75 yds.

⑤ length = 25 in.
width = 20 in.

⑥ length = 1/2 ft.
width = 3/4 ft.

⑦ length = 7 m
width = 3.2 m

⑧ length = 8 mi.
width = 4 mi.

⑨ length = 10 mi.
width = 8 mi.

⑩ length = 30 ft.
width = 20 ft.

⑪ length = 17 yds.
width = 6 yds.

⑫ length = 16 in.
width = 13 in.

Squares

Learning Objective: *We will learn to identify the square as a distinct geometric shape.*

A square is a special type of rectangle. It consists of four straight line segments of equal length.

EXAMPLE:

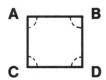

A square has four equal sides. Segments AB, CD, AC, and BD are all equal. AB is parallel to CD. AC is parallel to BD. Angles A, B, C, and D are right angles.

A Which line segments are equal in these squares?

①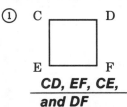
CD, EF, CE, and DF

②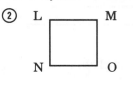
_____
_____

③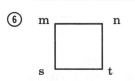
_____
_____

④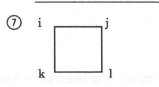
_____
_____

⑤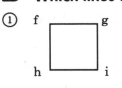
_____
_____

⑥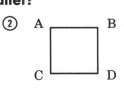
_____
_____

⑦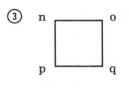
_____
_____

⑧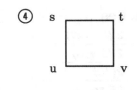
_____
_____

B Which lines are parallel?

①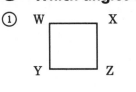
_____
_____

②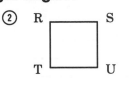
_____
_____

③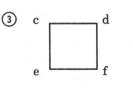
_____
_____

④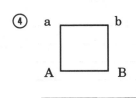
_____
_____

C Which angles are right angles?

① W X
Y Z
_____
_____

② R S
T U
_____
_____

③ c d
e f
_____
_____

④ a b
A B
_____
_____

REMINDER: *Write the definition of a square.*

_____
_____

Unit 133 cont'd 👉

Area is the amount of a surface. To measure the area of a square, use the formula A = LW. The answer is expressed in square units.

D **Find the areas of squares with the following lengths.**

① 5 inches

$A = LW$
$A = 5 \times 5$
$A = 25$ sq. in.

② 10 meters

③ 8 yards

④ 12 feet

⑤ 15 millimeters

⑥ 50 centimeters

⑦ 30 feet

⑧ 4 miles

⑨ 21 feet

⑩ 7 meters

⑪ 13 inches

⑫ 9 meters

Perimeter is the measure around. To measure the perimeter of a square, use the formula P = 2 (L + W).

E **Find the perimeters of squares with the following line lengths.**

① 5 inches

$P = 2 (L + W)$
$P = 2 (5 + 5)$
$P = 2(10)$
$P = 20$ sq. in.

② 35 feet

③ 6 inches

④ 20 centimeters

⑤ 10 inches

⑥ 18 miles

⑦ 100 feet

⑧ 16 yards

⑨ 2 miles

⑩ 71 centimeters

⑪ 500 millimeters

⑫ 11 meters

Quadrilaterals

Learning Objective: *We will learn to identify quadrilaterals as distinct geometric shapes.*

A quadrilateral is a geometric figure made up of four straight line segments. The opposite sides of a quadrilateral may or may not be equal; the sides may or may not be parallel.

EXAMPLES:

The figure at the left is a quadrilateral. It is comprised of straight line segments AB, CD, AC, and BD. Segments AB and CD are parallel but not equal. Segments AC and BD are neither parallel nor equal.

A Place a check (✓) beside each quadrilateral.

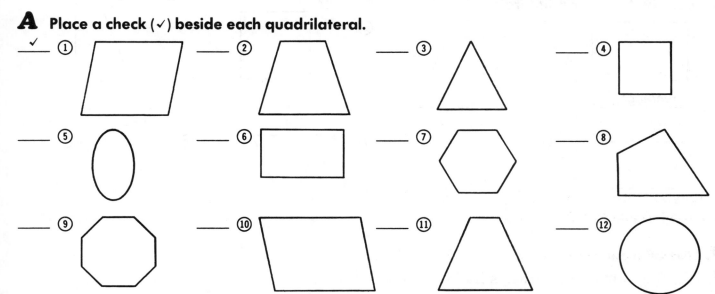

B Describe each of these quadrilaterals.

REMINDER: Write the definition of a quadrilateral.

_____

_____

Unit 134 cont'd ☞

Look at these different quadrilaterals.

square	rectangle	parallelogram	trapezoid	quadrilateral

Sides are parallel and equal. Two sides are parallel. None of its sides are equal nor parallel.

C Identify these quadrilaterals.

① _____
rectangle

② _____

③ _____

④ _____

⑤ _____

⑥ _____

⑦ _____

⑧ _____

D True or False

_t_ ① A quadrilateral always had four sides.

___ ② Rectangles, squares, parallelograms, and trapezoids are quadrilaterals.

___ ③ Some quadrilaterals have curved lines.

___ ④ Quadrilaterals must have sides that are parallel.

___ ⑤ A trapezoid has two sides that are parallel.

___ ⑥ A rectangle is a quadrilateral which has four right angles.

___ ⑦ Angles in a quadrilateral must always measure 90°.

___ ⑧ The opposite sides of a quadrilateral can never be equal.

___ ⑨ A square is always a quadrilateral, but a quadrilateral is not always a square.

___ ⑩ A square is a rectangle, a parallelogram, and a quadrilateral.

Triangles

Learning Objective: *We will learn to identify the triangle as a distinct geometric shape.*

A triangle consists of three straight line segments. These segments meet at points called vertices. The segments form three angles which total 180°.

EXAMPLE:

Triangle ABC consists of line segments AB, AC, and BC.
These segments meet at vertices A, B, and C.
Three angles are formed. Angle A equals 80°. Angle B equals 40°.
Angle C equals 60°. The total of angles A, B, and C is 180°.

A Which line segments make up each triangle?

①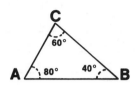

MN, NO, and MO

②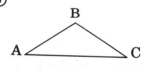

_____

③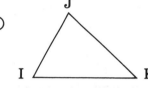

_____

④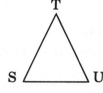

_____

⑤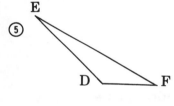

_____

⑥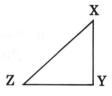

_____

⑦ (triangle IJK)

_____

⑧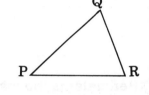

_____

B If we know the measure of two angles, we can easily figure the measure of the third angle. The total of the three angles always adds to 180°.
Find the measure of the third angle.

① ∠A = 50° ∠B = 85° ∠C = __45°__
   50 + 85 + 45 = 180

② ∠C = 60° ∠D = 60° ∠E = _____

③ ∠F = 90° ∠G = 45° ∠H = _____

④ ∠B = 35° ∠C = 85° ∠D = _____

⑤ ∠x = 67° ∠y = 43° ∠z = _____

⑥ ∠M = 22° ∠N = 78° ∠O = _____

REMINDER: Write the definition of a triangle.

_____

_____

Unit 135 cont'd ☞

Area is the amount of a surface. To measure the area of a triangle, use the formula $A = 1/2$ (base $\times$ height). The answer is expressed in square units.

C Find the areas of these triangles.

① base = 4 inches
height = 2 inches

$A = 1/2 \, (b \times h)$

$A = 1/2 \, (4 \times 2)$

$A = 1/2 \, (8)$

$A = 4$ sq. in.

② base = 11 miles
height = 12 miles

③ base = 20 millimeters
height = 10 millimeters

④ base = 12 centimeters
height = 8 centimeters

⑤ base = 7 yards
height = 4 yards

⑥ base = 15 inches
height = 3 inches

Perimeter is the measure around. To measure the perimeter of a triangle, add the measures of the three sides.

D Find the areas of these triangles.

① side 1 = 10 inches
side 2 = 8 inches
side 3 = 6 inches

$P = a + b + c$

$P = 10 + 8 + 6$

$P = 24$ inches

② side 1 = 37 feet
side 2 = 42 feet
side 3 = 80 feet

③ side 1 = 111 millimeters
side 2 = 118 millimeters
side 3 = 96 millimeters

④ side 1 = 73 centimeters
side 2 = 136 centimeters
side 3 = 90 centimeters

⑤ side 1 = 12 inches
side 2 = 24 inches
side 3 = 36 inches

⑥ side 1 = 50 yards
side 2 = 50 yards
side 3 = 100 yards

Comprehension Check

A Identify these shapes.

①
square

②

③

④

⑤

⑥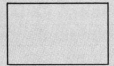

⑦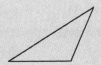

⑧

⑨

⑩

B Why are these shapes considered rectangles?

①

②

C Why are these shapes considered squares?

①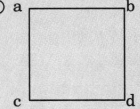

②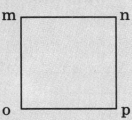

③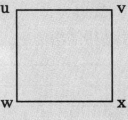

D Why are these shapes considered triangles?

①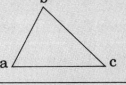

②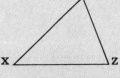

③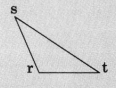

Test 27 cont'd 👉

E Find the area of each rectangle and square. Use A = LW.

① length = 6 inches
width = 3 inches

$A = LW$
$A = 6 \times 3$
$A = 18$ sq. in.

② length = 10 centimeters
width = 20 centimeters

③ length = 12 miles
width = 6 miles

④ 22 inches

⑤ 7 meters

⑥ 1 kilometer

⑦ length = 50 millimeters
width = 30 millimeters

⑧ length = 11 yards
width = 7 yards

⑨ length = 25 inches
width = 20 inches

⑩ 5 feet

⑪ 30 centimeters

⑫ 6 inches

F Find the areas of these triangles. Use A = 1/2 (b × h).

① base = 4 inches
height = 4 inches

② base = 10 feet
height = 12 feet

③ base = 8 meters
height = 10 meters

G Find the perimeters.

① rectangle
length = 20 feet
width = 10 feet

② square
17 inches

③ triangle
side 1 = 18 meters
side 2 = 12 meters
side 3 = 21 meters

Isosceles Triangles

Learning Objective: *We will learn to recognize an isosceles triangle.*

An isosceles triangle is a triangle with two equal sides.

EXAMPLE: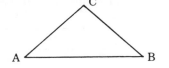

This triangle is an isosceles triangle. Segments AC and CB are equal; segment AB is called the base. Angles A and B are equal.

A Place a check (✓) beside each isosceles triangle.

✓ ①   — ②  — ③   — ④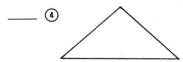

— ⑤   — ⑥ 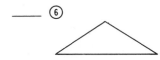 — ⑦  — ⑧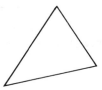

B Why is each of these triangles an isosceles triangle?

①   *BC = CD*

    ∠B = ∠D

② 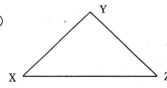   _____

    _____

③   _____

    _____

④ 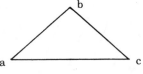   _____

    _____

⑤ 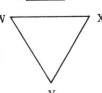   _____

    _____

⑥   _____

    _____

REMINDER: Write the definition of an isosceles triangle.

_____

_____

Unit 136 cont'd ☛

C If we know that an isosceles triangle has two equal sides, what can we assume about the dimensions of these isosceles triangles?

① △ABC
AB = 5 inches
BC = 5 inches
Side AC does not
measure 5 inches.
_____

② △LMN
LM = 13 meters
MN = 20 meters
_____
_____
_____

③ △RST
RS = 40 centimeters
RT = 40 centimeters
_____
_____
_____

④ △XYZ
XY = 16 feet
YZ = 21 feet
_____
_____
_____

⑤ △DEF
DE = 9 miles
DF = 9 miles
_____
_____
_____

⑥ △JKL
JK = 46 millimeters
KL = 60 millimeters
_____
_____
_____

D Answer the questions.

① What are the five isosceles triangles in this exercise? __△*ABC*, △*DEF*, △*GHI*,__
   __△*JKL*, and △*MNO*__

② Why is △ABC an isosceles triangle?
_____

③ What sides of △DEF are equal?
_____

④ What angles of △GHI are equal?
_____

⑤ What is the base of △MNO?
_____

⑥ Why is △JKL an isosceles triangle?
_____

⑦ How many equal sides does an isosceles triangle have? _____

⑧ Which of these triangles is the largest?
_____

⑨ Which of these triangles is the smallest?
_____

⑩ Define an isosceles triangle.
_____
_____

Scalene Triangles   Unit 137

A scalene triangle is a triangle with three unequal sides.

EXAMPLE: 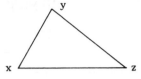 This triangle is a scalene triangle. None of segments xy, yz, and xz are equal. None of angles x, y, and z are equal.

A Place a check (✓) beside each scalene triangle.

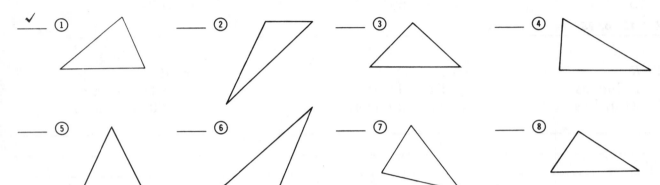

✓ ①   ___ ②   ___ ③   ___ ④

___ ⑤   ___ ⑥   ___ ⑦   ___ ⑧

B Why is each of these triangles a scalene triangle?

① 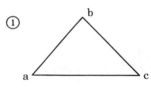 $ab \neq bc \neq ac$
                                $\angle a \neq \angle b \neq \angle c$

② 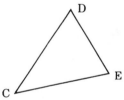   _____
                               _____

③ 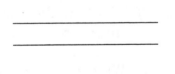   _____
                               _____

④ 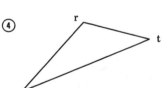   _____
                               _____

⑤ 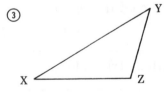   _____
                               _____

⑥ 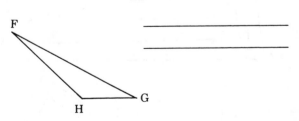   _____
                               _____

REMINDER: *Write the definition of a scalene triangle.*

_____

_____

C If we know that a scalene triangle has three unequal sides, what can we assume about the dimensions of these scalene triangles? What can we assume about the angles?

① △XYZ
XY = 12 feet
YZ = 16 feet
Side XZ does not measure
12 or 16 feet.
_____

∠X = 45°
∠Y = 75°
∠Z ≠ 45° or 75°

② △ABC
AB = 90 centimeters
AC = 110 centimeters
_____
_____

∠A = 60°
∠B = 55°
_____

③ △RST
RS = 10 yards
ST = 15 yards
_____
_____

∠R = 20°
∠S = 77°
_____

④ △UVW
UV = 18 inches
VW = 27 inches
_____
_____
_____

∠U = 42°
∠V = 11°
_____

⑤ △EFG
EF = 4 meters
FG = 3 meters
_____
_____
_____

∠E = 75°
∠F = 50°
_____

⑥ △NOP
NO = 100 millimeters
OP = 80 millimeters
_____
_____
_____

∠N = 32°
∠O = 100°
_____

D Answer the questions.

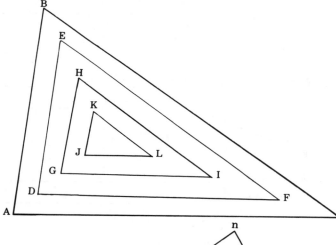

① What is a scalene triangle?
A scalene triangle has 3 unequal sides
and 3 unequal angles.

② What are the 8 scalene triangles in this exercise? _____

③ Why is △DEF a scalene triangle? _____

④ Which sides of △mno are not equal? _____

⑤ Which sides of △JKL are not equal? _____

⑥ Which angles of △pqr are not equal? _____

⑦ Which angles of △GIH are equal? _____

⑧ What kind of triangle is △stu? _____

Equilateral Triangles Unit 138

Learning Objective: *We will learn to recognize an equilateral triangle.*

An equilateral triangle is a triangle with three equal sides.

EXAMPLE: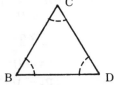

This triangle is an equilateral triangle. Segments BC, CD, and BD are all equal. Angles B, C, and D each equal 60°.

A Place a check (✓) beside each equilateral triangle.

✓ ①   — ②   — ③   — ④

— ⑤  — ⑥   — ⑦   — ⑧

B Why is each of these triangles an equilateral triangle?

① 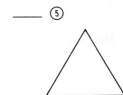 ② 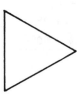 ③  ④

DE = EF = DF
∠D = ∠E = ∠F

_____   _____   _____

⑤ 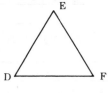 ⑥ 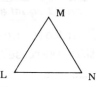 ⑦ 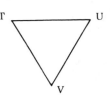 ⑧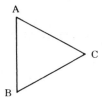

_____   _____   _____   _____

_____   _____   _____   _____

REMINDER: Write the definition of an equilateral triangle.

_____

_____

Unit 138 cont'd ☞

C If we know that an equilateral triangle has three equal sides and three equal angles, what can we assume about the dimensions of these equilateral triangles? What can we assume about the angles?

① △abc
ab = 10 inches
bc = 10 inches
ac = 10 inches

∠a = 60°
∠b = 60°
_∠c = 60°_

② △rst
rs = 7 yards
st = 7 yards
rt = 7 yards

∠r = 60°
∠s = 60°
_∠t = 60°_

③ △CDE
CD = 18 cm
CE = 18 cm
_DE = 18 cm_

∠C = 60°
∠D = 60°
_∠E = 60°_

④ △lmn
lm = 45 meters
ln = 45 meters
mn = 45 meters

∠l = 60°
∠m = 60°
_∠n = 60°_

⑤ △ghi
gh = 82 mm
hi = 82 mm
_gi = 82 mm_

∠g = 60°
∠h = 60°
_∠i = 60°_

⑥ △TUV
TU = 30 miles
UV = 30 miles
TV = 30 miles

∠T = 60°
∠U = 60°
_∠V = 60°_

⑦ △FGH
FG = 2 feet
FH = 2 feet
GH = 2 feet

∠F = 60°
∠H = 60°
_∠G = 60°_

⑧ △XYZ
XY = 21 inches
XZ = 21 inches
YZ = 21 inches

∠X = 60°
∠Z = 60°
_∠Y = 60°_

D Answer the questions.

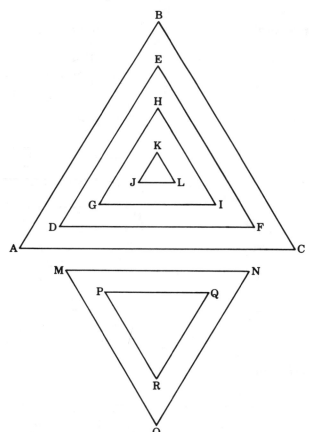

① What is an equilateral triangle?
An equilateral triangle has 3 equal sides
and 3 equal angles.

② What are the 6 equilateral triangles in this exercise? _____

③ Why is △DEF an equilateral triangle?

④ Why is △MNO an equilateral triangle?

⑤ Which sides of △ABC are equal?

⑥ Which sides of △PQR are equal?

⑦ Which sides of △JKL are equal?

⑧ Which angles of △GHI are equal?

⑨ Which angles of △MNO are equal?

⑩ What kind of triangles are in this exercise? _____

Circles

Learning
Objective: *We will learn to identify the circle as a distinct geometric shape.*

A circle is a closed curved line. All points on the line are the same distance from the center of the circle.

EXAMPLE:

 This is a circle.
The point marks
the center of
the circle.

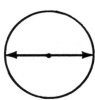 The diameter of a
circle is a straight
line which runs
through the center
of the circle.

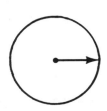 The radius of a circle
is a straight line
which runs from the
center of the circle
to the curved line
which forms the circle.

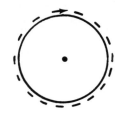 The circumference is
the measure of the
curved line which
forms the circle.

A We know that the diameter of a circle equals two times the radius. What is the diameter of a circle with each of these radii?

① 6 feet
2 × 6 = 12 ft.

② 10 inches

③ 8 miles

④ 14 meters

⑤ 2 miles

⑥ 25 inches

⑦ 50 millimeters

⑧ 5 kilometers

⑨ 80 feet

⑩ 41 centimeters

⑪ 11 feet

⑫ 17 yards

B We know that the radius of a circle equals 1/2 of the diameter. What is the radius of a circle with each of these diameters?

① 100 centimeters
100 ÷ 2 = 50 cm

② 4 feet

③ 42 inches

④ 10 miles

⑤ 12 feet

⑥ 22 millimeters

⑦ 35 meters

⑧ 90 inches

⑨ 1,000 inches

⑩ 66 yards

⑪ 1/2 inch

⑫ 36 centimeters

REMINDER: Write the definition of a circle.

Unit 139 cont'd ☛

To find the circumference of a circle, use the formula c = π d.

C Find the circumferences. (Use 3.14 for pi.)

① diameter = 5 feet

    c = π d

    c = 3.14 × 5

    c = 15.7 feet

② diameter = 2 miles

③ diameter = 10 meters

④ diameter = 20 inches

⑤ diameter = 12 centimeters

⑥ diameter = 3 yards

⑦ diameter = 8 inches

⑧ diameter = 9 feet

⑨ diameter = 15 millimeters

D Fill in the blanks.

① A circle is a closed _____*curved*_____ line.

② All points on a line which forms a circle are the same distance from the _____ of the circle.

③ The _____ is a straight line which runs through the center of the circle.

④ The _____ is a straight line which runs from the center of the circle to the curved line which forms the circle.

⑤ The _____ is the measure of the curved line which forms the circle.

⑥ The diameter equals _____ times the radius.

⑦ The radius equals _____ the diameter.

⑧ The formula for the circumference is _____.

⑨ In exercise C we used _____ for pi.

⑩ The symbol for pi is _____.

⑪ The diameter divides the circle into two _____.

⑫ The plural of "radius" is _____.

Mathematical Affixes   Unit 140

Learning Objective: *We will learn to identify mathematical prefixes and suffixes.*

A prefix is a word part put at the beginning of a word to change its meaning. A suffix is a word part put at the end of a word to change its meaning.

EXAMPLE:

angle   triangle

The prefix "tri" means "three." When we add "tri" to the word "angle," we designate three angles.

A Match the affixes and their meanings.

_h_ ① -sect	⑪ bi-	a. most	k. eight
② octa-	⑫ para-	b. half	l. between
③ -er	⑬ semi-	c. around	m. three
④ centi-	⑭ -ence	d. without	n. state of being
⑤ tri-	⑮ quadr-	e. two	o. through; across
⑥ -est	⑯ dia-	f. four	p. like
⑦ -al	⑰ penta-	g. more	q. not
⑧ intra-	⑱ dis-	h. to cut	r. one hundred
⑨ -less	⑲ peri-	i. within	s. beside
⑩ inter-	⑳ -meter	j. five	t. measure

B Identify the mathematical affixes. (Not all words have both prefixes and suffixes.)

	prefix	suffix		prefix	suffix
① intersect	*inter-*	*-sect*	⑧ parallel		
② centimeter			⑨ pentagon		
③ semicircle			⑩ kilogram		
④ perimeter			⑪ quadrangle		
⑤ octagon			⑫ identical		
⑥ circumference			⑬ equilateral		
⑦ milliliter			⑭ nanosecond		

REMINDER: Write the definitions of a prefix and a suffix.

_____

_____

Unit 140 cont'd ☛

C Many affixes denote numbers. Match these with their meanings.

① uni-	five		⑨ kilo-	seven	
② penta-	one		⑩ deci-	one tenth	
③ centi-	three		⑪ bi-	one thousand	
④ deca-	one hundred		⑫ hepta-	a hundred	
⑤ tri-	eight		⑬ hecto-	two	
⑥ hexa-	six		⑭ quadr-	four	
⑦ octa-	one thousandth		⑮ micro-	one billionth	
⑧ milli-	ten		⑯ nano-	one millionth	

D Write a word with each of these affixes.

① quadr- *quadrilateral*   ⑤ hepta- _____   ⑨ -tion _____

② centi- _____   ⑥ kilo- _____   ⑩ bi- _____

③ para- _____   ⑦ -meter _____   ⑪ -ar _____

④ -ence _____   ⑧ dia- _____   ⑫ deca- _____

E Name these shapes. Identify each prefix and tell how it applies to the name of the shape.

①

This is a quadrilateral.
"Quadr-" means "four."
A quadrilateral has four sides.

②

_____
_____
_____

③

_____
_____
_____

④

_____
_____
_____

⑤

_____
_____
_____

⑥

_____
_____
_____

Comprehension Check

A Fill in the blanks.

① A triangle is a figure with _____ *three* _____ sides.

② An isosceles triangle is a triangle with _____ equal sides.

③ An isosceles triangle has _____ equal angles.

④ A scalene triangle is a triangle with _____ equal sides.

⑤ A scalene triangle has _____ equal angles.

⑥ An equilateral triangle is a triangle with _____ equal sides.

⑦ An equilateral triangle has _____ equal angles.

⑧ Each angle of an equilateral triangle measures _____ .

⑨ A circle is a closed _____ line.

⑩ All points on a circle are the same distance from the _____ .

B Identify the figure described.

① Sides AB and BC of △ABC are equal. Angle A equals angle C.

_____

② Sides AB, BC, and AC of △ABC are equal. Each angle of △ABC measures 60°.

_____

③ Side AB of △ABC measures 6 centimeters. Side BC measures 4 centimeters. Side AC measures 11 centimeters.

_____

④ Side AB of △ABC measures 8 inches. Side BC measures 8 inches. Side AC measures 8 inches.

_____

⑤ Side AB of △ABC measures 13 millimeters. Side BC measures 13 millimeters. Side AC measures 11 millimeters.

_____

Test 28 cont'd 👉

C Identify each of these triangles.

① 9 cm, 11 cm, 22 cm

scalene

② 6 in., 6 in., 6 in.

③ 12 mm, 12 mm, 7 mm

④ 8 ft., 20 ft., 30 ft.

⑤ 10 m, 10 m, 15 m

⑥ 33 in., 39 in., 55 in.

⑦ 10 yds., 17 yds., 21 yds.

⑧ 15 ft., 15 ft., 15 ft.

D Find the diameters of circles with these radii.

① 7 inches

② 41 centimeters

③ 11 miles

④ 16 feet

E Find the radii of circles with these diameters.

① 20 millimeters

② 100 inches

③ 5 miles

④ 42 meters

F Match each affix with its definition.

① para-

② octa-

③ centi-

④ -sect

⑤ tri-

⑥ equi-

⑦ hexa-

a. one hundred

b. eight

c. beside

d. to cut

e. equal

f. six

g. three

G Write a word with each of these affixes.

① kilo-   kilogram

② semi-

③ inter-

④ para-

⑤ dia-

⑥ tri-

⑦ peri-

⑧ -tion

⑨ circum-

⑩ quadr-

⑪ penta-

⑫ deca-

Angles

Learning Objective: *We will learn to identify complementary and supplementary angles.*

An angle is the space between two lines that meet at a point. An angle is measured in degrees.

Two angles are complementary if their sum is 90°.
Two angles are supplementary if their sum is 180°.

A What is the complementary angle of each given angle?

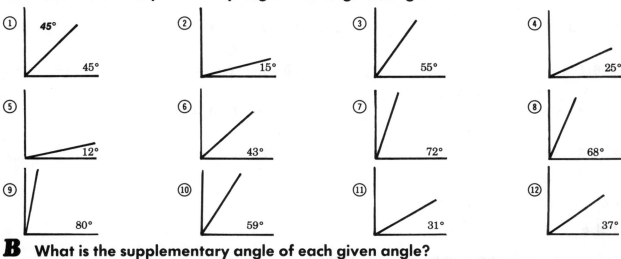

B What is the supplementary angle of each given angle?

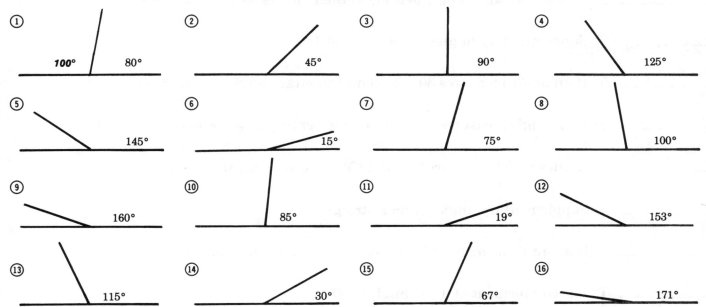

REMINDER: Write the definition of complementary and supplementary angles.

Unit 141 cont'd 👉

C Add each set of angles. Then identify if the set of angles is complementary (c) or supplementary (s).

_c_ ① 73° + 17° = **90°**

____ ② 111° + 69° =

____ ③ 5° + 85° =

____ ④ 123° + 57° =

____ ⑤ 60° + 120° =

____ ⑥ 3° + 87° =

____ ⑦ 36° + 54° =

____ ⑧ 143° + 37° =

____ ⑨ 91° + 89° =

____ ⑩ 19° + 161° =

____ ⑪ 1° + 179° =

____ ⑫ 50° + 40° =

____ ⑬ 107° + 73° =

____ ⑭ 21° + 69° =

____ ⑮ 170° + 10° =

____ ⑯ 97° + 83° =

D True or False

true ① Two angles are complementary if their sum is 90°.

____ ② Supplementary angles have a sum of 180°.

____ ③ If an angle measures 30°, its complementary angle would measure 150°.

____ ④ If an angle measures 110°, its supplementary angle would measure 70°.

____ ⑤ Angles which measure 25° and 65° are complementary.

____ ⑥ Supplementary angles form a straight line.

____ ⑦ If an angle measures 95°, its supplementary angle would also measure 95°.

____ ⑧ The complement of a 10° angle is 80°.

____ ⑨ If an angle measures 100°, its supplement measures 80°.

____ ⑩ If an angle measures 45°, its complement measures 45°.

Classifying Angles

Learning Objective: *We will learn to distinguish among acute, obtuse, right, and straight angles.*

An angle is the space between two lines that meet at a point. An angle is measured in degrees.

① This is an acute angle. It measures less than 90°.

② This is a right angle. It measures exactly 90°.

③ This is an obtuse angle. It measures more than 90° but less than 180°.

④ This is a straight angle. It measures exactly 180°.

A Classify each of these angles.

①  acute

②

③

④

⑤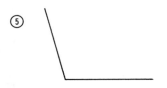

⑥

⑦

⑧

⑨

⑩

⑪

⑫

⑬

⑭

⑮

⑯

REMINDER: What are four classifications of angles?

_____

_____

Unit 142 cont'd ☞

B Classify each of these angle measures.

① 76° _____acute_____   ⑥ 180° _____   ⑪ 91° _____

② 155° _____   ⑦ 176° _____   ⑫ 49° _____

③ 90° _____   ⑧ 124° _____   ⑬ 107° _____

④ 22° _____   ⑨ 87° _____   ⑭ 179° _____

⑤ 116° _____   ⑩ 2° _____   ⑮ 66° _____

C Draw an example of each kind of angle.

① acute angle   ② right angle   ③ obtuse angle   ④ straight angle

D True or False

_____true_____ ① An angle that measures exactly 90° is a right angle.

_____ ② A 180° angle is a straight angle.

_____ ③ It takes three right angles to make one straight angle.

_____ ④ An acute angle measures less than 90°.

_____ ⑤ An obtuse angle measures between 90° and 180°.

_____ ⑥ An angle of 65° would be considered an obtuse angle.

_____ ⑦ A straight angle forms a straight line.

_____ ⑧ An angle of 45° would be considered an acute angle.

_____ ⑨ An angle of 91° would be considered a right angle.

_____ ⑩ An angle is measured in degrees.

Classifying Triangles

Unit 143

Learning Objective: *We will learn to recognize different kinds of triangles.*

A triangle is a geometric figure that has three sides. The sides form three angles.

① 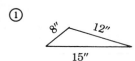 This is a scalene triangle. None of the sides are equal. None of the angles are equal.

② This is an isosceles triangle. Two of its sides are equal. Two of its angles are equal.

③ 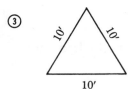 This is an equilateral triangle. All three sides are equal. All three angles are equal.

④ 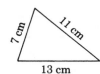 This is a right triangle. One of its angles forms a right angle.

A Classify each of these triangles.

①

equilateral

②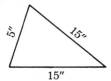

③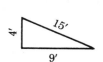

④

⑤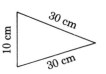

⑥

⑦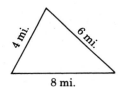

⑧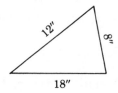

⑨

⑩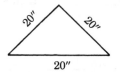

⑪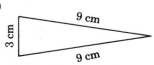

⑫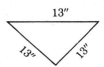

⑬

⑭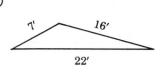

⑮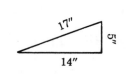

⑯

REMINDER: What are four classifications of triangles?

_____

_____

Unit 143 cont'd ☞

B Why are these triangles classified as they are?

① scalene triangle

11 cm 24 cm 37 cm

_____
_____
_____

② isosceles triangle

15" 15" 8"

_____
_____
_____

③ equilateral triangle

10" 10" 10"

_____
_____
_____

④ right triangle

14' 17" 6'

_____
_____
_____

C Draw an example of each kind of triangle.

① scalene   ② isosceles   ③ equilateral   ④ right

D Fill in the blanks.

① A triangle is a geometric figure that has _____*three*_____ sides.

② A triangle has _____ angles.

③ A scalene triangle has _____ equal sides and _____ equal angles.

④ An isosceles triangle has _____ equal sides.

⑤ An equilateral triangle has _____ equal sides.

⑥ One of the angles of a right triangle must be a _____ angle.

⑦ If a triangle measures 4" × 10" × 10", it is an _____ triangle.

⑧ If one angle of a triangle measures 90°, it is a _____ triangle.

⑨ If a triangle measures 6" × 6" × 6", it is an _____ triangle.

⑩ If a triangle measures 12 cm × 10 cm × 20 cm, it is a _____ triangle.

Congruent Angles

Learning Objective: *We will learn to identify congruent angles.*

Two angles are congruent if they have exactly the same size and shape.

EXAMPLE:

(a)
90°

(b)
45°

(c)
45°

Angles b and c are each 45°. Angle a is 90°. Angles b and c are congruent.

A Match the congruent angles.

b ①

_____ ⑥

a.

f.

_____ ②

_____ ⑦

b.

g.

_____ ③

_____ ⑧

c.

h.

_____ ④

_____ ⑨

d.

i.

_____ ⑤

_____ ⑩

e.

j.

B Identify a congruent angle for each of these angles.

① 100° _____ *100°* _____   ⑥ 32° _____   ⑪ 90° _____   ⑯ 85° _____

② 25° _____   ⑦ 5° _____   ⑫ 55° _____   ⑰ 130° _____

③ 61° _____   ⑧ 105° _____   ⑬ 170° _____   ⑱ 15° _____

④ 152° _____   ⑨ 120° _____   ⑭ 1° _____   ⑲ 179° _____

⑤ 47° _____   ⑩ 180° _____   ⑮ 109° _____   ⑳ 145° _____

REMINDER: Write the definition of congruent angles.

_____

_____

Unit 144 cont'd ☞

C Draw an angle congruent with each of these angles.

① ⑤

② ⑥

③ ⑦

④ ⑧

D Fill in the blanks.

① A right angle is congruent with another _____*right*_____ angle.

② Congruent angles must be the same _____ and _____.

③ An acute angle of 75° is congruent to another _____ angle.

④ A straight angle is congruent with another _____ angle.

⑤ Two 105° angles would be _____.

⑥ An obtuse angle of 97° is congruent to another _____ angle.

⑦ A 65° angle _____ congruent to a 165° angle.

⑧ A 5° angle is congruent with another _____ angle.

⑨ A 160° angle is congruent with another _____ angle.

⑩ A 30° angle is congruent with another _____ angle.

⑪ A 77° angle is congruent with another _____ angle.

⑫ A 121° angle is congruent with another _____ angle.

Congruent Figures

Learning Objective: *We will learn to identify figures which are congruent.*

Two figures are congruent when they are exactly the same shape and size.

EXAMPLE: (a)   (b)   (c)

Figures a, b, and c are all triangles. Figures a and b are the same size. Figure c is smaller. Therefore, figures a and b are congruent because they are the same shape and the same size.

A **Place a check (✓) beside each pair of congruent figures.**

 ①

—— ②

—— ③

—— ④

—— ⑤

—— ⑥

—— ⑦

—— ⑧

—— ⑨

—— ⑩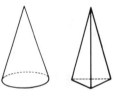

—— ⑪

—— ⑫

—— ⑬

—— ⑭

—— ⑮

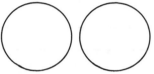

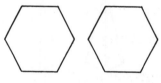
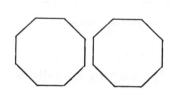

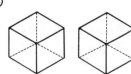
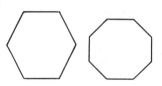

REMINDER: Write the definition of congruent figures.

_____

_____

Unit 145 cont'd ☛

B Classify the following pairs of figures as either congruent or incongruent. If they are incongruent, explain why.

①

congruent

②

③

④

⑤

⑥

⑦

⑧

⑨

C Answer the questions.

① Samuel roped off two sections of his yard. Both sections were squares, which he labeled A and B. Square A measured 20′ × 20′ × 20′ × 20′. Square B was congruent to square A. What were square B's dimensions? _____

② Mr. Overton's office measures 10′ × 12′ × 10′ × 12′. Ms. Kelso's office measures 10′ × 15′ × 10′ × 15′. Are the two offices congruent? _____
Why? _____

③ Liz has a corner table that measures 2′ × 2′ × 4′. She wants a shelf the same size to hang over the table. The shelf will be congruent to the top of the table. What is the shelf's dimensions?

_____

④ Joanna has two circular rugs. One rug has a diameter of six feet. The other has a diameter of four feet. The rugs are exactly the same in every respect except size. Are they congruent?

_____

⑤ Justin has two collies. He built each dog a doghouse. The houses were squares that measured 3′ × 3′ × 3′ × 3′. Were the houses congruent? _____

Comprehension Check

A Measure each of these angles.

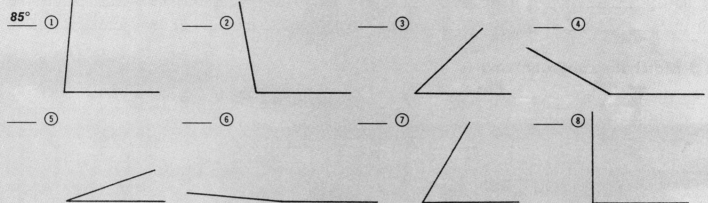

_85°_ ①   ②   ③   ④

⑤   ⑥   ⑦   ⑧

B Identify each kind of angle.

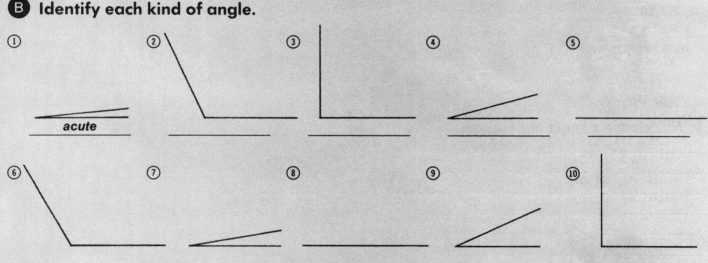

① _acute_   ②   ③   ④   ⑤

⑥   ⑦   ⑧   ⑨   ⑩

C Identify each kind of triangle.

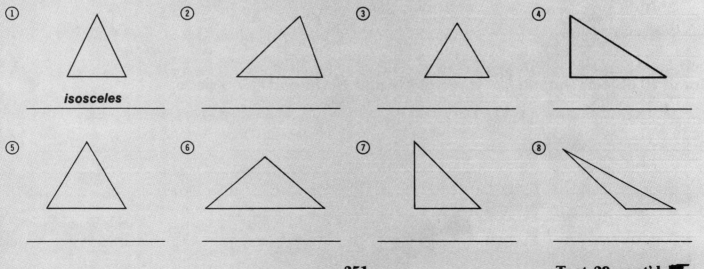

① _isosceles_   ②   ③   ④

⑤   ⑥   ⑦   ⑧

Test 29 cont'd

D **Identify a congruent angle for each of these angles.**

① 50° ___*50°*___   ④ 180° _____   ⑦ 20° _____   ⑩ 170° _____

② 90° _____   ⑤ 136° _____   ⑧ 45° _____   ⑪ 65° _____

③ 101° _____   ⑥ 72° _____   ⑨ 110° _____   ⑫ 18° _____

E **Match the congruent angles.**

_*b*_ ① 90°   ___ ④ 180°   a. 60°   d. 180°

___ ② 60°   ___ ⑤ 165°   b. 90°   e. 115°

___ ③ 115°   ___ ⑥ 45°   c. 165°   f. 45°

F **Match the congruent figures.**

_*c*_ ①   ___ ④   a.   d.

___ ②   ___ ⑤   b.   e.

___ ③   ___ ⑥   c.   f.

Name 10 objects shaped like a rectangle and 10 shaped like a circle.

rectangle   circle

① _____   ⑥ _____   ① _____   ⑥ _____

② _____   ⑦ _____   ② _____   ⑦ _____

③ _____   ⑧ _____   ③ _____   ⑧ _____

④ _____   ⑨ _____   ④ _____   ⑨ _____

⑤ _____   ⑩ _____   ⑤ _____   ⑩ _____

Perimeters

Learning Objective: *We will learn to calculate the perimeters of various figures.*

The perimeter is the measure of the outer boundary of a figure.

Use the following formulas to find the perimeter.

(a)

$$P = 2(L + W)$$
or
$$P = 2L + 2W$$

(b)

$$P = 2(L + W)$$
or
$$P = 2L + 2W$$
or
$$P = 4L$$

(c)

$$P = a + b + c$$

(d)

$$c = \pi d$$
or
$$c = 2\pi r$$

A Find the perimeters of these rectangles and squares.

① length = 6 cm
width = 3 cm

$P = 2(L + W)$
$P = 2(6 + 3)$
$P = 2(9)$
$P = 18$ cm

② length = 12 in.
width = 10 in.

③ length = 31 ft.
width = 24 ft.

④ length = 8 mi.
width = 5 mi.

⑤ side = 10 ft.

⑥ side = 50 mm

⑦ side = 13 mi.

⑧ side = 2 m

⑨ length = 15 mm
width = 5 mm

⑩ length = 7 m
width = 4 m

⑪ length = 200 cm
width = 100 cm

⑫ length = 75 in.
width = 50 in.

⑬ side = 18 yds.

⑭ side = 30 cm

⑮ side = 41 in.

⑯ side = 100 mm

REMINDER: Write the definition of perimeter.

Unit 146 cont'd

B Find the perimeters of these triangles.

① side 1 = 5 feet
side 2 = 10 feet
side 3 = 12 feet

$P = a + b + c$
$P = 5 + 10 + 12$
$P = 27$ feet

② side 1 = 11 cm
side 2 = 16 cm
side 3 = 8 cm

③ side 1 = 7 yards
side 2 = 9 yards
side 3 = 13 yards

④ side 1 = 100 meters
side 2 = 120 meters
side 3 = 150 meters

⑤ side 1 = 15 inches
side 2 = 18 inches
side 3 = 22 inches

⑥ side 1 = 25 mm
side 2 = 25 mm
side 3 = 50 mm

C The word "circumference" is another word for "perimeter." Find the circumference of these circles. (Use 3.14 for pi.)

① diameter = 6 inches

$c = \pi d$
$c = 3.14 \times 6$
$c = 18.84$ in.

② radius = 5 inches

③ diameter = 8 feet

④ radius = 12 yards

⑤ diameter = 25 cm

⑥ diameter = 50 mm

D Answer the questions.

① Bentley wants to put a fence around his yard. The yard measures 100' x 200' x 100' x 200'. How much fence will Bentley need?

② Chris has a circular flower bed that has a diameter of ten feet. If Chris plans to run a brick edge around the bed, how much brick will he need?

③ Ned taped around the edge of a table that measured 4' x 10' x 4' x 10'. How much tape did he use?

④ Ann sewed a lace ruffle around the hem of a skirt. The skirt has a diameter of three feet. How much lace did she use?

Areas

Learning Objective: *We will learn to calculate the areas of various figures.*

Area is the amount of a surface.

Use the following formulas to find the area.

(a)

$A = LW$

(b)

$A = LW$

(c)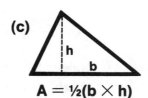

$A = \frac{1}{2}(b \times h)$

(d)

$A = \pi r^2$

A Find the areas of these rectangles and squares.

① length = 15 inches
  width = 10 inches
  $A = LW$
  $A = 15 \times 10$
  $A = 150$ sq. in.

② length = 3 miles
  width = 9 miles

③ length = 10 meters
  width = 5 meters

④ length = 21 cm
  width = 12 cm

⑤ side = 20 feet

⑥ side = 9 miles

⑦ side = 12 cm

⑧ side = 90 mm

⑨ length = 12 cm
  width = 8 cm

⑩ length = 32 meters
  width = 19 meters

⑪ length = 50 mm
  width = 40 mm

⑫ length = 7 feet
  width = 6 feet

⑬ length = 5 miles
  width = 9 miles

⑭ length = 40 cm
  width = 20 cm

⑮ length = 12 feet
  width = 2 feet

⑯ length = 100 mm
  width = 75 mm

REMINDER: Write the definition of area.

Unit 147 cont'd ☛

B Find the areas of these triangles.

① base = 6 inches
height = 4 inches

$A = ½(b \times h)$

$A = ½(6 \times 4)$

$A = ½(24)$

$A = 12$ sq. in.

② base = 9 meters
height = 9 meters

③ base = 100 cm
height = 70 cm

④ base = 10 yards
height = 8 yards

⑤ base = 20 inches
height = 16 inches

⑥ base = 8 miles
height = 6 miles

C Find the areas of these circles. (Use 3.14 for pi.)

① radius = 5 meters

$A = \pi r^2$

$A = 3.14(5)^2$

$A = 3.14 \times 25$

$A = 78.5$ sq. m

② radius = 4 feet

③ radius = 2 miles

④ radius = 11 millimeters

⑤ radius = 8 yards

⑥ radius = 10 centimeters

D Fill in the blanks.

① _____ is the amount of a surface.

② The formula A = LW stands for area equals _____ times _____ .

③ The formula A = ½(b × h) stands for area equals one-half times the product of the _____ times the _____ .

④ The formula A = πr^2 stands for area equals pi times the _____ squared.

⑤ Area is expressed in _____ units.

Square and Cubic Units

Unit 148

Learning Objective: **We will learn to figure square and cubic units.**

When two units are multiplied, the answer is expressed in square units. When three units are multiplied, the answer is expressed in cubic units.

EXAMPLES: (a) 2 inches $\times$ 2 inches = 4 square inches

(b) 2 inches $\times$ 2 inches $\times$ 2 inches = 8 cubic inches

A Multiply.

① 1 foot $\times$ 2 feet = **2 sq. ft.**

② 7 inches $\times$ 3 inches =

③ 10 meters $\times$ 5 meters =

④ 12 yards $\times$ 8 yards =

⑤ 9 miles $\times$ 3 miles =

⑥ 8 centimeters $\times$ 4 centimeters =

⑦ 11 inches $\times$ 4 inches =

⑧ 13 kilometers $\times$ 2 kilometers =

⑨ 20 feet $\times$ 10 feet =

⑩ 6 millimeters $\times$ 6 millimeters =

⑪ 5 miles $\times$ 5 miles =

⑫ 15 meters $\times$ 3 meters =

⑬ 17 meters $\times$ 2 meters =

⑭ 70 inches $\times$ 4 inches =

⑮ 3 yards $\times$ 30 yards =

⑯ 25 feet $\times$ 8 feet =

⑰ 4 millimeters $\times$ 4 millimeters $\times$ 4 millimeters =

⑱ 7 kilometers $\times$ 11 kilometers $\times$ 5 kilometers =

⑲ 9 centimeters $\times$ 10 centimeters $\times$ 2 centimeters =

⑳ 20 inches $\times$ 10 inches $\times$ 15 inches =

㉑ 41 miles $\times$ 32 miles $\times$ 18 miles =

㉒ 8 centimeters $\times$ 8 centimeters $\times$ 8 centimeters =

REMINDER: Write the definition of square and cubic units.

_____

_____

Unit 148 cont'd ☞

B Would the answer to each of these multiplication problems be expressed in square (s) or cubic (c) units?

s ① 15 feet
×4 feet
60

_____ ② 11 inches
×5 inches
55
×3 inches
165

_____ ③ 30 meters
×8 meters
240
×6 meters
1,440

_____ ④ 96 cm
×9 cm
864

_____ ⑤ 100 mm
×10 mm
1000
×7 mm
7,000

_____ ⑥ 13 yards
×11 yards
13
13
143
×2 yards
286

_____ ⑦ 412 inches
×21 inches
412
824
8,652

_____ ⑧ 401 feet
×153 feet
1203
2005
401
61,353

_____ ⑨ 77 meters
×42 meters
154
308
3,234

_____ ⑩ 147 feet
×20
2940
×10 feet
29,400

_____ ⑪ 1,000 cm
×100 cm
100,000

_____ ⑫ 212 inches
×51 inches
212
1060
10,812

C Match the problems with their answers.

d ① 6 cm × 4 cm × 8 cm

_____ ② 18 mi. × 32 mi.

_____ ③ 11 mm × 11 mm × 11 mm

_____ ④ 9 mi. × 9 mi. × 7 mi.

_____ ⑤ 4 in. × 24 in. × 2 in.

_____ ⑥ 72 mm × 66 mm

_____ ⑦ 4 m × 48 m

_____ ⑧ 6 mm × 8 mm × 99 mm

_____ ⑨ 11 ft. × 121 ft.

_____ ⑩ 6 mi. × 3 mi. × 32 mi.

a. 192 cubic inches

b. 4,752 cubic millimeters

c. 1,331 cubic millimeters

d. 192 cubic centimeters

e. 192 square meters

f. 576 square miles

g. 1,331 square feet

h. 4,752 square millimeters

i. 567 cubic miles

j. 576 cubic miles

Volume

Learning Objective: *We will learn to calculate the volume of a container.*

Volume measures the total space an object occupies. It is based on the measurement of the cube. It is expressed in cubic units.

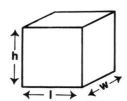

We use volume to determine how much a container, such as a box, can hold.

To measure volume, we must know the length, the width, and the height of the container. We use the formula V = LWH.

A Find the volumes.

① length = 4 cm
width = 2 cm
height = 3 cm

V = LWH
V = 4 × 2 × 3
V = 24 cu. cm

② length = 5 in.
width = 5 in.
height = 2 in.

③ length = 8 mm
width = 10 mm
height = 6 mm

④ length = 7 ft.
width = 4 ft.
height = 4 ft.

⑤ length = 12 in.
width = 12 in.
height = 12 in.

⑥ length = 15 cm
width = 12 cm
height = 10 cm

⑦ length = 9 ft.
width = 11 ft.
height = 6 ft.

⑧ length = 40 mm
width = 30 mm
height = 20 mm

⑨ length = 20 cm
width = 30 cm
height = 10 cm

⑩ length = 17 in.
width = 10 in.
height = 5 in.

⑪ length = 15 in.
width = 8 in.
height = 3 in.

⑫ length = 26 cm
width = 21 cm
height = 17 cm

⑬ length = 100 mm
width = 50 mm
height = 25 mm

⑭ length = 32 in.
width = 22 in.
height = 20 in.

REMINDER: Write the definition of volume.

Unit 149 cont'd ☞

Remember that to calculate volume, you must know length, width, and height. Ask yourself if the object is a solid or if it can be filled with something. If the answer is yes, then you can determine the object's volume.

B Place a check (✓) beside the objects for which we can determine the volume.

✓ ① a box in which we put old magazines

_____ ② a swimming pool

_____ ③ a room in the school

_____ ④ the top of a table

_____ ⑤ a square hole in the yard

_____ ⑥ a tin box in which we store tea

_____ ⑦ a box filled with candy

_____ ⑧ an empty box

_____ ⑨ the floor of the gym

_____ ⑩ a sheet of paper

_____ ⑪ a crate full of oranges

_____ ⑫ a photograph of your house

_____ ⑬ a carton full of M & M's

_____ ⑭ a rectangular piggy bank full of new pennies

_____ ⑮ a thick piece of fudge

C Find the volume for the object described in each paragraph.

① Lucy needs a box that is 20 inches long, 15 inches wide, and 6 inches deep.

$V = LWH$
$V = 20 \times 15 \times 6$
$V = 1,800$ *cu. in.*

② Brad built a rabbit cage that is 10 feet long, 16 feet wide, and 5 feet tall.

③ Sharon bought a set of wooden blocks for the Smith's baby. Each block is 14 centimeters long, 14 centimeters wide, and 14 centimeters high.

④ Jamison has a book that is 12 inches long, 8 inches wide, and 6 inches thick.

⑤ Cam needs a box that is 17 inches long, 11 inches wide, and 2 inches deep.

⑥ Alvira's room is 14'x16'. The ceiling is 8 feet above the floor.

Using Formulas

Learning Objective: *We will learn which formulas apply to given situations.*

A formula is a rule for doing something.

Formulas for Area

a. of a rectangle $\longrightarrow$ **A = LW**
   or square

b. of a triangle $\longrightarrow$ **A = ½(b × h)**

c. of a circle $\longrightarrow$ **A = πr²**

Formula for Volume

of a cube $\longrightarrow$ **V = LWH**

Formulas for Perimeter

a. of a rectangle $\longrightarrow$ **P = 2(L + W)**
   or
   P = 2L + 2W

b. of a square $\longrightarrow$ **P = 2(L + W)**
   or
   P =2L + 2W
   or
   P = 4L

c. of a triangle $\longrightarrow$ **P = a + b + c**

d. of a circle $\longrightarrow$ **c = πd**
   or
   c = 2πr

A Answer the questions.

① What is the formula for finding the perimeter of a rectangle? <u>*P = 2(L + W) or*</u>
   <u>*P = 2L + 2W*</u>

② What is the formula for finding the area of a rectangle? _____

③ What is the formula for finding the volume of a cube? _____

④ What is the formula for finding the perimeter of a circle? _____

⑤ What is the formula for finding the area of a triangle? _____

⑥ What is the formula for finding the area of a square? _____

⑦ What is the formula for finding the perimeter of a triangle? _____

⑧ What is the formula for finding the area of a circle? _____

⑨ What is the formula for finding the perimeter of a square? _____
   _____

⑩ What does it mean when two symbols are written beside each other, as the "L" and
   "W" in A = LW? _____

REMINDER: Write the definition of a formula.

_____

_____

Unit 150 cont'd 👉

The answer for area is expressed in square units. The answer for perimeter is expressed in the same units as the individual measures. The answer for volume is expressed in cubic units.

B How would the answers to these problems be expressed?

① the area of a square measured in feet _____ *square feet* _____

② the volume of a cube measured in centimeters _____

③ the perimeter of a circle measured in inches _____

④ the area of a triangle measured in meters _____

⑤ the perimeter of a rectangle measured in yards _____

⑥ the area of a rectangle measured in millimeters _____

⑦ the perimeter of a triangle measured in meters _____

⑧ the area of a circle measured in miles _____

⑨ the perimeter of a square measured in kilometers _____

⑩ the area of a square measured in inches _____

C Work the problems.

① Ted wants to build a storage crate. If he builds one 10 feet long, 6 feet wide, and 8 feet tall, how much will the crate hold?

② The Norton Company has a square grain tank that measures 30 feet long, 30 feet wide, and 30 feet deep. How much grain will it hold?

③ The Jacksons' yard is 200 feet long and 500 feet wide. What is the area of their yard?

④ Priscilla's room is 16′ x 20′ x 16′ x 20′. How many square feet is her room?

⑤ Alexis needs a border to go around the edge of a bulletin board. The board measures 60″ x 40″ x 60″ x 40″. How much border does she need?

⑥ Les has a circular flower bed with a diameter of five feet. He wants to run a metal edger on the border of the bed. How much border material does he need?

Comprehension Check Test 30

A Fill in the blanks.

① The ____perimeter____ is the measure of the outer boundary of a figure.

② The perimeter of a circle is called the _____ .

③ _____ is the amount of a surface.

④ _____ measures the space an object occupies.

⑤ Area is expressed in _____ units. Volume is expressed in _____ units.

⑥ We use volume to determine _____ a container can hold.

⑦ We use area to determine the space an object _____ .

⑧ We use perimeter to determine the distance _____ an object.

⑨ A _____ is a rule for doing something.

⑩ The number _____ is frequently used for pi.

B Match the formula with the situation for which it is used.

_b/j_ ① A = LW   ____ ④ V = LWH   ____ ⑦ c = πd   ____ ⑩ c = 2πr
____ ② A = ½(b × h)   ____ ⑤ P = 2(L + W)   ____ ⑧ P = 2L + 2W   ____ ⑪ d = 2r
____ ③ A = πr²   ____ ⑥ P = 4L   ____ ⑨ P = a + b + c   ____ ⑫ R = ½d

a. perimeter of a square
b. area of a rectangle
c. radius of a circle
d. volume of a cube
e. perimeter of a triangle
f. perimeter of a rectangle

g. area of a triangle
h. diameter of a circle
i. circumference of a circle
j. area of a square
k. perimeter of a circle
l. area of a circle

C Would you find the area (a), perimeter (p), or volume (v)?

_a_ ① the space a rug covers
____ ② how much a box holds
____ ③ the fence around a yard
____ ④ the lace trim around a collar
____ ⑤ the space a couch covers

____ ⑥ the space a painting covers
____ ⑦ how much a carton holds
____ ⑧ how much a pool holds
____ ⑨ the space a house covers
____ ⑩ the frame of a picture

Test 30 cont'd 👉

D Find the areas.

① length = 10 in.
width = 10 in.
$A = LW$
$A = 10 \times 10$
$A = 100$ sq. in.

② base = 7 ft.
height = 3 ft.
_____
_____
_____
_____

③ radius = 2 m
_____
_____
_____
_____

④ length = 6 yds.
width = 3 yds.
_____
_____
_____

⑤ base = 11 in.
height = 9 in.
_____
_____
_____
_____

⑥ length = 4 cm
width = 4 cm
_____
_____
_____

⑦ length = 20 in.
width = 10 in.
_____
_____
_____

⑧ radius = 7 km
_____
_____
_____
_____

E Find the perimeters.

① length = 5 ft.
width = 3 ft.
_____
_____
_____

② length = 10 m
width = 10 m
_____
_____
_____

③ side 1 = 6 cm
side 2 = 5 cm
side 3 = 8 cm
_____
_____
_____

④ radius = 3 in.
_____
_____
_____

F Find the volumes.

① length = 8 m
width = 4 m
height = 2 m
_____
_____
_____

② length = 10 ft.
width = 7 ft.
height = 4 ft.
_____
_____
_____

③ length = 20 in.
width = 18 in.
height =10 in.
_____
_____
_____

④ length = 9 cm
width = 9 cm
height = 9 cm
_____
_____
_____

Write a paragraph describing when you would need to find area, perimeter, and volume.

_____
_____
_____
_____
_____
_____
_____
_____

Line Graphs

Learning Objective: *We will learn to read a line graph.*

A line graph is a graph on which points are connected with a line.

EXAMPLE:

Line graphs are ideal for illustrating change over a period of time. The graph at the right shows one person's weight changes over a period of several years.

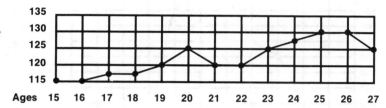

A Record the given information on line graphs.

①
Day	No. of Fish
1	2
2	3
3	4
4	6
5	8
6	10
7	9
8	9
9	10
10	8

Larry's Fishing Trips

②
Week	Total Diners
1	25
2	30
3	30
4	25
5	10
6	50
7	40
8	50
9	35
10	55

People Eating at Cafe

③
Week	Miles
1	3
2	3.5
3	3
4	4.5
5	2.5
6	3
7	4.5
8	4
9	5.5
10	5

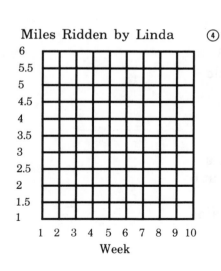

Miles Ridden by Linda

④
Day	Number Present
1	20
2	25
3	24
4	26
5	28
6	30
7	32
8	24
9	22
10	20

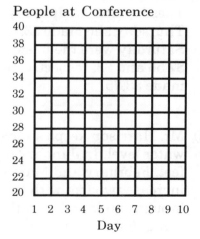

People at Conference

REMINDER: Write the definition of a line graph.

Unit 151 cont'd ☞

This graph records the pounds of dog food used at Robison's Kennels from January through December.

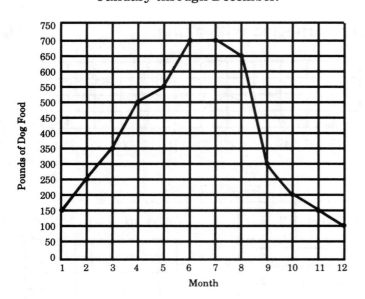

① How many pounds were used in February? __*250*__

② How many pounds were used in May? _____

③ During which two months was the same amount of food used? _____

_____

④ Did the pounds of food always increase? _____

⑤ During which two months was the most food used? _____

⑥ When was dog food consumption the lowest? _____

⑦ When was the smallest increase? _____

_____

⑧ When was the largest decrease? _____

⑨ During which two months did consumption increase by 150 pounds? _____

⑩ Why do you believe the pounds of dog food used was higher in June and July? _____

C Read the paragraphs and record the information on a line graph.

① Christina kept a record of the tips she made during a week. On Monday she made $2.50. Tuesday and Wednesday she made $4.75. On Thursday she made $3.25. Because Friday and Saturday were the busiest days, Christina made $7.50 and $8, respectively. On Sunday she made $3.75.

② Mr. Harrison keeps a record of the Black River's water level. In January of 1983 the river stood at 6 feet. February and March each saw the river increase two feet with the spring thaw. April rains brought an increase of three feet, and May through June saw the river level being steady. From July through September the river dropped two feet a month, but in October the rains brought it back up three feet. In November the river level dropped one foot, and in December of 1983 it was at the same level it had been in January.

Bar Graphs

Learning Objective: *We will learn to read vertical and horizontal bar graphs.*

A bar graph uses a vertical or horizontal bar to record information.

EXAMPLE: Bar graphs are well suited for comparisons of groups.

A vertical bar graph, like the one below, uses vertical bars to record information.

A horizontal bar graph, like the one below, uses horizontal bars to record information.

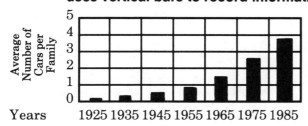

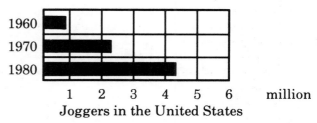

Joggers in the United States

A Record the given information on a bar graph. Then answer the questions.

I.

Professors	per 100 passed
Jamison	78
Moisan	83
Thompson	60
Harris	65
Jay	74
Reynolds	85
Barker	68

Number per 100 of Students Who Passed English II

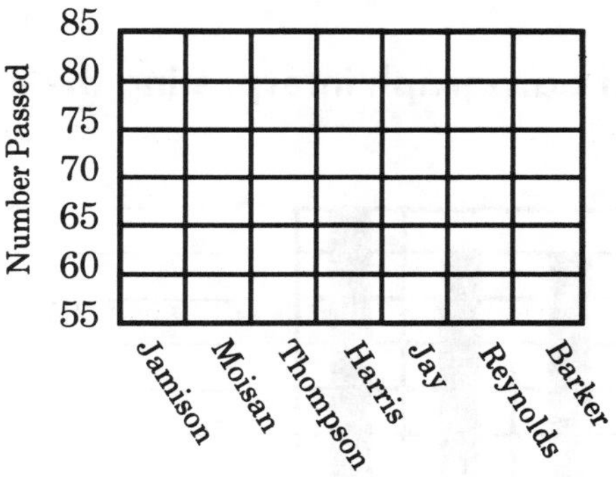

(Grid with Number Passed axis: 85, 80, 75, 70, 65, 60, 55; labels Jamison, Moisan, Thompson, Harris, Jay, Reynolds, Barker)

① Which professor passed the least number of students?

_____

② Who passed the most?

_____

③ How many professors are there?

_____

④ What kind of bar graph is this?

_____

II. Approximate Distance in Miles

① Willow Springs to Alexandria 200
② Sullivan to Kirksville 200
③ Hayti to Ste. Genevieve 500
④ Poplar Bluff to St. Louis 150
⑤ Princeton to Gainesville 300
⑥ Warrensburg to Hayti 400
⑦ St. Joseph to Ironton 350
⑧ Kennett to Bethany 500

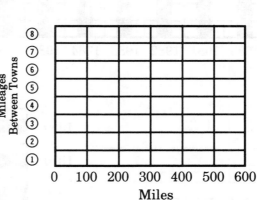

Miles

① How many distances are recorded? _____
② Which is the shortest? _____
③ How many are over 250 miles? _____
④ What kind of bar graph is this? _____

REMINDER: Write the definition of a bar graph.

_____

_____

Unit 152 cont'd ☞

B Construct a vertical bar graph to record the information given.

Preference of Dinner Food—200 people results: 30-hamburger, 25-steak, 45-chicken, 30-pork, 50-fish, 20-other

C Construct a horizontal bar graph to record the information given.

Candy Bar Sales—8 people results: Cathy-70, Larry-65, Rita-50, Liz-45, John-40, Jerry-40, Rick-35, Marci-20

D Read each graph and write a short paragraph interpreting the information.

①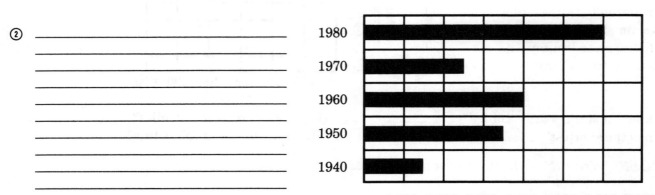

②

Circle Graphs

Learning Objective: *We will learn to read circle graphs.*

A circle graph uses a circle to record information.

EXAMPLE:

The circle graph at right shows the percent of children who eat lunch at the school's cafeteria, bring their lunch to school, and walk home to eat lunch.

100 children
  50% eat at school
  25% bring lunch
  25% walk home for lunch

A Record the given information on the circle graphs.

① Twenty-five percent of American women have black hair. Another twenty-five percent have red hair. The remaining fifty percent is equally divided between women who have brown or blonde hair.

② Sixty percent of college graduates earn over $10,000 per year. Twenty-five percent earn over $19,500 a year. Ten percent earn over $40,000 per year, and five percent earn over $65,000 per year.

③ Seventy-five of every one hundred school children learn the basics of reading, writing, and arithmetic. The other twenty-five percent of the children fail in one or more areas.

④ Sixty of every one hundred homes in the United States have one television. Another thirty of the one hundred have two televisions, and ten in every one hundred have three or more.

REMINDER: Write the definition of a circle graph.

_____

_____

 Unit 153 cont'd ☛

B Study the circle graphs and answer the questions.

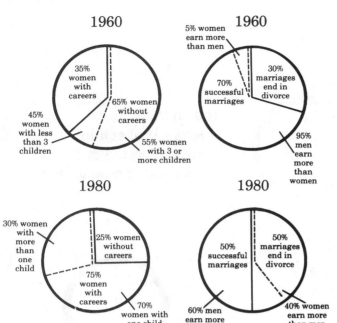

1960

1960

1980

1980

① In 1960, what percent of women had no career? _**65%**_

② In 1960, how many successful marriages were there? _____

③ Which year saw women with one child or less? _____

④ When did most women have a career? _____

⑤ When were half of all marriages ending in divorce? _____

⑥ What percent of men earned more than women in 1960? _____ 1980? _____

⑦ What was the percent of successful marriage in 1980? _____

⑧ How many years do these graphs cover? _____

C Study the graphs and write a short paragraph interpreting the information.

①

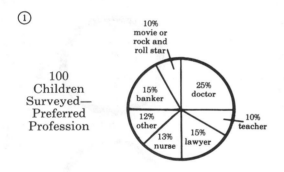

100 Children Surveyed— Preferred Profession

_____
_____
_____
_____
_____
_____
_____
_____
_____
_____
_____
_____
_____
_____

② _____
_____
_____
_____
_____
_____
_____
_____
_____
_____
_____
_____

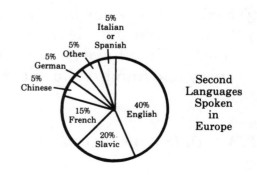

Second Languages Spoken in Europe

Reading Graphs

Learning Objective: **We will learn to interpret information on a graph.**

A graph is a visual aid for presenting numerical information.

EXAMPLE: Bar graphs are well suited for comparisons of groups. This vertical bar graph illustrates the number of college graduates in millions.

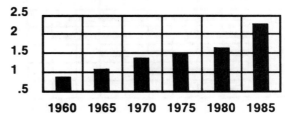

A Study each graph and answer the questions.

I.

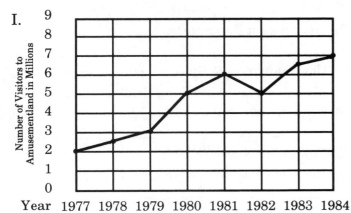

Year 1977 1978 1979 1980 1981 1982 1983 1984

① Which years does this graph cover?
   1977-1984

② What does this graph illustrate?

③ What kind of graph is this?

④ When was visitation the lowest?

   The highest? _____

⑤ Was there always an increase?

⑥ How many visited the park in 1980?

II. ① How many age groups does this graph cover? _____ **6** _____
② What does this graph illustrate? _____
③ What kind of graph is this? _____
④ Which age group spends the least? _____ The most? _____

⑤ When is the sharpest increase?

   The sharpest decrease?

⑥ How much does the average thirty-year old spend on entertainment per year?
   _____ Ten-year-old? _____
   Sixty-year-old? _____
   Fifty-year-old? _____

⑦ How much money is covered on the graph? _____

REMINDER: Write the definition of a graph.

B Study each graph and answer the questions.

I. Most Preferred One Pizza Topping

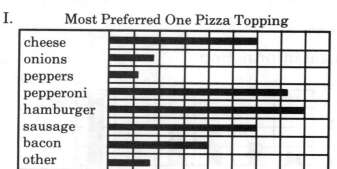

II. 1980 College Majors at A.C.U.

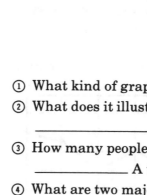

① What kind of graph is this? _____
   horizontal bar graph

② What does it illustrate? _____
_____

③ How many people were surveyed? _____

④ Which topping is most preferred? _____
   _____ Least preferred? _____

⑤ Name one topping "other" could be. _____
_____

⑥ How many people chose cheese? _____

⑦ How many people chose onions? _____

⑧ How many people chose sausage? _____

① What kind of graph is this? _____

② What does it illustrate? _____
_____

③ How many people chose a business major?
   _____ A teaching field? _____

④ What are two majors "other" could be?
_____

⑤ How many chose "other"? _____

⑥ Name one job included in art and science?
_____

C True or False

__f__ ① Circle graphs use points to plot information.

_____ ② Horizontal bar graphs use vertical bars to plot information.

_____ ③ Line graphs use points and lines to plot information.

_____ ④ Bar graphs are well suited for comparing groups.

_____ ⑤ Circle graphs are cut into pie-shaped wedges.

_____ ⑥ Line graphs are only used with numbers less than 100.

_____ ⑦ Horizontal bar graphs never show percents.

_____ ⑧ Vertical bar graphs may show increases.

_____ ⑨ Circle graphs may only use percent.

_____ ⑩ Line graphs may show increases or decreases.

_____ ⑪ Circle graphs show increases and decreases.

_____ ⑫ Horizontal and vertical bar graphs use bars to illustrate information.

372

Using a Table to Predict Results

Unit 155

Learning Objective: **We will learn to preduct results.**

A prediction is an educated guess about something that may happen.

EXAMPLE:

The line graph at the right shows Tom Shelly's income from age 20 through 45. From it, we can predict that Tom will make at least $37,000 when he is 50 because he is making that amount at age 45.

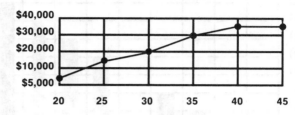

A Study the graph below and answer the questions.

Christmas Items Sold

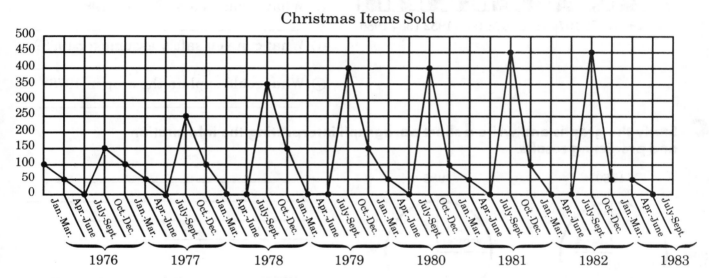

① What kind of graph is this? _____ *line graph* _____
② What does it illustrate? _____
③ How many years are covered? _____
④ What can be predicted about future April-June sales? _____

⑤ What can be predicted about future July-September sales? _____

⑥ What can be predicted about sales in 1983 for October-December? _____

⑦ What can be predicted about sales in January-March of 1984? _____

⑧ What can be predicted about future October-December sales? _____

REMINDER: Write the definition of a prediction.

_____

_____

Unit 155 cont'd 👉

B Study the graph and answer the questions.

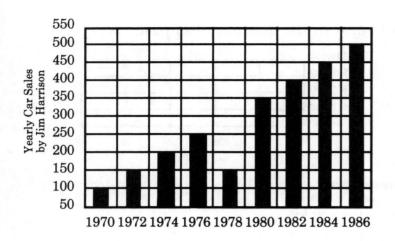

① What kind of graph is this?
vertical bar graph

② What does the graph illustrate?
_____

③ If the graph ended with 1976, what would your prediction about Jim Harrison's car sales be?
_____

④ With the exception of 1978, would your prediction in ③ be correct for the years shown on the graph? _____

⑤ What would you predict for 1988?
_____

⑥ What can you safely assume for 1988?
_____

⑦ What could explain the drop in 1978?
_____

C Study the graphs and write a short paragraph interpreting the information and predicting results.

①   1960   1985

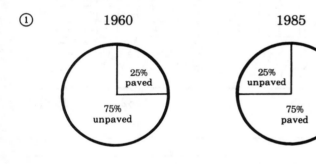

Paved Roads in Rural Areas

_____
_____
_____
_____
_____
_____
_____
_____
_____
_____
_____

② _____
_____
_____
_____
_____
_____
_____
_____
_____
_____
_____

College Enrollment at H.S.U.

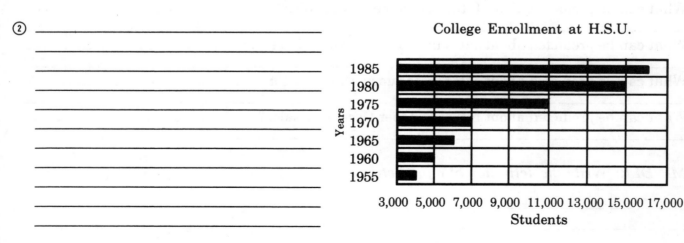

374

Comprehension Check

A Record the given information on a line graph.

① Week Visitors

Week	Visitors
1	20
2	25
3	25
4	28
5	20
6	27

Visitors to Yellow Rock Cave

② Roses

Week	Sold
1	10
2	12
3	15
4	8
5	9
6	6

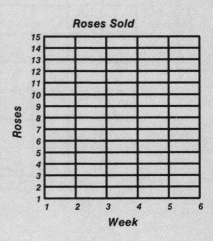

Roses Sold

B Record the given information on a vertical bar graph.

Town	Population
Bay	52,000
Harrison	42,300
Millerson	15,000
Ironville	35,000
Stoker	23,600
Twiller	10,000

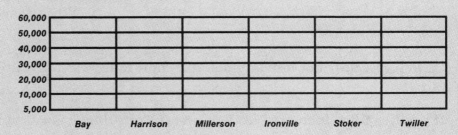

C Record the given information on a horizontal bar graph.

Vacation Preferences
650 People

amusement parks - 75
beach - 275
skiing - 150
mountain climbing - 50
spelunking - 25
travel - 75

amusement parks						
beach						
skiing						
mountain climbing						
spelunking						
traveling						

50 100 150 200 250 300

D Record the given information on a circle graph.

30 people favor dogs as pets
20 people favor cats as pets
10 people favor fish as pets
15 people favor hamsters as pets
25 people favor no pets

Test 31 cont'd 👉

E Study the graph and answer the questions.

① What kind of graph is this? _____
   line graph

② What does it illustrate _____
   _____

③ Does the number filled always increase?
   _____

④ How many years does the graph cover?
   _____

⑤ How many cavities were filled
   in 1973? _____ 1975? _____
   1977? _____

⑥ What year saw the sharpest increase?
   _____

⑦ If Dr. Tyrer does not lose any patients, how many cavities can he expect to fill
   in 1978 _____

⑧ If cavities filled increased at their present rate, how many - at least - will Dr. Tyrer fill
   in 1979? _____ 1980? _____ 1981? _____

F Using the graph from exercise A question one, answer the following questions.

① How many visitors, at the least, can Yellow Rock Cave expect during week 7? _____

② If visitors continue to increase by their present average, how many will visit in
   week 7? _____ Week 8? _____ Week 9? _____

Define.

① graph _____
② line graph _____
③ vertical _____
④ horizontal _____
⑤ bar graph _____
⑥ circle graph _____
⑦ interpret _____
⑧ prediction _____

Time Zones

Learning Objective: *We will learn to read time zones.*

A time zone is a geographical region in which the same standard time is used.

The continental United States is divided into four time zones.

A Complete the charts.

Pacific	Mountain	Central	Eastern
2:15 a.m.	3:15 a.m.	4:15 a.m.	5:15 a.m.
	6:30 p.m.		
		1:00 p.m.	
			8:05 a.m.
			2:30 p.m.
		7:00 a.m.	
	4:09 p.m.		
3:50 p.m.			
11:59 a.m.			

Pacific	Mountain	Central	Eastern
	6:19 a.m.		
	9:00 p.m.		
			5:10 a.m.
			10:00 p.m.
2:00 p.m.			
1:20 a.m.			
		5:45 a.m.	
		8:45 p.m.	
3:00 a.m.			

B If it is 2 a.m. in San Francisco, CA, what time is it in these cities?

① Detroit, MI ___5 a.m.___ ⑥ Billings, MT _____ ⑪ Atlanta, GA _____

② El Paso, TX _____ ⑦ Buffalo, NY _____ ⑫ Reno, NV _____

③ Cleveland, OH _____ ⑧ Phoenix, AZ _____ ⑬ Des Moines, IA _____

④ Salt Lake City, UT _____ ⑨ Boise, ID _____ ⑭ Chicago, IL _____

⑤ Wichita, KS _____ ⑩ Portland, OR _____ ⑮ Memphis, TN _____

REMINDER: Write the definition of a time zone.

_____

_____

Unit 156 cont'd ☞

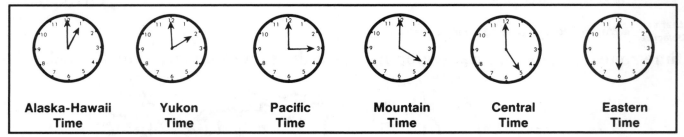

Alaska-Hawaii Time	Yukon Time	Pacific Time	Mountain Time	Central Time	Eastern Time

C Complete the chart.

Alaska-Hawaii Time	Yukon Time	Pacific Time	Mountain Time	Central Time	Eastern Time
Tuesday 11:00 p.m.	Wednesday 12:00 a.m.	Wednesday 1:00 a.m.	Wednesday 2:00 a.m.	Wednesday 3:00 a.m.	Wednesday 4:00 a.m.
Saturday 4:15 p.m.					
			Saturday 12:45 a.m.		
	Monday 4:30 a.m.				
		Sunday 10:15 p.m.			
					Wednesday 1:00 p.m.
Saturday 8:55 p.m.					
				Thursday 3:15 p.m.	

D Answer the questions.

① Robin lived in Missouri. Her mother lived in New York. When it was 6 o'clock at Robin's home, what time was it at her mother's home?

_____

② Jean called Liz at 8 o'clock in the evening. Jean was in Boston. Liz was in Los Angeles. What time did Liz receive the call?

_____

③ Toby called his parents on Monday, but they received the call on Tuesday. How do you explain the different days?

_____

④ Howard's plane left at 4 p.m. from Atlanta. It arrived at Denver at 6 p.m. It was a four-hour flight. How do you explain only a two-hour difference in time?

_____

Reading Maps

Learning Objective: *We will learn to read a simple map.*

A map is a representation of an actual area.

EXAMPLE:

A **Read the map above and answer these questions.**

① In which state is San Francisco located? _____ *California* _____
② In which state is Salt Lake City located? _____
③ Which states border California? _____
④ Which states border Montana? _____
⑤ Which states border Indiana? _____
⑥ Which state borders Arkansas on the north? _____
⑦ Which state borders Arizona on the east? _____
⑧ Which state borders North Carolina on the west? _____
⑨ Which state borders Minnesota on the south? _____
⑩ Which states border Wyoming on the south? _____
⑪ Which states border Nebraska? _____
⑫ In which part of Florida is Miami? _____
⑬ In which part of Tennessee is Memphis? _____
⑭ Which states' names begin with the word "north"? _____
⑮ Which states' names begin with the word "new"? _____
⑯ Which states have the shortest names? _____
⑰ Which state's name begins with the word "west"? _____
⑱ Which area marked on this map is not a state? _____

REMINDER: Write the definition of a map.

_____
_____

Unit 157 cont'd ☞

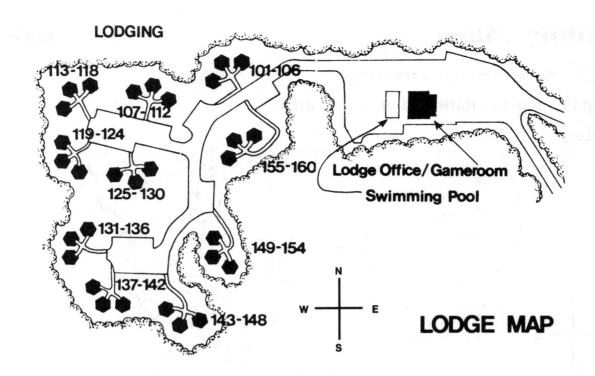

LODGING

113-118
107-112
119-124
125-130
131-136
137-142
143-148
101-106
155-160

Lodge Office/Gameroom
Swimming Pool

N
W — E
S

LODGE MAP

B Read the map above and answer these questions.

① What does this map show? _a vacation lodge map_

② What is the first building as you enter the area? _____

③ Where is the swimming pool? _____

④ How many cabins are there? _____

⑤ What are the cabins' numbers _____

⑥ To get to cabin 112, which cabins would you pass? _____

⑦ Is cabin 125 near 130? _____

⑧ Is there a restaurant on this map? _____

⑨ In which direction do you travel to exit the area? _____

⑩ Which cabins are closest to the office? _____

⑪ Where is the gameroom located? _____

⑫ What surrounds the lodge area? _____

⑬ How many roads lead to and from the lodge? _____

⑭ Which cabins are farthest south? _____

⑮ Where are cabins 143-148 in relation to cabins 137-142? _____

⑯ Where are cabins 101-106 in relation to cabins 155-160? _____

⑰ Where are cabins 113-118 in relation to cabins 107-112? _____

⑱ Where are cabins 149-154 in relation to cabins 131-136? _____

⑲ How many cabins are in each cluster? _____

⑳ How many cabin clusters are there? _____

Reading Scales on Maps

Learning Objective: *We will learn to use a scale when reading a map.*

A scale marks how the distances between objects on a map correspond to real distances.

EXAMPLE: If you measure the scale at right, you will find that it is 2 inches in length. It tells us that, on any map using this scale, 2 inches will equal 48 miles and 1 inch will equal 24 miles.

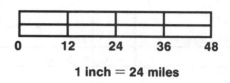

1 inch = 24 miles

A Complete each of the following computations.

scale: 1 inch = 5 miles

1 inch = **5 miles**
1/2 inch =
2 inches =
3 inches =
2 1/2 inches =
5 inches =
10 inches =
8 inches =
20 inches =
25 inches =

scale: 1 inch = 10 miles

1 inch =
2 inches =
3 inches =
4 inches =
5 inches =
6 inches =
7 inches =
8 inches =
9 inches =
10 inches =

scale: 1 inch = 8 miles

1/4 inch =
1/2 inch =
3/4 inch =
1 inch =
1 1/2 inches =
2 inches =
2 1/4 inches =
3 inches =
3 3/4 inches =
4 inches =

scale: 1/2 inch = 1 mile

1/4 inch =
1/2 inch =
3/4 inch =
1 inch =
1 1/2 inches =
2 inches =
2 1/2 inches =
3 inches =
3 1/2 inches =
4 inches =

scale: 1 inch = 100 miles

1/4 inch =
1/2 inch =
3/4 inch =
1 inch =
2 inches =
3 inches =
4 inches =
5 inches =
6 inches =
7 inches =

scale: 1 inch = 150 miles

1/3 inch =
2/3 inch =
1 inch =
2 inches =
2 1/3 inches =
3 inches =
3 2/3 inches =
4 inches =
5 inches =
5 1/2 inches =

REMINDER: Write the definition of a scale.

_____

_____

Unit 158 cont'd ☞

B Read the map and answer the questions.

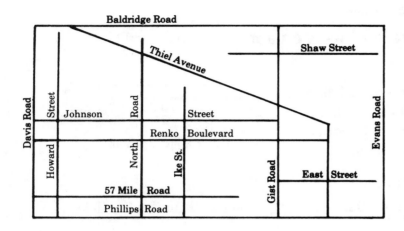

scale: 1/2 inch = 1/2 mile

① How long is Shaw Street? ___*1 1/2 miles*___
② How long is Johnson Street? _____
③ How long is Howard Street? _____
④ How long is East Street? _____
⑤ How long is Thiel Avenue? _____

⑥ Which is longer, Howard Street or Gist Road? _____
⑦ Which is longer, North Road or Shaw Street? _____
⑧ Which is longer, Baldridge Road or Phillips Road? _____
_____
⑨ If you traveled Renko Boulevard to Gist Road, how far did you travel?
_____
⑩ How far does 57 Mile Road run from North Road? _____
⑪ If you traveled all of East Street, all of Thiel Avenue, and all of Howard Street, how far have you traveled?
_____
⑫ Is Davis Road longer north of Renko Boulevard or south of it?
_____

C Work the problems. Use the scale of 1 inch = 10 miles.

① Highway 39 measures 14 inches, Highway 10 measures 9 inches, and Highway 16 measures 18 inches. How many miles do these highways make?

② Interstate 22 runs 20 inches on the map. If you travel half of it, how far have you gone?

③ Highway 17 measures 9 inches on the map. If you traveled the length of Highway 17 four times, how far have you traveled?

④ Road 216 measures 5 inches. Highway 81 measures 14 inches. How much longer is Highway 81 than Road 216?

Road Maps

Learning Objective: *We will learn to read a road map.*

A map is a representation of an actual area.

EXAMPLE:

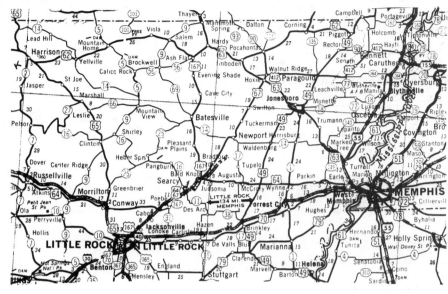

A Use the map above to answer these questions.

① What are the two largest cities on this map? ___*Little Rock and Memphis*___

② Which interstate connects Little Rock and Memphis? _____

③ Which interstate enters Memphis from the north? _____

④ Which road connects Jonesboro with Harrisburg? _____

⑤ Which road connects Jonesboro with Hoxie? _____

⑥ What town do you pass when going from Helena to Forest City on state highway 1? _____

⑦ Do you cross a state line when going from Jonesboro to Memphis? _____

⑧ What runs along the eastern border of Arkansas? _____

⑨ Which direction is Clinton from Marshall? _____

⑩ What road connects Clinton and Marshall? _____

⑪ What town do you pass between Marshall and Harrison? _____

⑫ What town is east of Harrison on U.S. Highway 62? _____

⑬ What road runs south of Yellville? _____

⑭ What U.S. highway runs south of Ash Flat? _____

⑮ What town is south of Cave City on U.S. Highway 167? _____

⑯ Which interstate cuts east and west across Arkansas? _____

⑰ Which interstate exits Little Rock on the southwest? _____

⑱ Which interstate exits Memphis on the south? _____

REMINDER: Write the definition of a map.

_____

_____

Unit 159 cont'd ☞

B Use the map at the right to answer these questions.

① What is the largest city on this map?
Salt Lake City

② What interstate enters Salt Lake City on the east? _____

③ What interstate exits Salt Lake City on the west? _____

④ What desert does Interstate 80 cross? _____

⑤ In which direction from Salt Lake City is Ogden? _____

⑥ Does Interstate 84 cross a state line? _____

⑦ In which direction from Salt Lake City is Provo? _____

⑧ On which road is Park Valley? _____

⑨ On which road is Vernon? _____

⑩ Do any roads cross the Great Salt Lake? _____

C True or False

false ① A road map shows only roads.

_____ ② A road map shows only paved roads.

_____ ③ A road map is very helpful when planning long trips by car.

_____ ④ A road map will indicate the number of miles between cities.

_____ ⑤ A road map uses symbols to indicate different kinds of roads.

_____ ⑥ Road maps do not show state or country boundaries.

_____ ⑦ A road map may concentrate only on roads within a city.

_____ ⑧ Road maps do not indicate the sizes of towns.

_____ ⑨ You would probably need a road map to go from Ohio to Utah.

_____ ⑩ An interstate is a multilane highway that crosses state lines.

Latitude and Longitude

Unit 160

Learning Objective: *We will learn to read lines of latitude and longitude.*

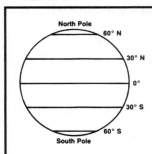

Latitude is the distance north or south from the equator. The equator is 0° latitude.

Lines of latitude are called parallels.

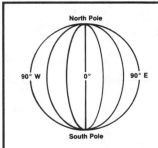

Longitude is the distance east or west from Greenwich, England. The line at Greenwich is 0° longitude.

Lines of longitude are called meridians.

A Fill in the blanks.

① _____*Latitude*_____ runs north and south from the equator.

② _____ runs east and west from the prime meridian at Greenwich, England.

③ The equator is _____ latitude.

④ The prime meridian is _____ longitude.

⑤ Lines of latitude are called _____ .

⑥ Lines of longitude are called _____ .

⑦ North latitudes are _____ the equator. South latitudes are _____ the equator.

⑧ Both latitude and longitude are measured in _____ .

⑨ If you were traveling west, you would cross lines of _____ .

⑩ The northernmost line of latitude is at the _____ . The southernmost line of latitude is at the _____ .

⑪ All meridians meet at the _____ .

⑫ A point indicated at 10° E would be on a line of _____ . A point indicated at 10° S would be on a line of _____ .

REMINDER: Write the definitions of latitude and longitude.

_____

_____

Unit 160 cont'd 👉

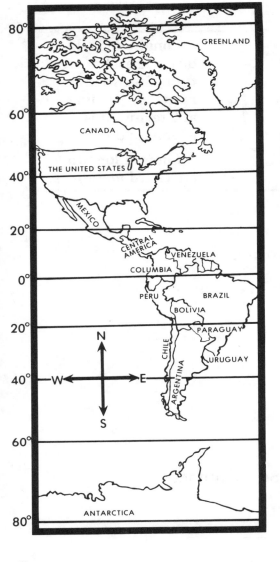

B **Use the map on the left to answer these questions.**

① Which parallel of latitude is the equator? _____ *0°* _____

② Which parallel of latitude runs across the United States? _____

③ Is the United States north or south of the equator? _____

④ Which country lies entirely between the equator and 20° south parallel? _____

⑤ Which continent lies entirely below the 60° south parallel? _____

⑥ The 80° north parallel runs through which countries? _____

⑦ The 40° south parallel runs through which countries? _____

⑧ Which direction would you have to go to cross more than one parallel of latitude? _____

⑨ Does Uruguay lie north or south of the equator? _____

⑩ Does the equator run through Brazil? _____

⑪ Does the equator run through Mexico? _____

⑫ Does South America lie north or south of the equator? _____

_____

C **Answer these questions.**

① Diane is traveling west from Dallas, Texas. Will she cross lines of latitude or longitude?

_____

② Millie is traveling north from Miami, Florida. Will she cross lines of latitude or longitude?

_____

③ How far north can a person go? _____
How far south can a person go? _____

④ Does the equator cross the prime meridian? _____
Does the prime meridian cross the equator? _____

⑤ Do the equator and the prime meridian ever run in the same direction? _____

Comprehension Check

A Study these clocks and fill in the table.

Pacific
Time

Mountain
Time

Central
Time

Eastern
Time

Pacific Time	Mountain Time	Central Time	Eastern Time
Monday 1:30 a.m.	Tuesday 2:30 a.m.	Tuesday 3:30 a.m.	Tuesday 4:30 a.m.
	Thursday 12:00 a.m.		
			Friday 3:00 p.m.
Sunday 9:00 p.m.			
			Tuesday 6:45 a.m.
		Saturday 3:47 a.m.	
	Thursday 8:15 p.m.		
	Monday 6:00 p.m.		
		Saturday 1:59 a.m.	
Saturday 10:20 p.m.			

B Answer true or false to these statements about maps.

_t_ ① There are many different kinds of maps.

____ ② A map can help you get from one side of town to the other.

____ ③ North on a map is usually to the left.

____ ④ All roads on a map look alike.

____ ⑤ A scale will help you determine real distance.

____ ⑥ A road map uses symbols to indicate different kinds of roads.

____ ⑦ Maps show both land areas and bodies of water.

____ ⑧ Maps are only used when traveling by car.

____ ⑨ Some maps show more than one country.

____ ⑩ Latitude lines run east and west; longitude lines run north and south.

Test 32 cont'd ☞

C Study the map above and answer these questions.

① Which country is northernmost on this map? ___*Canada*___

② What body of water lies on the east? _____

③ What body of water lies on the south? _____

④ What country lies south of Texas? _____

⑤ Does this map show the western border of the United States? _____

⑥ Which state is surrounded on three sides by Great Lakes? _____

⑦ What rivers are named on this map? _____

_____

⑧ Which way is north? _____ South? _____ East? _____ West? _____

⑨ Which state is north of Kansas? _____

⑩ Which states are west of Tennessee? _____

⑪ Which state is east of Mississippi? _____

⑫ Which state is south of Iowa? _____

⑬ How many states border Oklahoma? _____

⑭ Does this map list any cities? _____

⑮ How are land borders defined on this map? _____

Write a paragraph describing five instances where maps are used.

_____

_____

_____

_____

_____

_____

_____

388

Reading Charts

Learning Objective: *We will learn to read and interpret a chart.*

A chart is a map, a diagram, a graph, or a list which makes information more accessible and easier to understand.

EXAMPLE: A chart may give information about many things. For example, a chart may present weather information.

AVERAGE WEIGHTS OF GIRLS AGES 9-12

Height in Inches	9 Years	10 Years	11 Years	12 Years
45	45			
46	48			
47	50	50		
48	52	53	53	
49	55	56	56	
50	58	59	61	62
51	61	61	63	65
52	64	64	65	67
53	67	68	68	69
54	70	70	71	71
55	74	74	74	75
56	76	78	78	79
57	80	82	82	82
58		84	86	86
59		87	90	90
60		91	95	95
61			99	100
62			104	105
63				110
64				114
65				118

A Use the weight chart at the left to answer these questions. First find the height in inches; then follow across to the person's age. The weight is given in pounds.

① What is the average weight for these girls?

(a) Carolyn, age 10, height 50 inches _____ *59 lbs.*

(b) Lisa Ann, age 10, height 51 inches _____

(c) Brenda, age 9, height 48 inches _____

(d) Karen, age 12, height 62 inches _____

(e) Tricia, age 11, height 56 inches _____

(f) Donna, age 11, height 50 inches _____

(g) Freda, age 12, height 59 inches _____

(h) Judy, age 9, height 57 inches _____

(i) Ginger, age 9, height 46 inches _____

(j) Melanie, age 10, height 55 inches _____

(k) Pamela, age 11, height 52 inches _____

(l) Deborah, age 9, height 56 inches _____

(m) Nina, age 12, height 64 inches _____

(n) Roxanne, age 10, height 58 inches _____

(o) Susan, age 9, height 47 inches _____

② Does this chart show average weights for boys? _____

③ What ages are covered on this chart? _____

④ Is the average weight for a girl, age 9, height 58 inches given on this chart? _____

_____

⑤ What is the height span on this chart? _____

REMINDER: Write the definition of a chart.

_____

_____

Unit 161 cont'd 👉

Mileage Chart

	Chicago, Ill.	Dallas, Texas	Denver, Colo.	Houston, Texas	Kansas City, Mo.	Los Angeles, Calif.	Milwaukee, Wis.	Mpls.-St. Paul, Minn.	St. Louis, Mo.	Salt Lake City, Utah	San Francisco, Calif.	Seattle, Wash.
Albuquerque, N. Mex.	1289	639	419	829	787	797	1341	1206	1040	614	1125	1482
Austin, Texas	1130	196	908	162	749	1386	1203	1150	839	1297	1790	2168
Baton Rouge, La.	908	421	1205	282	764	1819	989	1184	664	1662	2185	2533
Bismarck, N. Dak.	829	1175	685	1417	783	1661	754	428	980	953	1625	1216
Boise, Idaho	1731	1607	842	1797	1410	856	1721	1443	1660	358	650	505
Carson City, Nev.	1969	1667	1052	1857	1652	447	1992	1781	1902	543	221	772
Cheyenne, Wyo.	965	871	102	1113	648	1163	988	794	898	462	1212	1267
Chicago, Ill.		936	1012	1085	499	2090	89	399	288	1427	2177	2052
Dallas, Texas	936		784	245	499	1398	1009	956	645	1241	1764	2112
Davenport, Iowa	164	846	849	1024	349	1940	202	346	228	1264	2014	1929
Denver, Colo.	1012	784		1026	616	1128	1035	841	856	495	1245	1347
Des Moines, Iowa	330	704	679	947	201	1795	358	253	336	1094	1844	1773
Duluth, Minn.	474	1109	996	1352	601	2053	399	147	665	1352	2064	1655
El Paso, Texas	1434	622	654	755	935	793	1486	1339	1178	869	1197	1740
Houston, Texas	1085	245	1026		742	1548	1158	1199	794	1431	1952	2302
Jackson, Miss.	747	403	1191	429	661	1805	832	1053	498	1648	2171	2519
Jefferson City, Mo.	390	565	750	780	146	1720	463	510	130	1255	2005	2016
Kansas City, Mo.	499	499	616	742		1591	554	454	253	1110	1860	1872
Lincoln, Nebr.	526	630	486	874	216	1613	551	385	465	912	1662	1672
Little Rock, Ark.	644	331	957	441	396	1701	717	825	353	1456	2025	2277
Los Angeles, Calif.	2090	1398	1128	1548	1591		2142	1940	1841	720	401	1144
Memphis, Tenn.	537	464	1035	561	459	1831	619	846	288	1534	2155	2331
Milwaukee, Wis.	89	1009	1035	1158	554	2142		324	364	1450	2200	1974
Oklahoma City, Okla.	794	210	615	455	347	1352	868	804	504	1108	1676	1962
Omaha, Nebr.	472	656	547	899	202	1656	497	359	454	955	1705	1667
Peoria, Ill.	152	812	900	964	350	1941	220	429	170	1326	2076	2025
Phoenix, Ariz.	1725	1005	818	1155	1226	390	1777	1636	1476	669	797	1451
Pierre, S. Dak.	768	968	523	1212	595	1552	701	395	823	851	1601	1310
Portland, Oreg.	2123	2043	1278	2233	1846	969	2045	1709	2096	789	639	175
St. Louis, Mo.	288	645	856	794	253	1841	364	552		1360	2110	2109
Salt Lake City, Utah	1427	1241	495	1431	1110	720	1450	1239	1360		751	857
San Antonio, Texas	1209	279	938	201	772	1362	1282	1227	918	1314	1766	2185
San Diego, Calif.	2078	1341	1171	1491	1579	120	2130	1989	1829	778	521	1274
San Francisco, Calif.	2177	1764	1245	1952	1860	401	2200	1989	2110	751		814
Santa Fe, N. Mex.	1253	630	360	820	754	853	1300	1142	1006	611	1187	1482
Seattle, Wash.	2052	2112	1347	2302	1872	1144	1974	1638	2109	857	814	
Spokane, Wash.	1763	1896	1112	2138	1583	1220	1685	1349	1820	732	909	277
Topeka, Kans.	562	492	541	735	63	1532	610	515	315	1053	1803	1831
Tulsa, Okla.	690	265	684	510	244	1448	766	698	402	1177	1772	2031

B Answer these questions using the mileage chart at the left.

① What is the mileage between these cities?

(a) Austin and Chicago   _1,130_

(b) Boise and Seattle   _____

(c) Dallas and St. Louis   _____

(d) El Paso and Dallas   _____

(e) Lincoln and Houston   _____

(f) Peoria and Salt Lake City   _____

(g) St. Louis and Denver   _____

(h) Spokane and San Francisco   _____

(i) Tulsa and Chicago   _____

(j) Jackson and Chicago   _____

(k) Duluth and Los Angeles   _____

(l) Milwaukee and Dallas   _____

(m) Omaha and St. Louis   _____

(n) Pierre and St. Paul   _____

(o) San Diego and Los Angeles   _____

(p) Portland and Salt Lake City   _____

(q) Des Moines and St. Louis   _____

(r) Sante Fe and Seattle   _____

(s) Cheyenne and Milwaukee   _____

(t) Little Rock and Seattle   _____

(u) Topeka and Denver   _____

(v) Davenport and Chicago   _____

(w) Bismarck and Kansas City   _____

② Will it take longer to go from Albuquerque to Denver than from Albuquerque to St. Louis? _____

③ Which is longer — from Memphis to Dallas to Los Angeles or from Memphis to Los Angeles? _____

④ How much farther is it from Portland to Chicago than from Portland to Houston? _____

⑤ Is Minneapolis-St. Paul farther or nearer to Des Moines than is Chicago? _____

⑥ Which city is nearer to Kansas City — Duluth, Jackson, or Omaha? _____

Reading Meters

Learning
Objective: *We will learn to read meters.*

A meter is a mechanical device by which products are measured.

This is a parking meter. Inserting a nickel and turning the knob will result in buying 30 minutes of parking time. Inserting more money will result in buying more time.

A Study each meter and determine how much money was inserted to buy the parking time.

①

10¢

②

③

④

⑤

⑥

⑦

⑧

SENEX
UNLEADED

$ ☐ ☐ 2 . 5 0 price
☐ ☐ 5 . 0 0 gallons
$ ☐ ☐ . 5 0 price per gal.

This is a gasoline meter. The price number shows how much is owed for the gallons shown. The price per gallon shows how much each gallon of gasoline costs. Five gallons at fifty cents a gallon costs $2.50.

B Read each gas meter and determine how much money is owed.

① $ ☐ 1 0 . 0 0 price
☐ 1 0 . 0 0 gallons
$ ☐ 1 . 0 0 price per gal.

10 × $1 = $10

② $ ☐ ☐ 7 . 5 0 price
☐ 1 0 . 0 0 gallons
$ ☐ ☐ . 7 5 price per gal.

③ $ ☐ ☐ 9 . 1 3 price
☐ 1 1 . 0 0 gallons
$ ☐ ☐ . 8 3 price per gal.

④ $ ☐ 1 1 . 2 5 price
☐ 1 5 . 0 0 gallons
$ ☐ ☐ . 7 5 price per gal.

⑤ $ ☐ 1 4 . 0 8 price
☐ 1 6 . 0 0 gallons
$ ☐ ☐ . 8 8 price per gal.

⑥ $ ☐ ☐ 7 . 1 4 price
☐ ☐ 7 . 0 0 gallons
$ ☐ 1 . 0 2 price per gal.

⑦ $ ☐ ☐ 3 . 4 0 price
☐ ☐ 2 . 0 0 gallons
$ ☐ 1 . 7 0 price per gal.

⑧ $ ☐ 1 3 . 4 4 price
☐ ☐ 8 . 0 0 gallons
$ ☐ 1 . 6 8 price per gal.

REMINDER: Write the definition of a meter.

Unit 162 cont'd ☞

C Study each meter and answer the questions.

1. What kind of meter is this? ___*parking meter*___
2. How much time will 1¢ buy? _____
   5¢ buy? _____ 10¢ buy? _____
3. How much would 30 minutes of time cost? _____
4. How much would 45 minutes cost? _____
5. How much would 1 hour 15 minutes cost? _____
6. How much would 3 hours cost? _____
7. How much would 4 hours 12 minutes cost? _____
8. How much would 4 hours 45 minutes cost? _____

1. What kind of meter is this? ___*gasoline meter*___
2. How much does the gasoline cost? _____
3. How much gas will $2 buy? _____
4. How much gas will $5 buy? _____
5. How much gas will $11 buy? _____
6. How much will 10 gallons cost? _____
7. How much will 8 gallons cost? _____
8. How much will 16 gallons cost? _____

D Solve each problem.

1. Judy's car will hold ten gallons of gas. She needs eight gallons to fill it up. How much will it cost her to fill her gasoline tank if the gas costs 78¢ a gallon?

   _____

2. Harold needs to park his truck for approximately two and one-half hours so that he can run errands. If 5¢ will buy 30 minutes of parking time, 20¢ will buy two hours of time, and 25¢ will buy three hours of time, how much money should he put in the meter? _____

3. Jeremy bought two hours and forty-five minutes worth of parking time. If 1¢ bought 15 minutes, 5¢ bought 30 minutes and 10¢ bought one hour, how much money did Jeremy put in the machine.

   _____

4. Karrie bought $11.77 worth of gasoline. If the gas cost $1.07 per gallon, how many gallons did she buy? _____

392

Reading Scales

Learning Objective: **We will learn to read scales.**

A scale measures products in terms of weight.

EXAMPLE: This is a scale. It measures products in terms of pounds. There are 16 ounces in a pound. This scale shows 8/16 or 1/2 pound.

16 = 1 pound

A Study each scale and determine the weight in ounces.

① **13 ounces**   ②   ③   ④

⑤   ⑥   ⑦   ⑧

B These scales weigh in different measurements. Study each carefully and determine the weight.

① grams **3 grams**   ② tons   ③ kilograms   ④ pounds

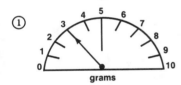

⑤ ounces   ⑥ metric tons   ⑦ metric tons   ⑧ grams

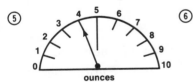 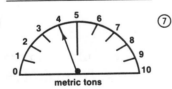 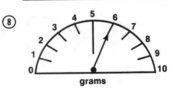

⑨ tons   ⑩ kilograms   ⑪ ounces   ⑫ grams

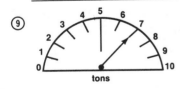 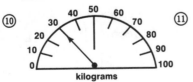 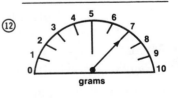

REMINDER: Write the definition of a scale.

Unit 163 cont'd ☞

This is a weight scale. It is normally used to tell a person's weight. The pointer on this scale is stationary and the dial in the scale rotates to the correct weight when it is stepped on. This scale shows 135 pounds.

C Study each scale and determine the weight.

①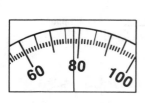

78 pounds

②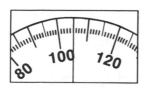

③

④

⑤

⑥

⑦

⑧

D Read each paragraph and find the answer.

① Mrs. Robinson wants to buy 24 ounces of white grapes at 50¢ per pound. How much will the grapes cost? _____

②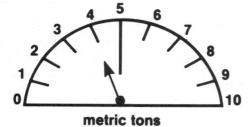

metric tons

Mr. Lennis contracted with Rains Livestock for delivery of 8 metric tons of grain on November 10. The scales from Rains Livestock are shown above. Did Mr. Lennis meet his obligation? _____ How much does he lack? _____

③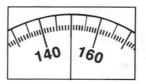

On July 1 Larry weighed 175 pounds. He wanted to lose 25 pounds by September 30. The scales above show how Larry's scales looked on September 30. Did Larry accomplish his goal? _____

④ Lezli wants to buy 10 pounds of potatoes, 2 pounds of onions, and 4 pounds of apples. Each product costs the same at 65¢ per pound. How much will the food cost Lezli? _____

Reading Gauges

Learning Objective: *We will learn to read gauges.*

A gauge may be used to measure pressure or volume.

This is a tire gauge. It measures how much air is in a tire. It measures pounds of air pressure per square inch (psi). This gauge shows 35 psi. The average vehicle tire needs 32 psi. This gauge shows too much air in the tire.

A Study each tire gauge and determine the air pressure per square inch. Does the tire need air or does it have too much?

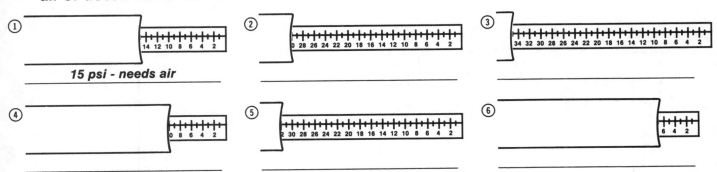

① 15 psi - needs air

This is a gasoline gauge. It measures the gas in the tank of a vehicle. Most gas gauges measure gas in sixteenths. This gas gauge shows 10/16, or a little over a half a tank of gas.

B Study each gas gauge and determine the amount of gasoline in the tank.

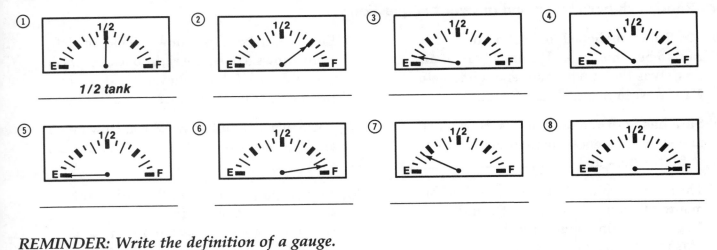

① 1/2 tank

REMINDER: *Write the definition of a gauge.*

   Unit 164 cont'd 👉

This is a rain gauge. It measures the inches of rainfall. This gauge shows .5 or 1/2 inch of rain.

C Study each gauge and determine the rainfall amount.

① _____ _____

② _____ _____

③ _____ _____

④ _____

⑤ _____ _____

D Read each paragraph and answer the questions.

① Mr. Browning hoped for .9 of an inch of rain to help his crops. It rained 3/10 of an inch. Was the rain amount enough to help Mr. Browning? ___no___

② Bob's right front tire shows 30 psi, the left front shows 32 psi, the right back shows 30 psi, and the left back shows 29 psi. Which tire does not need any air? _____

③ Sara has 8/16 of a tank of gas. How much more of a tank does she need to buy of gas to fill the tank up? _____

④ Carmen's tires all show 28 psi. How much air does each tire need? _____

⑤ The average rainfall for Texas during the month of August is 3 inches. During August the rain gauge only showed 1.3. Was this normal? _____
How much more did Texas need? _____
_____

⑥ Janet's gas gauge shows 2/16 of a tank. Is she closer to empty or full? _____
How much does she need to fill the tank 1/2 full? _____
How much does she need to fill the tank completely? _____

Math Symbols

Learning Objective: *We will learn to identify various mathematical symbols.*

A symbol is a sign that stands for something else.

Common Symbols							
$+$	$=$	$\geqq$	{ }	$\angle$	π	$\varnothing$	$\cup$
$-$	$>$	$\leqq$	( )	$\triangle$	$\circ$	$\in$	$\cap$
$\div$	$<$	$\mathbb{A}$	[ ]	$\perp$	$\therefore$	$\notin$	$\equiv$
$\times$	$\neq$	$\not\forall$		$\parallel$	$\because$	$\subseteq$	$\not\subseteq$

A Answer these questions.

___=___ ① Which symbol indicates one number is equal to another?

_____ ② Which symbol indicates a number is less than another?

_____ ③ Which symbol indicates that the enclosed members are a set?

_____ ④ Which symbol indicates the operation of multiplication?

_____ ⑤ Which symbol indicates an angle?

_____ ⑥ Which symbol stands for the word "therefore"?

_____ ⑦ Which symbol stands for the empty set?

_____ ⑧ Which symbol indicates the operation of addition?

_____ ⑨ Which symbol indicates a number is greater than another?

_____ ⑩ Which symmbol indicates a number is greater than or equal to another?

_____ ⑪ Which symbol stands for the Greek letter "pi"?

_____ ⑫ Which symbol indicates one set is a subset of another set?

_____ ⑬ Which symbol indicates a number is not greater than another?

_____ ⑭ Which symbol stands for "triangle"?

_____ ⑮ Which symbol indicates the operation of subtraction?

_____ ⑯ Which symbol indicates the operation within it is to be done first?

_____ ⑰ Which symbol indicates a set is the union of two other sets?

_____ ⑱ Which symbol indicates a line is parallel to another line?

_____ ⑲ Which symbol indicates the operation of division?

_____ ⑳ Which symbol stands for the word "degrees"?

_____ ㉑ Which symbol indicates a number is not equal to another?

_____ ㉒ Which symbol stands for the word "since"?

_____ ㉓ Which symbol indicates a number is not less than another?

_____ ㉔ Which symbol indicates a member is an element of a larger set?

_____ ㉕ Which symbol indicates a set is the intersection of two other sets?

_____ ㉖ Which symbol indicates two lines are perpendicular?

REMINDER: Write the definition of a symbol.

_____

_____

Unit 165 cont'd 👉

B Supply the correct symbols.

① $27 \underline{\ <\ } 96$

② $100 \underline{\hspace{1cm}} 100$

③ $25 \underline{\hspace{1cm}} 5 = 5$

④ $\angle A = 90$

⑤ $\underline{\hspace{1cm}} = 3.14$

⑥ $17 \underline{\hspace{1cm}} 13 = 30$

⑦ $412 \underline{\hspace{1cm}} 250$

⑧ $3 \underline{\hspace{1cm}} 4 = 12$

⑨ $1 \underline{\hspace{1cm}} 1{,}000$

⑩ $A = \{1, 2, 3, 4\}$
$B = \{3, 4, 5, 6\}$
$A \underline{\hspace{1cm}} B = \{3, 4\}$

⑪ $A = \{10, 20, 30\}$
$B = \{15, 25, 35\}$
$10 \underline{\hspace{1cm}} Set A$

⑫ $C = \{50, 500, 750\}$
$D = \{25, 250, 800\}$
$25 \underline{\hspace{1cm}} Set C$

⑬ $\angle A = 45°$
$\angle B = 40°$
$\angle A + \angle B = 85$

⑭ $\square ABCD$
$AB \parallel CD$
$AC \underline{\hspace{1cm}} BD$

⑮ $\triangle ABC$
$\angle A + \angle B = 120°$
$C = 60°$

⑯ $50 \underline{\hspace{1cm}} 7 = 43$

⑰ $900 \underline{\hspace{1cm}} 100 = 1{,}000$

⑱ $212 \underline{\hspace{1cm}} 312$

C Interpret each of these mathematical sentences.

① $20 + 17 = 37$
Twenty plus seventeen is equal to thirty-seven.
_____

⑥ $500 \div 100 = 5$
_____
_____

② $76 > 73$
_____
_____

⑦ $\triangle ABC \equiv \triangle DEF$
_____
_____

③ $\{1, 2, 3\} \subseteq Set C$
_____
_____

⑧ $210 \nless 200$
_____
_____

④ $\angle A = 60°$
_____
_____

⑨ $AB \perp CD$
_____
_____

⑤ $2 + (3 - 1) = 4$
_____
_____

⑩ $17 \in \{16, 17, 18, 19\}$
_____
_____

Comprehension Check

A Read each parking meter and determine how much money each amount of time costs.

① ② ③ ④

_____ _____ _____ _____

B Study the gas meter and answer the questions.

$ ☐☐☐ . ☐☐ price
☐☐☐ . ☐☐ gallons
$ ☐☐ . 7 8 price per gal.

① What is the price per gallon? _____
② How much would 10 gallons cost? _____
③ How much would 8 gallons cost? _____
④ How much gas will $10 buy? _____ $1 buy? _____
⑤ How much gas will $5 buy? _____ $2 buy? _____

C Study each scale carefully and determine each weight.

① 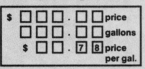 ②  ③  ④

5 pounds _____ _____ _____

⑤  ⑥  ⑦  ⑧

_____ _____ _____ _____

D Name each gauge, what it measures, the measurement on the gauge, and any additional information necessary.

① 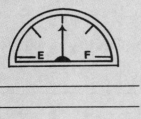 ② ③ _____

Test 33 cont'd ☞

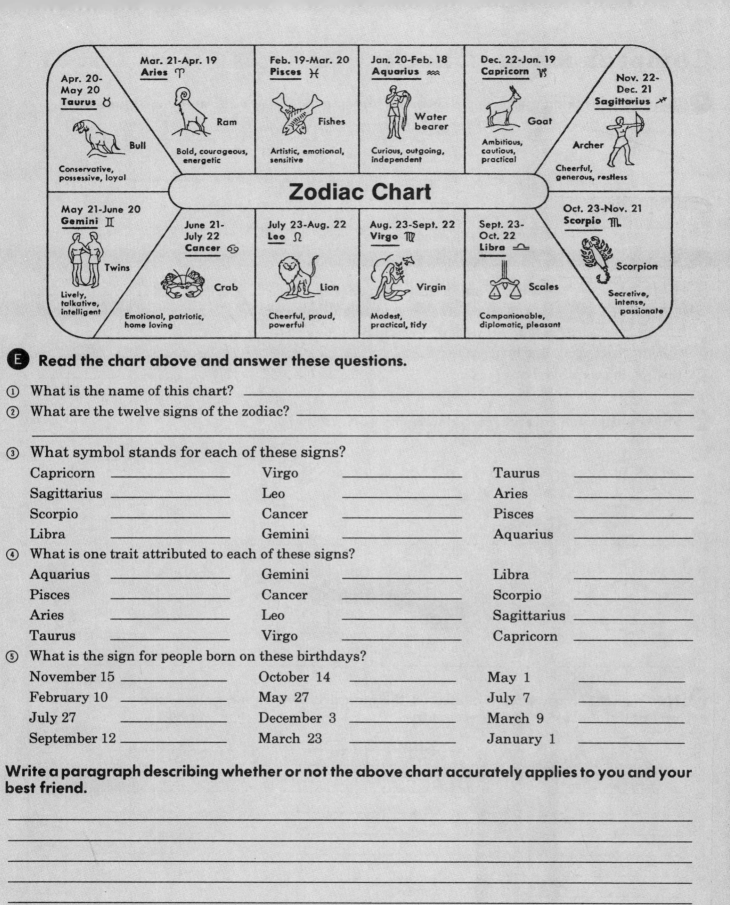

Zodiac Chart

Apr. 20-May 20
Taurus ♉
Bull
Conservative, possessive, loyal

Mar. 21-Apr. 19
Aries ♈
Ram
Bold, courageous, energetic

Feb. 19-Mar. 20
Pisces ♓
Fishes
Artistic, emotional, sensitive

Jan. 20-Feb. 18
Aquarius ♒
Water bearer
Curious, outgoing, independent

Dec. 22-Jan. 19
Capricorn ♑
Goat
Ambitious, cautious, practical

Nov. 22-Dec. 21
Sagittarius ♐
Archer
Cheerful, generous, restless

May 21-June 20
Gemini ♊
Twins
Lively, talkative, intelligent

June 21-July 22
Cancer ♋
Crab
Emotional, patriotic, home loving

July 23-Aug. 22
Leo ♌
Lion
Cheerful, proud, powerful

Aug. 23-Sept. 22
Virgo ♍
Virgin
Modest, practical, tidy

Sept. 23-Oct. 22
Libra ♎
Scales
Companionable, diplomatic, pleasant

Oct. 23-Nov. 21
Scorpio ♏
Scorpion
Secretive, intense, passionate

E Read the chart above and answer these questions.

① What is the name of this chart? _____

② What are the twelve signs of the zodiac? _____
_____

③ What symbol stands for each of these signs?

Capricorn _____	Virgo _____	Taurus _____
Sagittarius _____	Leo _____	Aries _____
Scorpio _____	Cancer _____	Pisces _____
Libra _____	Gemini _____	Aquarius _____

④ What is one trait attributed to each of these signs?

Aquarius _____	Gemini _____	Libra _____
Pisces _____	Cancer _____	Scorpio _____
Aries _____	Leo _____	Sagittarius _____
Taurus _____	Virgo _____	Capricorn _____

⑤ What is the sign for people born on these birthdays?

November 15 _____	October 14 _____	May 1 _____
February 10 _____	May 27 _____	July 7 _____
July 27 _____	December 3 _____	March 9 _____
September 12 _____	March 23 _____	January 1 _____

Write a paragraph describing whether or not the above chart accurately applies to you and your best friend.

_____
_____
_____
_____
_____